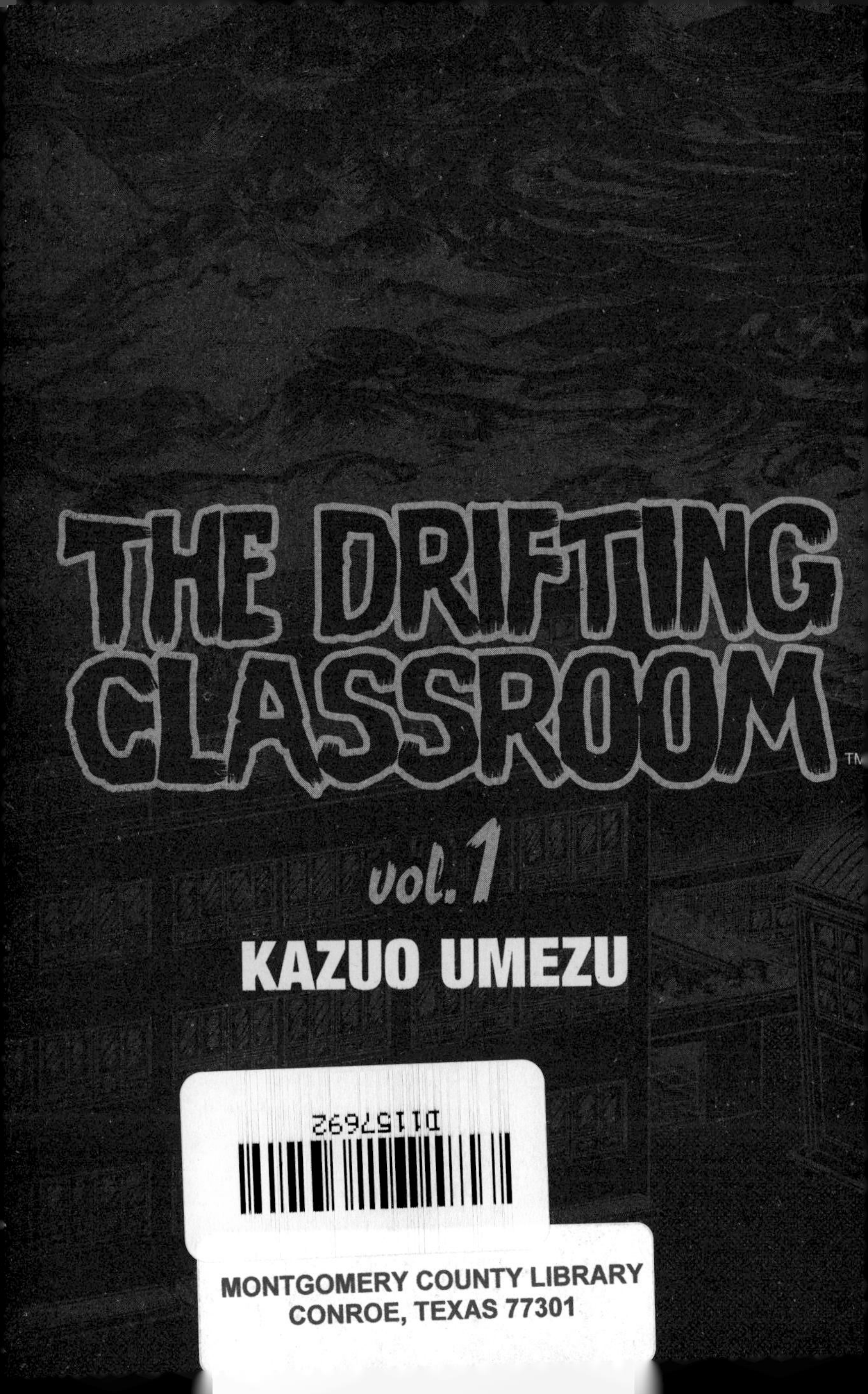

THE DRIFTING CLASSROOM™

vol. 1

KAZUO UMEZU

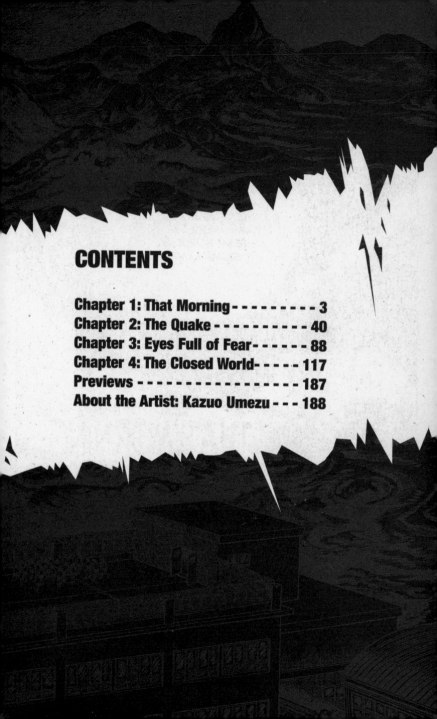

CONTENTS

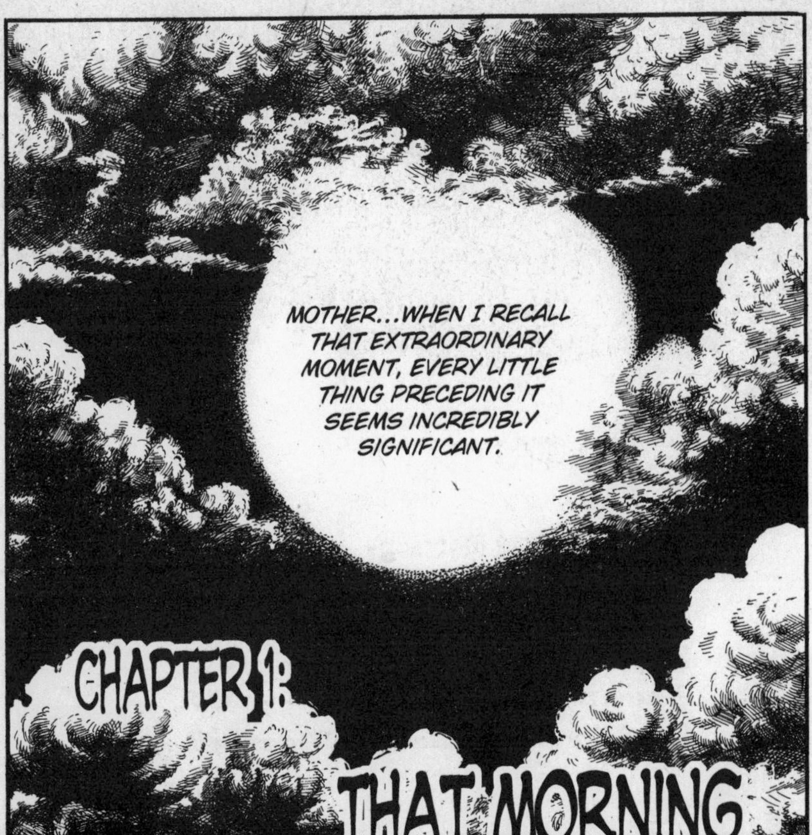
MOTHER...WHEN I RECALL THAT EXTRAORDINARY MOMENT, EVERY LITTLE THING PRECEDING IT SEEMS INCREDIBLY SIGNIFICANT.
CHAPTER 1:
THAT MORNING

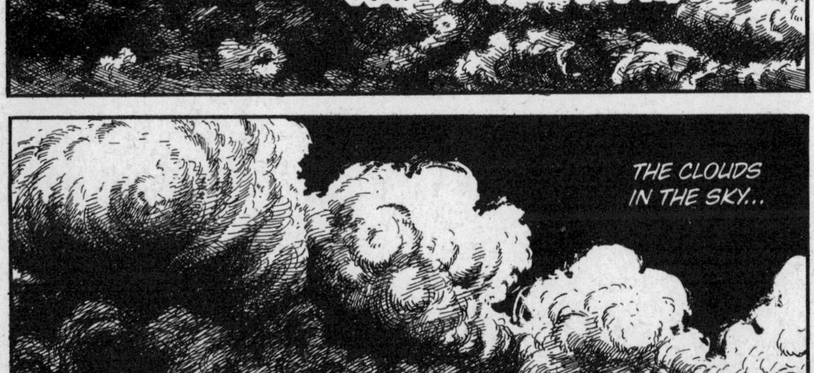
THE CLOUDS IN THE SKY...

THE TREES I SAW EVERY DAY...

THE OVER-GROWN WEEDS I KEPT ON TRYING TO TRAMPLE.

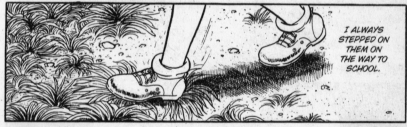

I ALWAYS STEPPED ON THEM ON THE WAY TO SCHOOL.

EVEN THE FLIES BUZZING OVER THE GARBAGE... I CAN NEVER FORGET THEM NOW.

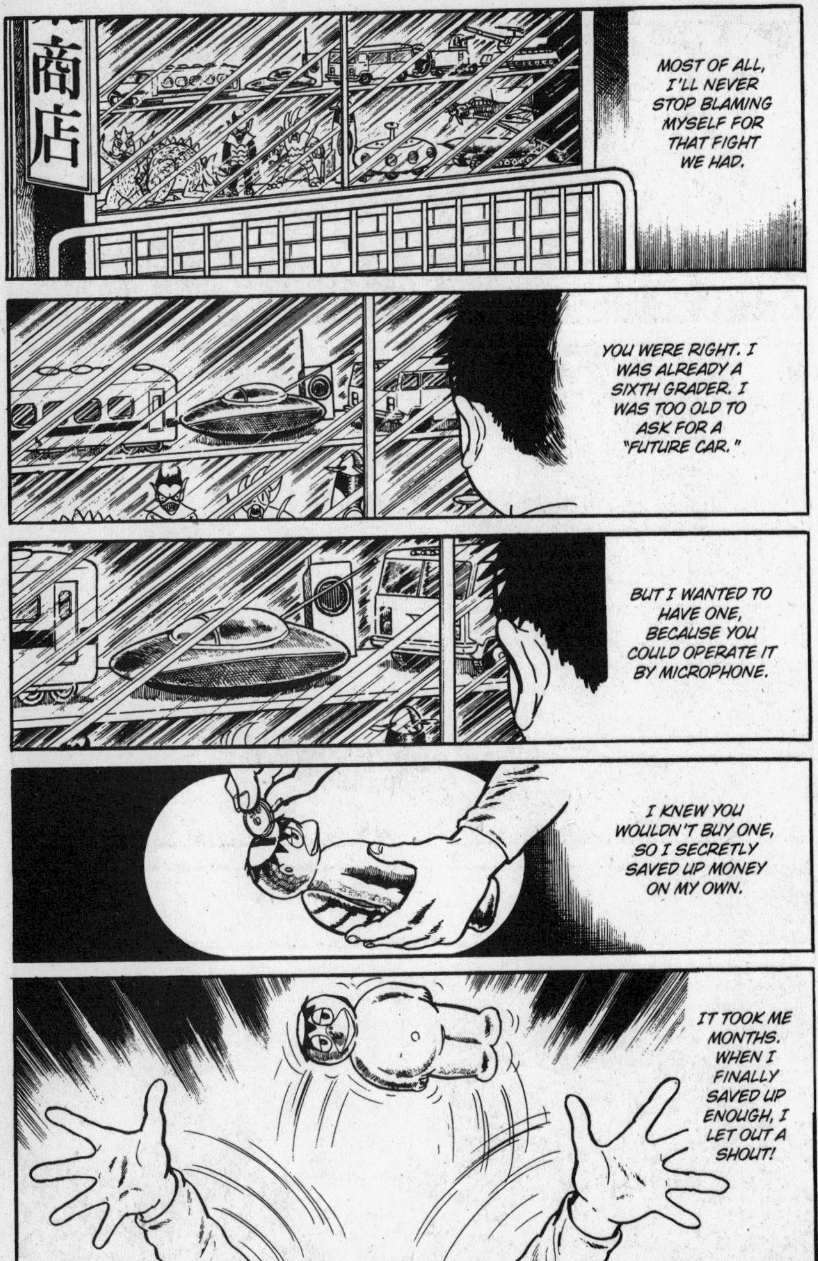
MOST OF ALL, I'LL NEVER STOP BLAMING MYSELF FOR THAT FIGHT WE HAD.
商店
YOU WERE RIGHT. I WAS ALREADY A SIXTH GRADER. I WAS TOO OLD TO ASK FOR A "FUTURE CAR."
BUT I WANTED TO HAVE ONE, BECAUSE YOU COULD OPERATE IT BY MICROPHONE.
I KNEW YOU WOULDN'T BUY ONE, SO I SECRETLY SAVED UP MONEY ON MY OWN.
IT TOOK ME MONTHS. WHEN I FINALLY SAVED UP ENOUGH, I LET OUT A SHOUT!

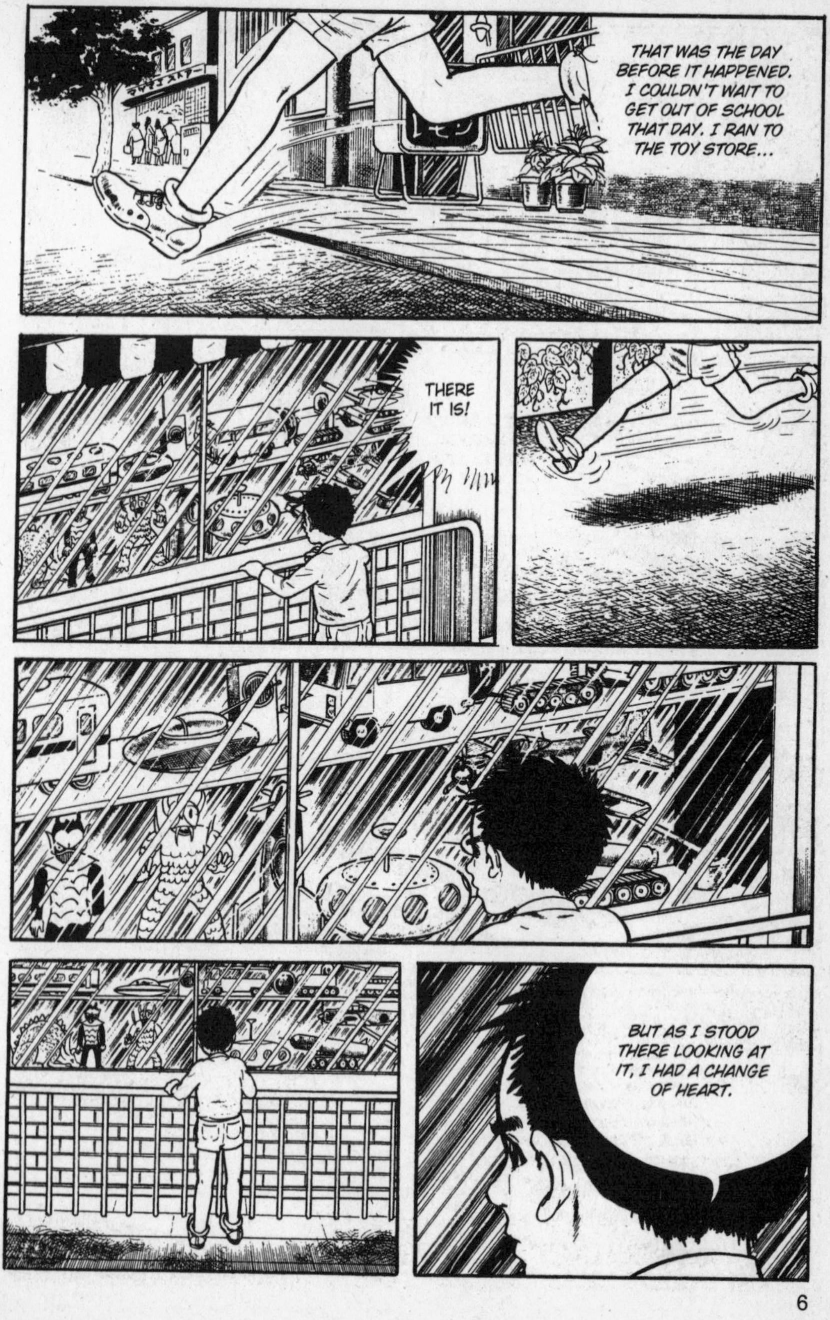
THAT WAS THE DAY BEFORE IT HAPPENED. I COULDN'T WAIT TO GET OUT OF SCHOOL THAT DAY. I RAN TO THE TOY STORE...
THERE IT IS!
BUT AS I STOOD THERE LOOKING AT IT, I HAD A CHANGE OF HEART.

I DECIDED NOT TO BUY THE FUTURE CAR. INSTEAD, I SPENT MY SAVINGS ON A WRISTWATCH...AS A GIFT FOR YOU, MOTHER.

I REMEMBERED YOU SAID YOU WANTED A NEW WATCH!

VRRR

OH!!

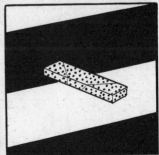

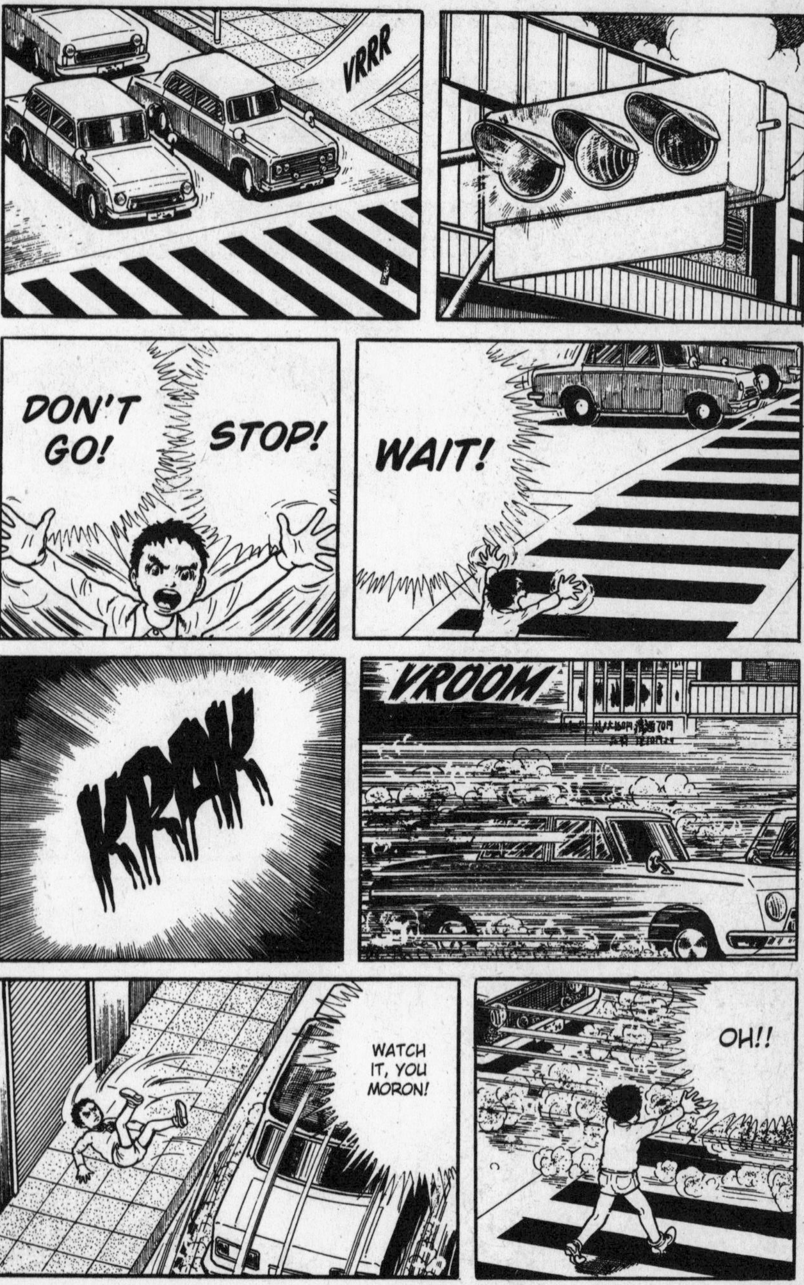
VRRR
WAIT!
STOP!
DON'T GO!
VROOM
KRAK
OH!!
WATCH IT, YOU MORON!

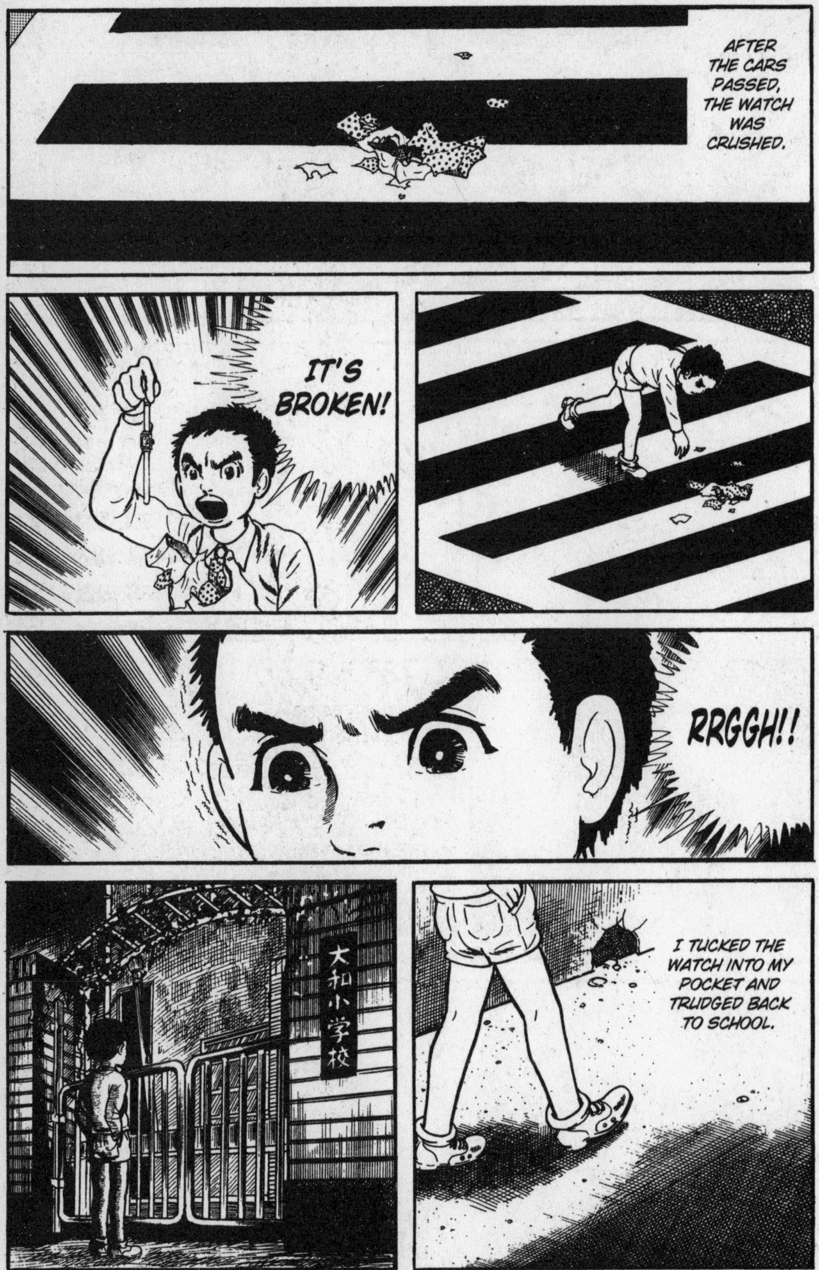
AFTER THE CARS PASSED, THE WATCH WAS CRUSHED.
IT'S BROKEN!
RRGGH!!
I TUCKED THE WATCH INTO MY POCKET AND TRUDGED BACK TO SCHOOL.
大和小学校

*SIGN=YAMATO ELEMENTARY SCHOOL

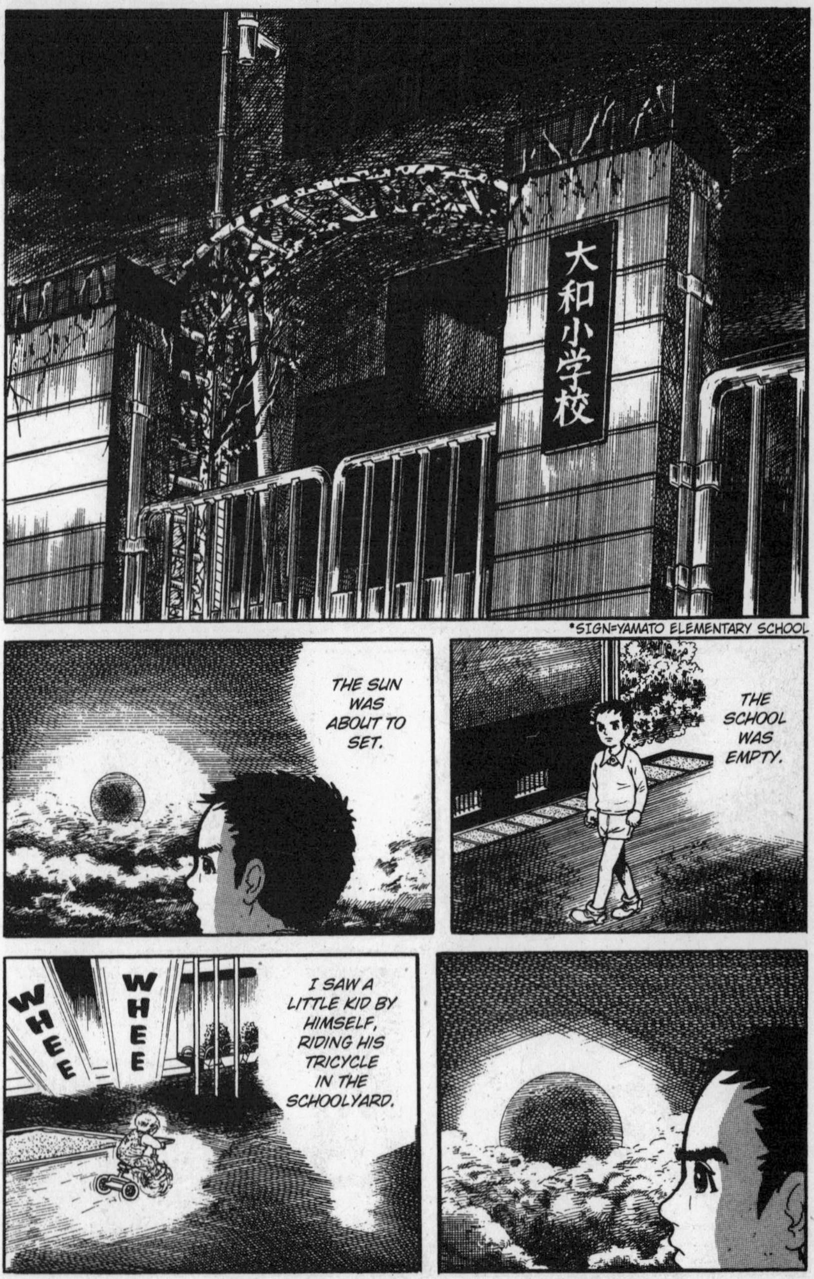
大和小学校
*SIGN=YAMATO ELEMENTARY SCHOOL
THE SCHOOL WAS EMPTY.
THE SUN WAS ABOUT TO SET.
I SAW A LITTLE KID BY HIMSELF, RIDING HIS TRICYCLE IN THE SCHOOLYARD.
WHEE
WHEE

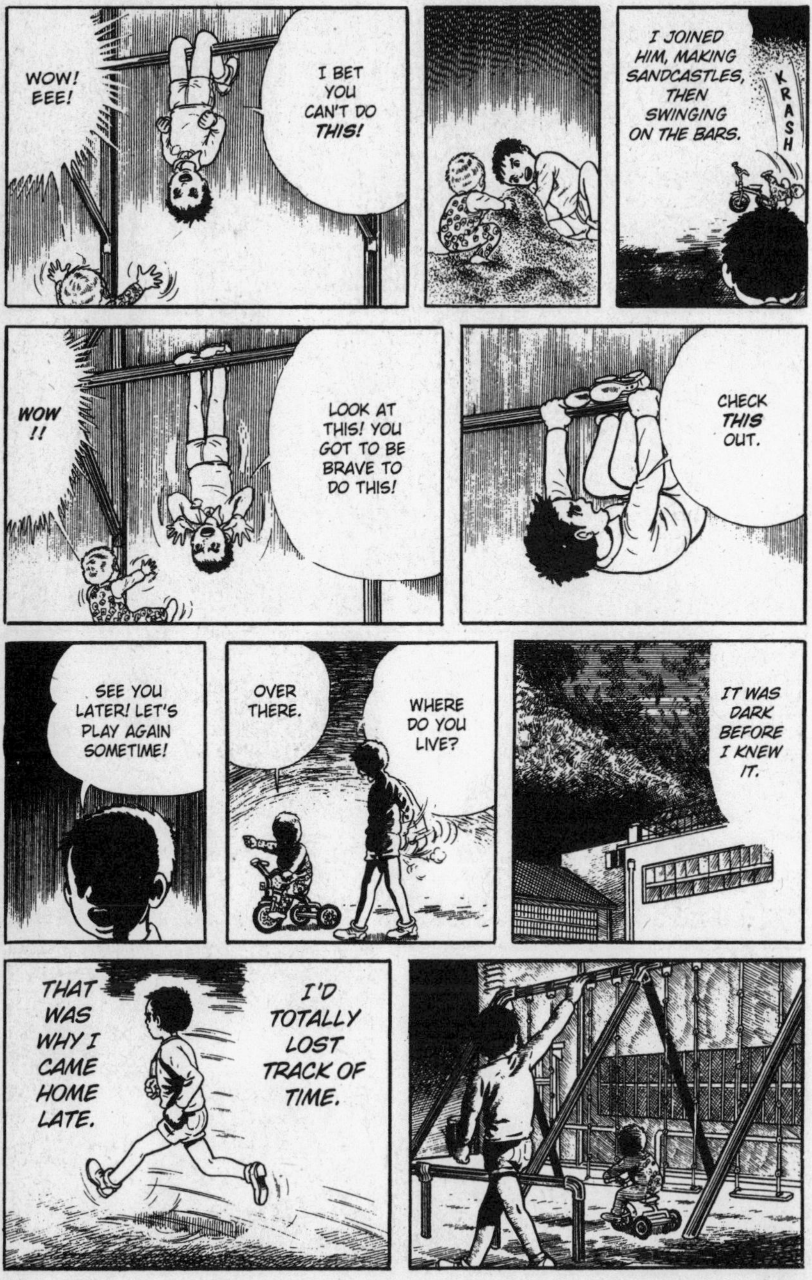
I JOINED HIM, MAKING SANDCASTLES, THEN SWINGING ON THE BARS.
KRASH
I BET YOU CAN'T DO THIS!
WOW! EEE!
CHECK THIS OUT.
LOOK AT THIS! YOU GOT TO BE BRAVE TO DO THIS!
WOW !!
IT WAS DARK BEFORE I KNEW IT.
WHERE DO YOU LIVE?
OVER THERE.
SEE YOU LATER! LET'S PLAY AGAIN SOMETIME!
I'D TOTALLY LOST TRACK OF TIME.
THAT WAS WHY I CAME HOME LATE.

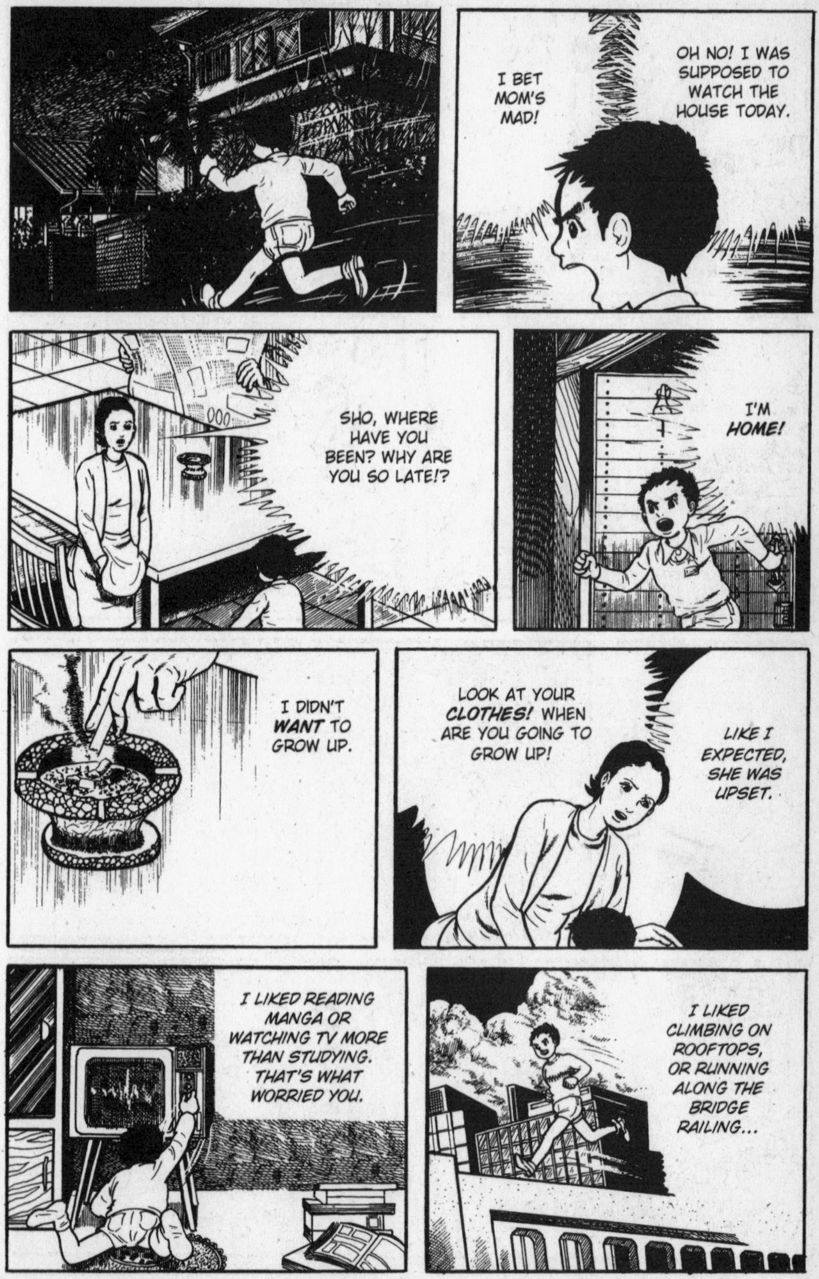
OH NO! I WAS SUPPOSED TO WATCH THE HOUSE TODAY.
I BET MOM'S MAD!
I'M HOME!
SHO, WHERE HAVE YOU BEEN? WHY ARE YOU SO LATE!?
LOOK AT YOUR CLOTHES! WHEN ARE YOU GOING TO GROW UP!
LIKE I EXPECTED, SHE WAS UPSET.
I DIDN'T WANT TO GROW UP.
I LIKED CLIMBING ON ROOFTOPS, OR RUNNING ALONG THE BRIDGE RAILING...
I LIKED READING MANGA OR WATCHING TV MORE THAN STUDYING. THAT'S WHAT WORRIED YOU.

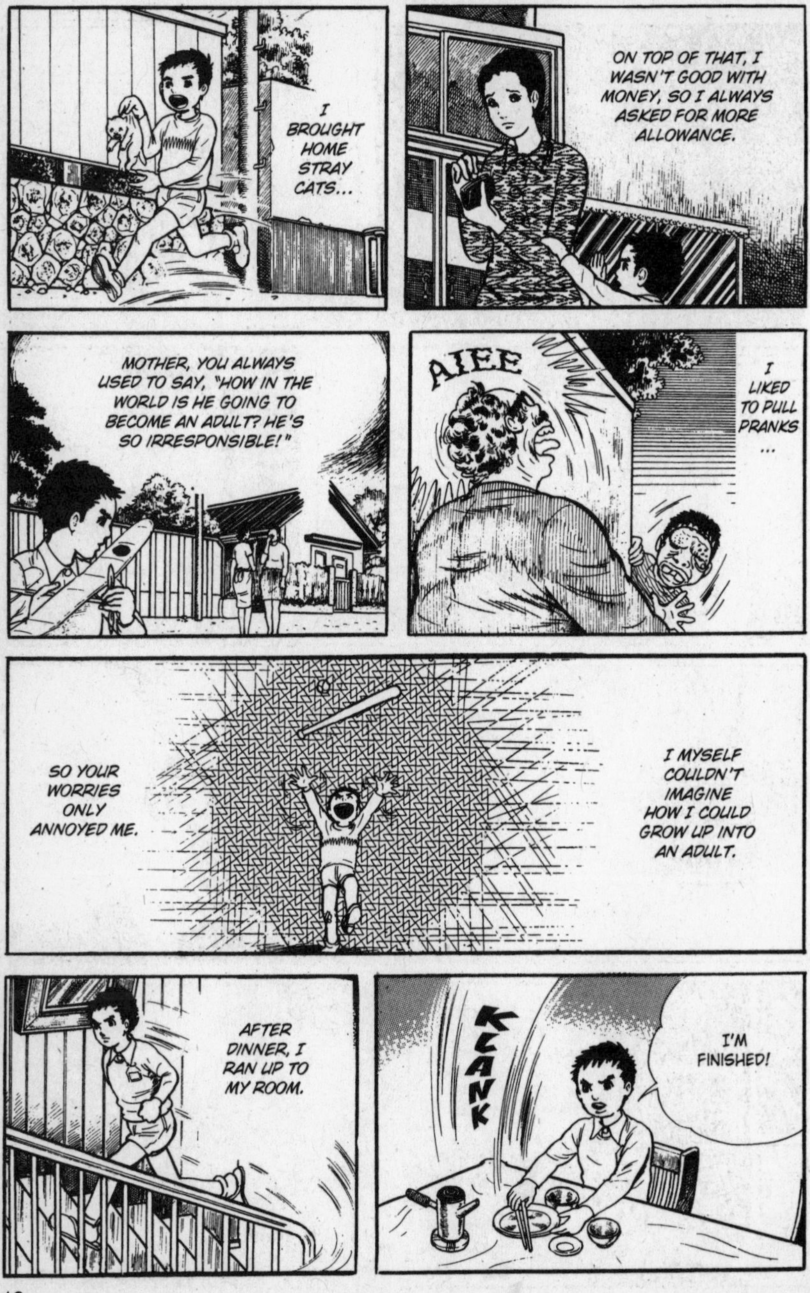
ON TOP OF THAT, I WASN'T GOOD WITH MONEY, SO I ALWAYS ASKED FOR MORE ALLOWANCE.
I BROUGHT HOME STRAY CATS...
I LIKED TO PULL PRANKS ...
AIEE
MOTHER, YOU ALWAYS USED TO SAY, "HOW IN THE WORLD IS HE GOING TO BECOME AN ADULT? HE'S SO IRRESPONSIBLE!"
I MYSELF COULDN'T IMAGINE HOW I COULD GROW UP INTO AN ADULT.
SO YOUR WORRIES ONLY ANNOYED ME.
I'M FINISHED!
KLANK
AFTER DINNER, I RAN UP TO MY ROOM.

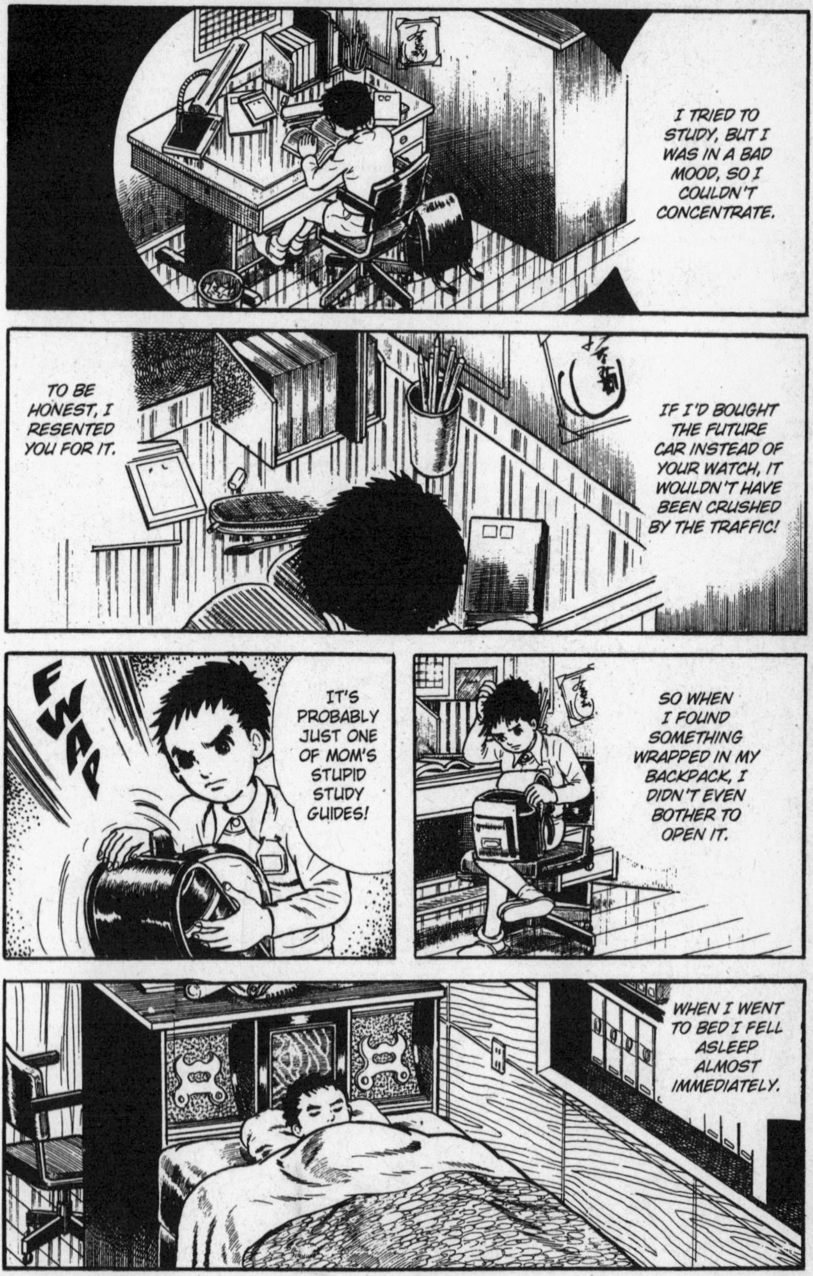
I TRIED TO STUDY, BUT I WAS IN A BAD MOOD, SO I COULDN'T CONCENTRATE.
TO BE HONEST, I RESENTED YOU FOR IT.
IF I'D BOUGHT THE FUTURE CAR INSTEAD OF YOUR WATCH, IT WOULDN'T HAVE BEEN CRUSHED BY THE TRAFFIC!
SO WHEN I FOUND SOMETHING WRAPPED IN MY BACKPACK, I DIDN'T EVEN BOTHER TO OPEN IT.
IT'S PROBABLY JUST ONE OF MOM'S STUPID STUDY GUIDES!
FWAP
WHEN I WENT TO BED I FELL ASLEEP ALMOST IMMEDIATELY.

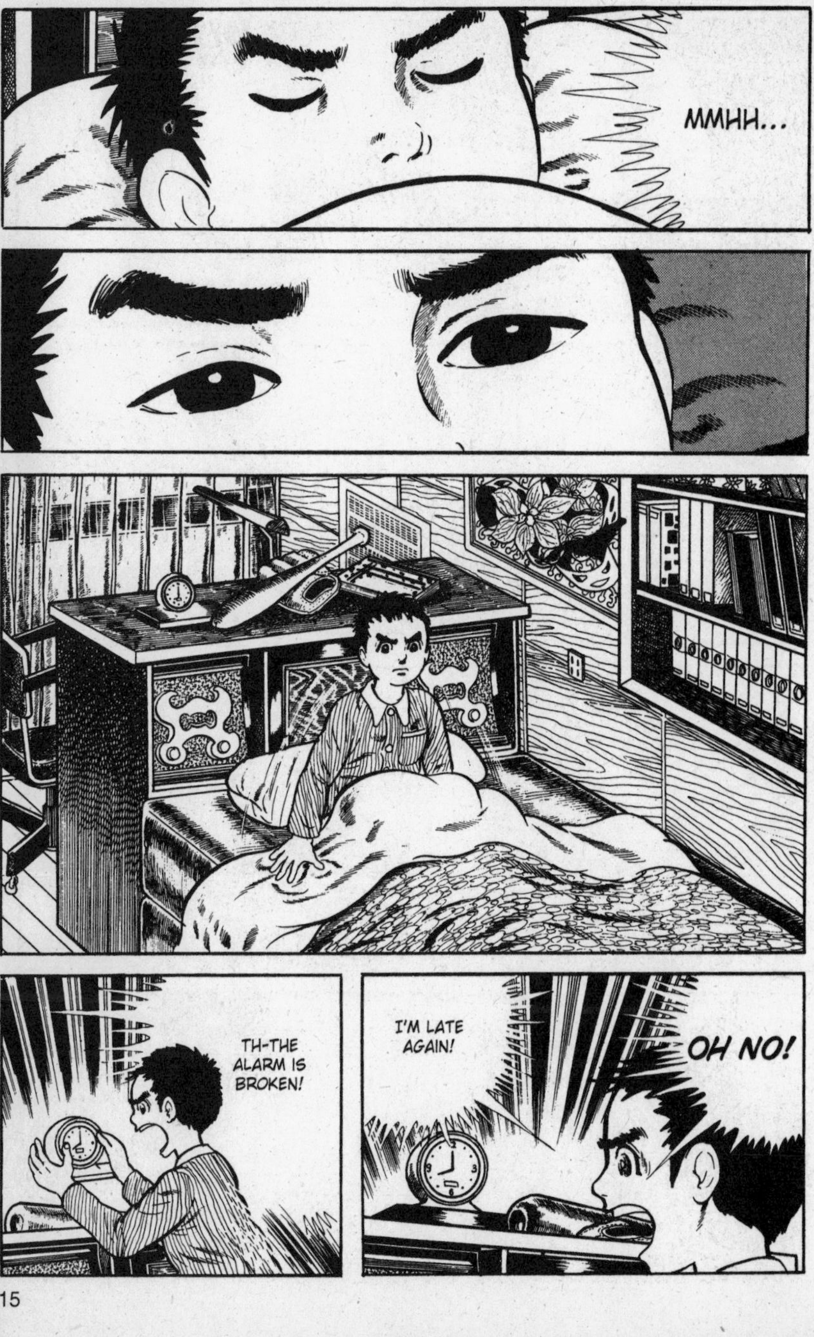
MMHH...
OH NO!
I'M LATE AGAIN!
TH-THE ALARM IS BROKEN!

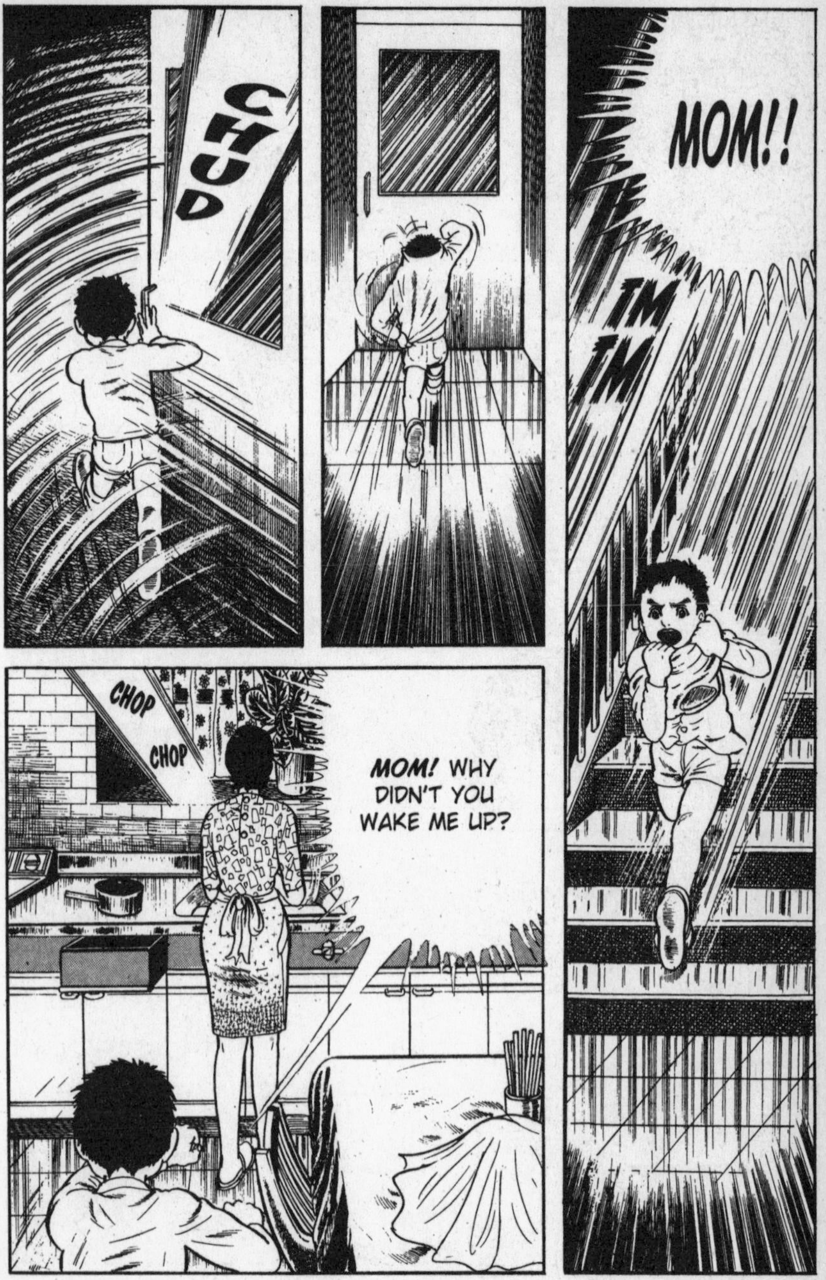
MOM!!
TM
TM
CHUD
CHOP
CHOP
MOM! WHY DIDN'T YOU WAKE ME UP?

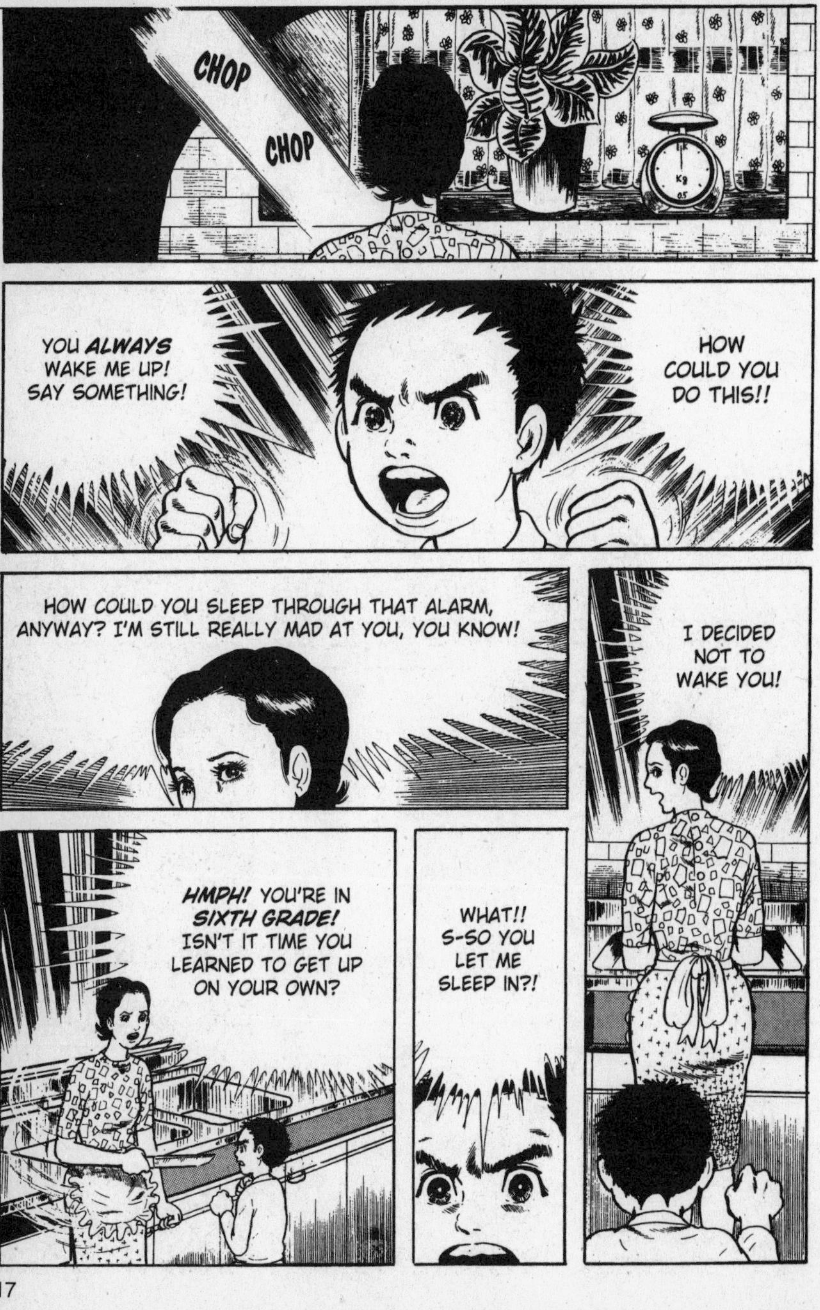
CHOP
CHOP
HOW COULD YOU DO THIS!!
YOU ALWAYS WAKE ME UP! SAY SOMETHING!
I DECIDED NOT TO WAKE YOU!
HOW COULD YOU SLEEP THROUGH THAT ALARM, ANYWAY? I'M STILL REALLY MAD AT YOU, YOU KNOW!
WHAT!! S-SO YOU LET ME SLEEP IN?!
HMPH! YOU'RE IN SIXTH GRADE! ISN'T IT TIME YOU LEARNED TO GET UP ON YOUR OWN?

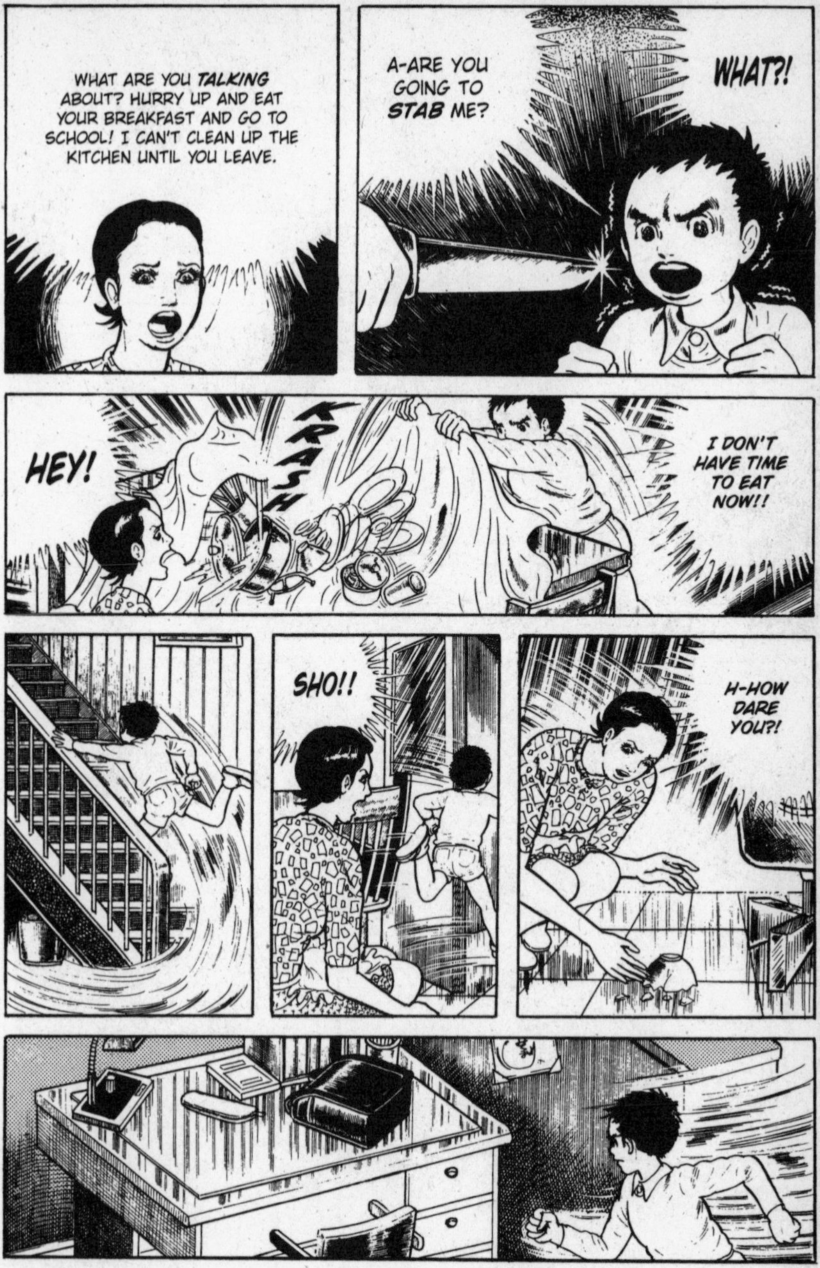
WHAT?!
A-ARE YOU GOING TO STAB ME?
WHAT ARE YOU TALKING ABOUT? HURRY UP AND EAT YOUR BREAKFAST AND GO TO SCHOOL! I CAN'T CLEAN UP THE KITCHEN UNTIL YOU LEAVE.
I DON'T HAVE TIME TO EAT NOW!!
KRASH
HEY!
H-HOW DARE YOU?!
SHO!!

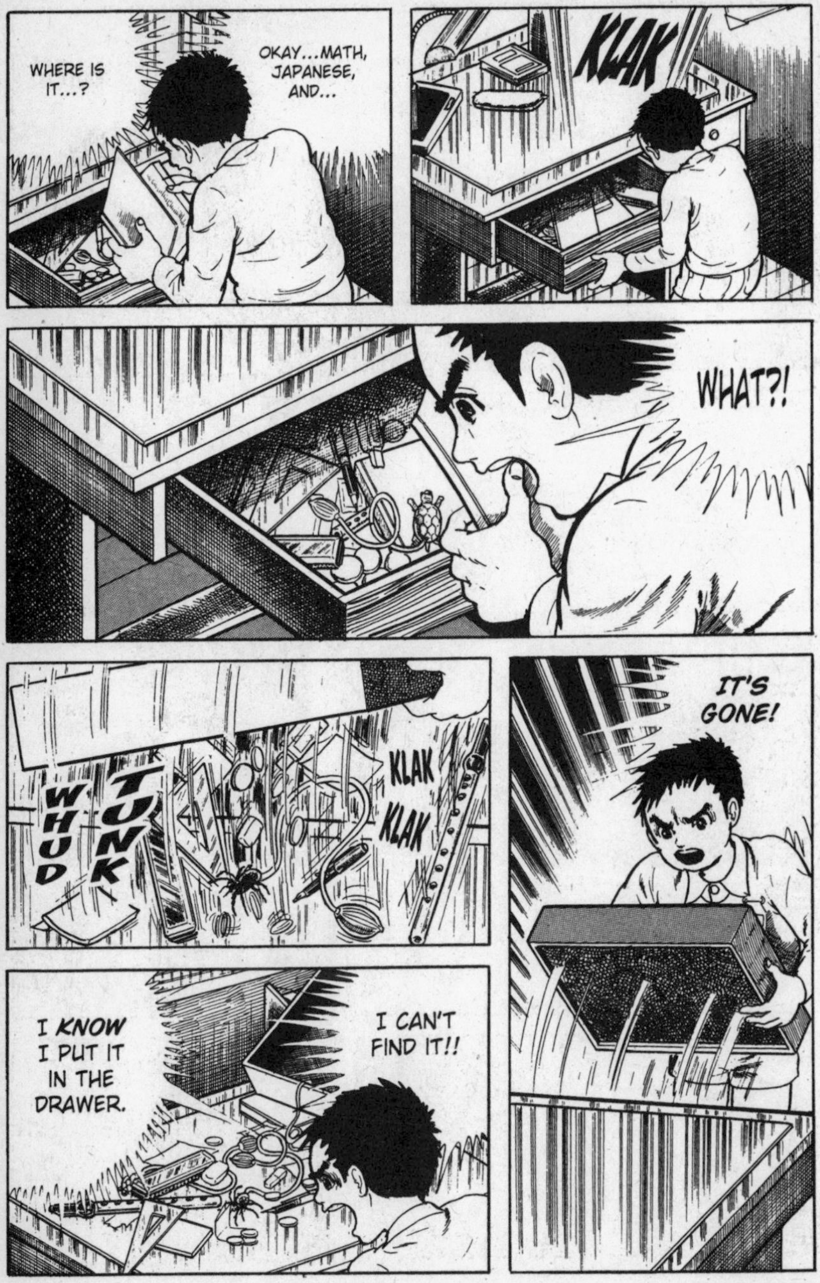
KLAK
OKAY...MATH, JAPANESE, AND...
WHERE IS IT...?
WHAT?!
IT'S GONE!
KLAK
KLAK
TUNK
WHUD
I CAN'T FIND IT!!
I KNOW I PUT IT IN THE DRAWER.

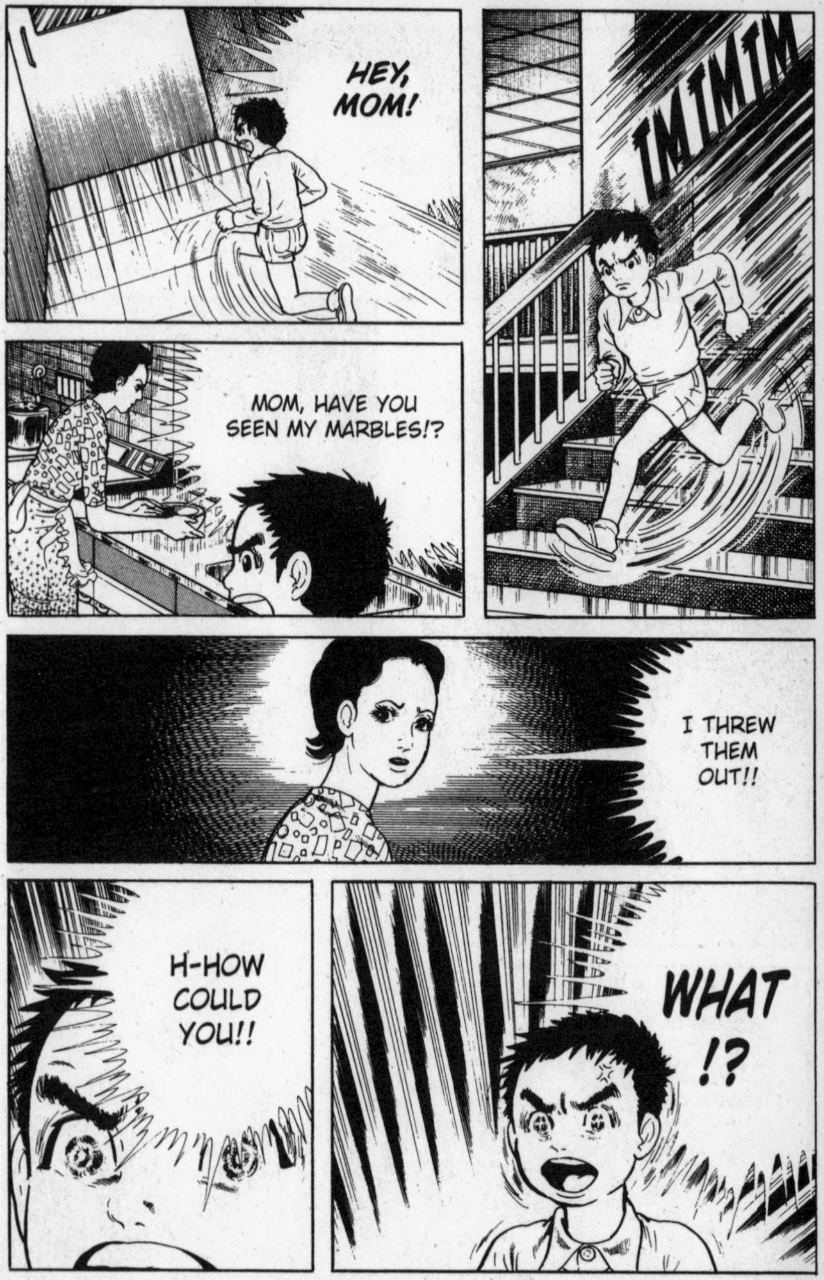
TMTMTM
HEY, MOM!
MOM, HAVE YOU SEEN MY MARBLES!?
I THREW THEM OUT!!
WHAT !?
H-HOW COULD YOU!!

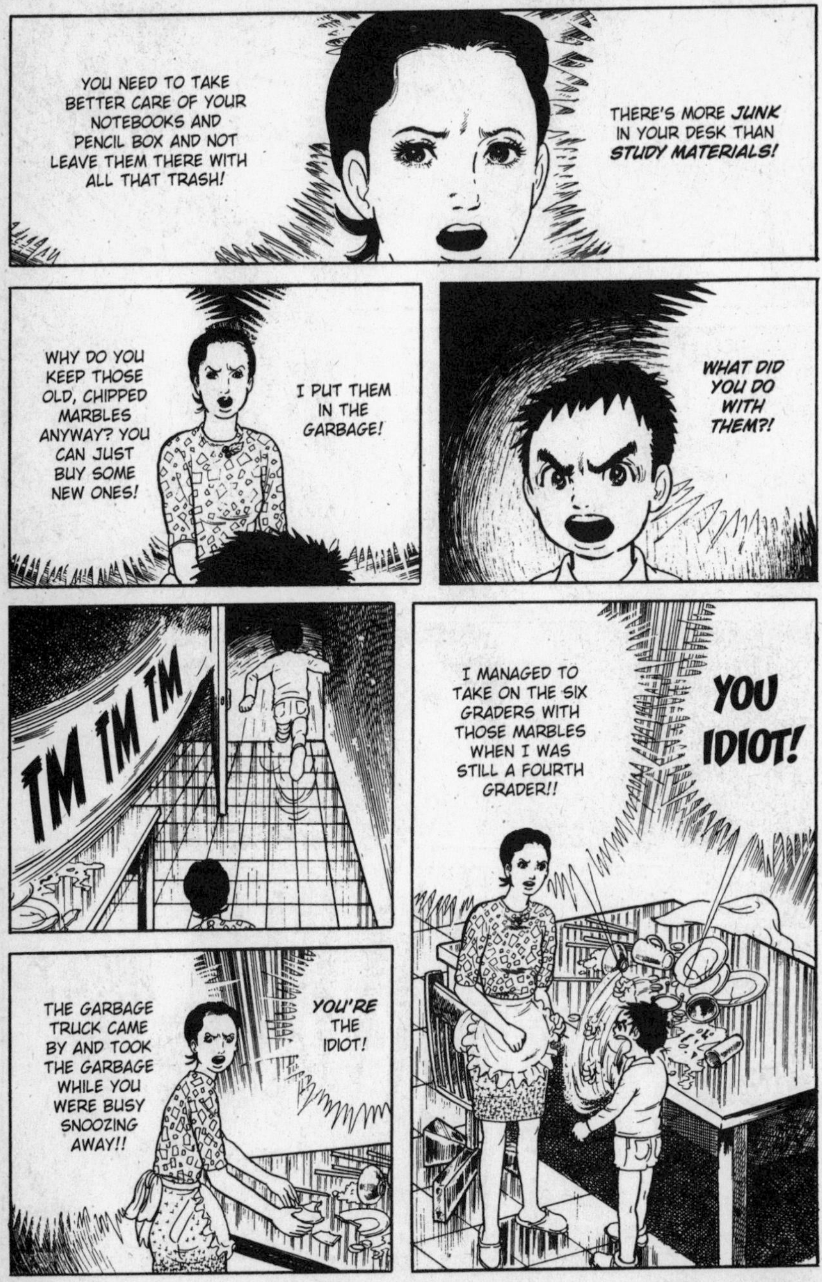
THERE'S MORE JUNK IN YOUR DESK THAN STUDY MATERIALS!
YOU NEED TO TAKE BETTER CARE OF YOUR NOTEBOOKS AND PENCIL BOX AND NOT LEAVE THEM THERE WITH ALL THAT TRASH!
WHAT DID YOU DO WITH THEM?!
I PUT THEM IN THE GARBAGE!
WHY DO YOU KEEP THOSE OLD, CHIPPED MARBLES ANYWAY? YOU CAN JUST BUY SOME NEW ONES!
YOU IDIOT!
I MANAGED TO TAKE ON THE SIX GRADERS WITH THOSE MARBLES WHEN I WAS STILL A FOURTH GRADER!!
TM TM TM
YOU'RE THE IDIOT!
THE GARBAGE TRUCK CAME BY AND TOOK THE GARBAGE WHILE YOU WERE BUSY SNOOZING AWAY!!

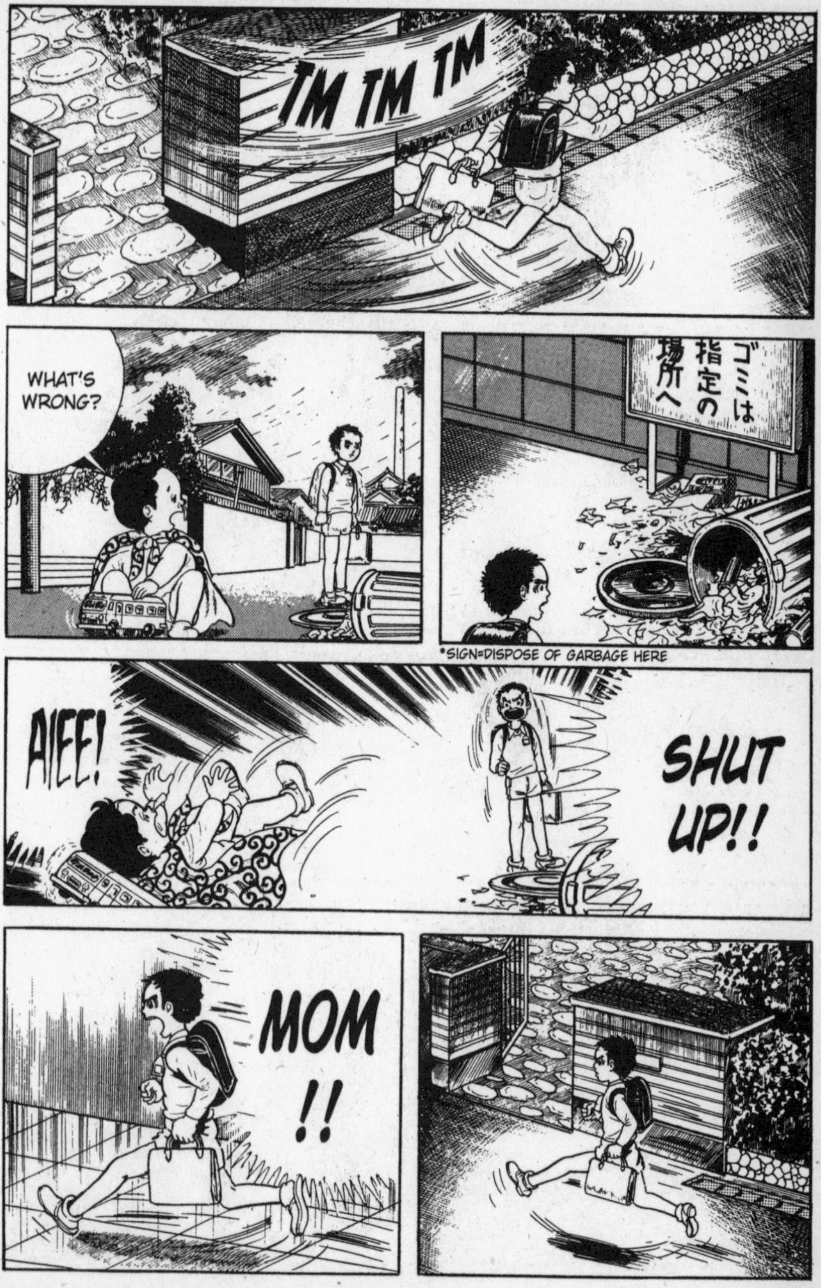
TM TM TM
ゴミは指定の場所へ
*SIGN=DISPOSE OF GARBAGE HERE
WHAT'S WRONG?
SHUT UP!!
AIEE!
MOM !!

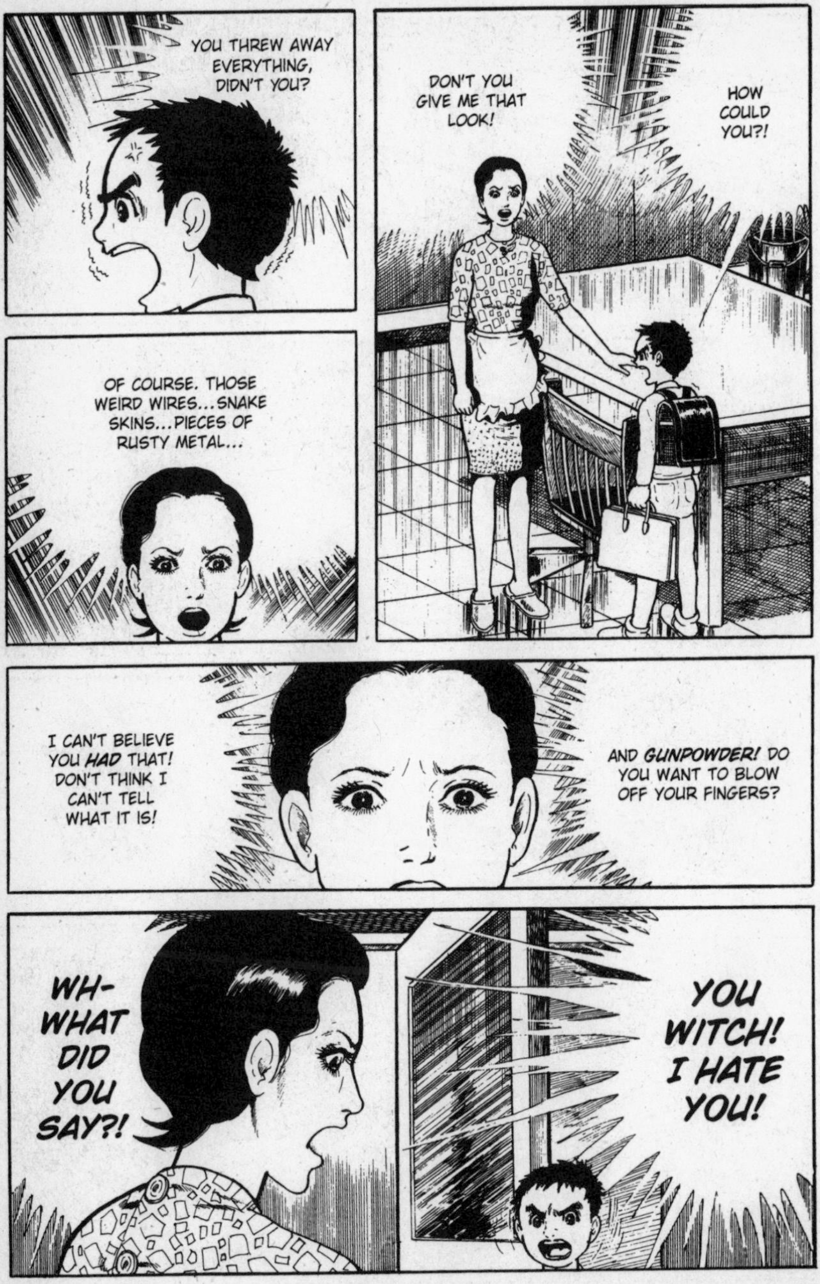
HOW COULD YOU?!
DON'T YOU GIVE ME THAT LOOK!
YOU THREW AWAY EVERYTHING, DIDN'T YOU?
OF COURSE. THOSE WEIRD WIRES... SNAKE SKINS... PIECES OF RUSTY METAL...
AND ***GUNPOWDER!*** DO YOU WANT TO BLOW OFF YOUR FINGERS?
I CAN'T BELIEVE YOU ***HAD*** THAT! DON'T THINK I CAN'T TELL WHAT IT IS!
YOU WITCH! I HATE YOU!
WH-WHAT DID YOU SAY?!

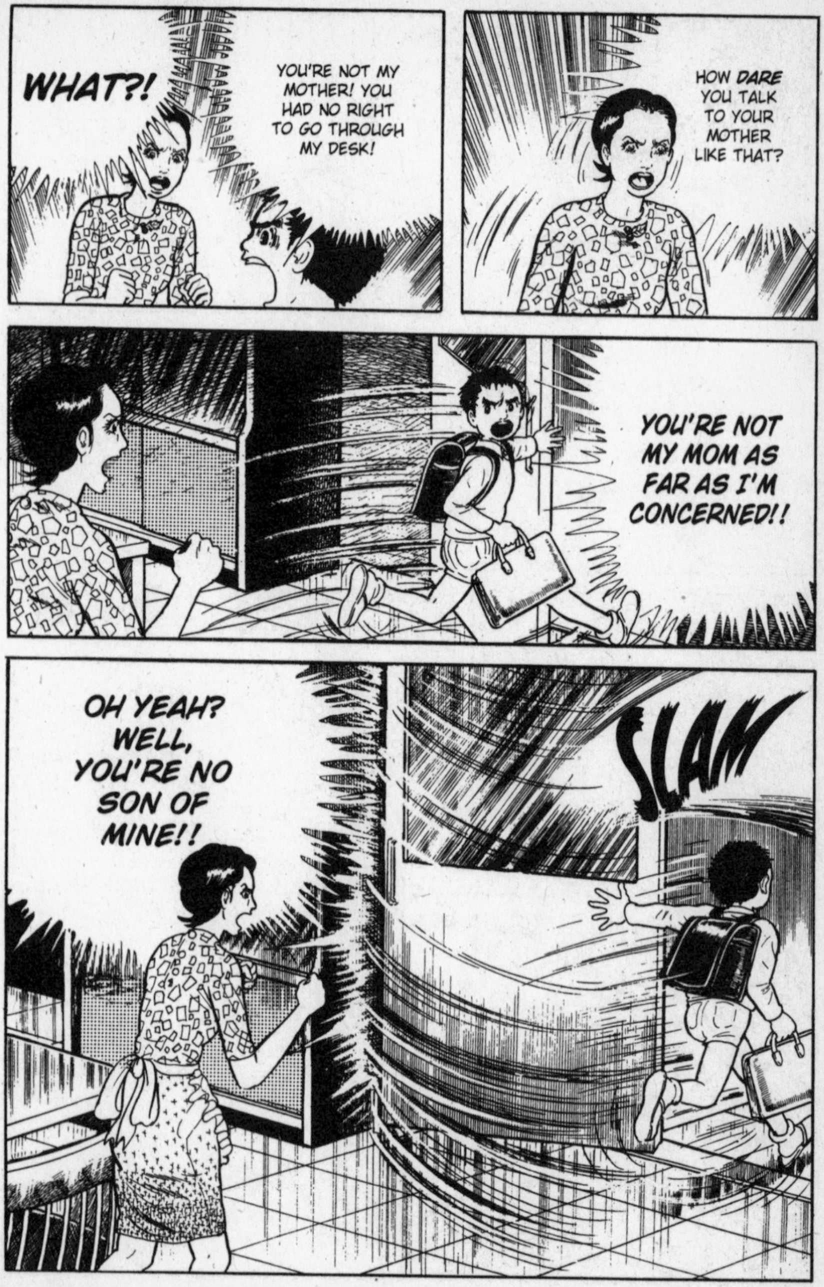
YOU'RE NOT MY MOTHER! YOU HAD NO RIGHT TO GO THROUGH MY DESK!
WHAT?!
HOW DARE YOU TALK TO YOUR MOTHER LIKE THAT?
YOU'RE NOT MY MOM AS FAR AS I'M CONCERNED!!
SLAM
OH YEAH? WELL, YOU'RE NO SON OF MINE!!

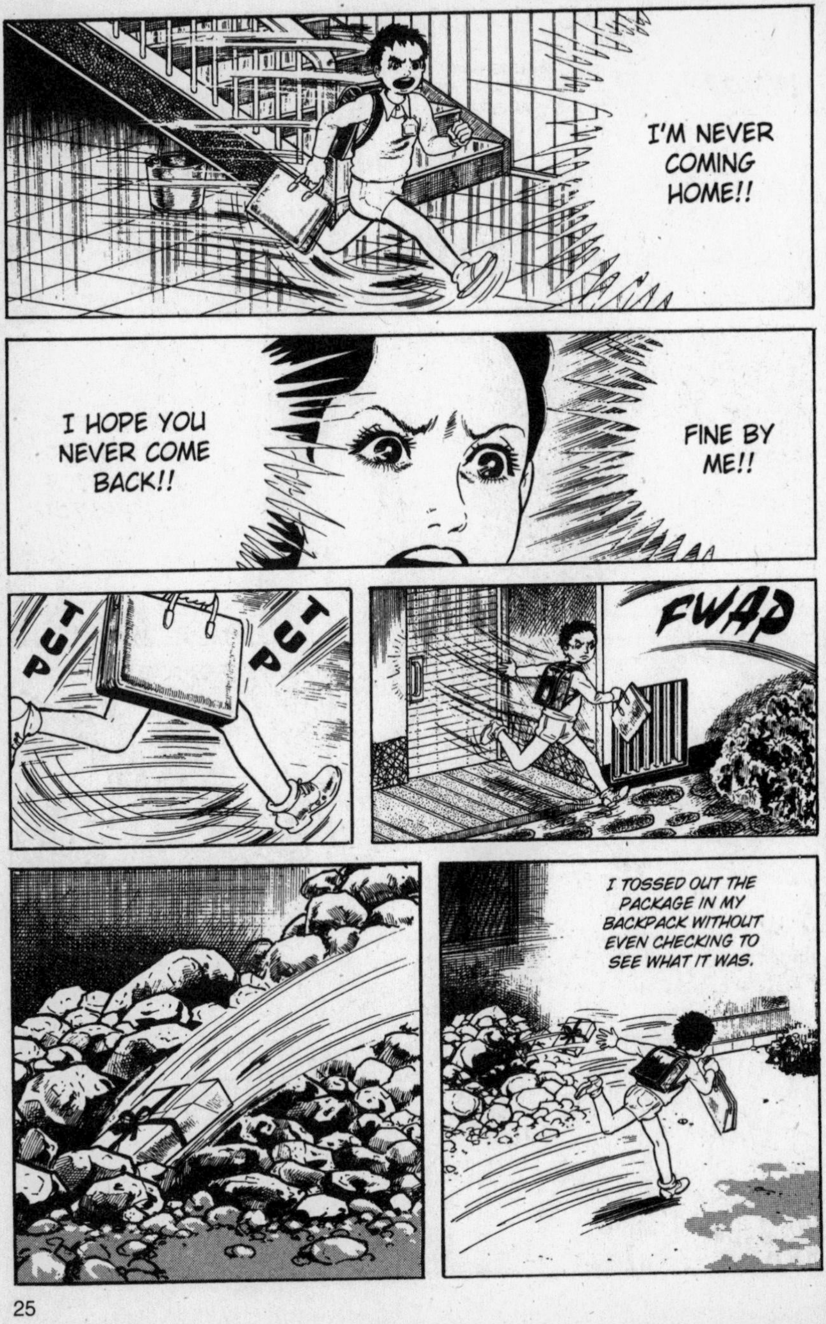
I'M NEVER COMING HOME!!
FINE BY ME!!
I HOPE YOU NEVER COME BACK!!
FWAP
TUP
TUP
I TOSSED OUT THE PACKAGE IN MY BACKPACK WITHOUT EVEN CHECKING TO SEE WHAT IT WAS.

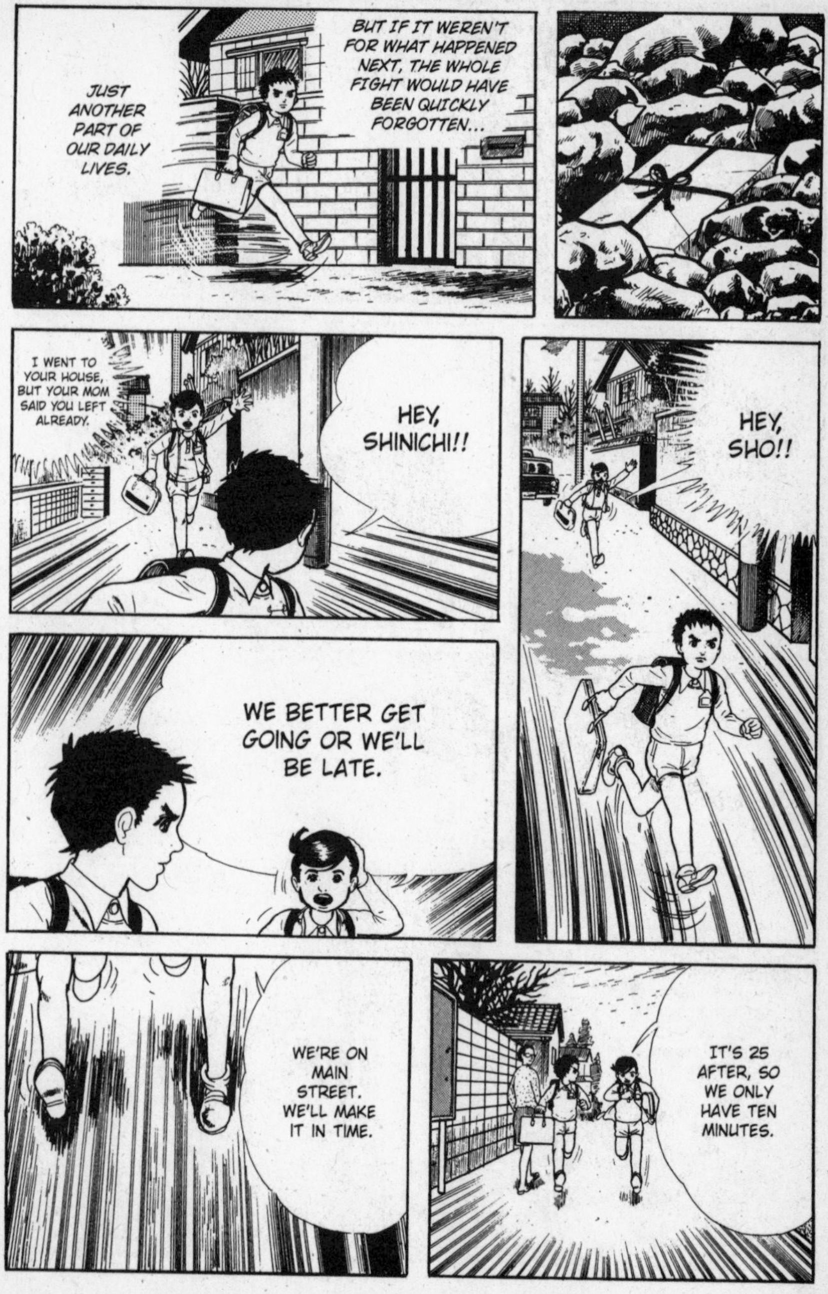
BUT IF IT WEREN'T FOR WHAT HAPPENED NEXT, THE WHOLE FIGHT WOULD HAVE BEEN QUICKLY FORGOTTEN...
JUST ANOTHER PART OF OUR DAILY LIVES.
HEY, SHO!!
HEY, SHINICHI!!
I WENT TO YOUR HOUSE, BUT YOUR MOM SAID YOU LEFT ALREADY.
WE BETTER GET GOING OR WE'LL BE LATE.
IT'S 25 AFTER, SO WE ONLY HAVE TEN MINUTES.
WE'RE ON MAIN STREET. WE'LL MAKE IT IN TIME.

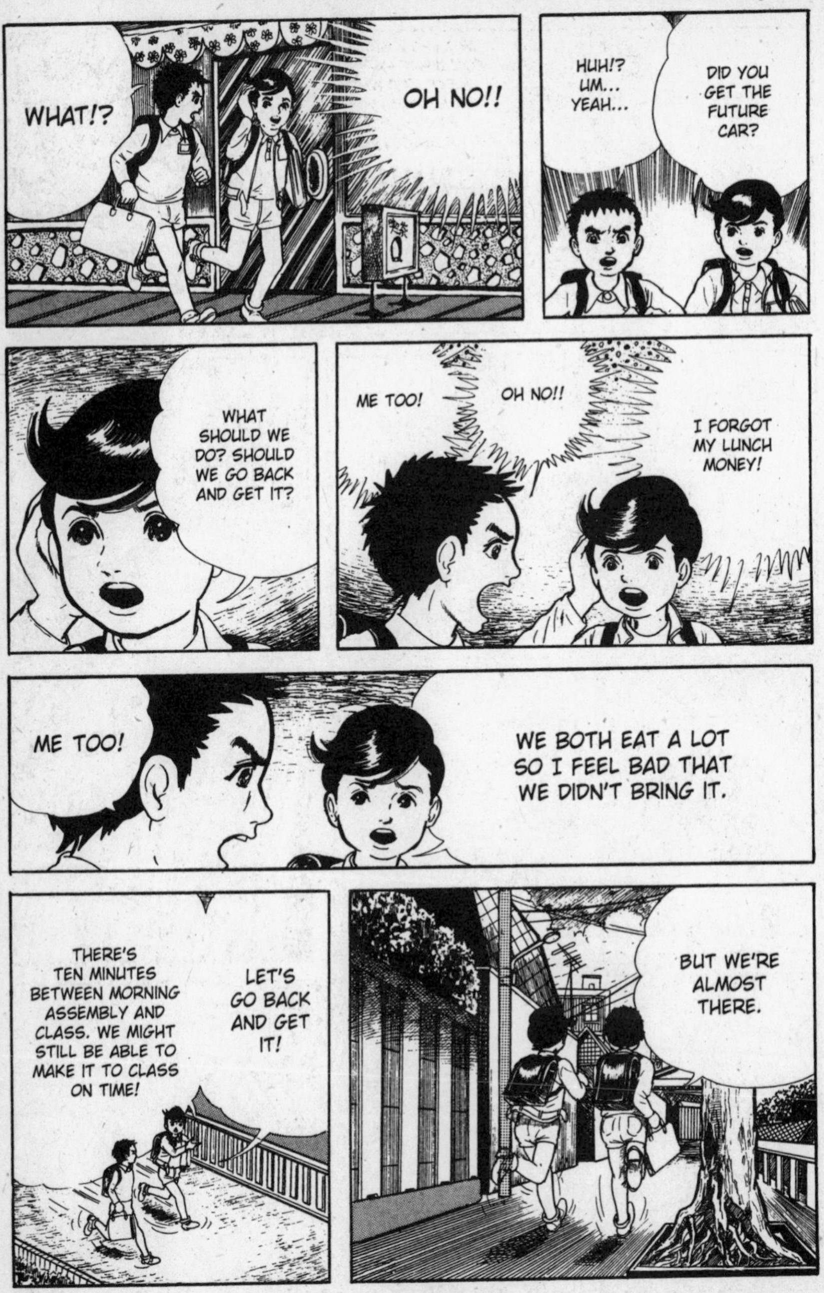
DID YOU GET THE FUTURE CAR?
HUH!? UM... YEAH...
OH NO!!
WHAT!?
I FORGOT MY LUNCH MONEY!
OH NO!!
ME TOO!
WHAT SHOULD WE DO? SHOULD WE GO BACK AND GET IT?
WE BOTH EAT A LOT SO I FEEL BAD THAT WE DIDN'T BRING IT.
ME TOO!
BUT WE'RE ALMOST THERE.
LET'S GO BACK AND GET IT!
THERE'S TEN MINUTES BETWEEN MORNING ASSEMBLY AND CLASS. WE MIGHT STILL BE ABLE TO MAKE IT TO CLASS ON TIME!

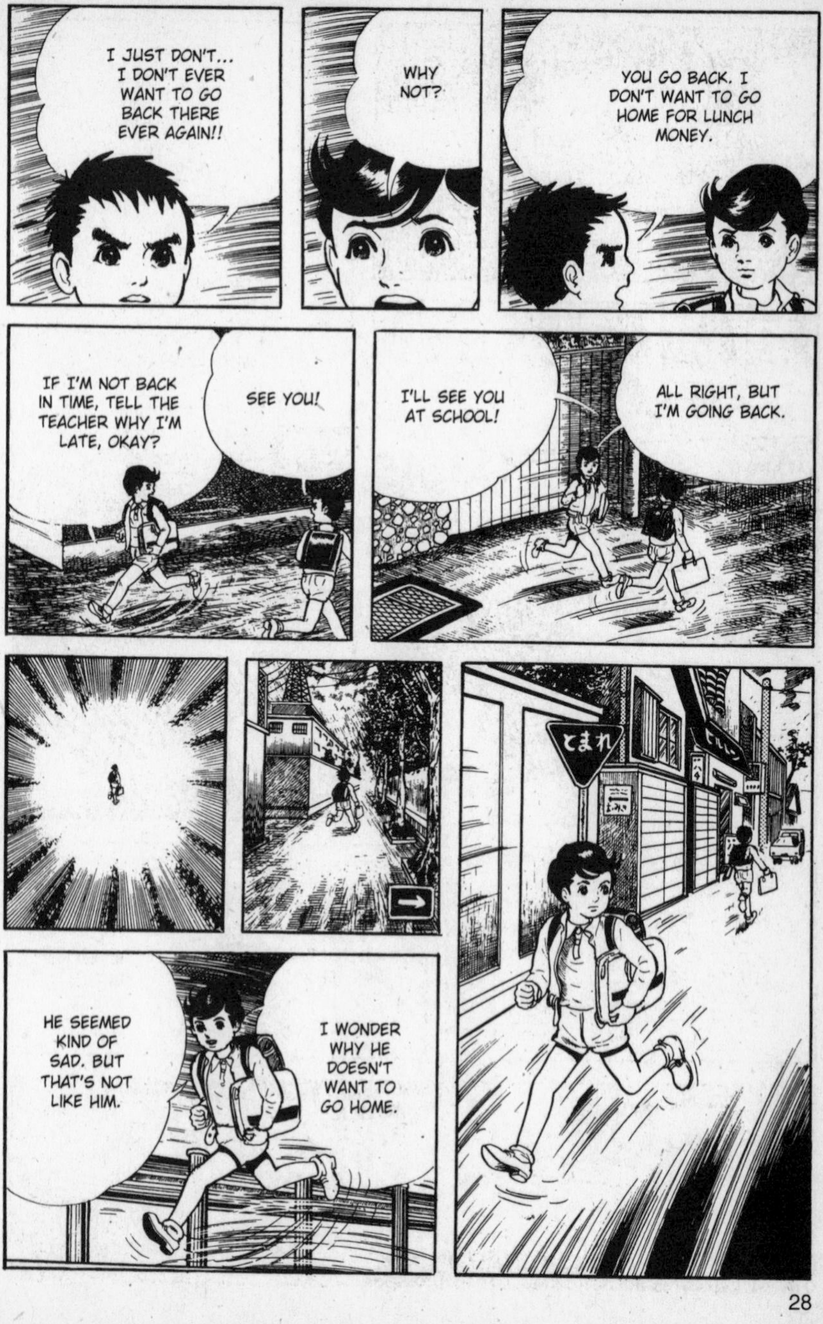
YOU GO BACK. I DON'T WANT TO GO HOME FOR LUNCH MONEY.
WHY NOT?
I JUST DON'T... I DON'T EVER WANT TO GO BACK THERE EVER AGAIN!!
ALL RIGHT, BUT I'M GOING BACK.
I'LL SEE YOU AT SCHOOL!
SEE YOU!
IF I'M NOT BACK IN TIME, TELL THE TEACHER WHY I'M LATE, OKAY?
とまれ
I WONDER WHY HE DOESN'T WANT TO GO HOME.
HE SEEMED KIND OF SAD. BUT THAT'S NOT LIKE HIM.

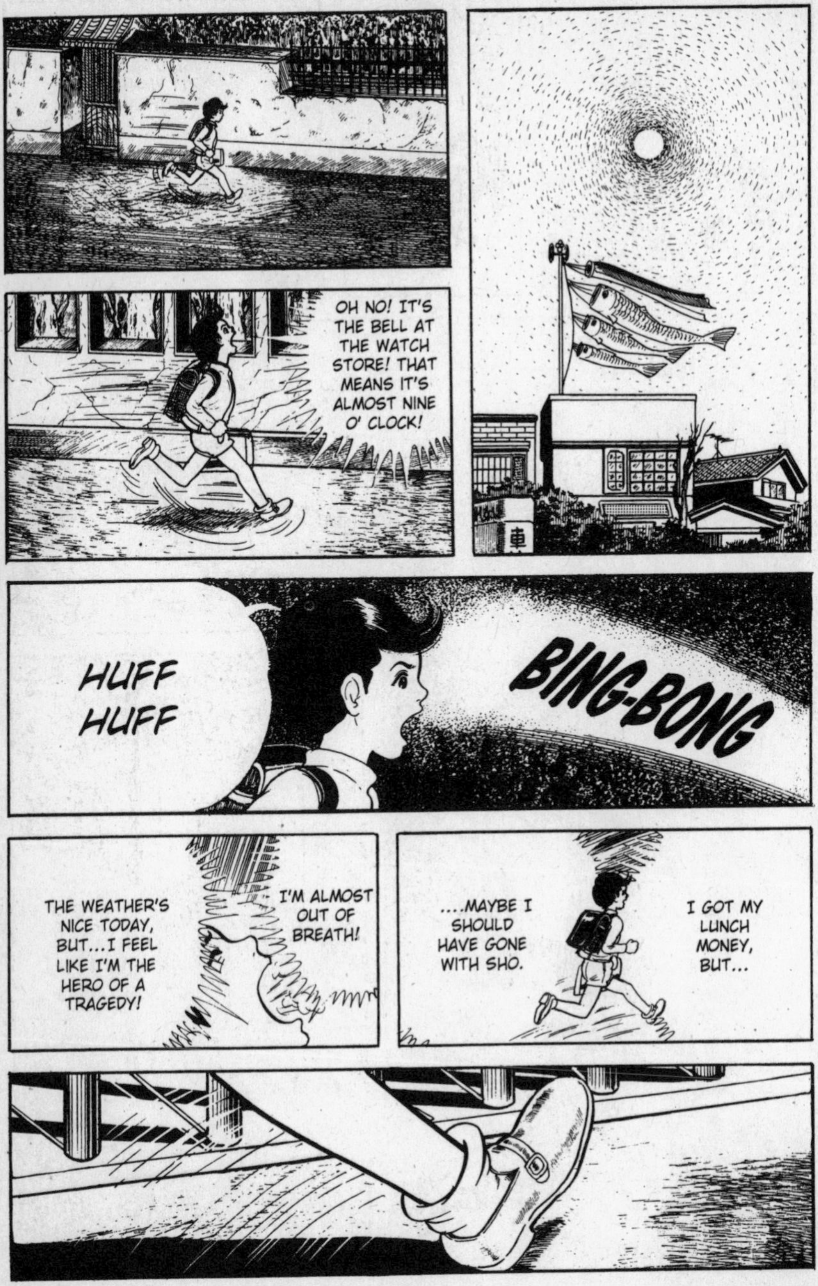
OH NO! IT'S THE BELL AT THE WATCH STORE! THAT MEANS IT'S ALMOST NINE O' CLOCK!
BING-BONG
HUFF HUFF
I GOT MY LUNCH MONEY, BUT...
....MAYBE I SHOULD HAVE GONE WITH SHO.
I'M ALMOST OUT OF BREATH!
THE WEATHER'S NICE TODAY, BUT...I FEEL LIKE I'M THE HERO OF A TRAGEDY!

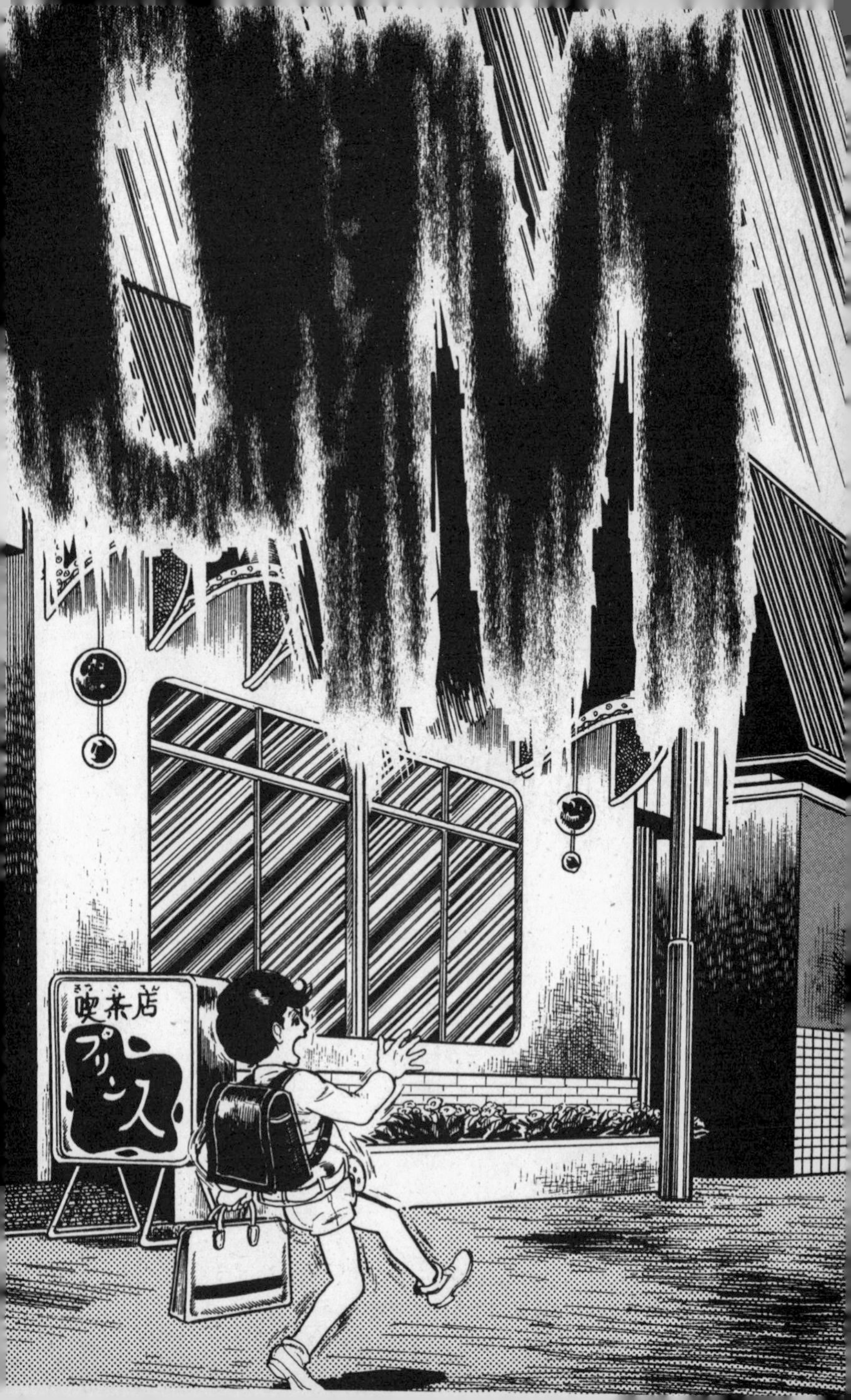
喫茶店
プリンス

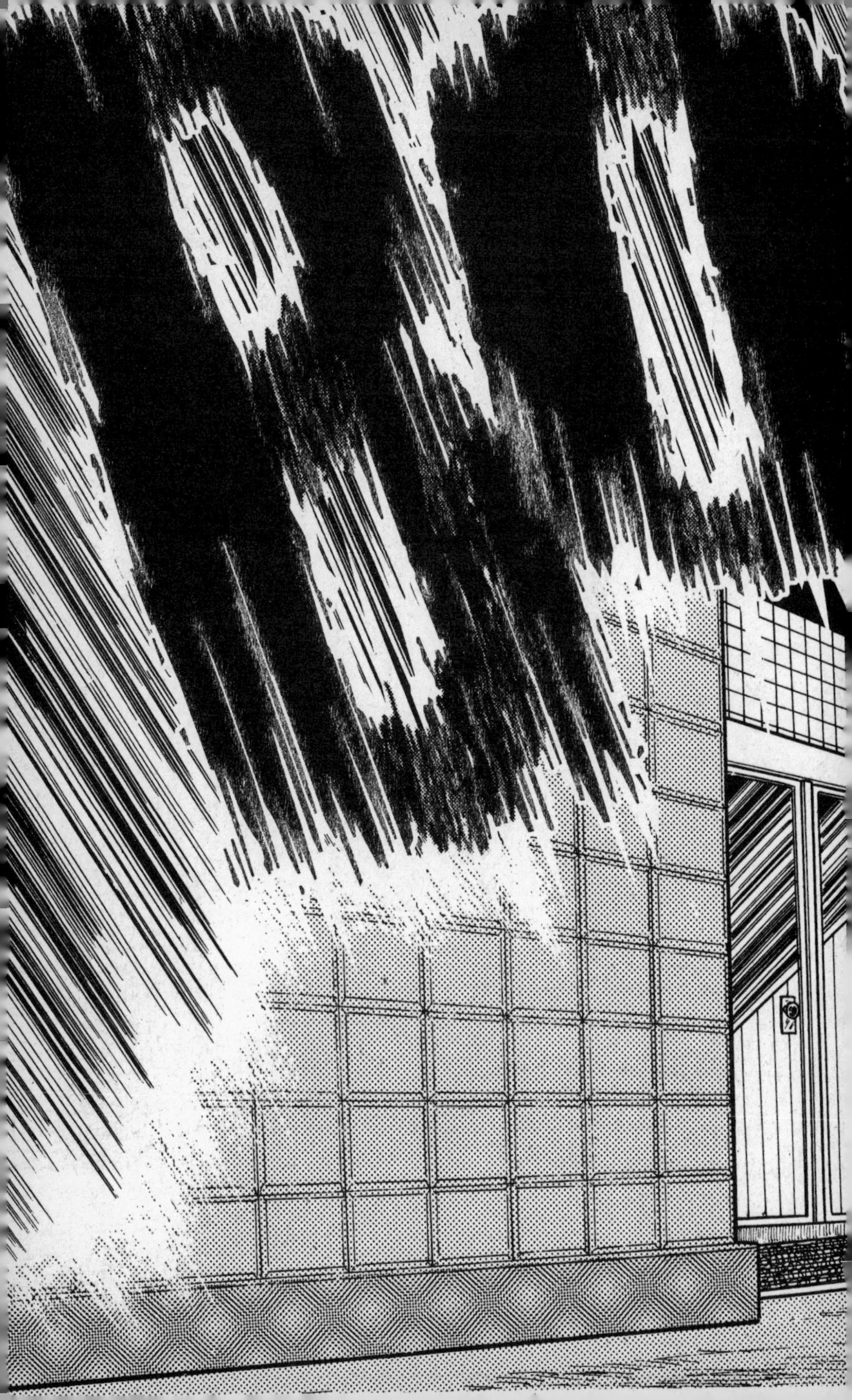

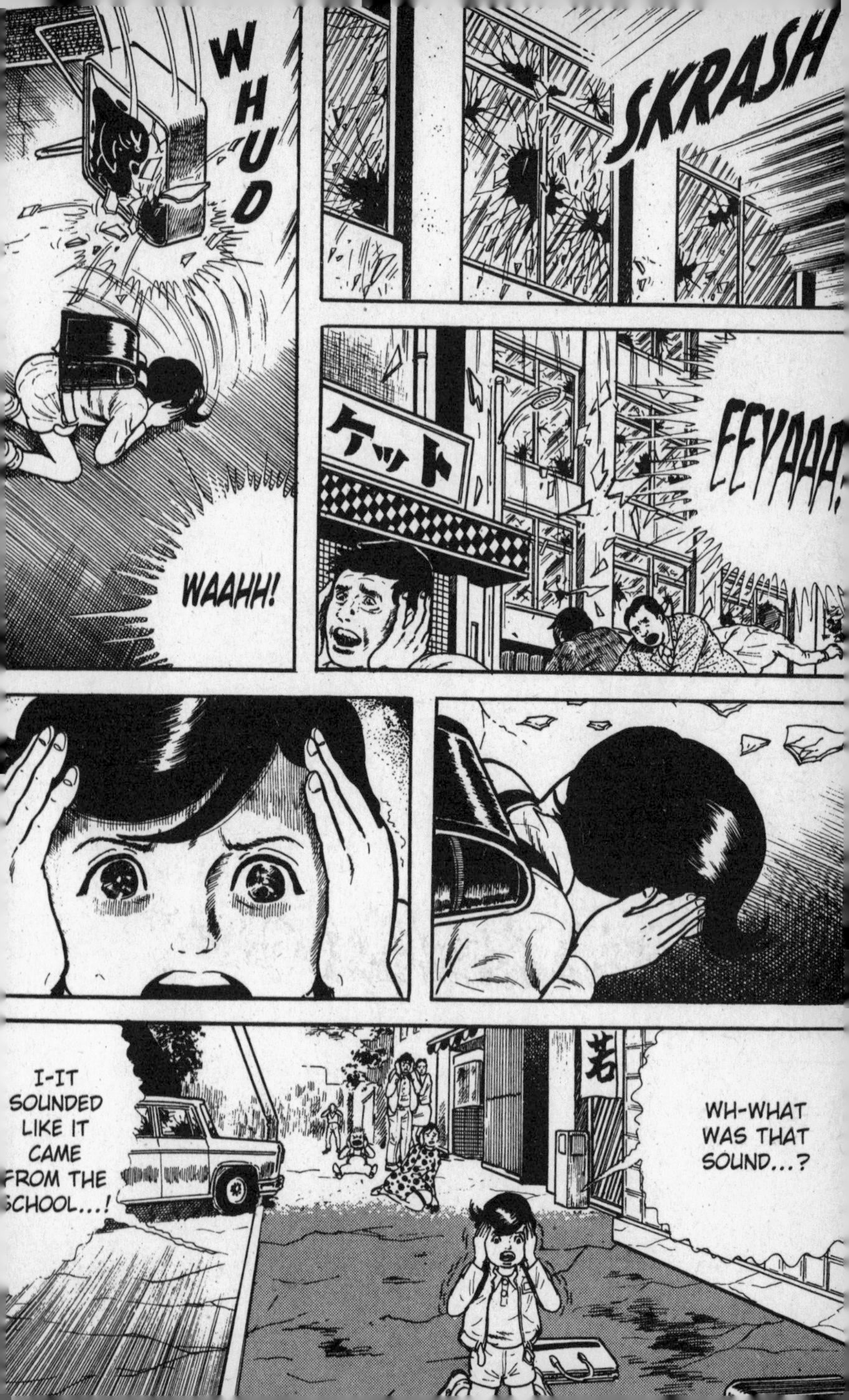
SKRASH
ケット
EEYAAA!
WHUD
WAAHH!
若
WH-WHAT WAS THAT SOUND...?
I-IT SOUNDED LIKE IT CAME FROM THE SCHOOL...!

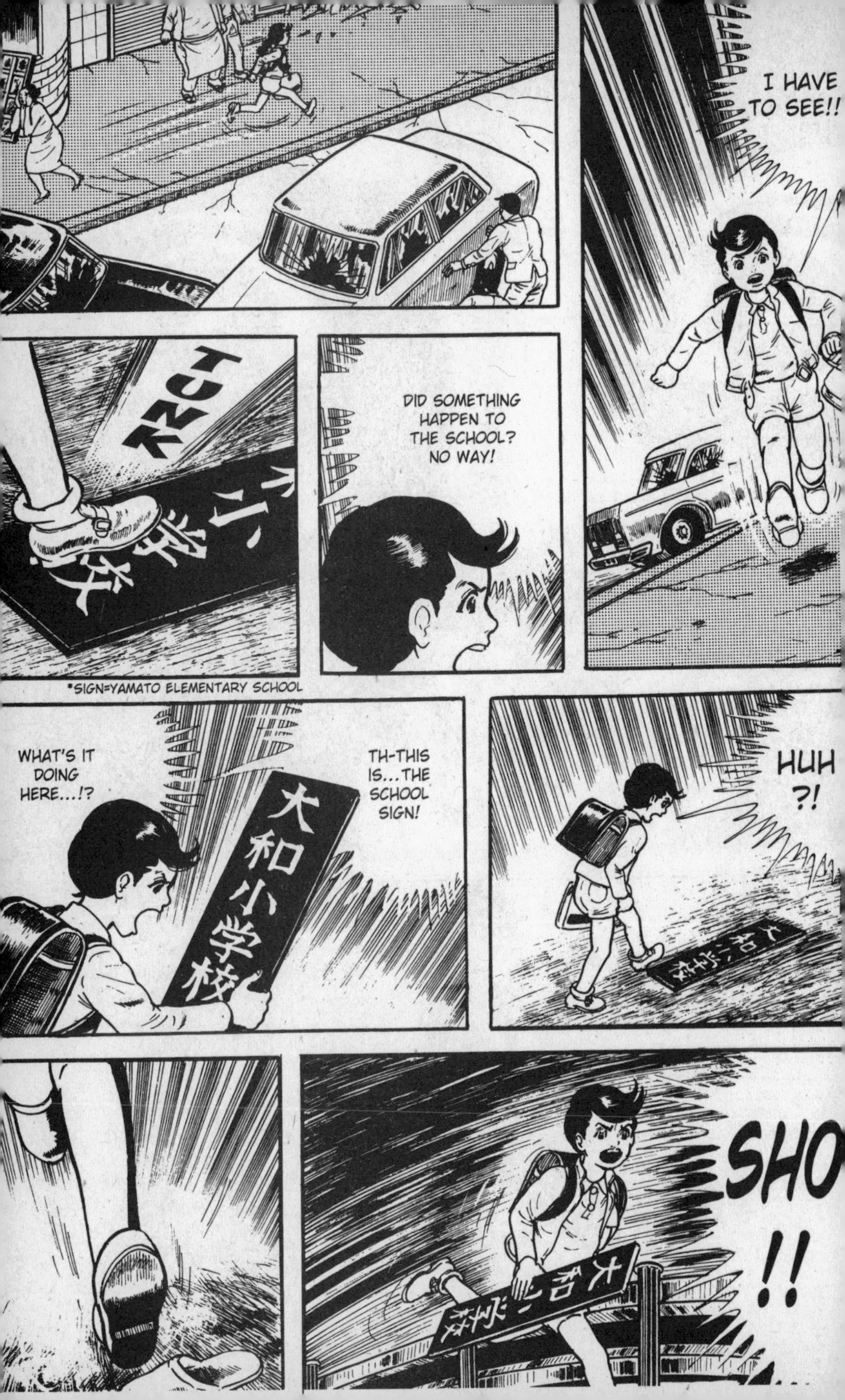
I HAVE TO SEE!!
DID SOMETHING HAPPEN TO THE SCHOOL? NO WAY!
JUNK
*SIGN=YAMATO ELEMENTARY SCHOOL
HUH ?!
TH-THIS IS...THE SCHOOL SIGN!
WHAT'S IT DOING HERE...!?
大和小学校
SHO !!

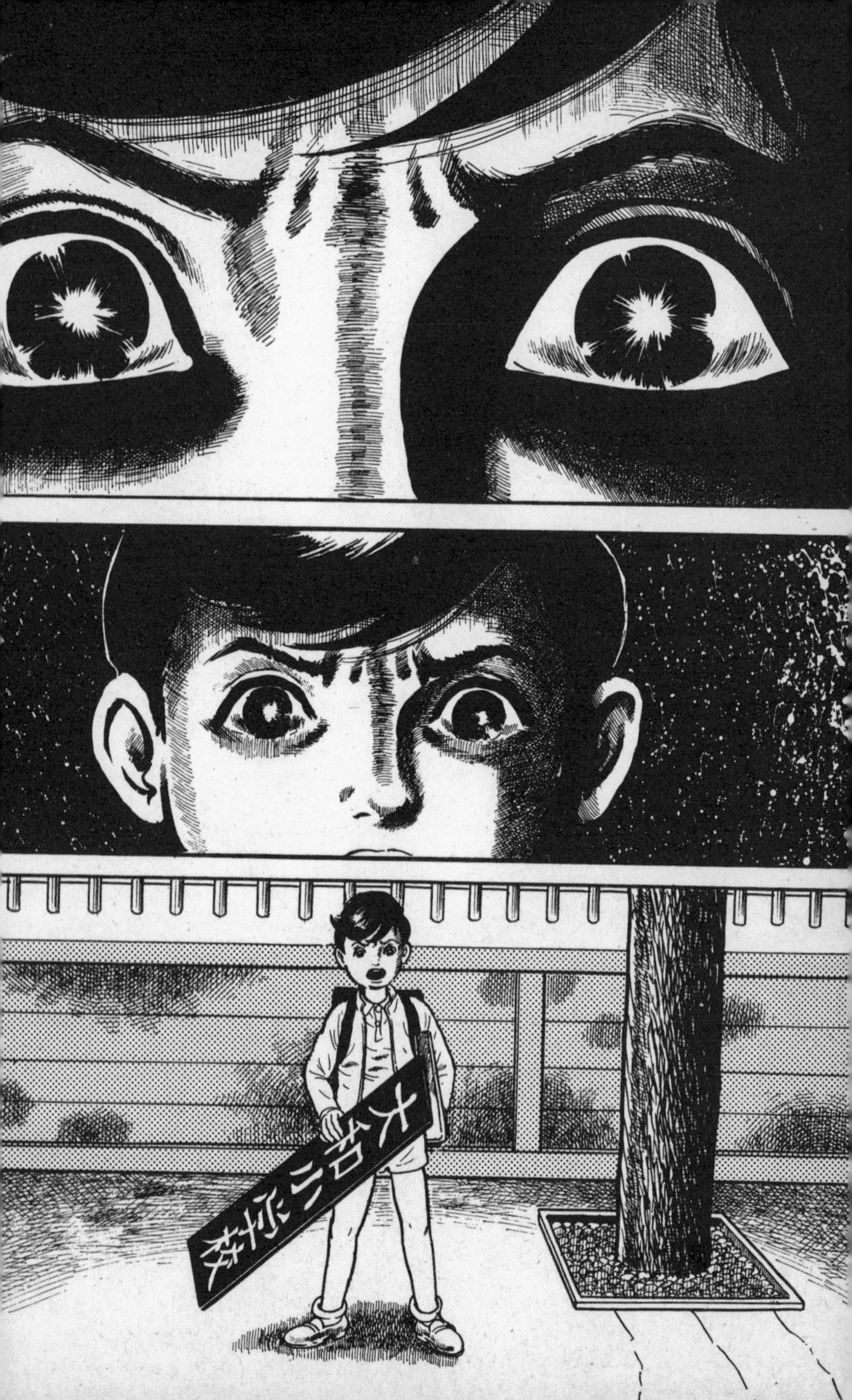

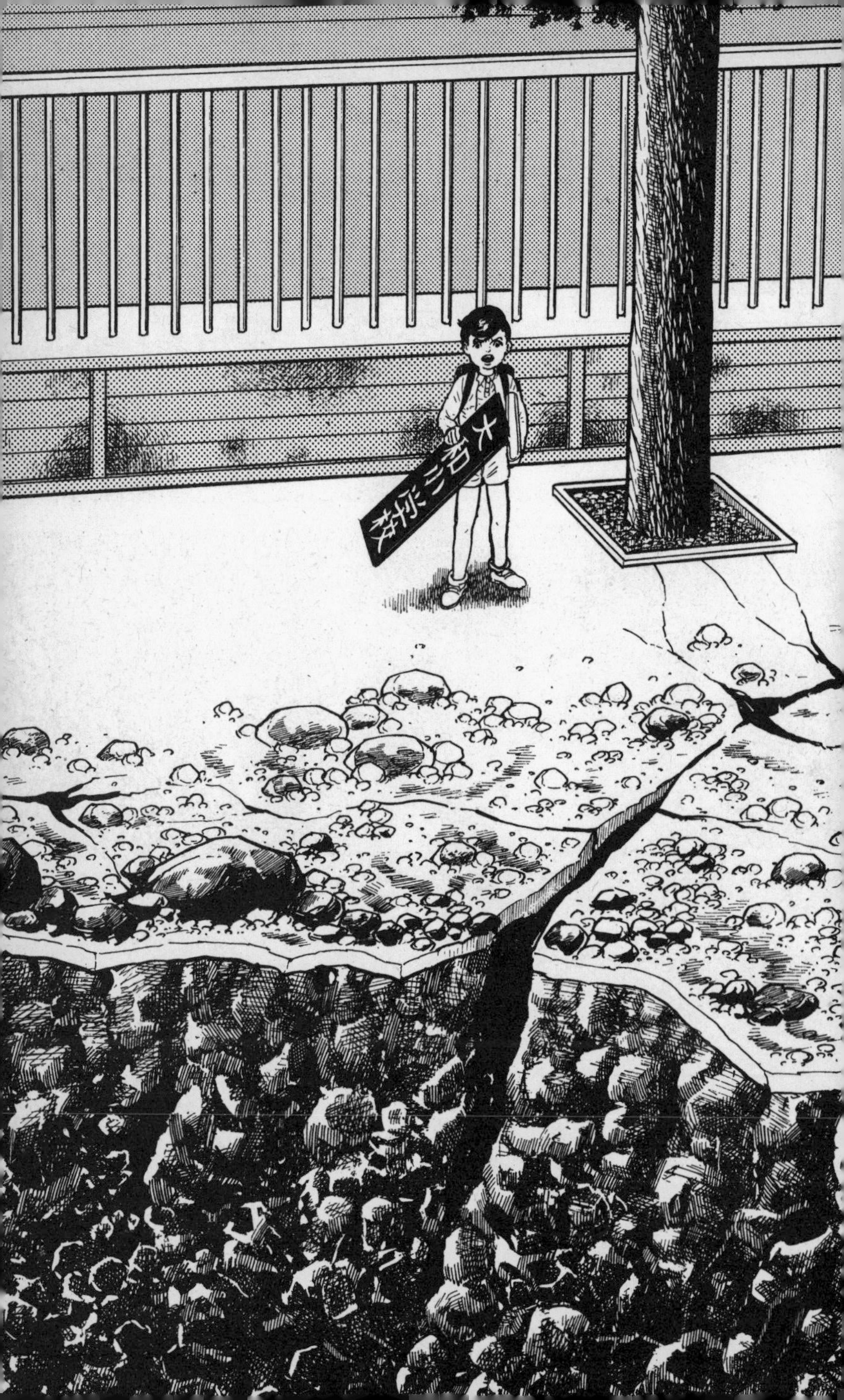

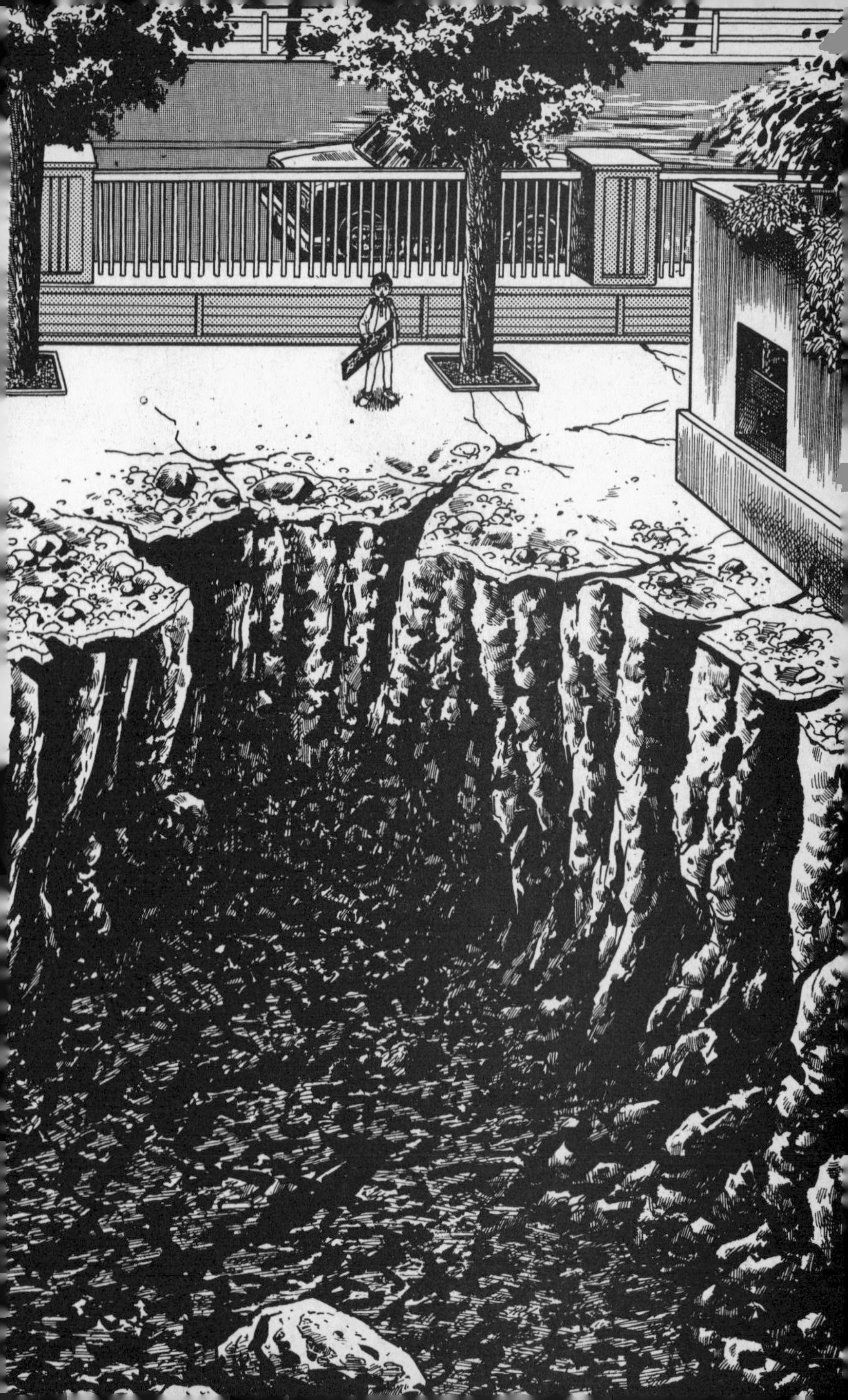

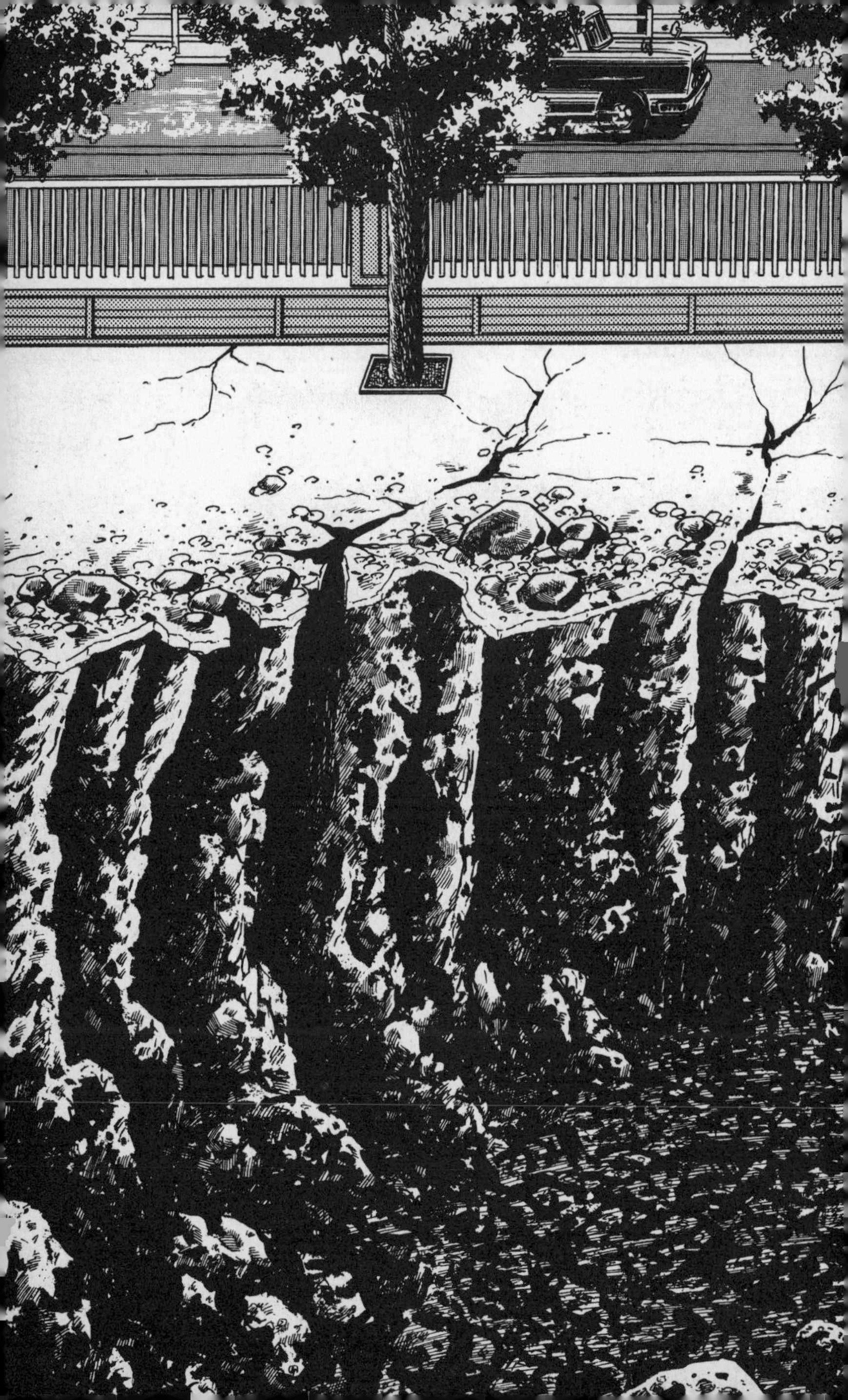

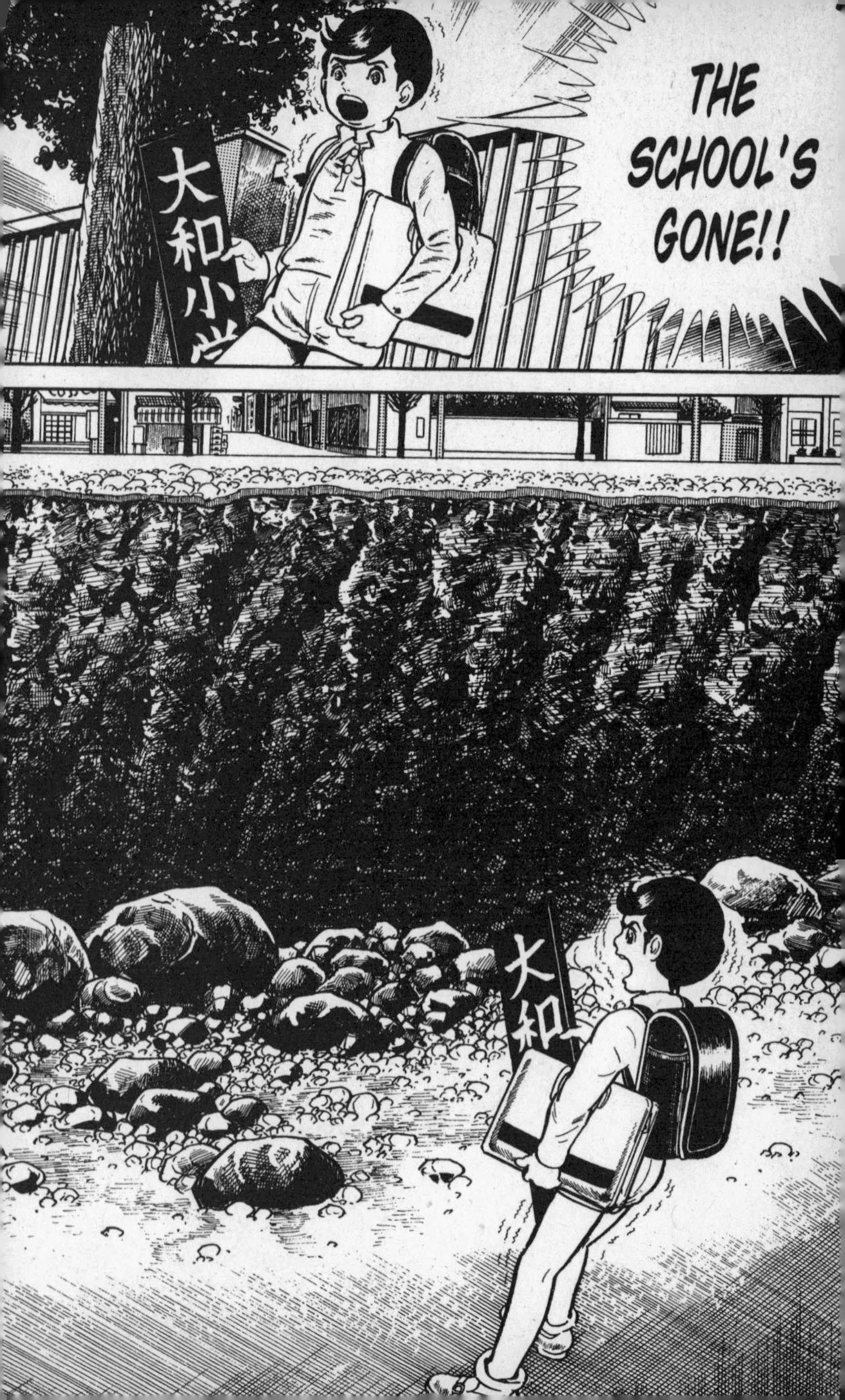
THE SCHOOL'S GONE!!
大和小学
大和

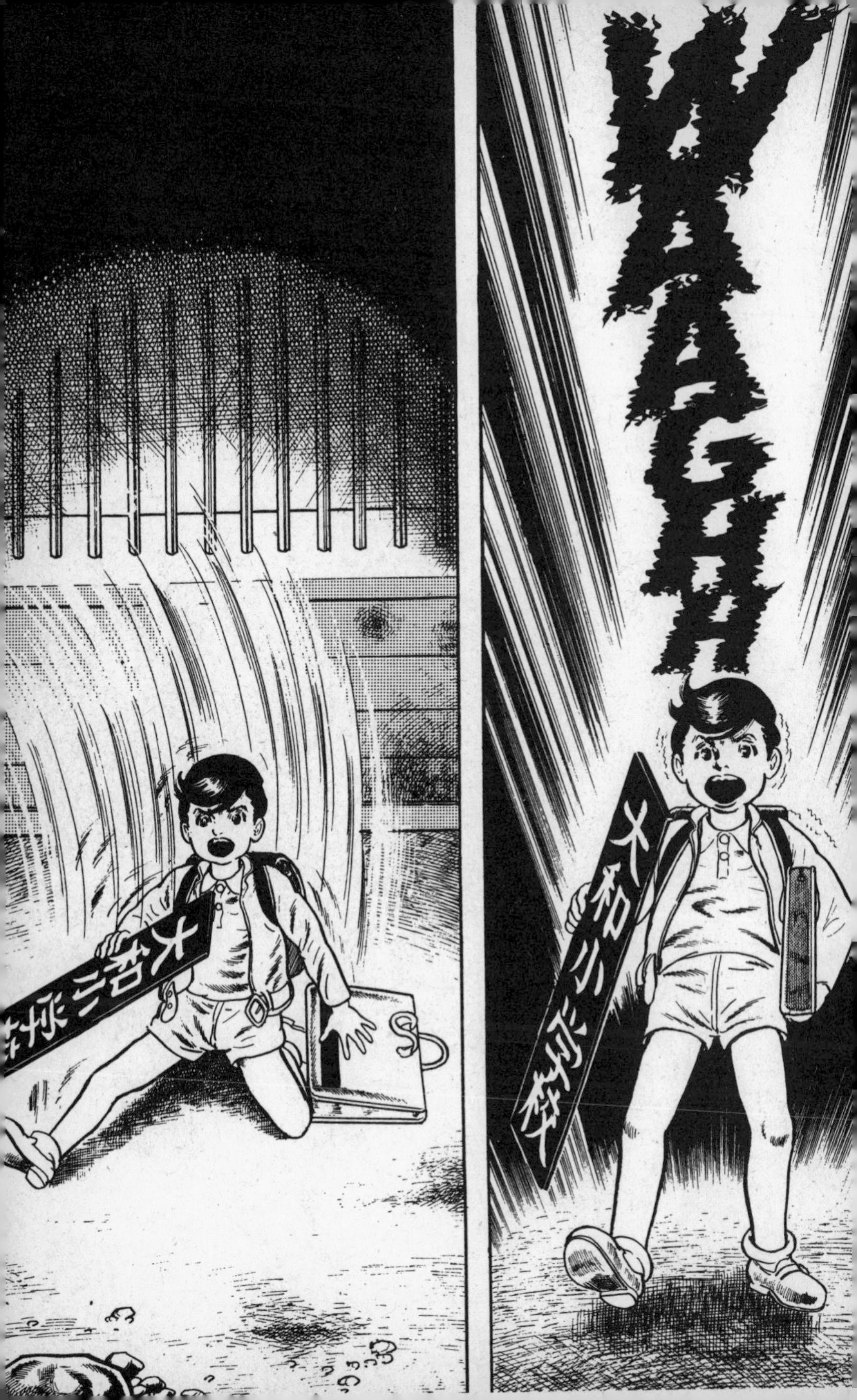
WAAGHH
大和小学校

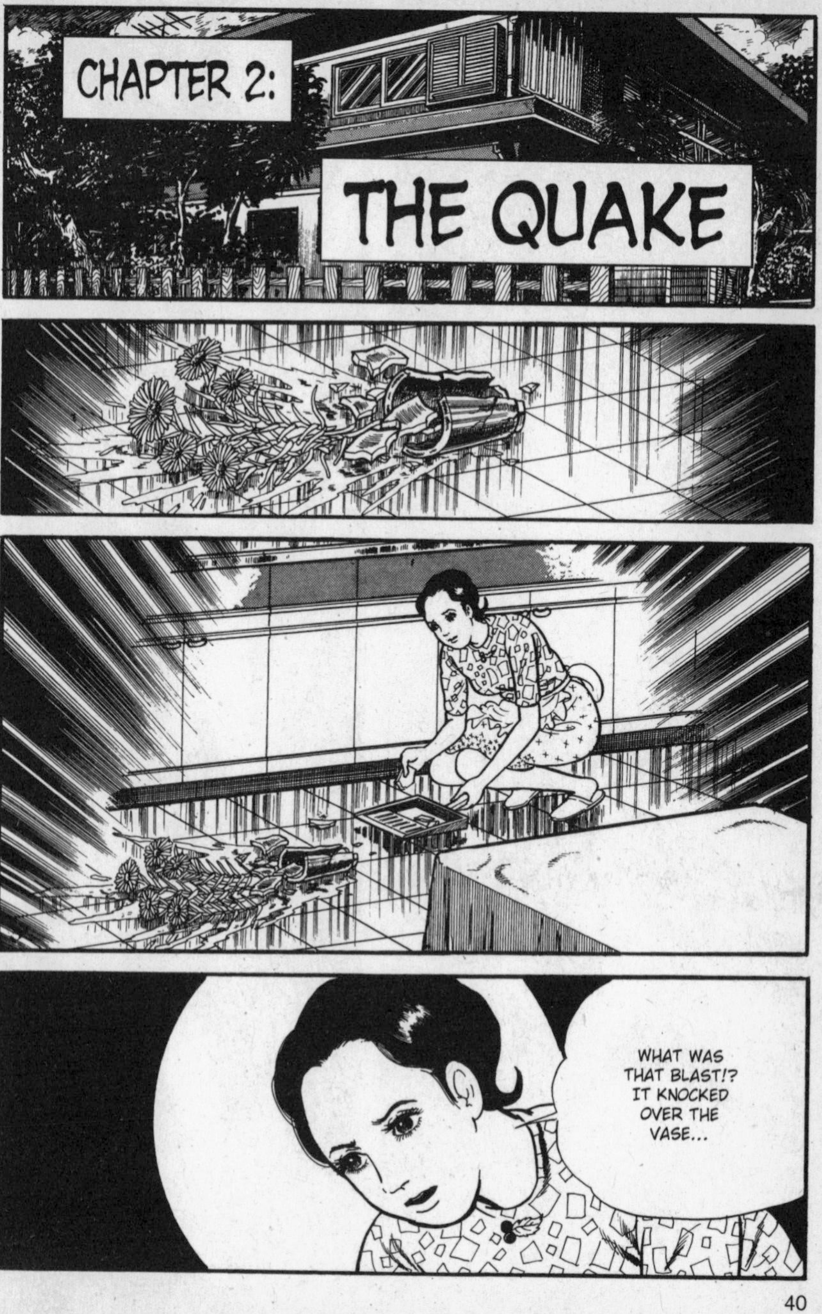
CHAPTER 2:
THE QUAKE
WHAT WAS THAT BLAST!? IT KNOCKED OVER THE VASE...

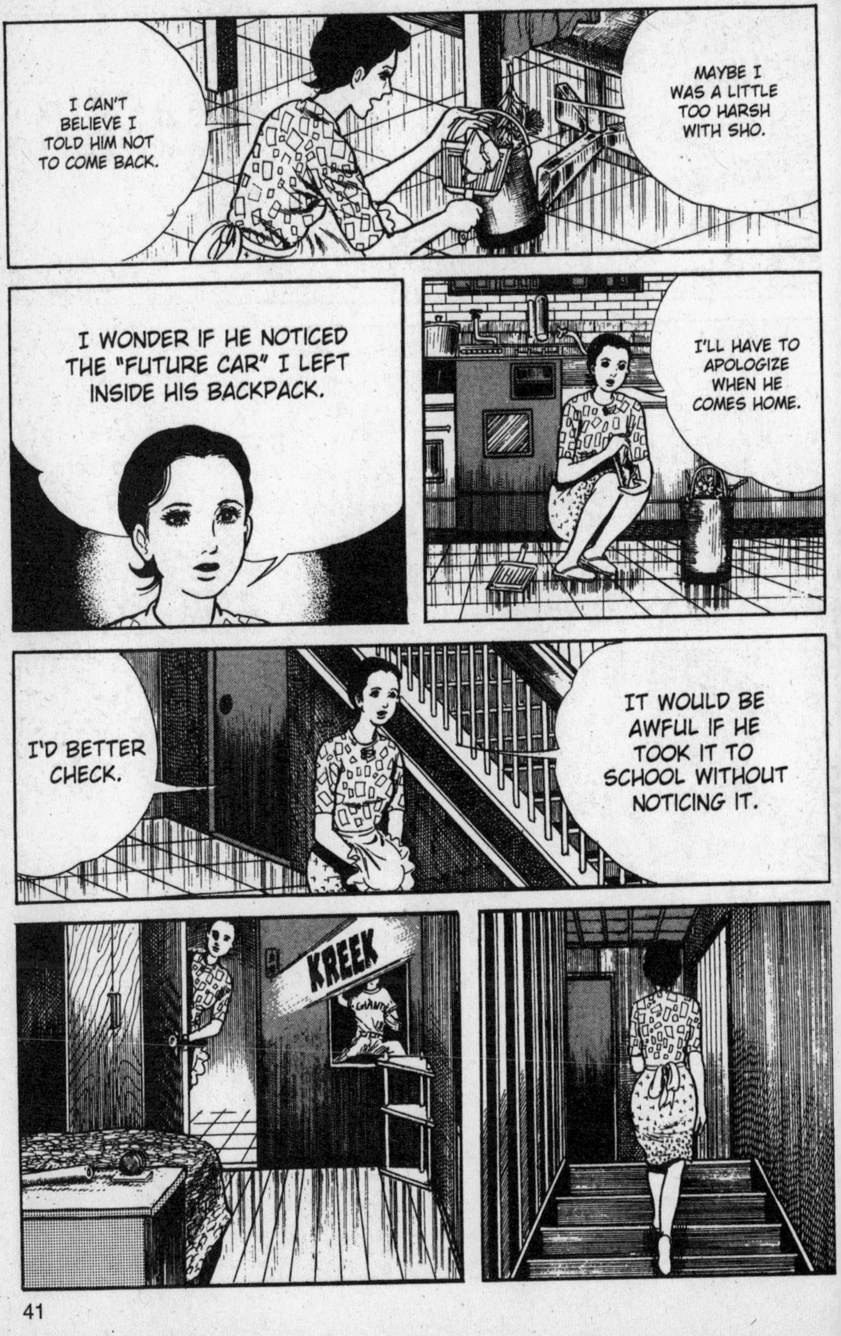
MAYBE I WAS A LITTLE TOO HARSH WITH SHO.
I CAN'T BELIEVE I TOLD HIM NOT TO COME BACK.
I'LL HAVE TO APOLOGIZE WHEN HE COMES HOME.
I WONDER IF HE NOTICED THE "FUTURE CAR" I LEFT INSIDE HIS BACKPACK.
IT WOULD BE AWFUL IF HE TOOK IT TO SCHOOL WITHOUT NOTICING IT.
I'D BETTER CHECK.
KREEK

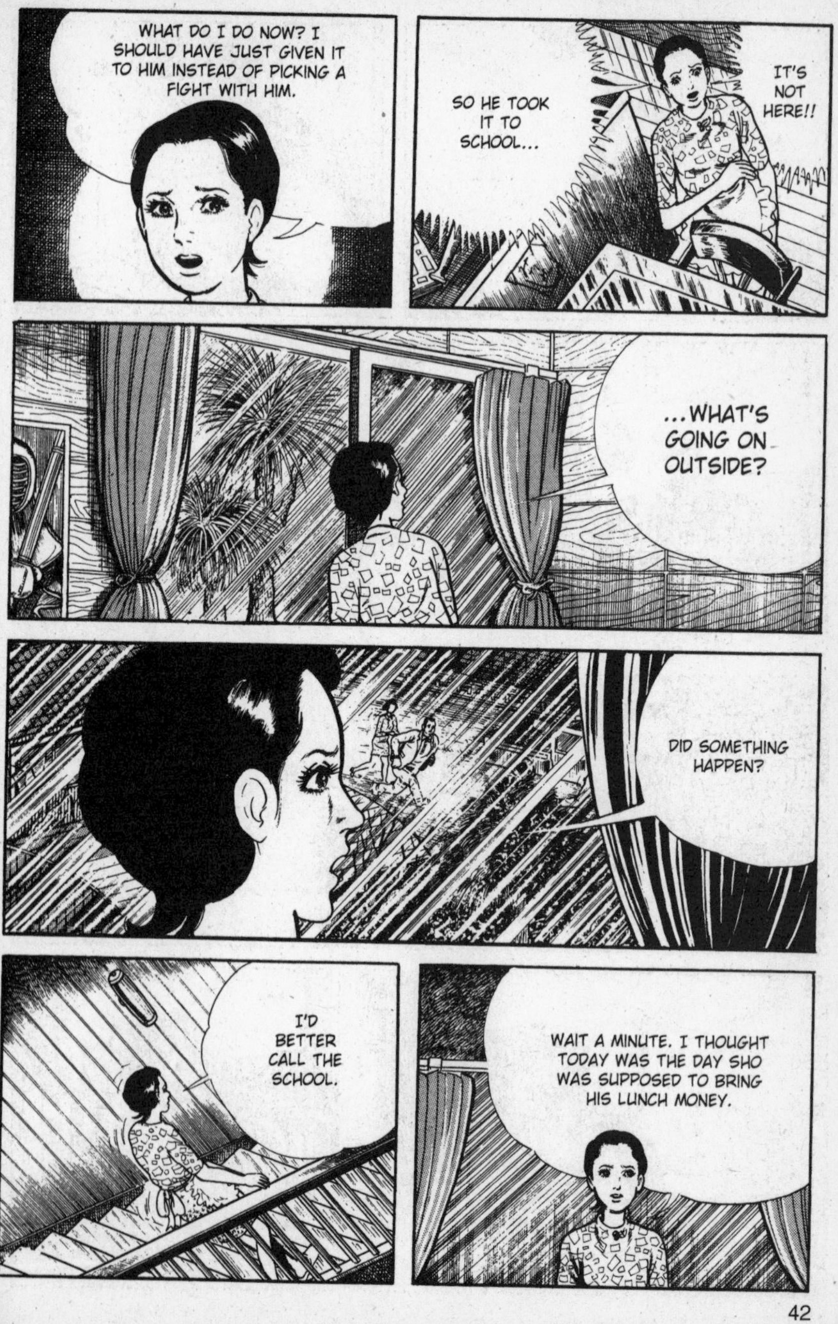
IT'S NOT HERE!!
SO HE TOOK IT TO SCHOOL...
WHAT DO I DO NOW? I SHOULD HAVE JUST GIVEN IT TO HIM INSTEAD OF PICKING A FIGHT WITH HIM.
...WHAT'S GOING ON OUTSIDE?
DID SOMETHING HAPPEN?
WAIT A MINUTE. I THOUGHT TODAY WAS THE DAY SHO WAS SUPPOSED TO BRING HIS LUNCH MONEY.
I'D BETTER CALL THE SCHOOL.

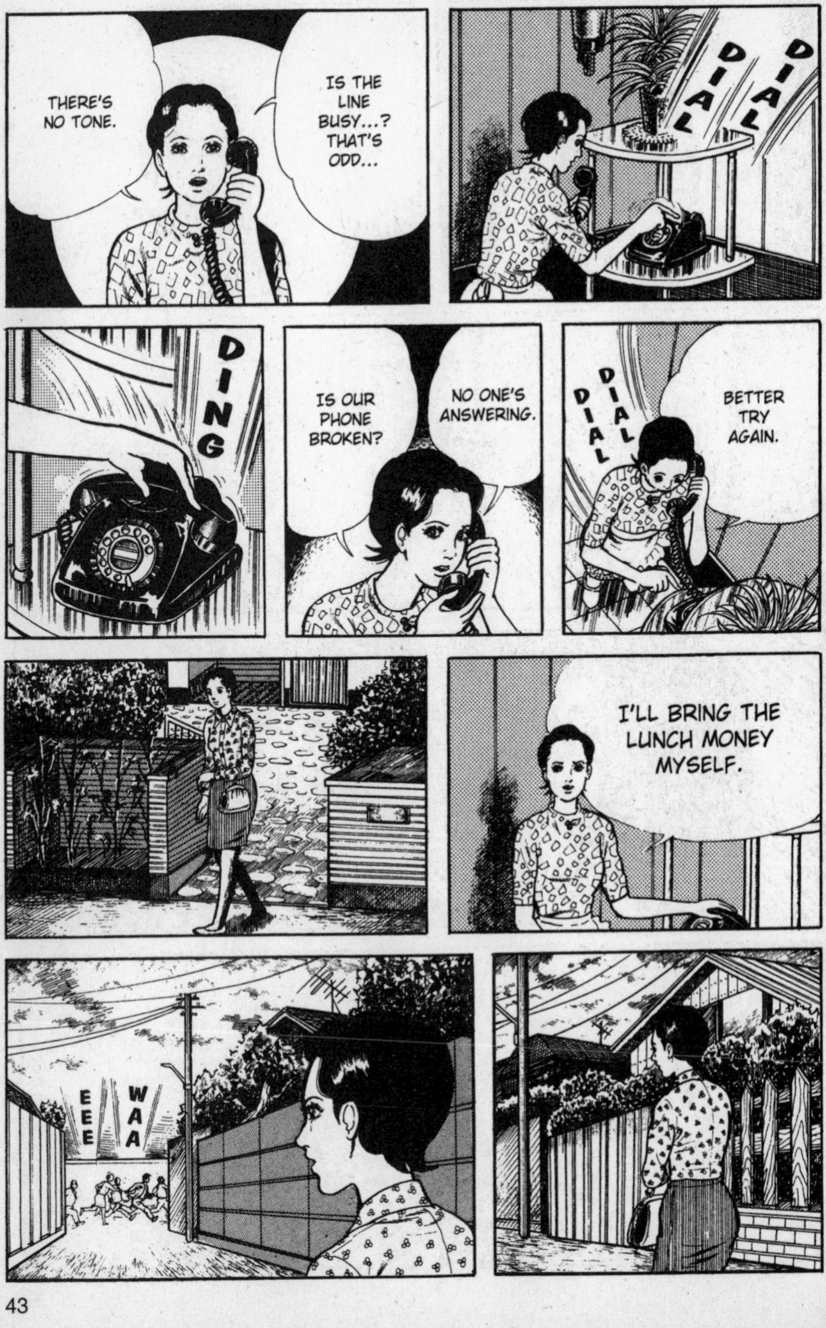
DIAL DIAL
IS THE LINE BUSY...? THAT'S ODD...
THERE'S NO TONE.
BETTER TRY AGAIN.
DIAL DIAL
NO ONE'S ANSWERING.
IS OUR PHONE BROKEN?
DING
I'LL BRING THE LUNCH MONEY MYSELF.
WAA
EEE

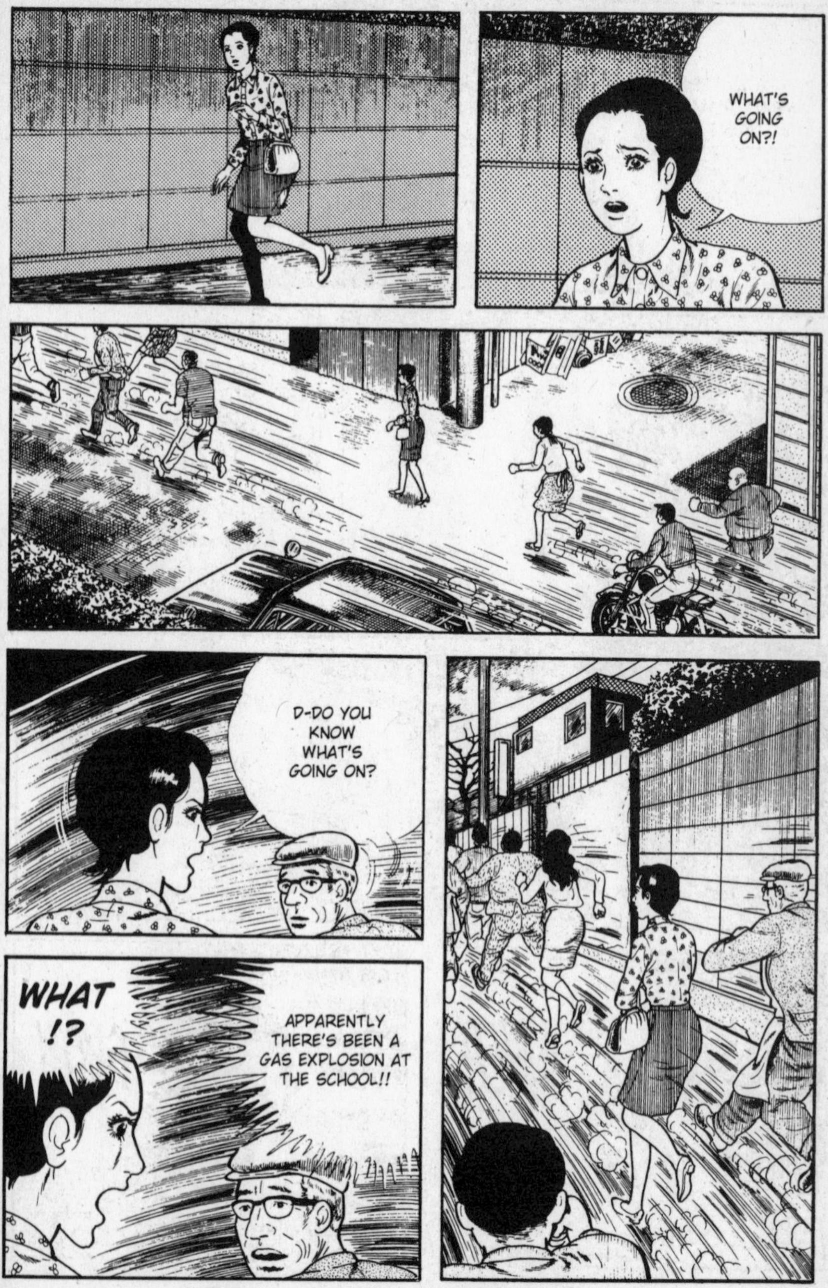
WHAT'S GOING ON?!
D-DO YOU KNOW WHAT'S GOING ON?
APPARENTLY THERE'S BEEN A GAS EXPLOSION AT THE SCHOOL!!
WHAT !?

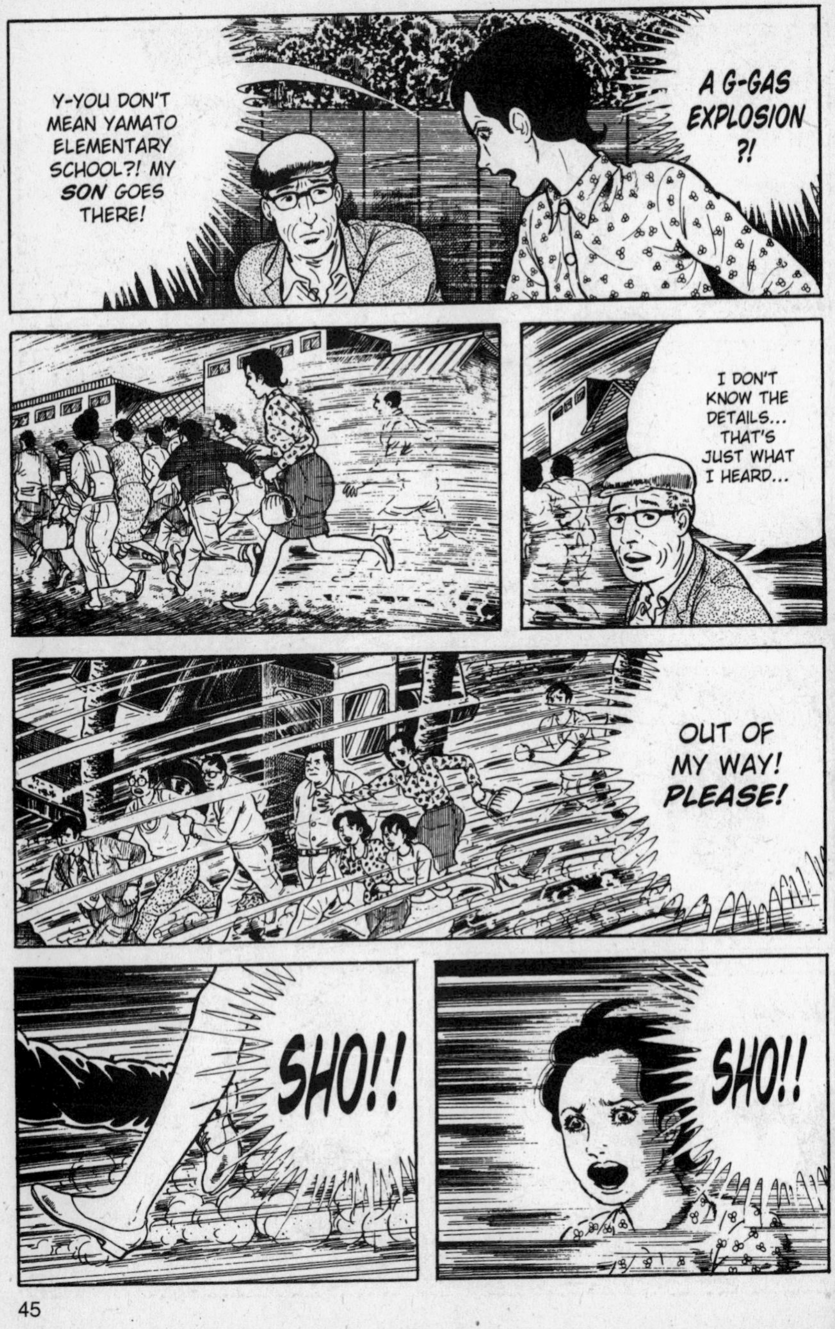
A G-GAS EXPLOSION ?!
Y-YOU DON'T MEAN YAMATO ELEMENTARY SCHOOL?! MY **SON** GOES THERE!
I DON'T KNOW THE DETAILS... THAT'S JUST WHAT I HEARD...
OUT OF MY WAY! ***PLEASE!***
SHO!!
SHO!!

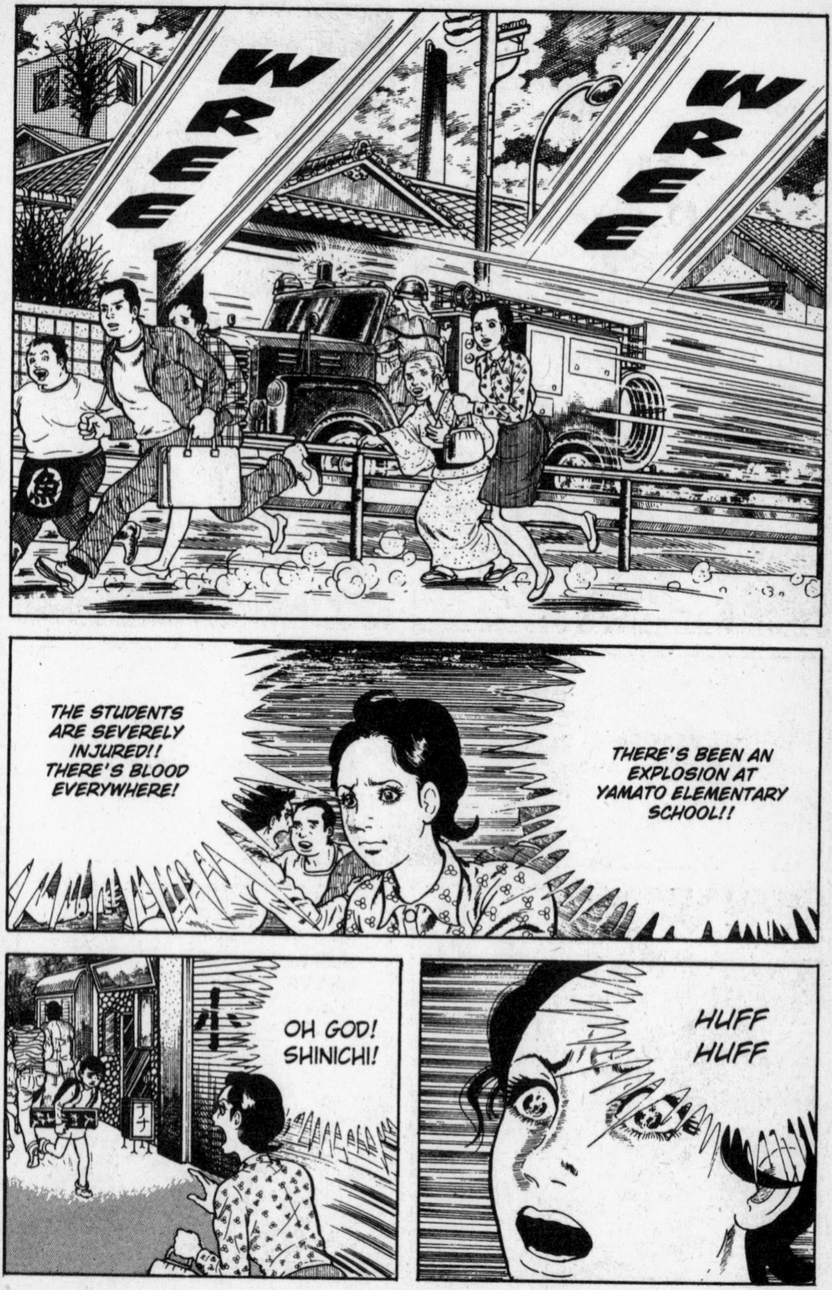
WREE
WREE
THERE'S BEEN AN EXPLOSION AT YAMATO ELEMENTARY SCHOOL!!
THE STUDENTS ARE SEVERELY INJURED!! THERE'S BLOOD EVERYWHERE!
HUFF HUFF
OH GOD! SHINICHI!

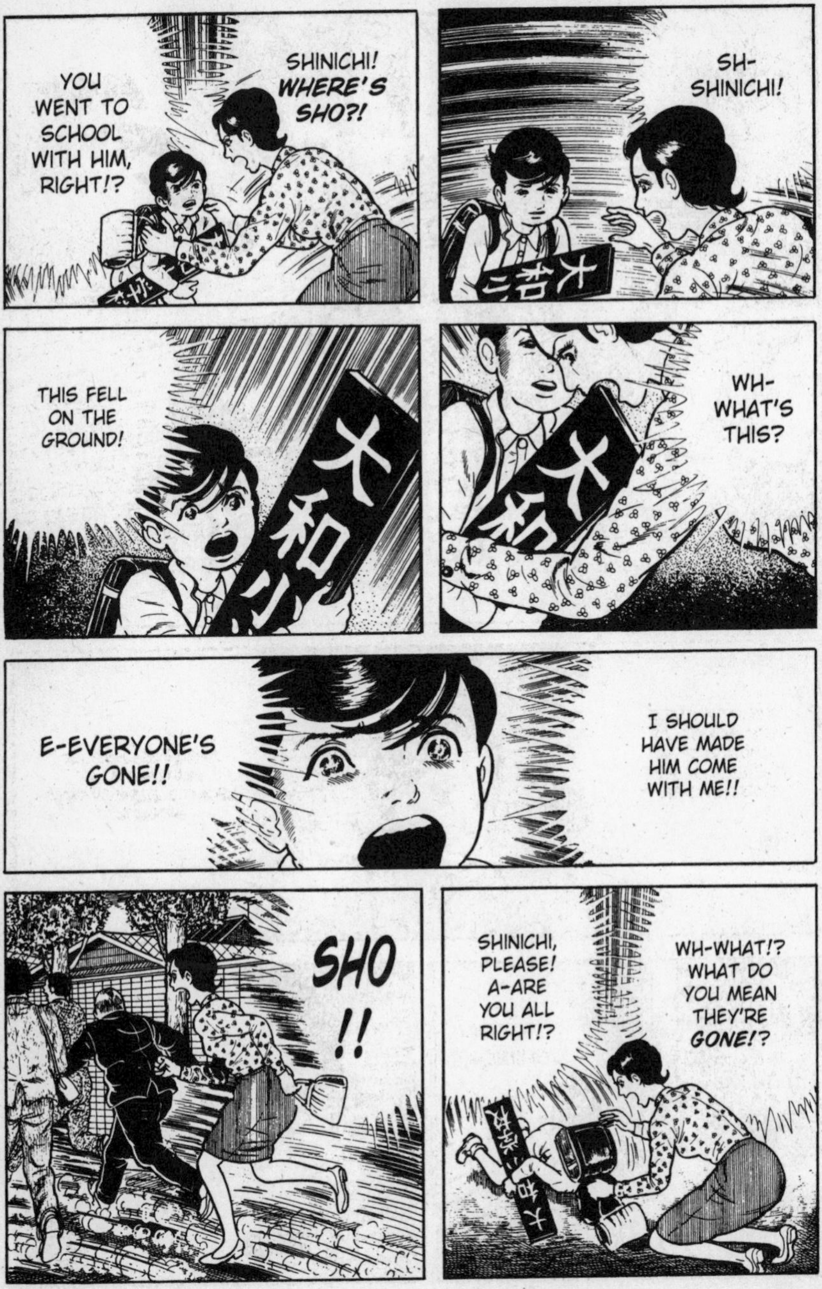
SH-
SHINICHI!
SHINICHI! *WHERE'S SHO?!*
YOU WENT TO SCHOOL WITH HIM, RIGHT!?
WH- WHAT'S THIS?
THIS FELL ON THE GROUND!
I SHOULD HAVE MADE HIM COME WITH ME!!
E-EVERYONE'S GONE!!
WH-WHAT!? WHAT DO YOU MEAN THEY'RE *GONE!?*
SHINICHI, PLEASE! A-ARE YOU ALL RIGHT!?
SHO !!

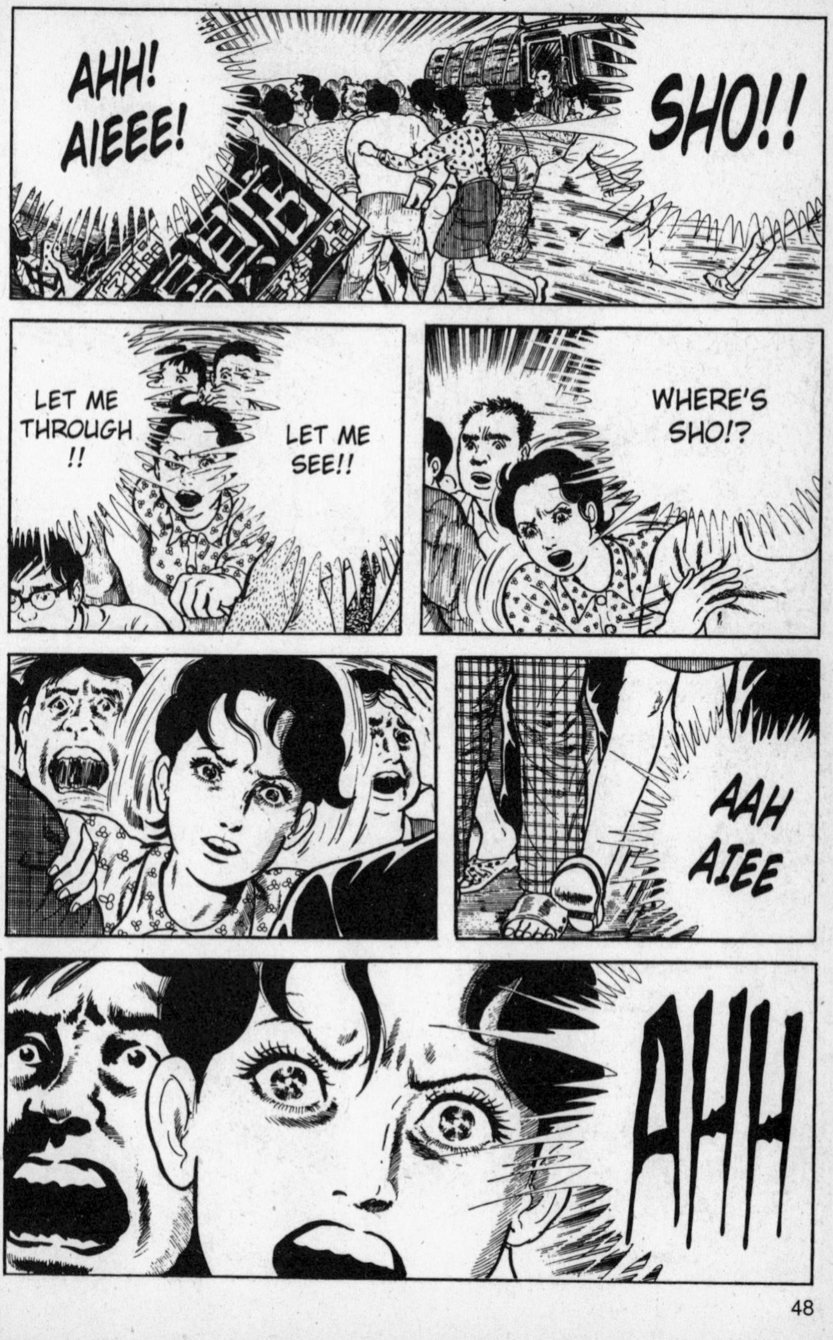

SHO!!
AHH! AIEEE!
WHERE'S SHO!?
LET ME SEE!!
LET ME THROUGH!!
AAH AIEE
AHH

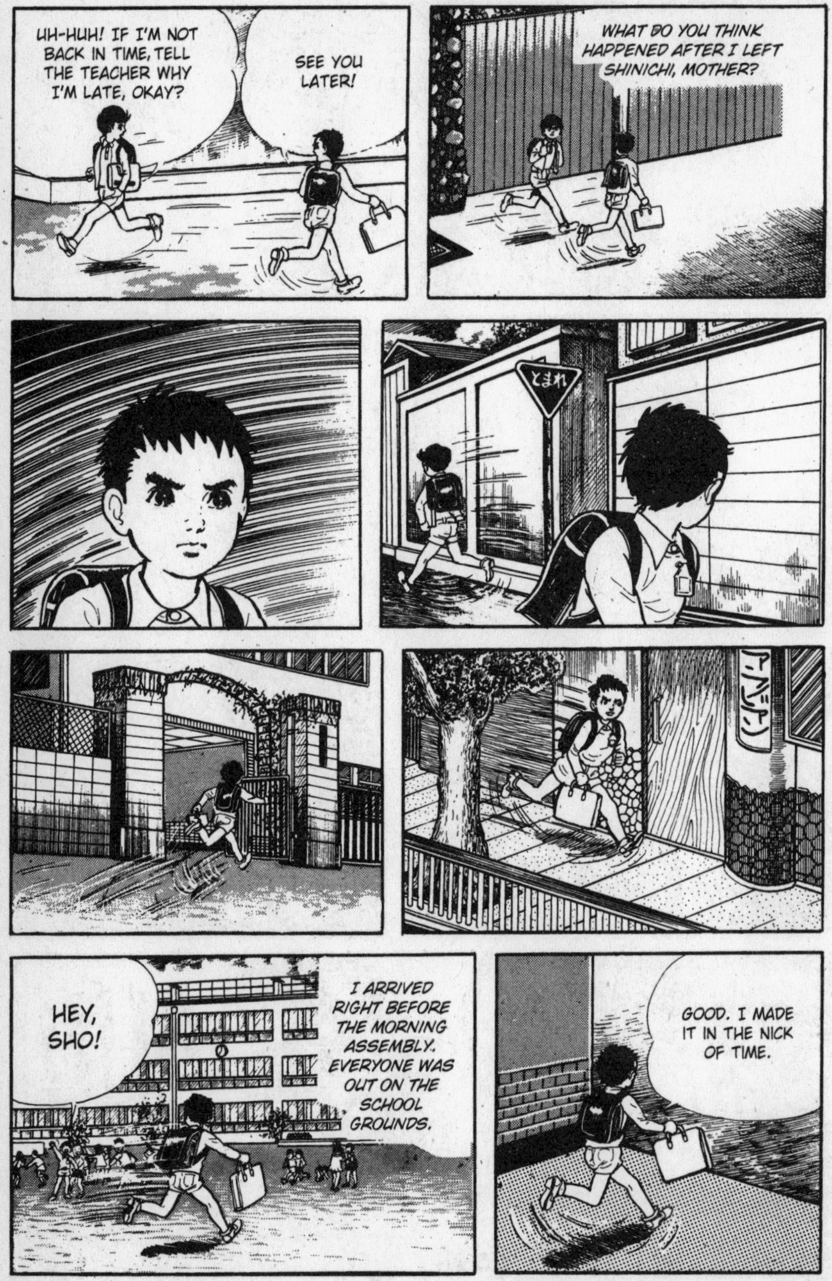
WHAT DO YOU THINK HAPPENED AFTER I LEFT SHINICHI, MOTHER?
SEE YOU LATER!
UH-HUH! IF I'M NOT BACK IN TIME, TELL THE TEACHER WHY I'M LATE, OKAY?
とまれ
GOOD. I MADE IT IN THE NICK OF TIME.
I ARRIVED RIGHT BEFORE THE MORNING ASSEMBLY. EVERYONE WAS OUT ON THE SCHOOL GROUNDS.
HEY, SHO!

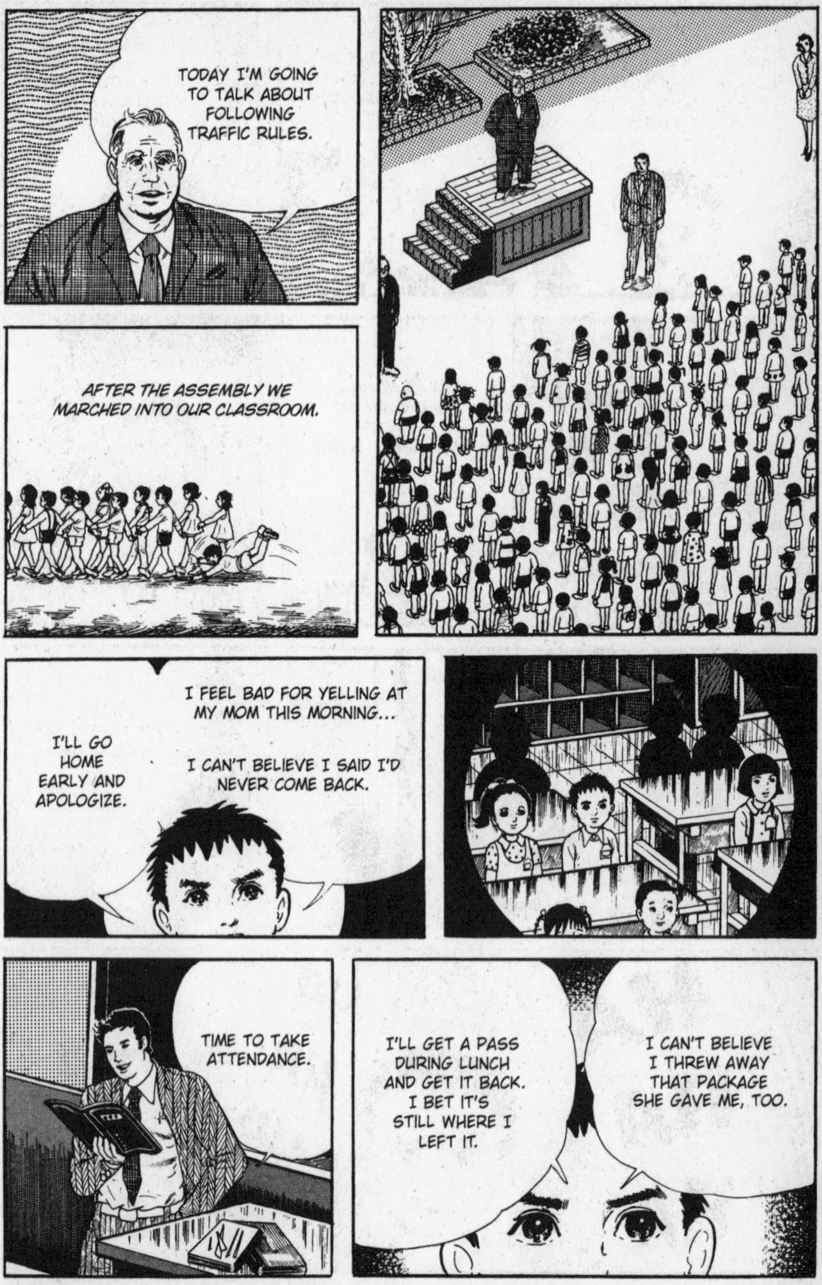
TODAY I'M GOING TO TALK ABOUT FOLLOWING TRAFFIC RULES.
AFTER THE ASSEMBLY WE MARCHED INTO OUR CLASSROOM.
I FEEL BAD FOR YELLING AT MY MOM THIS MORNING...
I CAN'T BELIEVE I SAID I'D NEVER COME BACK.
I'LL GO HOME EARLY AND APOLOGIZE.
I CAN'T BELIEVE I THREW AWAY THAT PACKAGE SHE GAVE ME, TOO.
I'LL GET A PASS DURING LUNCH AND GET IT BACK. I BET IT'S STILL WHERE I LEFT IT.
TIME TO TAKE ATTENDANCE.

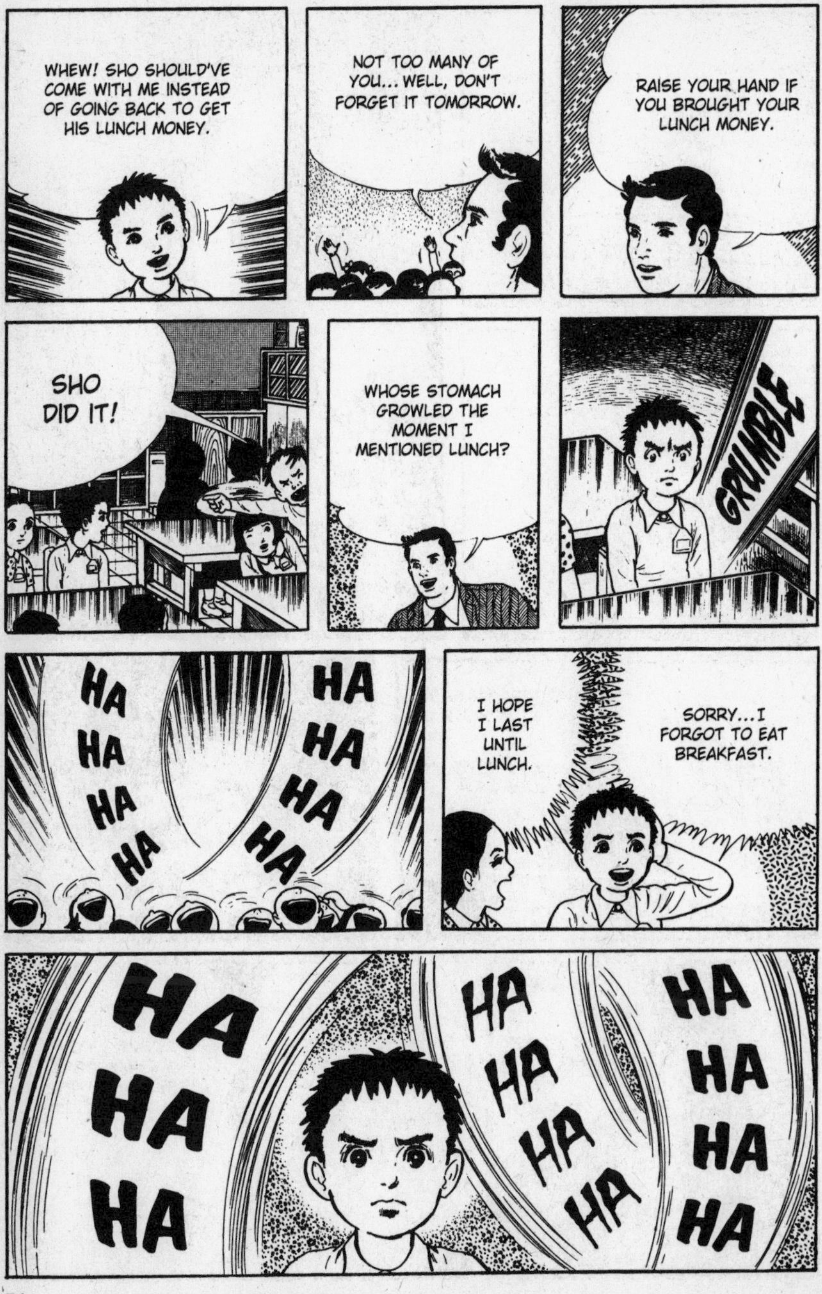
RAISE YOUR HAND IF YOU BROUGHT YOUR LUNCH MONEY.
NOT TOO MANY OF YOU... WELL, DON'T FORGET IT TOMORROW.
WHEW! SHO SHOULD'VE COME WITH ME INSTEAD OF GOING BACK TO GET HIS LUNCH MONEY.
GRUMBLE
WHOSE STOMACH GROWLED THE MOMENT I MENTIONED LUNCH?
SHO DID IT!
SORRY...I FORGOT TO EAT BREAKFAST.
I HOPE I LAST UNTIL LUNCH.
HA HA HA HA
HA HA HA HA
HA HA HA HA
HA HA HA HA
HA HA HA

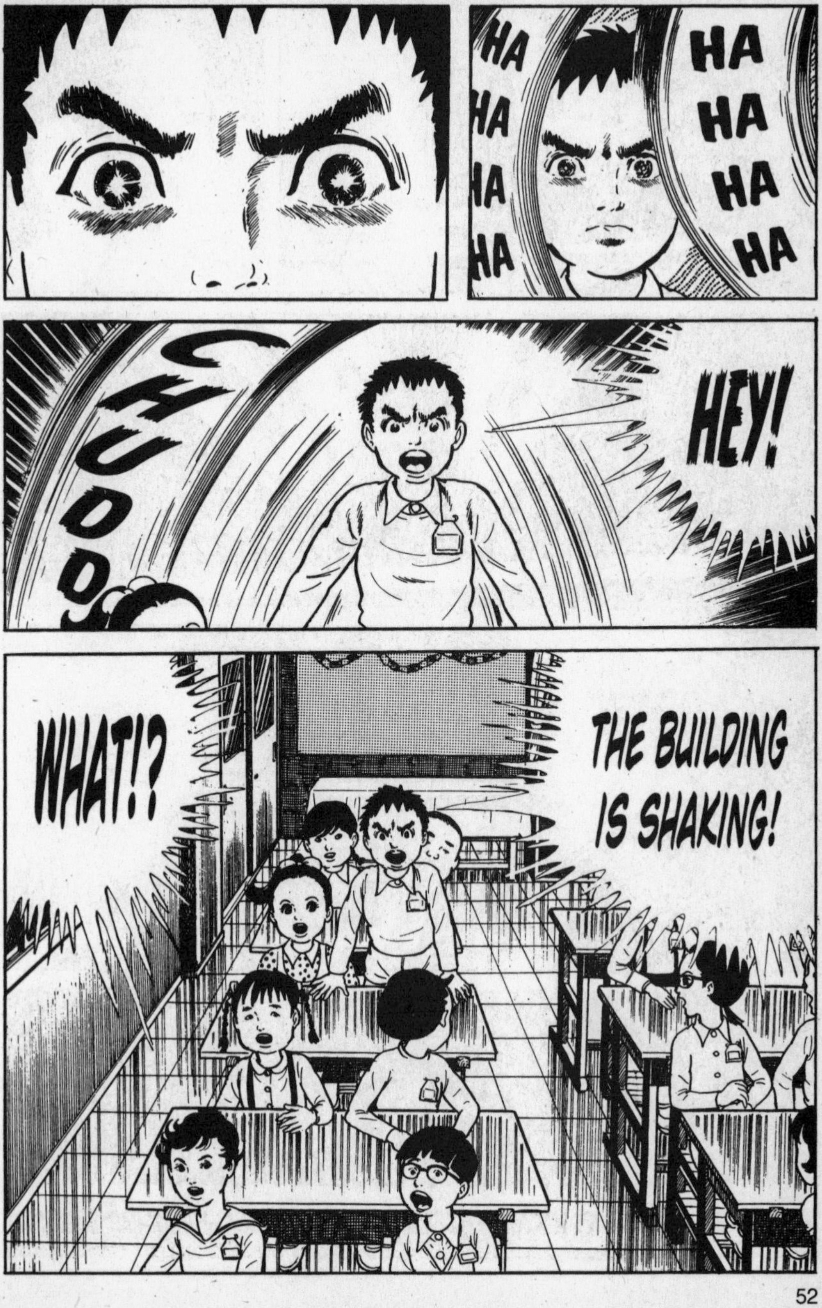
HA HA HA HA HA
HA HA HA HA
HEY!
CHUDD
THE BUILDING IS SHAKING!
WHAT!?

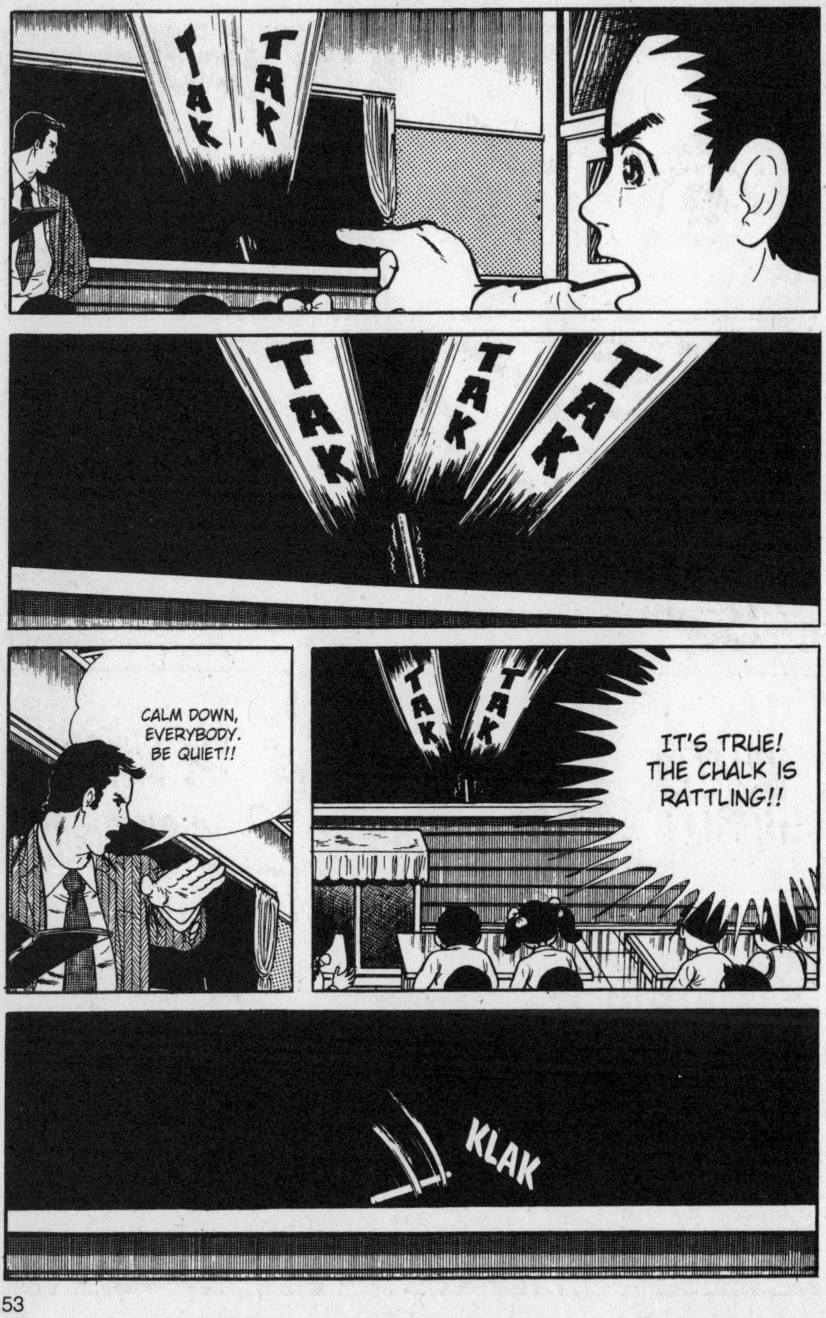
TAK
TAK
TAK
TAK
TAK
TAK
TAK
IT'S TRUE! THE CHALK IS RATTLING!!
CALM DOWN, EVERYBODY. BE QUIET!!
KLAK

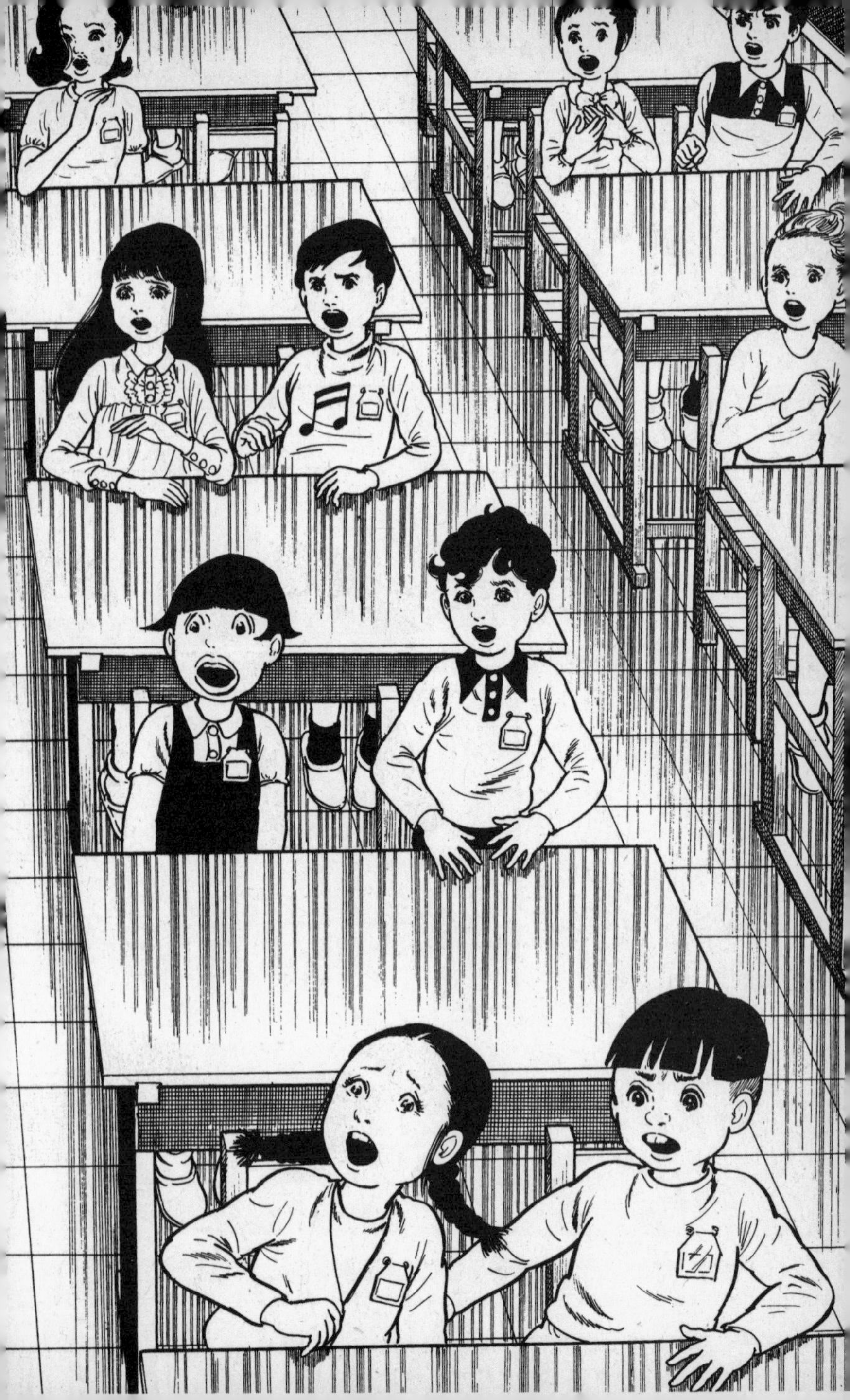

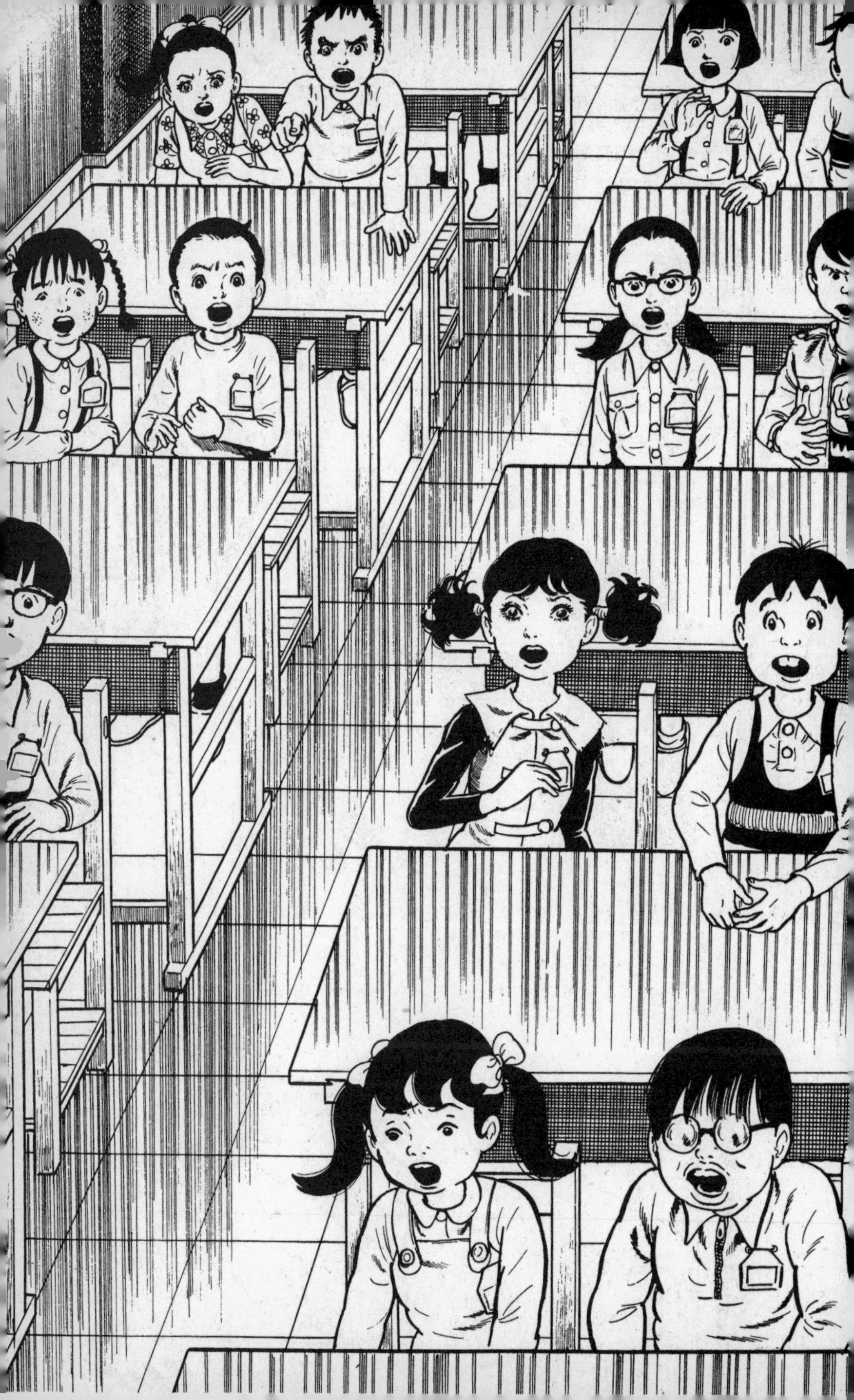

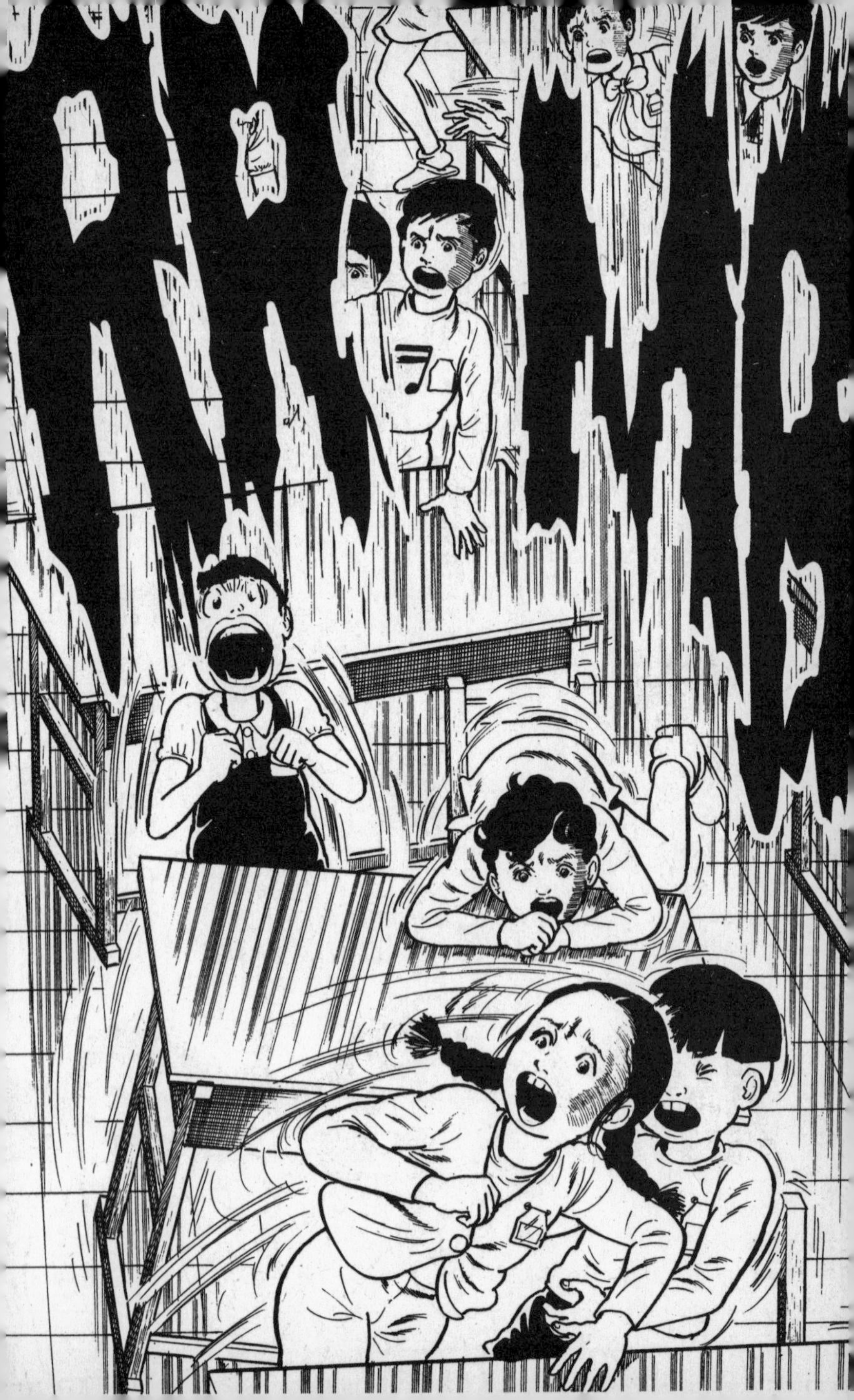

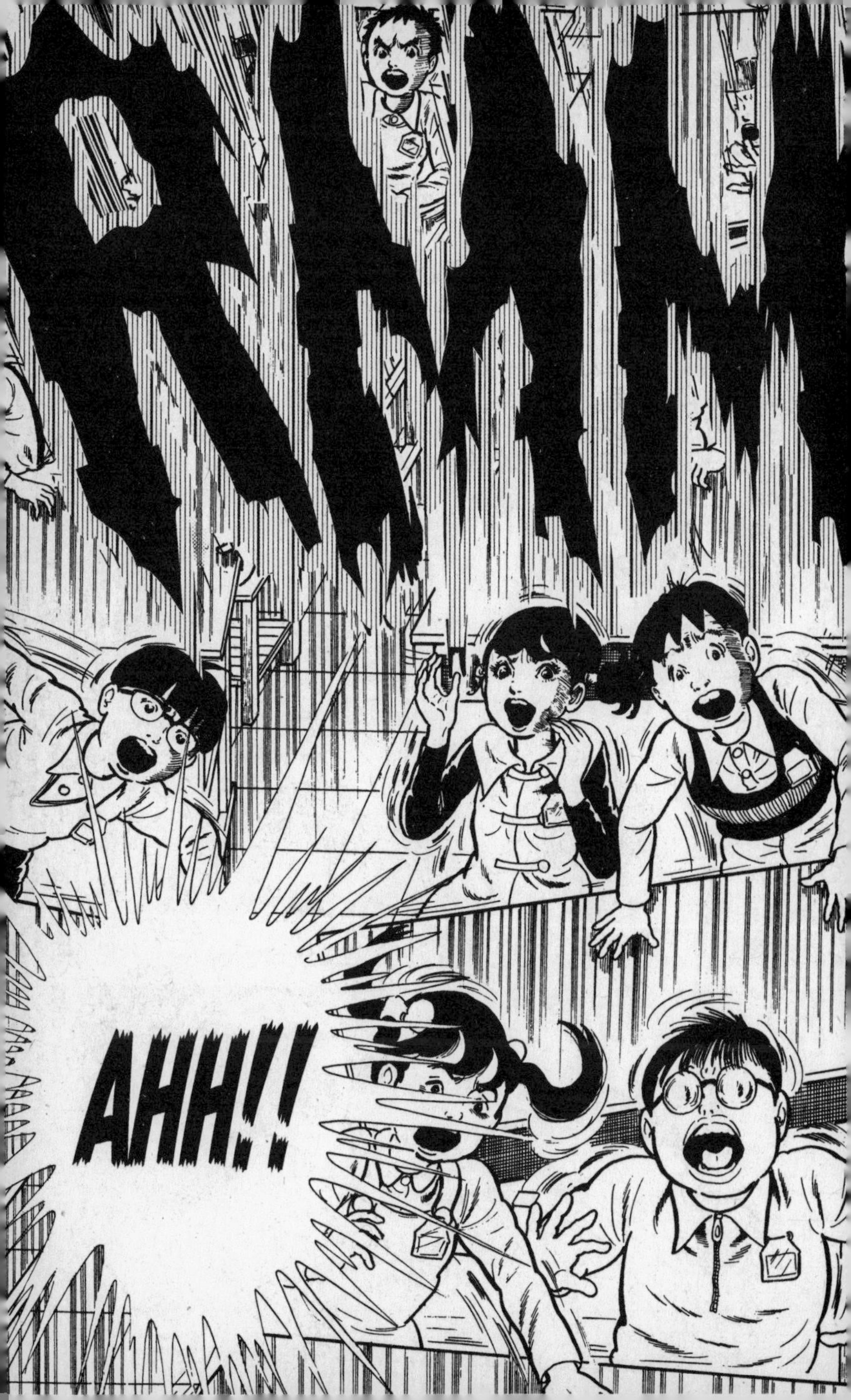
AHH!!

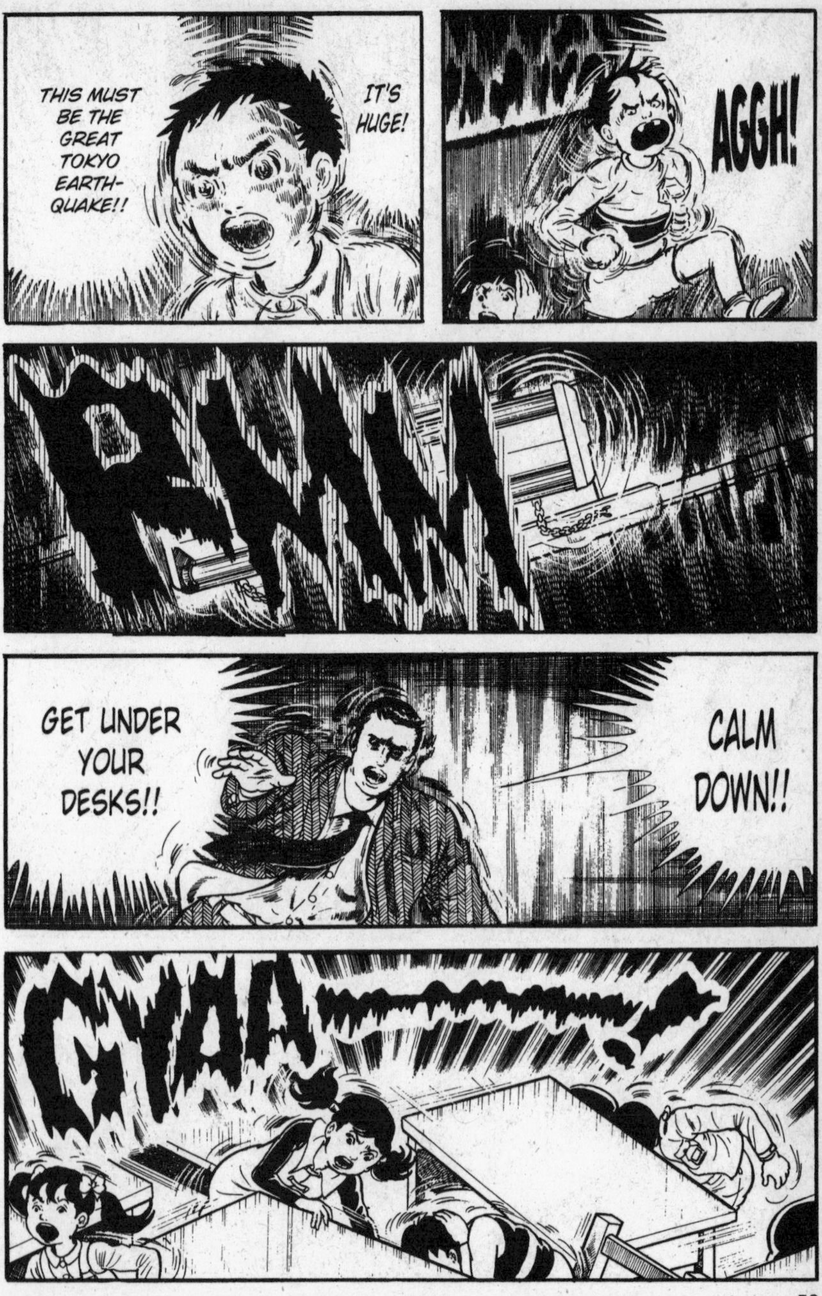
AGGH!
IT'S HUGE!
THIS MUST BE THE GREAT TOKYO EARTH-QUAKE!!
CALM DOWN!!
GET UNDER YOUR DESKS!!
GYAA

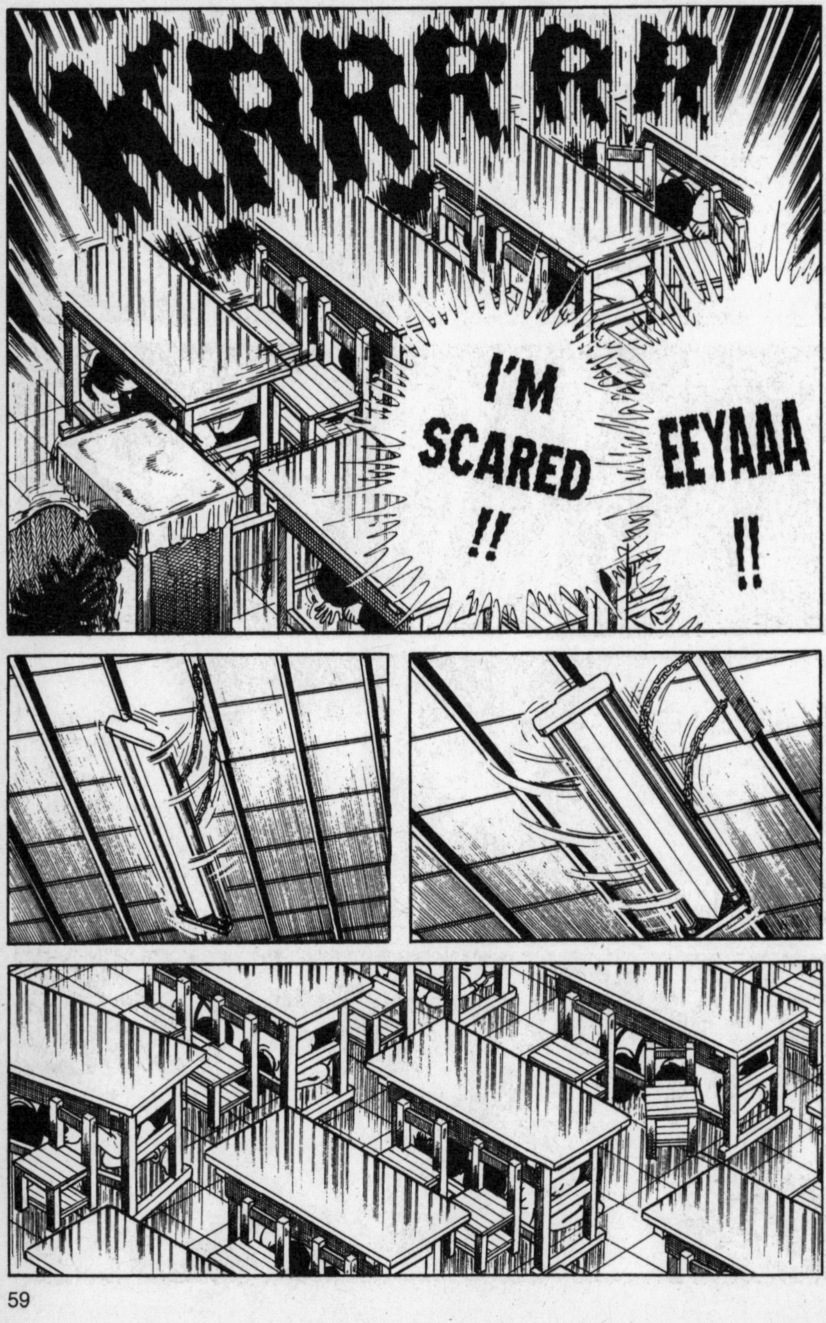
KRRRRR
EEYAAA!!
I'M SCARED!!

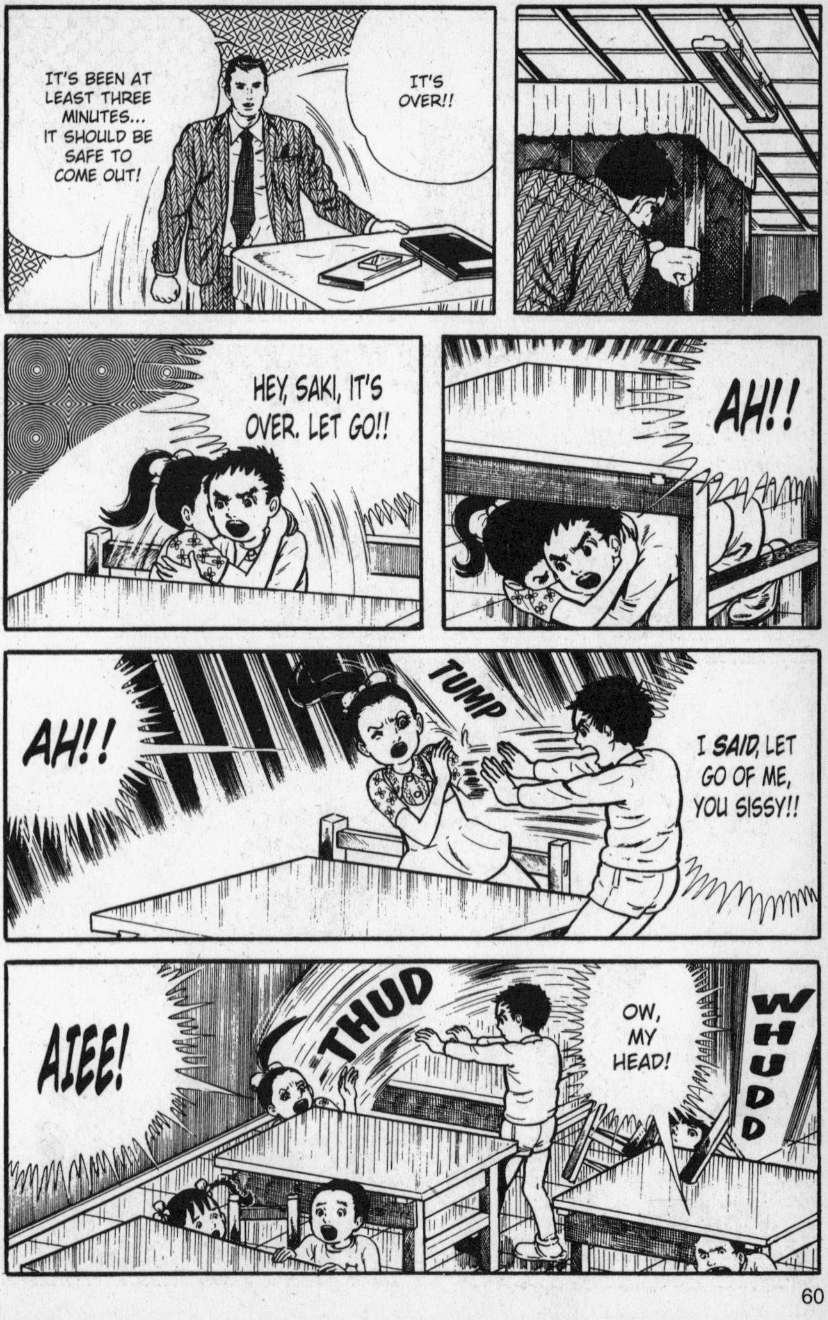
IT'S OVER!!
IT'S BEEN AT LEAST THREE MINUTES... IT SHOULD BE SAFE TO COME OUT!
AH!!
HEY, SAKI, IT'S OVER. LET GO!!
I SAID, LET GO OF ME, YOU SISSY!!
TUMP
AH!!
WHUDD
OW, MY HEAD!
THUD
AIEE!

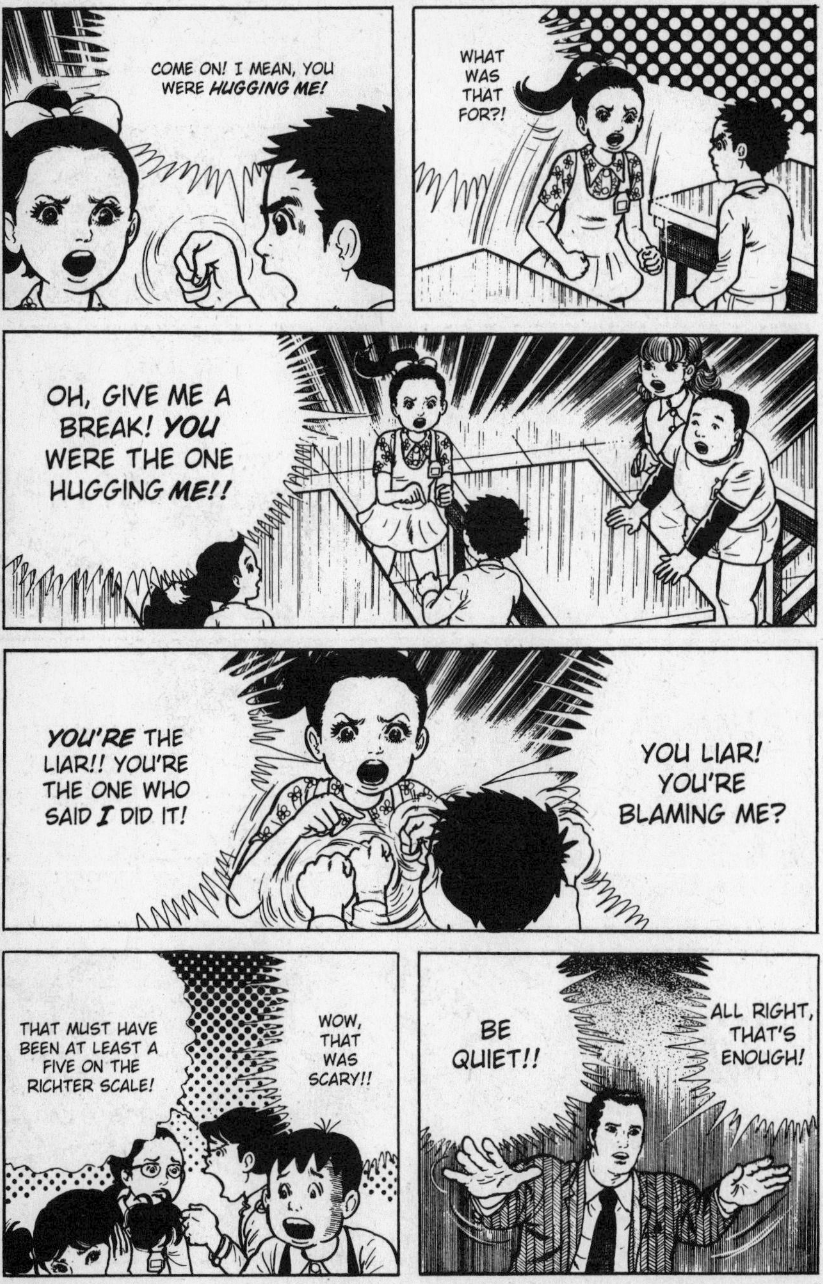
WHAT WAS THAT FOR?!
COME ON! I MEAN, YOU WERE HUGGING ME!
OH, GIVE ME A BREAK! YOU WERE THE ONE HUGGING ME!!
YOU LIAR! YOU'RE BLAMING ME?
YOU'RE THE LIAR!! YOU'RE THE ONE WHO SAID I DID IT!
ALL RIGHT, THAT'S ENOUGH!
BE QUIET!!
WOW, THAT WAS SCARY!!
THAT MUST HAVE BEEN AT LEAST A FIVE ON THE RICHTER SCALE!

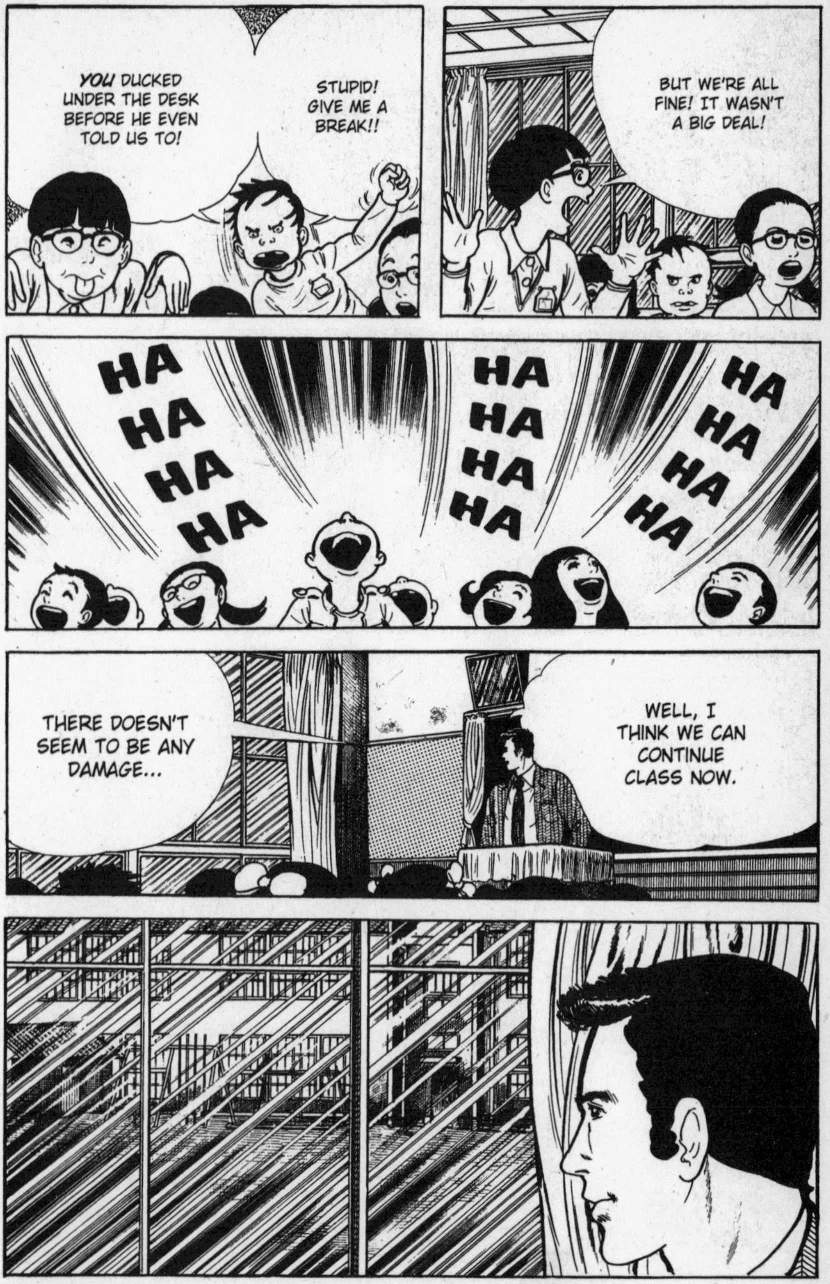
BUT WE'RE ALL FINE! IT WASN'T A BIG DEAL!
STUPID! GIVE ME A BREAK!!
YOU DUCKED UNDER THE DESK BEFORE HE EVEN TOLD US TO!
HA HA HA HA
HA HA HA HA
HA HA HA HA
WELL, I THINK WE CAN CONTINUE CLASS NOW.
THERE DOESN'T SEEM TO BE ANY DAMAGE...

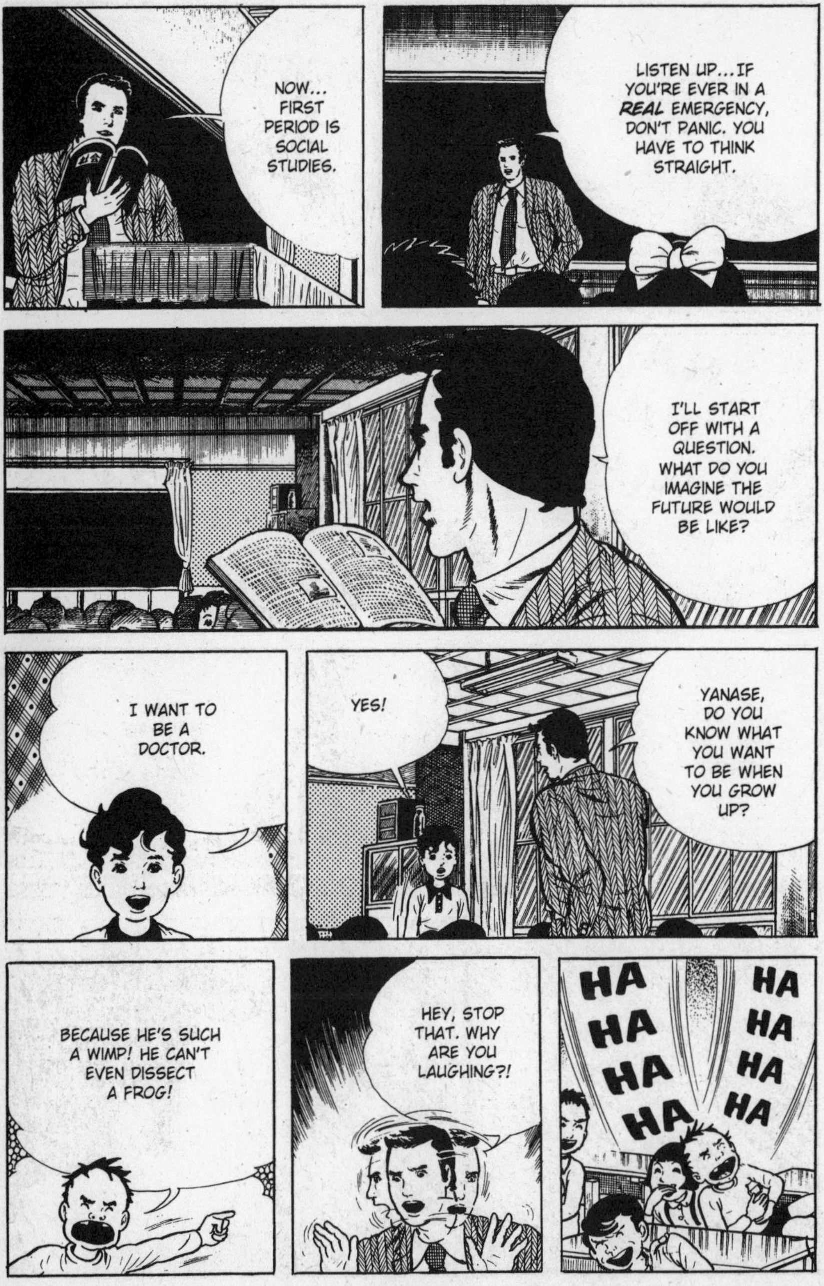
LISTEN UP...IF YOU'RE EVER IN A REAL EMERGENCY, DON'T PANIC. YOU HAVE TO THINK STRAIGHT.
NOW... FIRST PERIOD IS SOCIAL STUDIES.
I'LL START OFF WITH A QUESTION. WHAT DO YOU IMAGINE THE FUTURE WOULD BE LIKE?
YANASE, DO YOU KNOW WHAT YOU WANT TO BE WHEN YOU GROW UP?
YES!
I WANT TO BE A DOCTOR.
HA HA HA HA
HA HA HA HA
HEY, STOP THAT. WHY ARE YOU LAUGHING?!
BECAUSE HE'S SUCH A WIMP! HE CAN'T EVEN DISSECT A FROG!

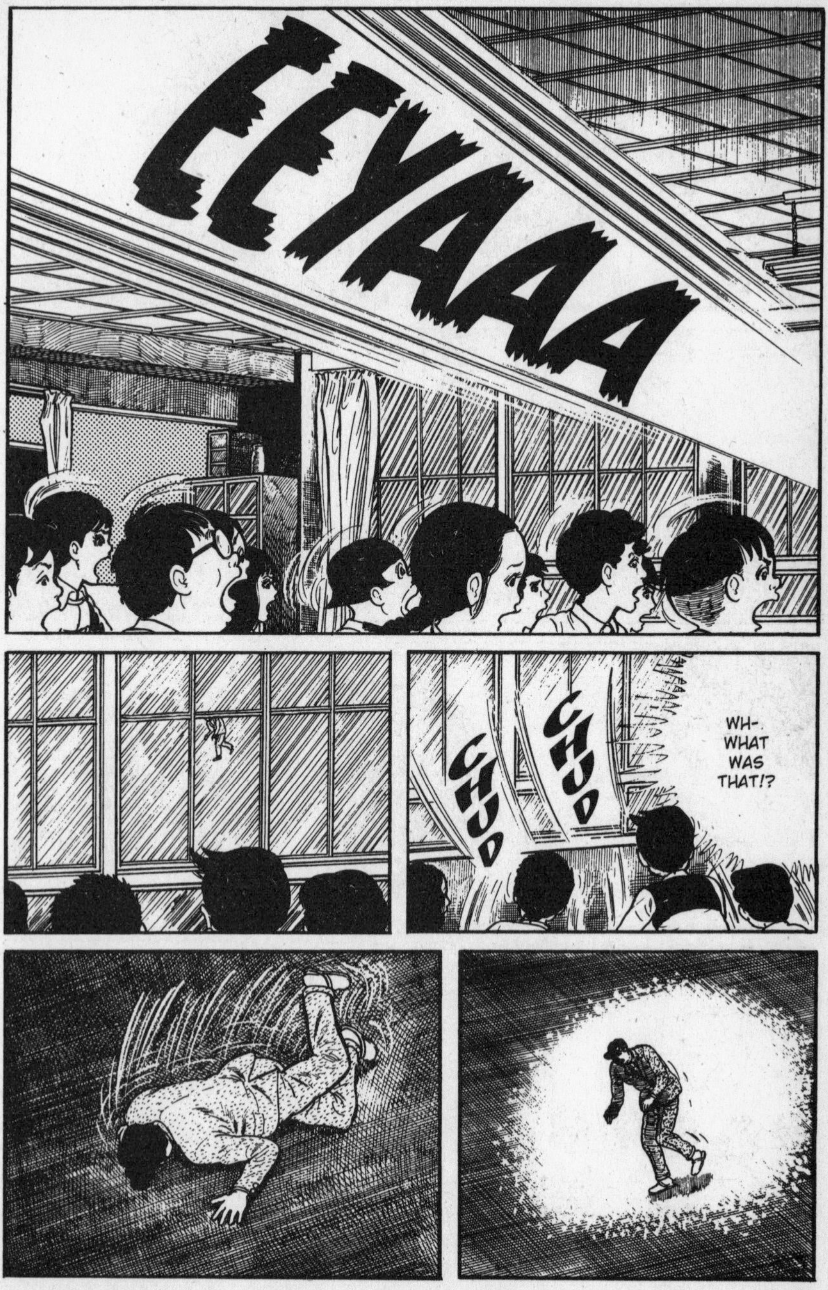
EEYAAA
CHUD
CHUD
WH-WHAT WAS THAT!?

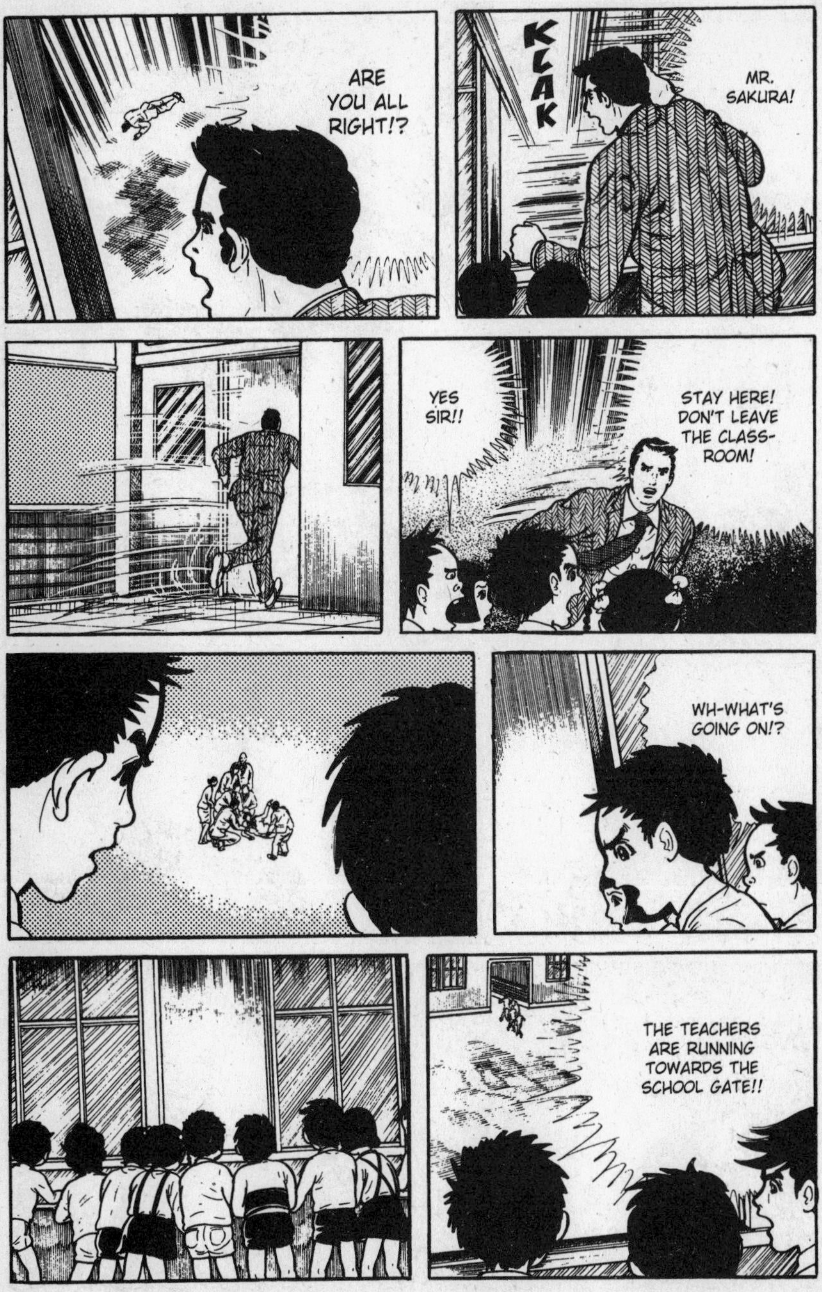
KLAK
MR. SAKURA!
ARE YOU ALL RIGHT!?
STAY HERE! DON'T LEAVE THE CLASS-ROOM!
YES SIR!!
WH-WHAT'S GOING ON!?
THE TEACHERS ARE RUNNING TOWARDS THE SCHOOL GATE!!

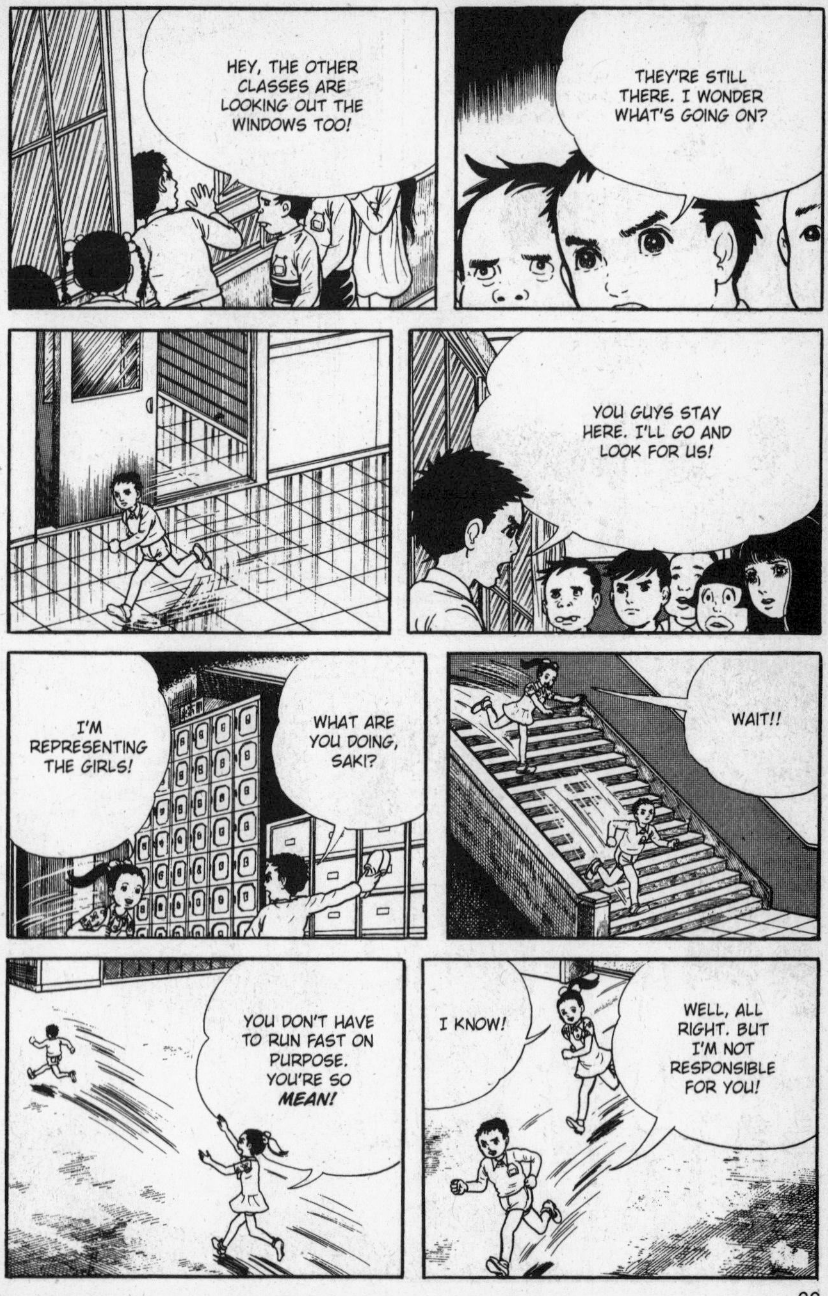
THEY'RE STILL THERE. I WONDER WHAT'S GOING ON?
HEY, THE OTHER CLASSES ARE LOOKING OUT THE WINDOWS TOO!
YOU GUYS STAY HERE. I'LL GO AND LOOK FOR US!
WAIT!!
WHAT ARE YOU DOING, SAKI?
I'M REPRESENTING THE GIRLS!
WELL, ALL RIGHT. BUT I'M NOT RESPONSIBLE FOR YOU!
I KNOW!
YOU DON'T HAVE TO RUN FAST ON PURPOSE. YOU'RE SO ***MEAN!***

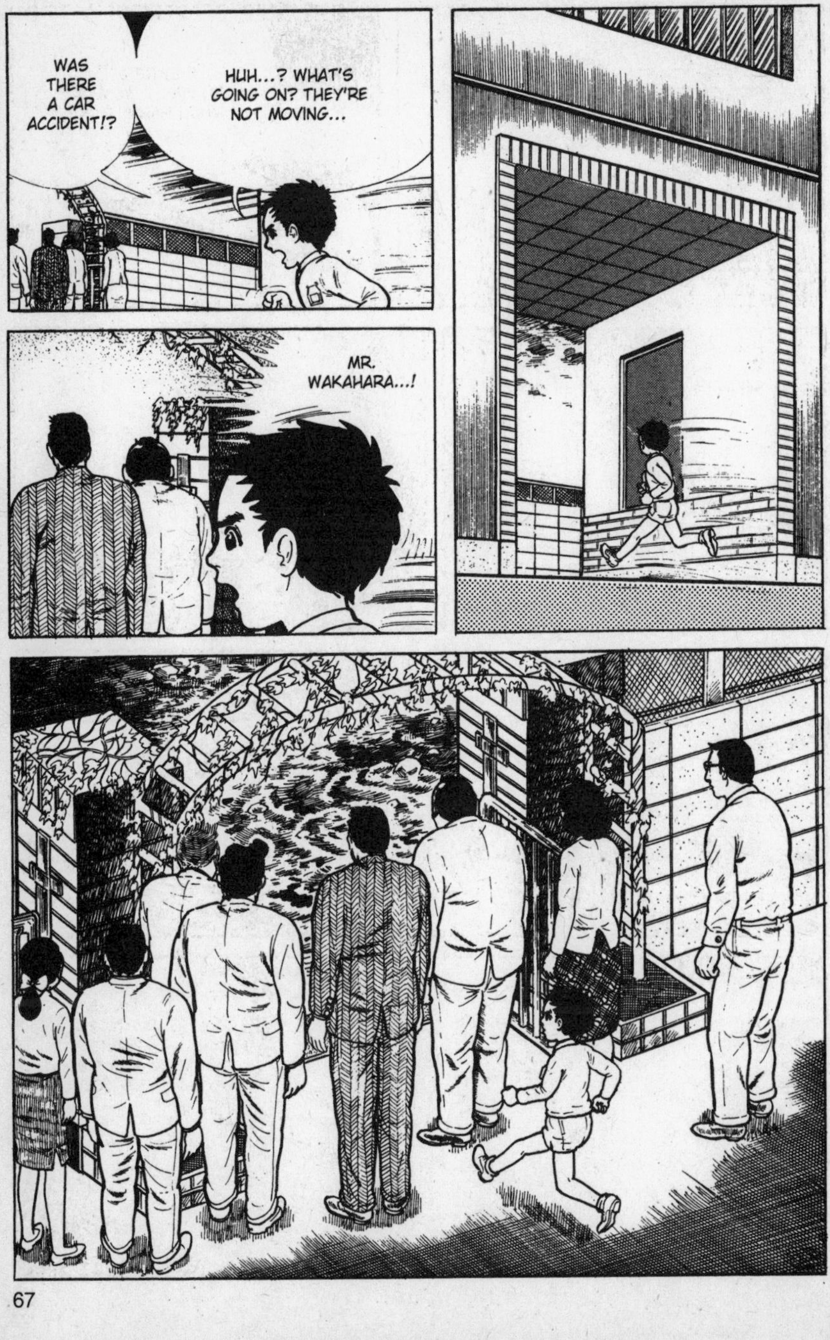
HUH...? WHAT'S GOING ON? THEY'RE NOT MOVING...
WAS THERE A CAR ACCIDENT!?
MR. WAKAHARA...!

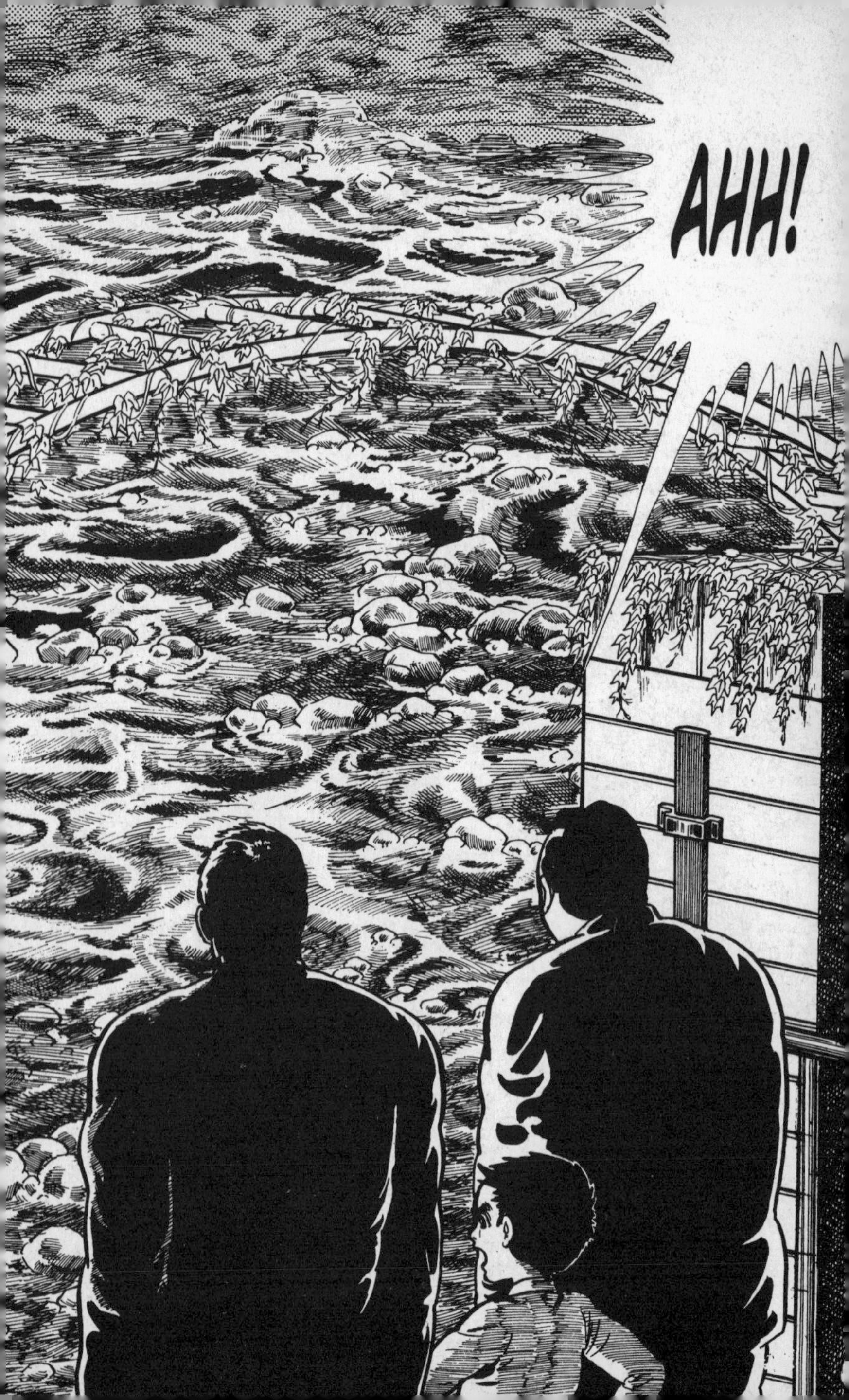
AHH!

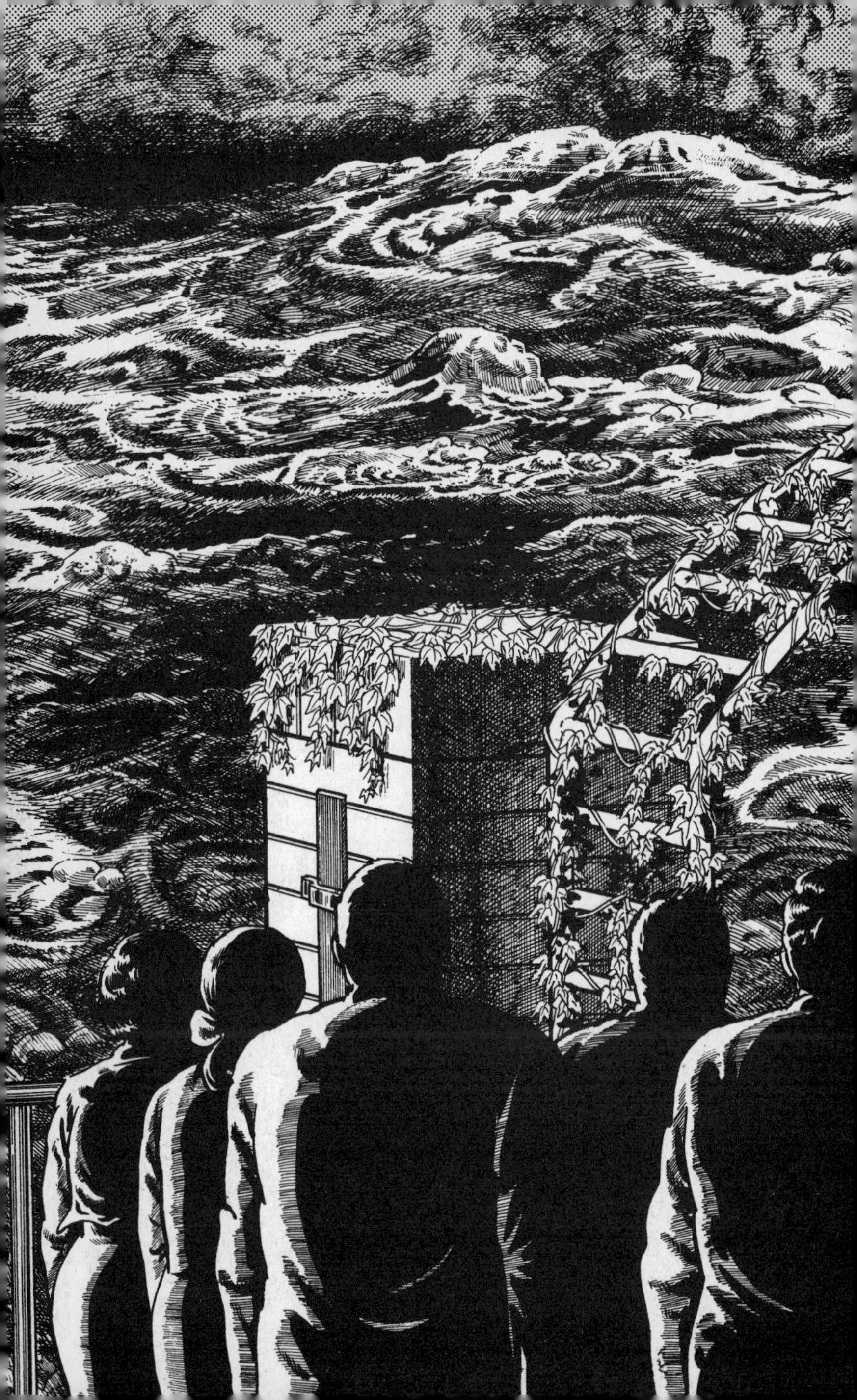

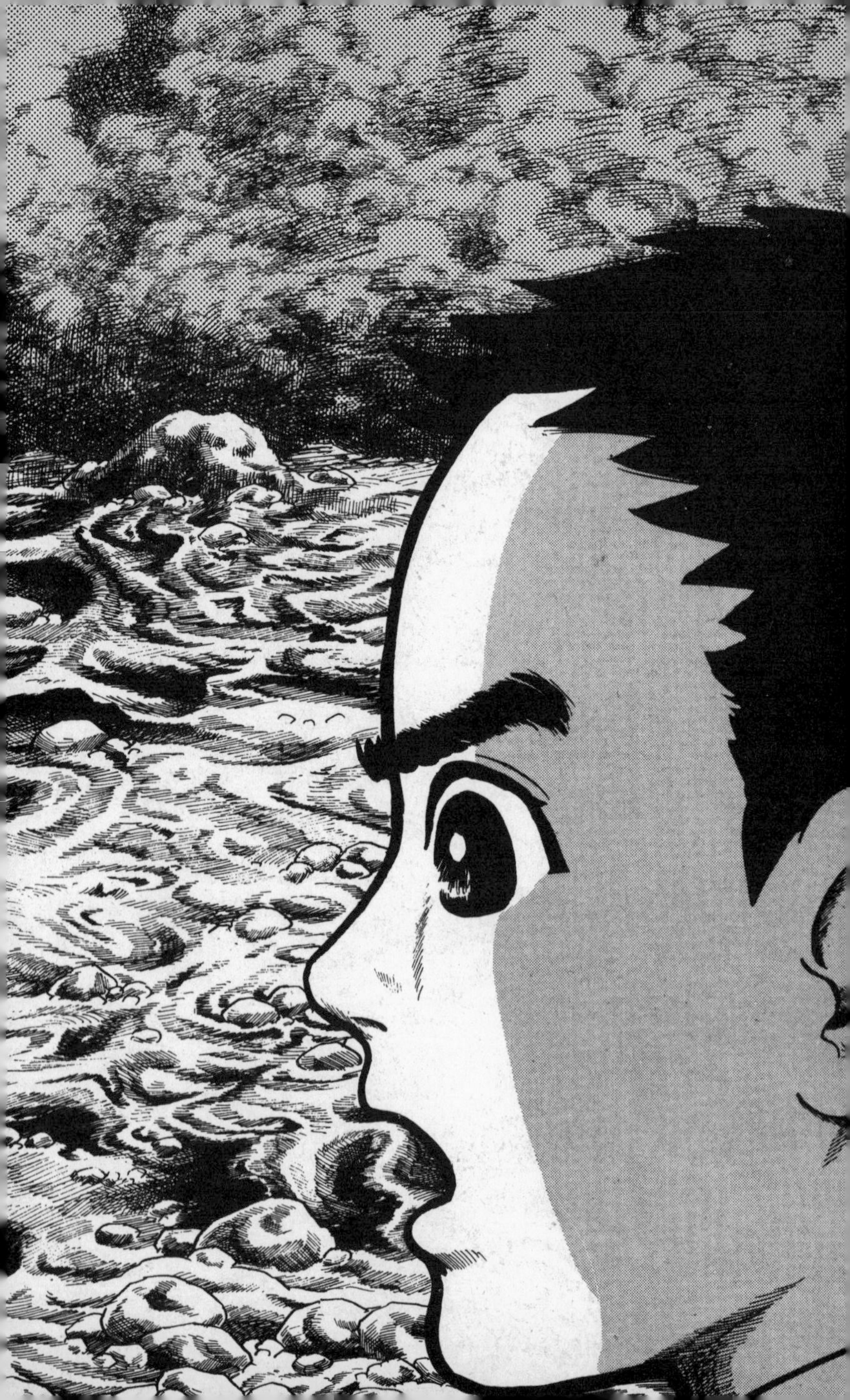

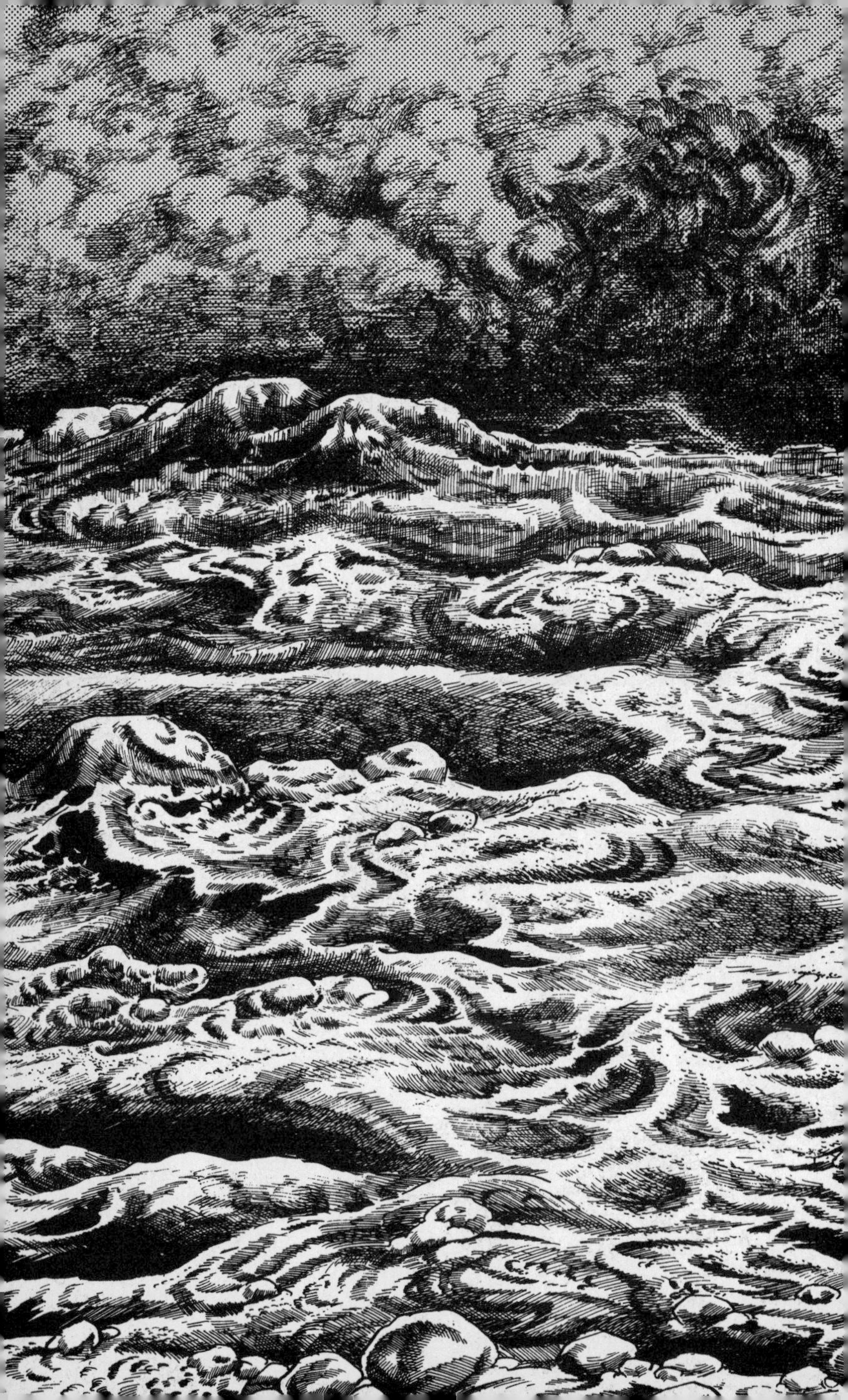

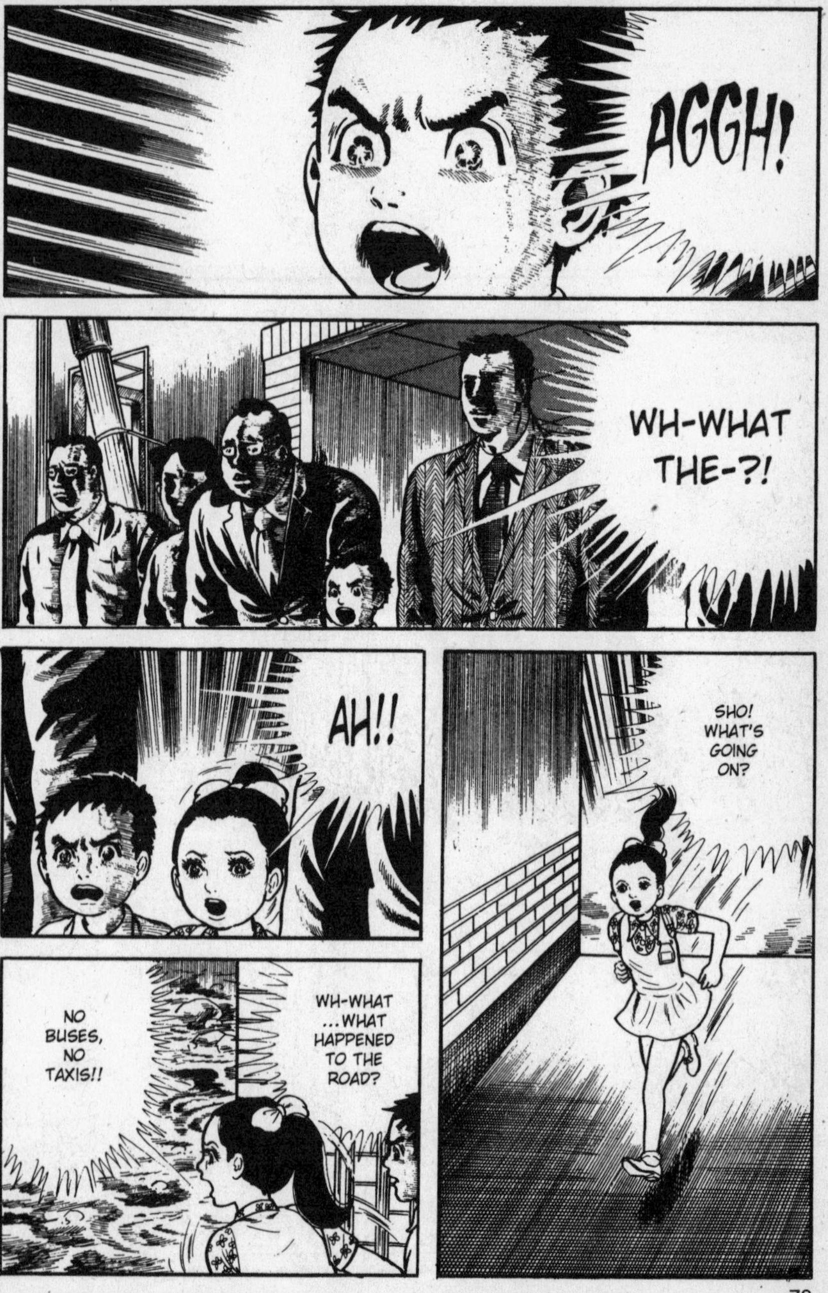
AGGH!
WH-WHAT THE-?!
SHO! WHAT'S GOING ON?
AH!!
WH-WHAT ...WHAT HAPPENED TO THE ROAD?
NO BUSES, NO TAXIS!!

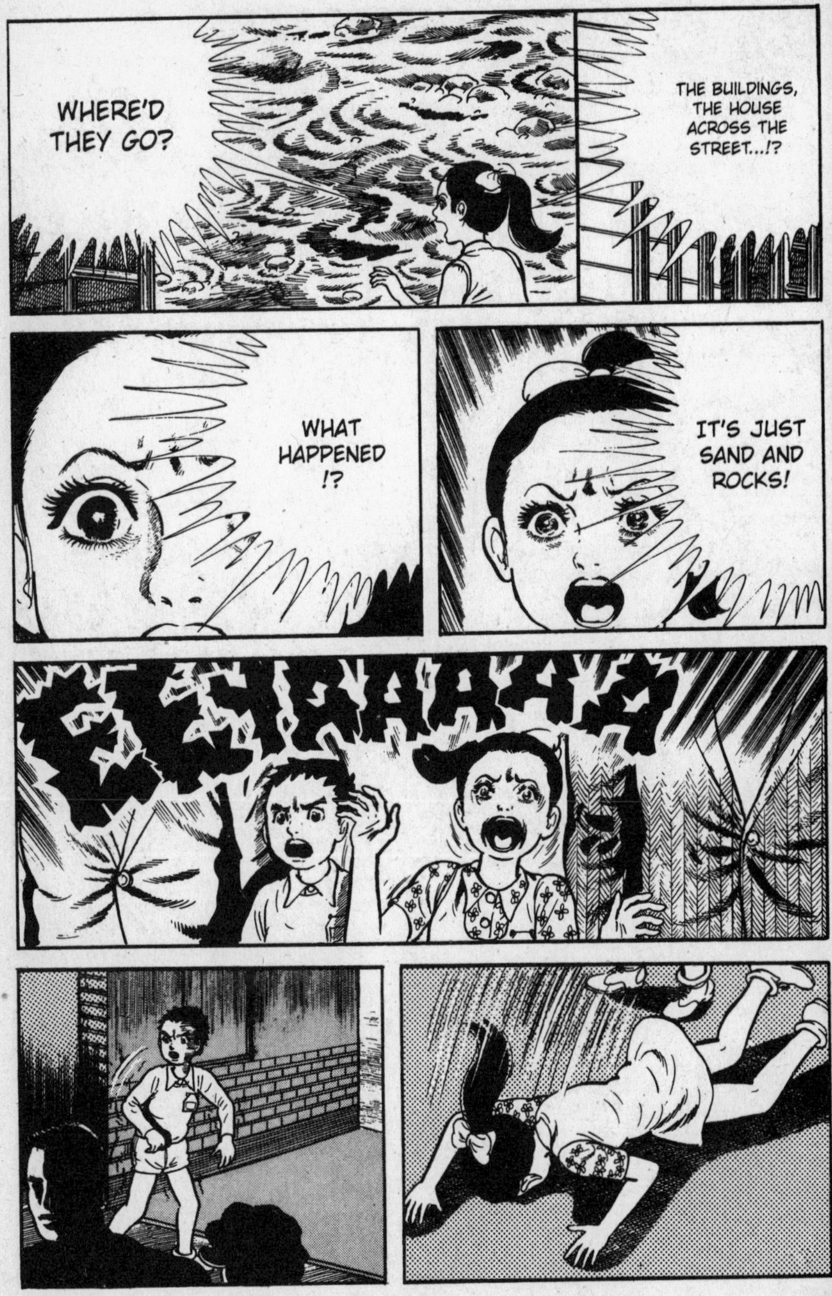
THE BUILDINGS, THE HOUSE ACROSS THE STREET...!?
WHERE'D THEY GO?
IT'S JUST SAND AND ROCKS!
WHAT HAPPENED !?

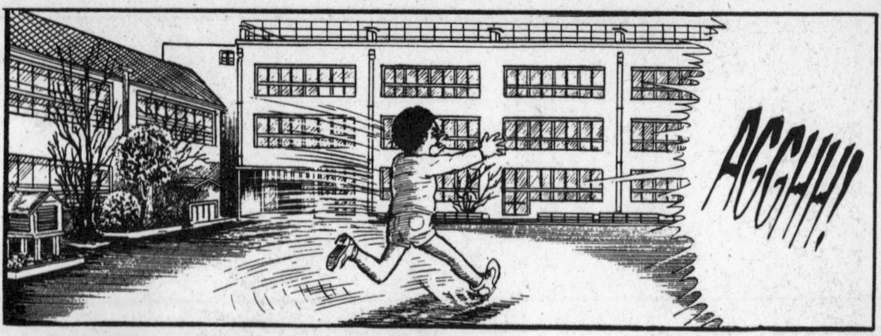
AGGHH!

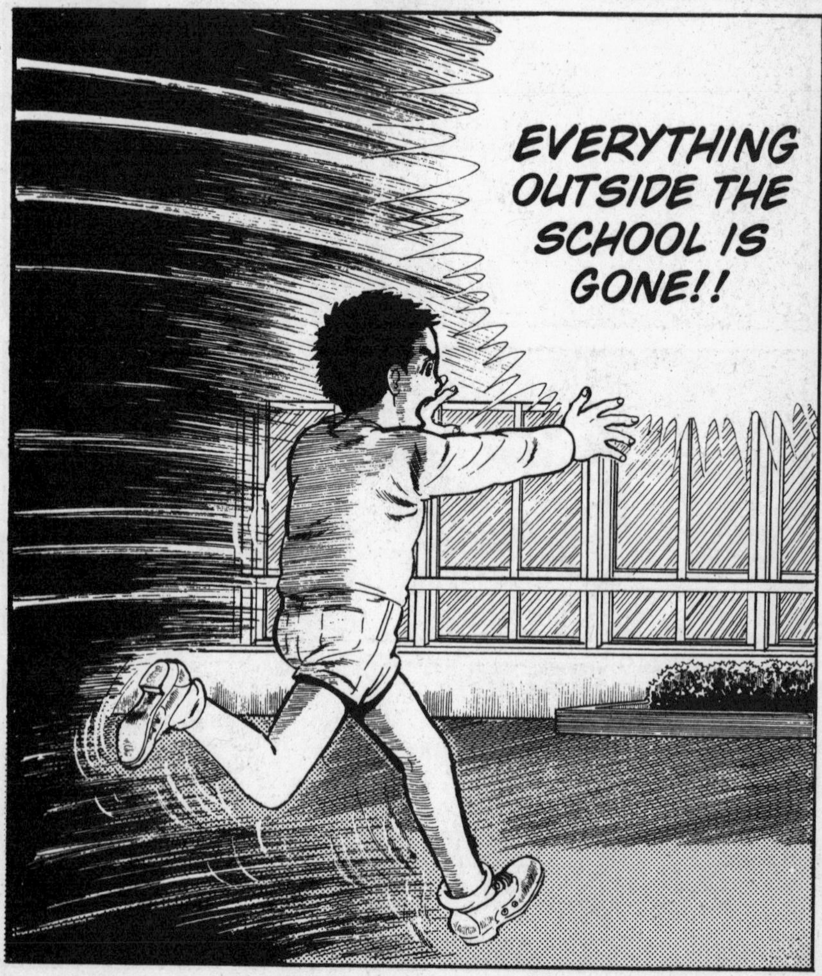
EVERYTHING OUTSIDE THE SCHOOL IS GONE!!

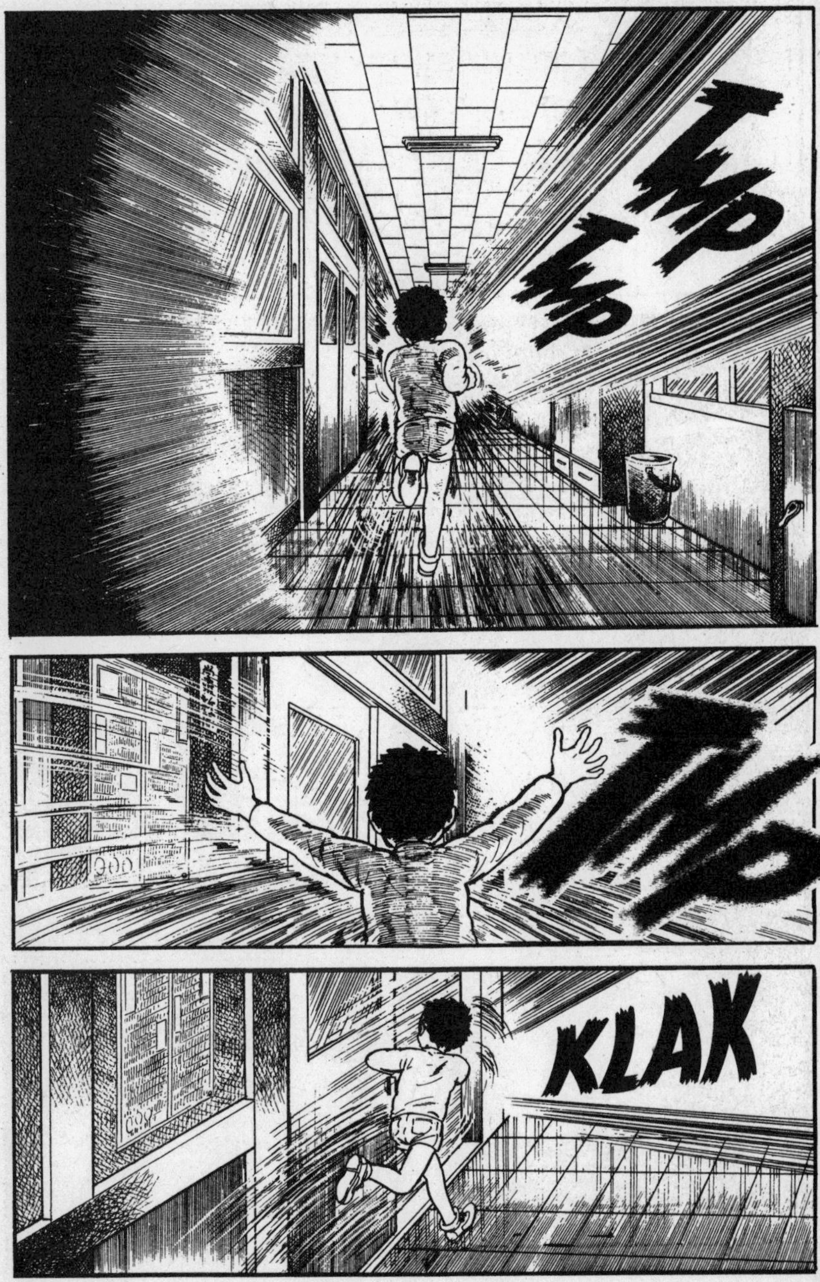
TMP TMP
THP
KLAK

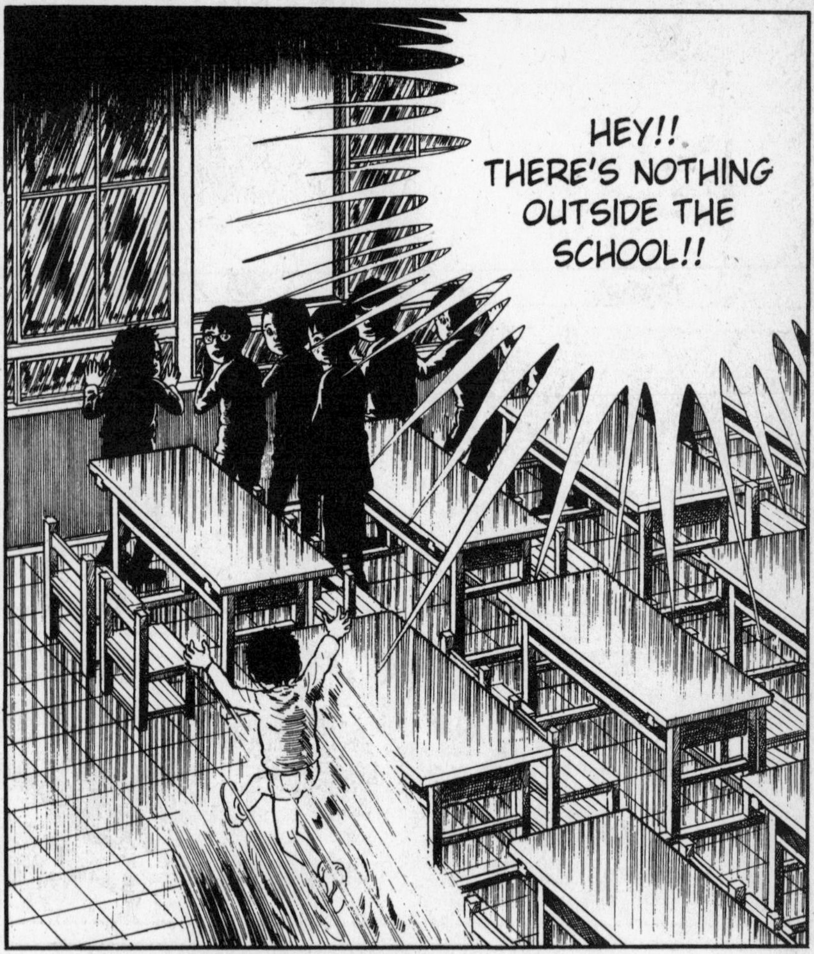
HEY!! THERE'S NOTHING OUTSIDE THE SCHOOL!!

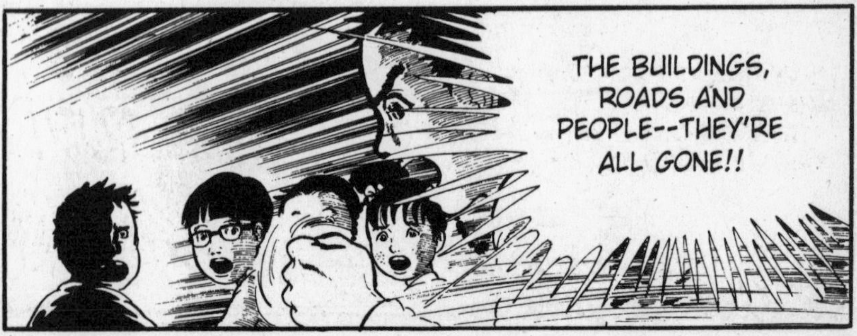
THE BUILDINGS, ROADS AND PEOPLE--THEY'RE ALL GONE!!

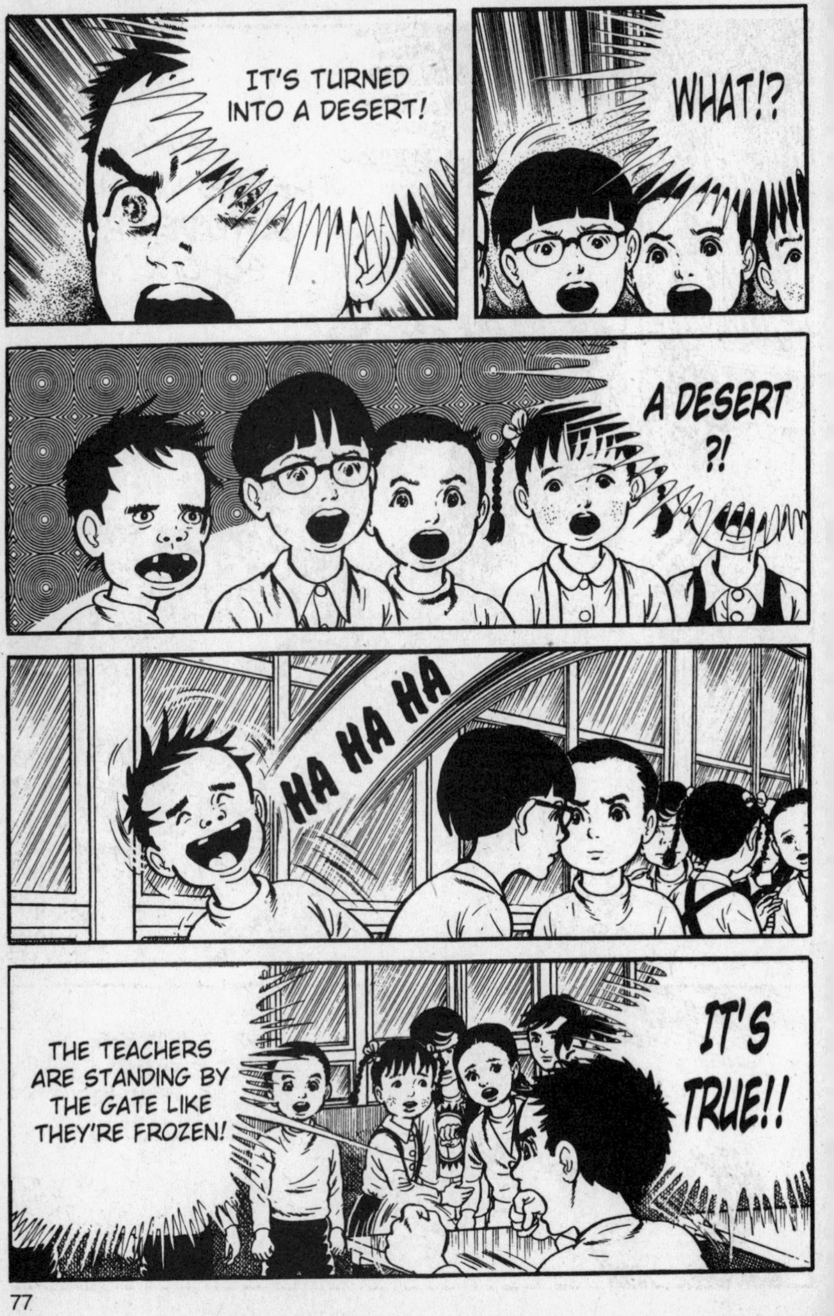
IT'S TURNED INTO A DESERT!
WHAT!?
A DESERT ?!
HA HA HA
THE TEACHERS ARE STANDING BY THE GATE LIKE THEY'RE FROZEN!
IT'S TRUE!!

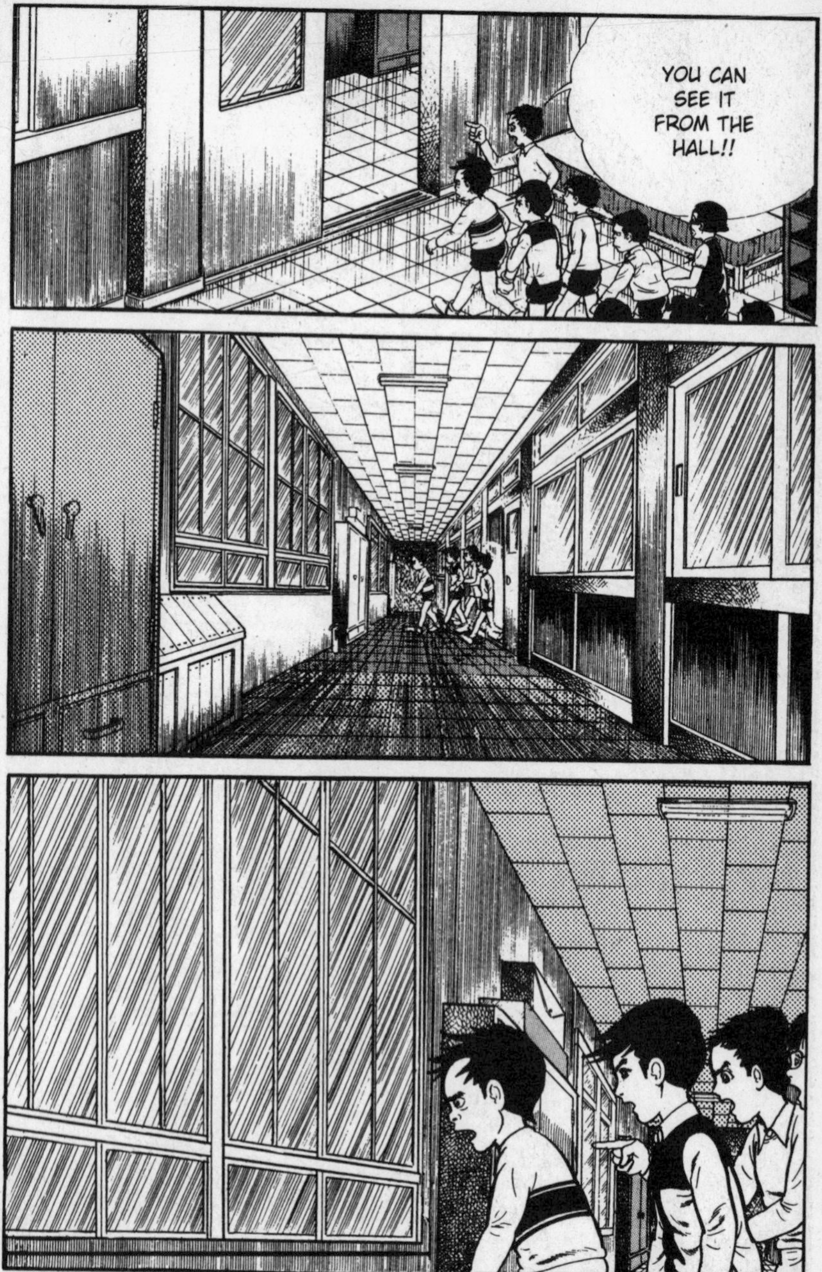
YOU CAN SEE IT FROM THE HALL!!

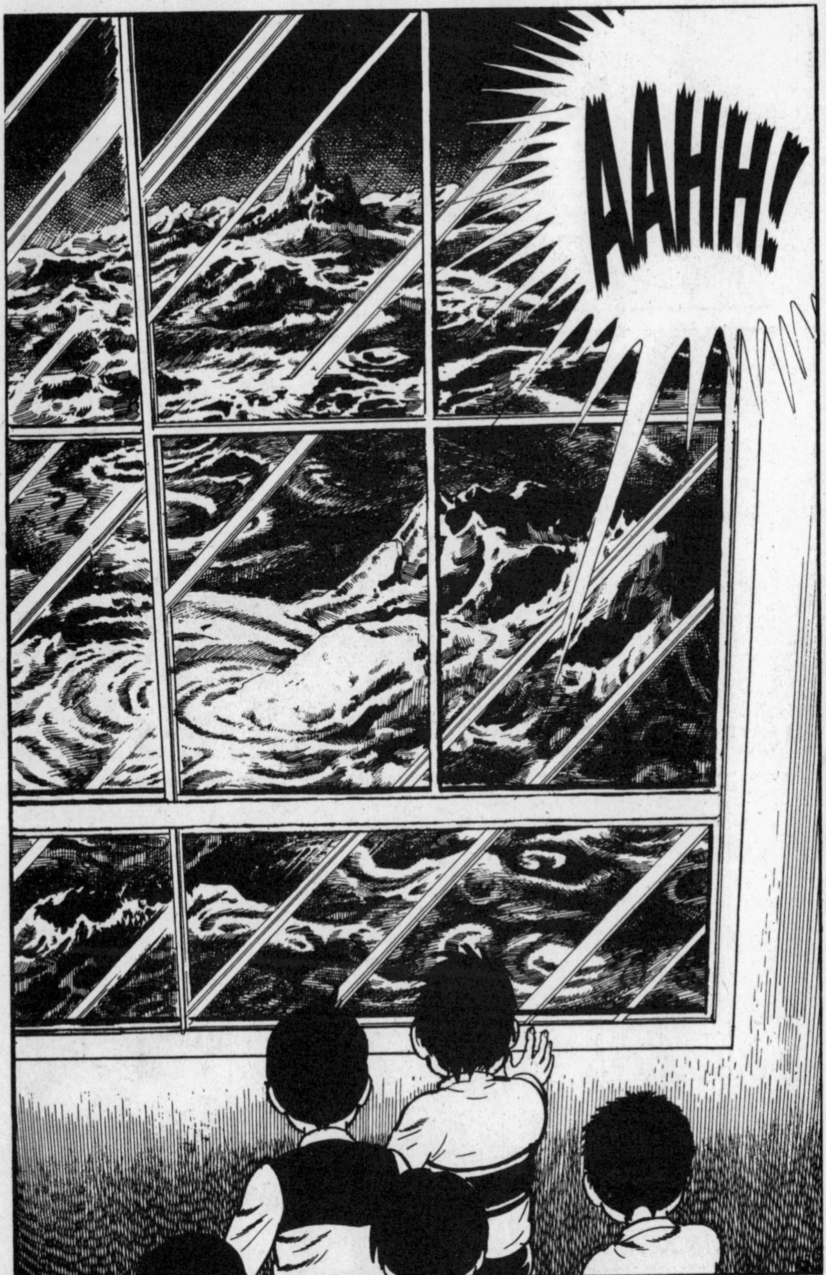
AAHH!

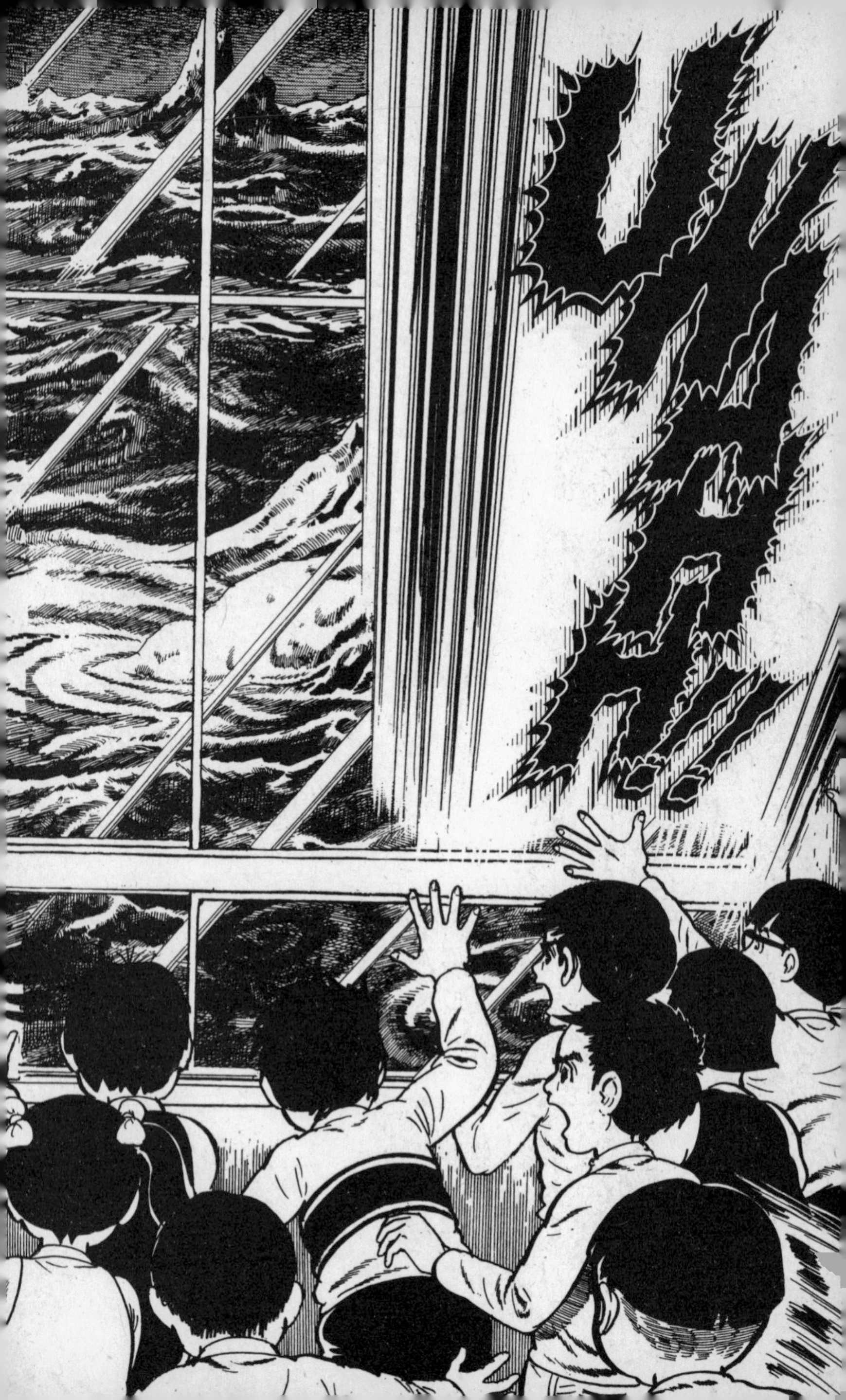

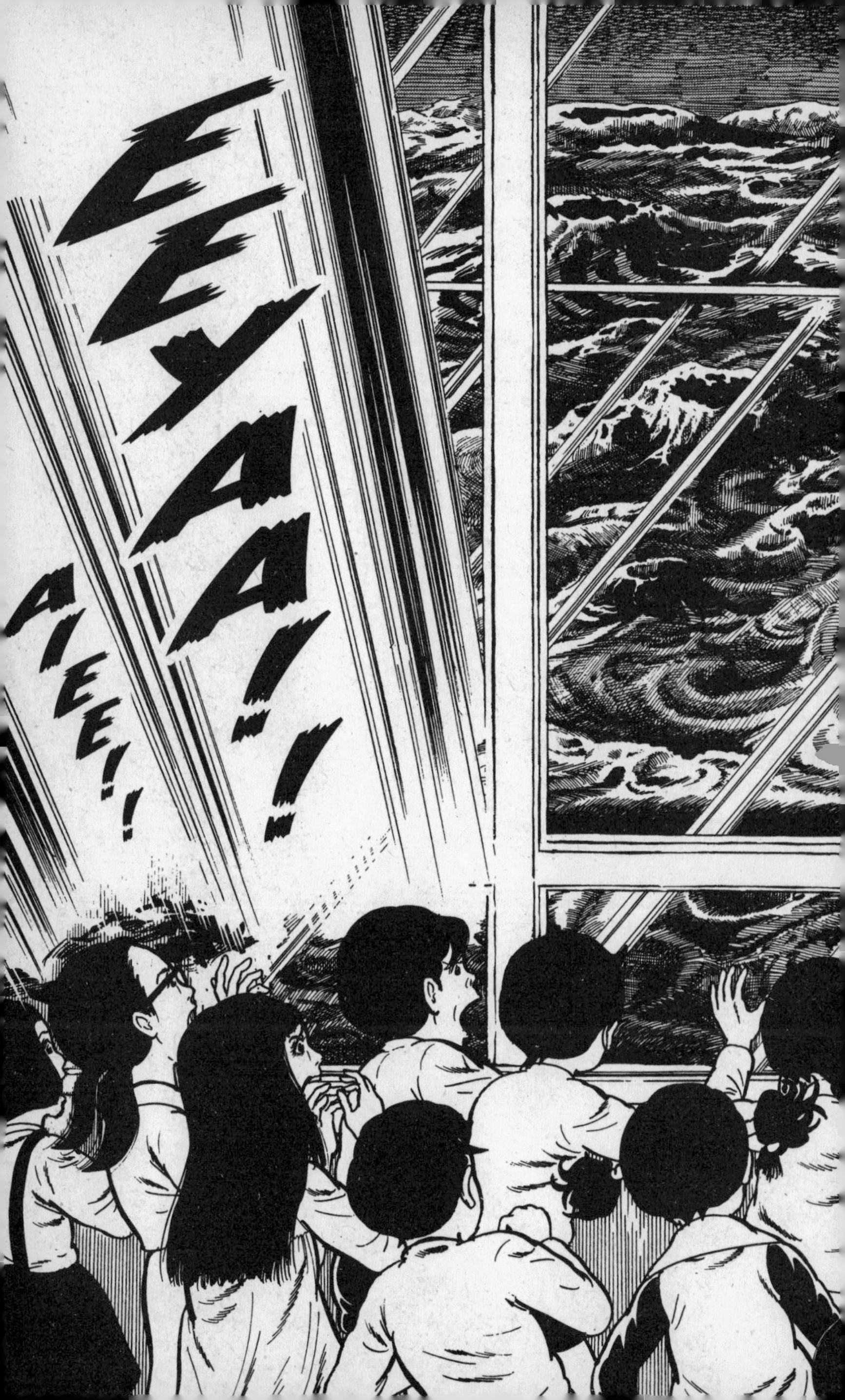
EEYAAA!!!
AIEEE!!!

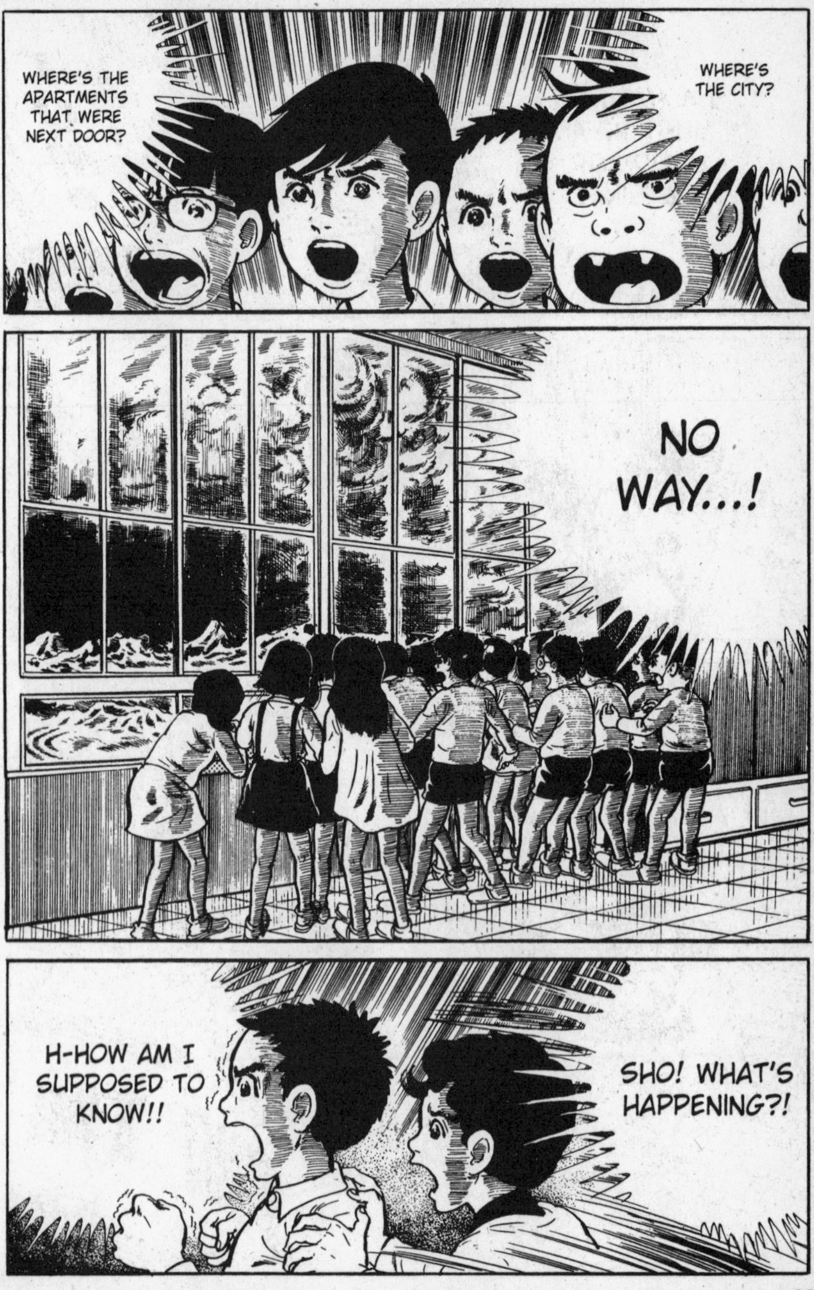
WHERE'S THE CITY?
WHERE'S THE APARTMENTS THAT WERE NEXT DOOR?
NO WAY...!
SHO! WHAT'S HAPPENING?!
H-HOW AM I SUPPOSED TO KNOW!!

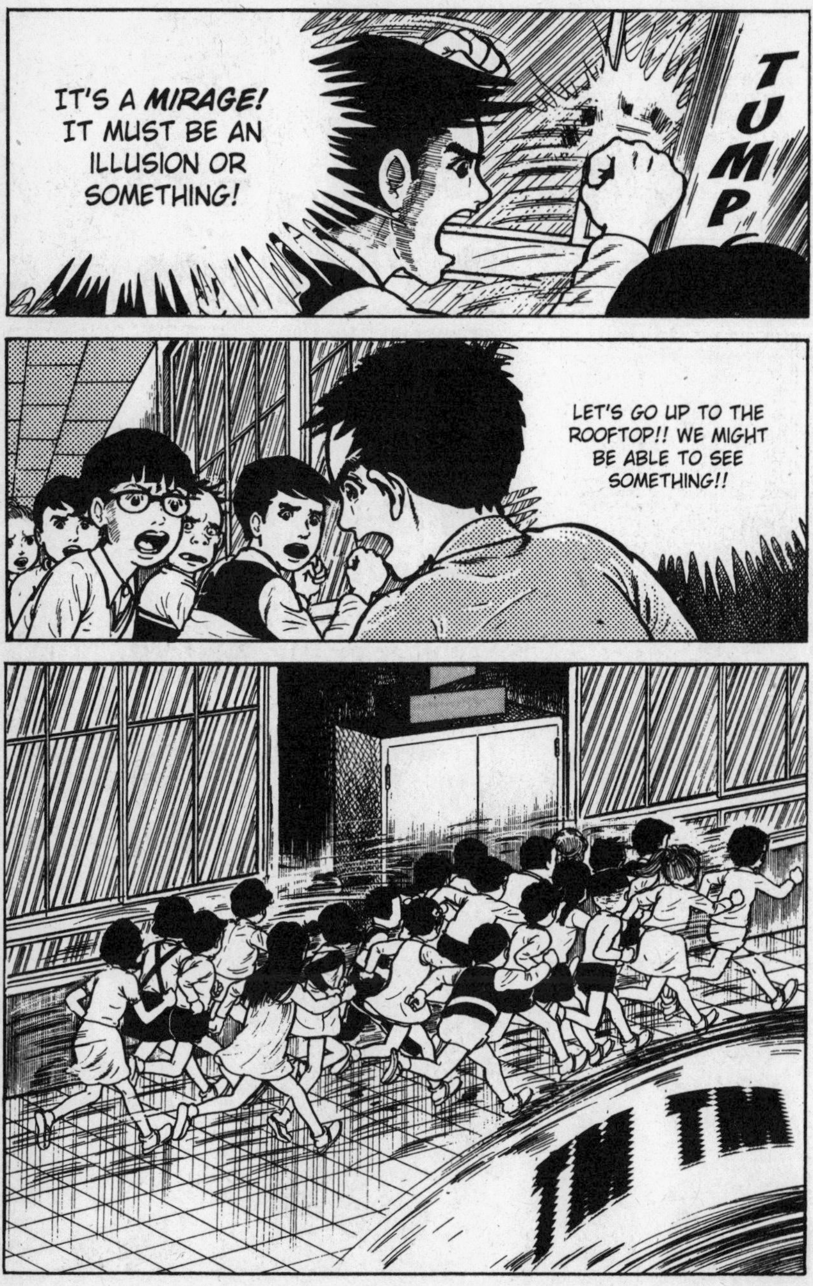
TUMP
IT'S A MIRAGE! IT MUST BE AN ILLUSION OR SOMETHING!
LET'S GO UP TO THE ROOFTOP!! WE MIGHT BE ABLE TO SEE SOMETHING!!
TM TM

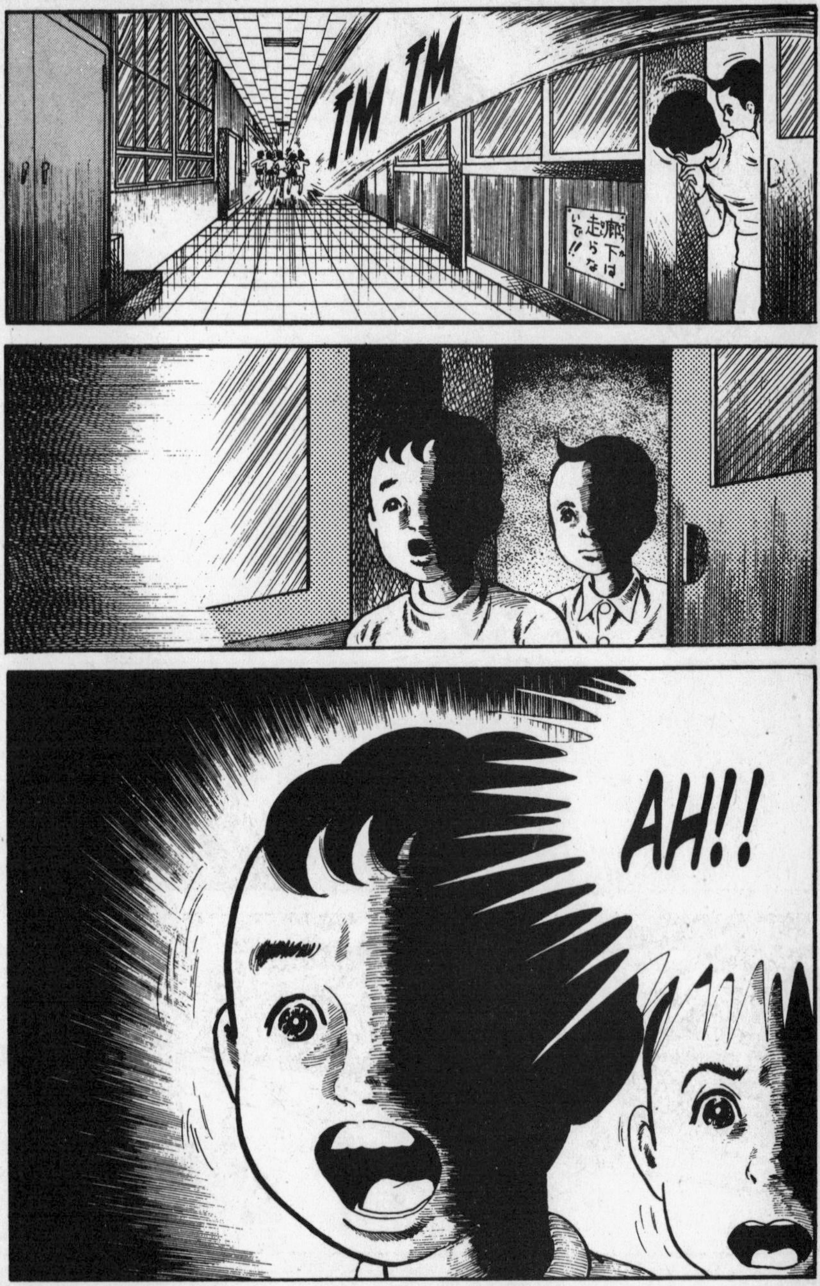
TM TM
廊下は走らないで!!
AH!!

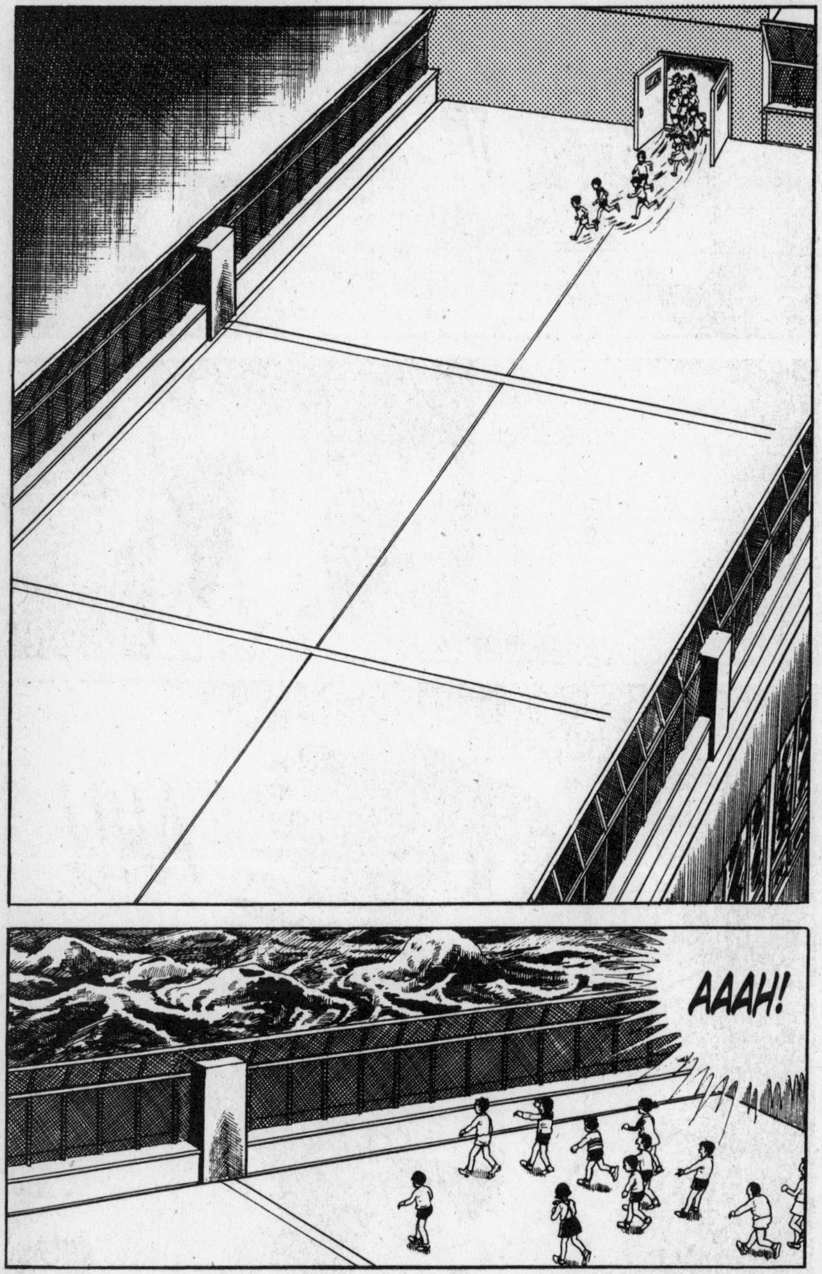
AAAH!

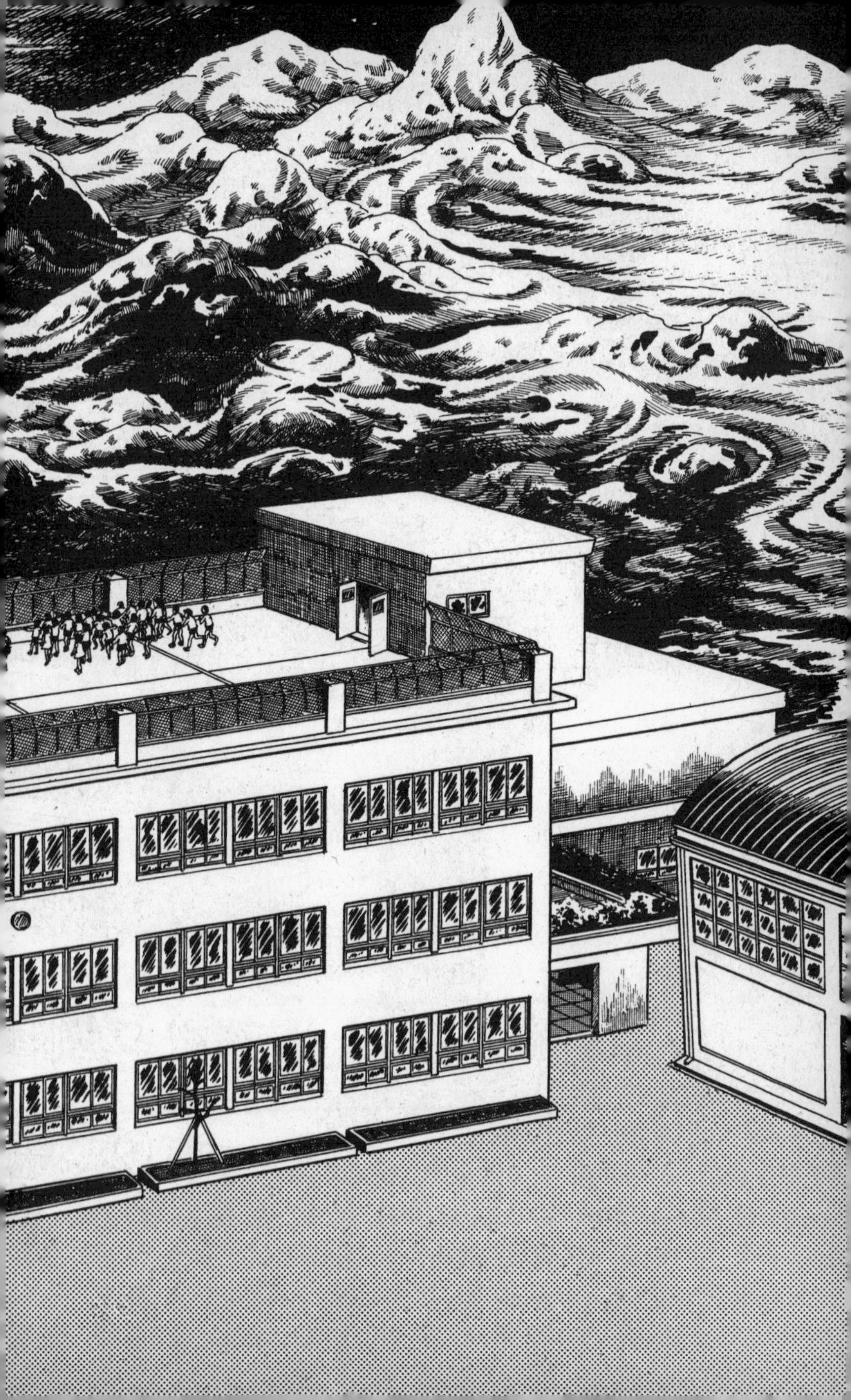

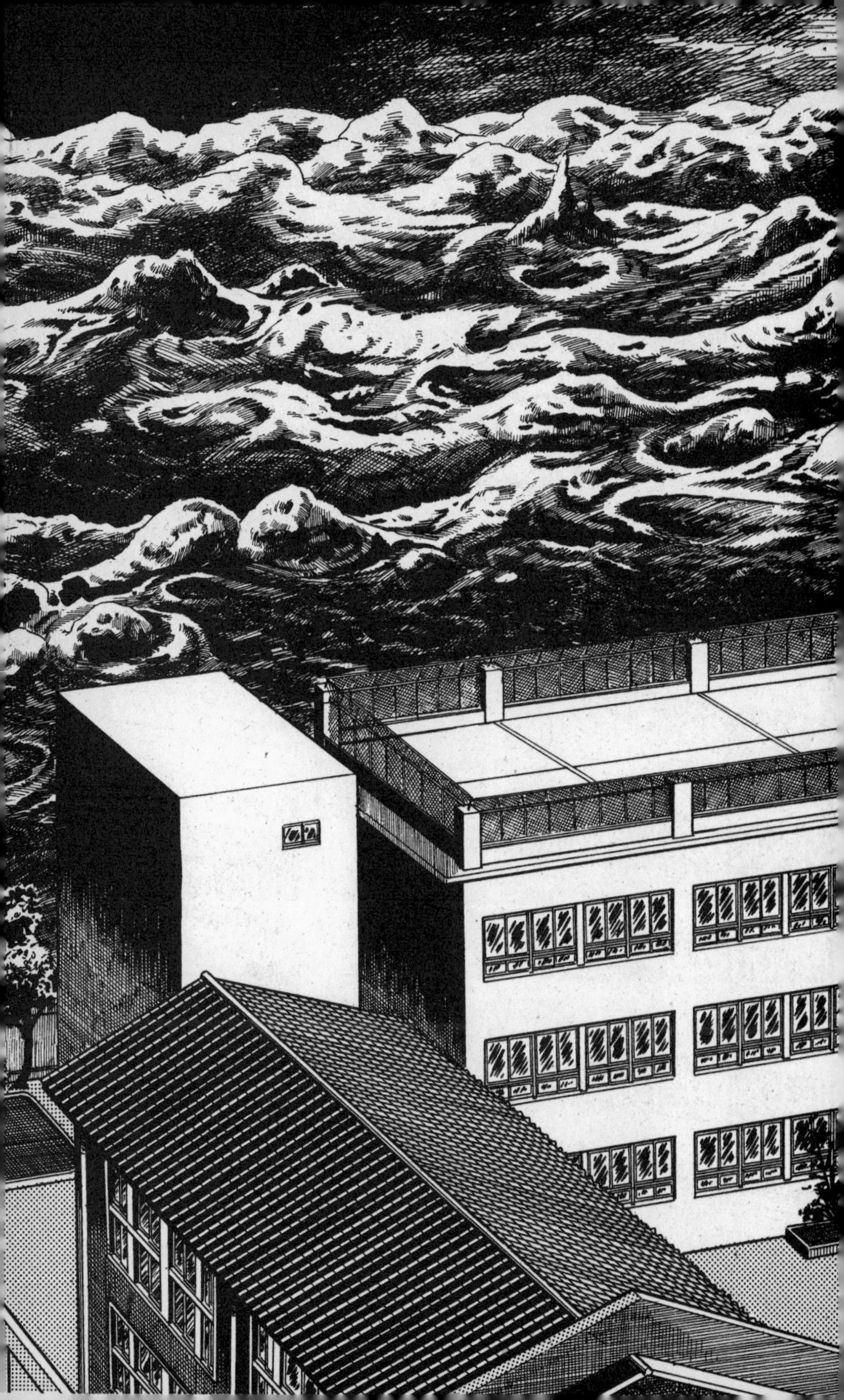

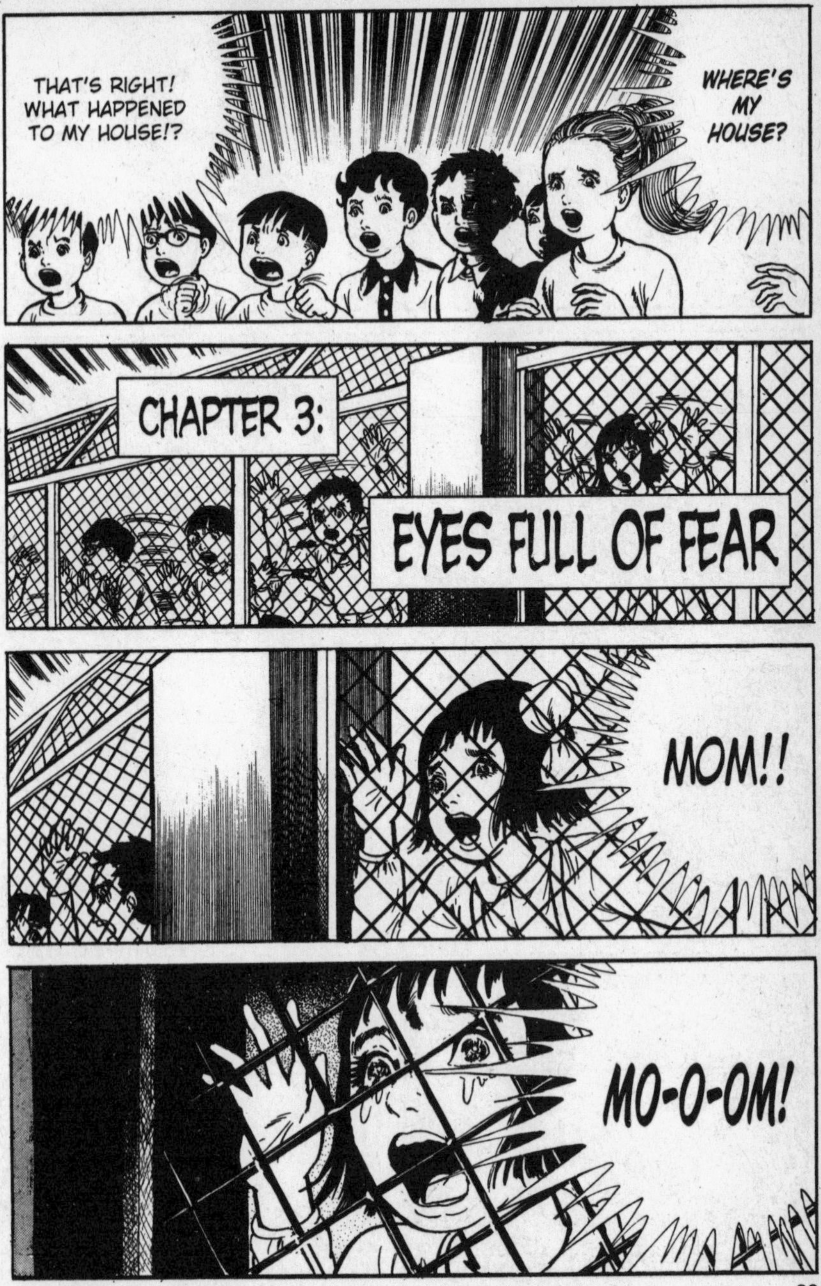
WHERE'S MY HOUSE?
THAT'S RIGHT! WHAT HAPPENED TO MY HOUSE!?
CHAPTER 3:
EYES FULL OF FEAR
MOM!!
MO-O-OM!

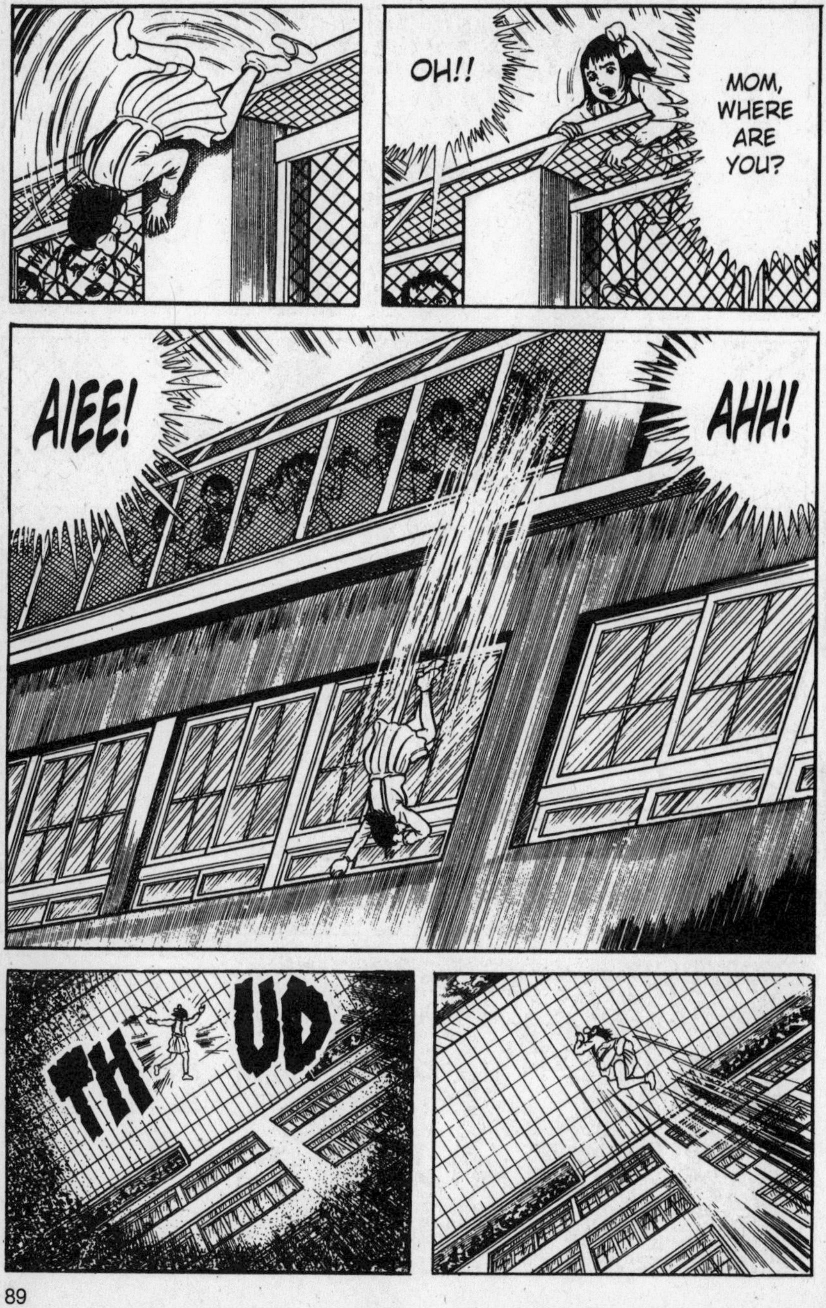
MOM, WHERE ARE YOU?
OH!!
AHH!
AIEE!
THUD

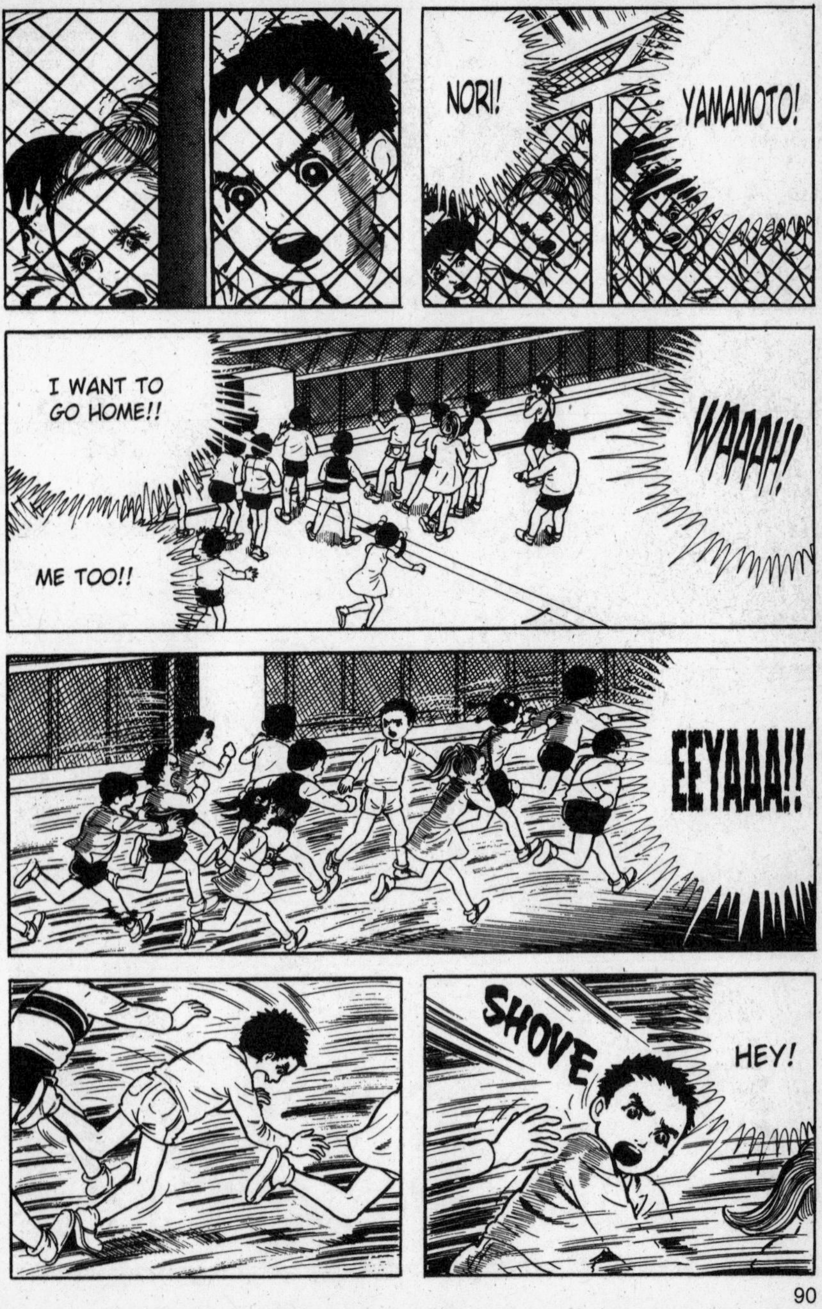
YAMAMOTO!
NORI!
WAAAH!
I WANT TO GO HOME!!
ME TOO!!
EEYAAA!!
SHOVE
HEY!

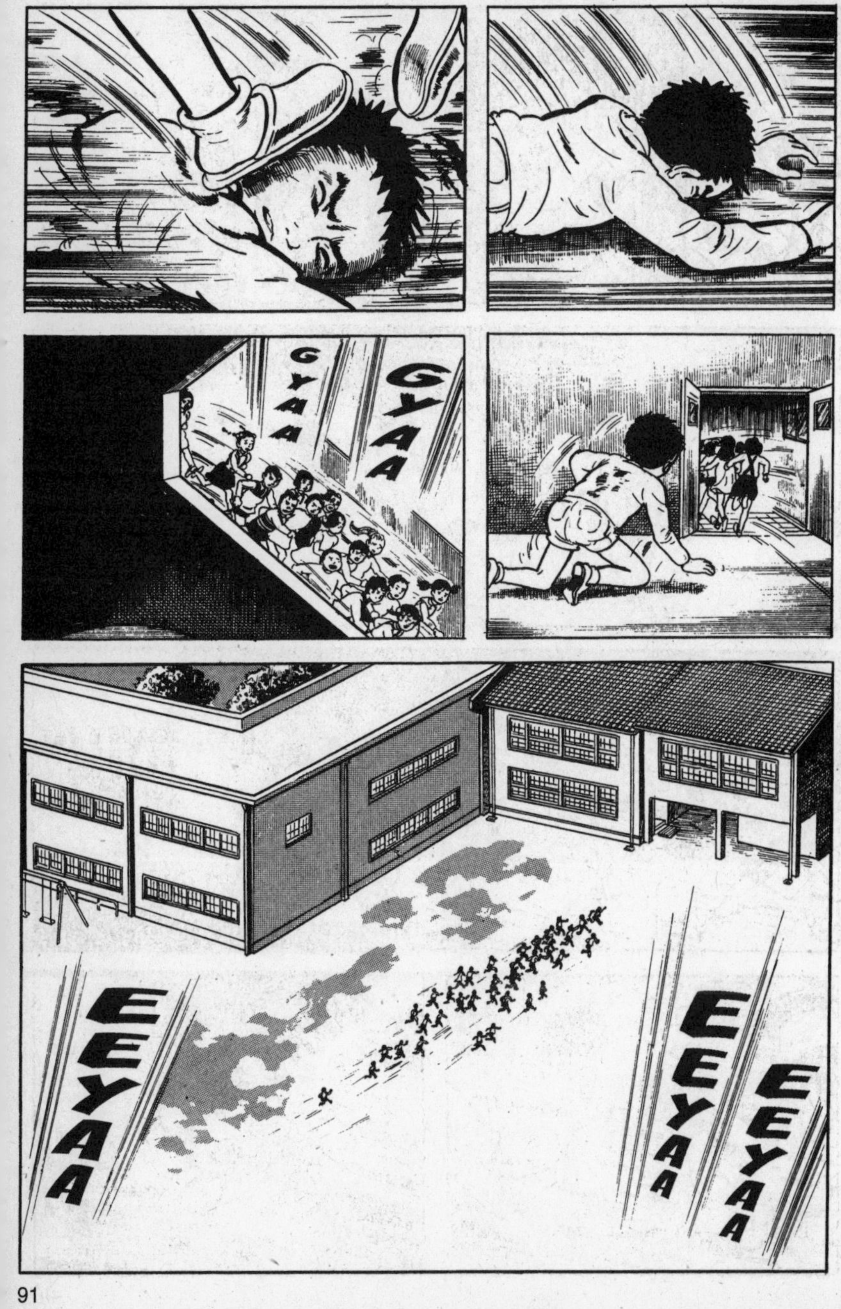
GYAA
GYAA
EEYAA
EEYAA
EEYAAA

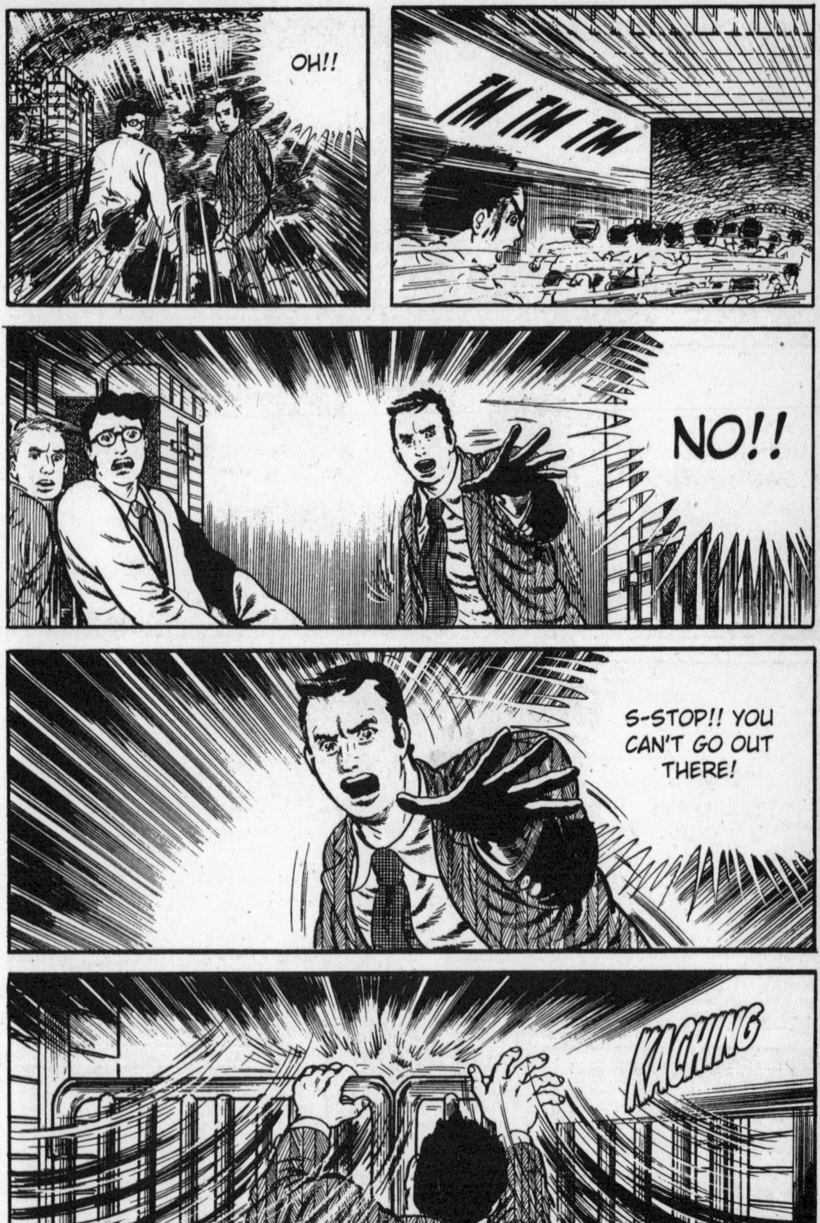
TIM TIM TIM
OH!!
NO!!
S-STOP!! YOU CAN'T GO OUT THERE!
KACHING

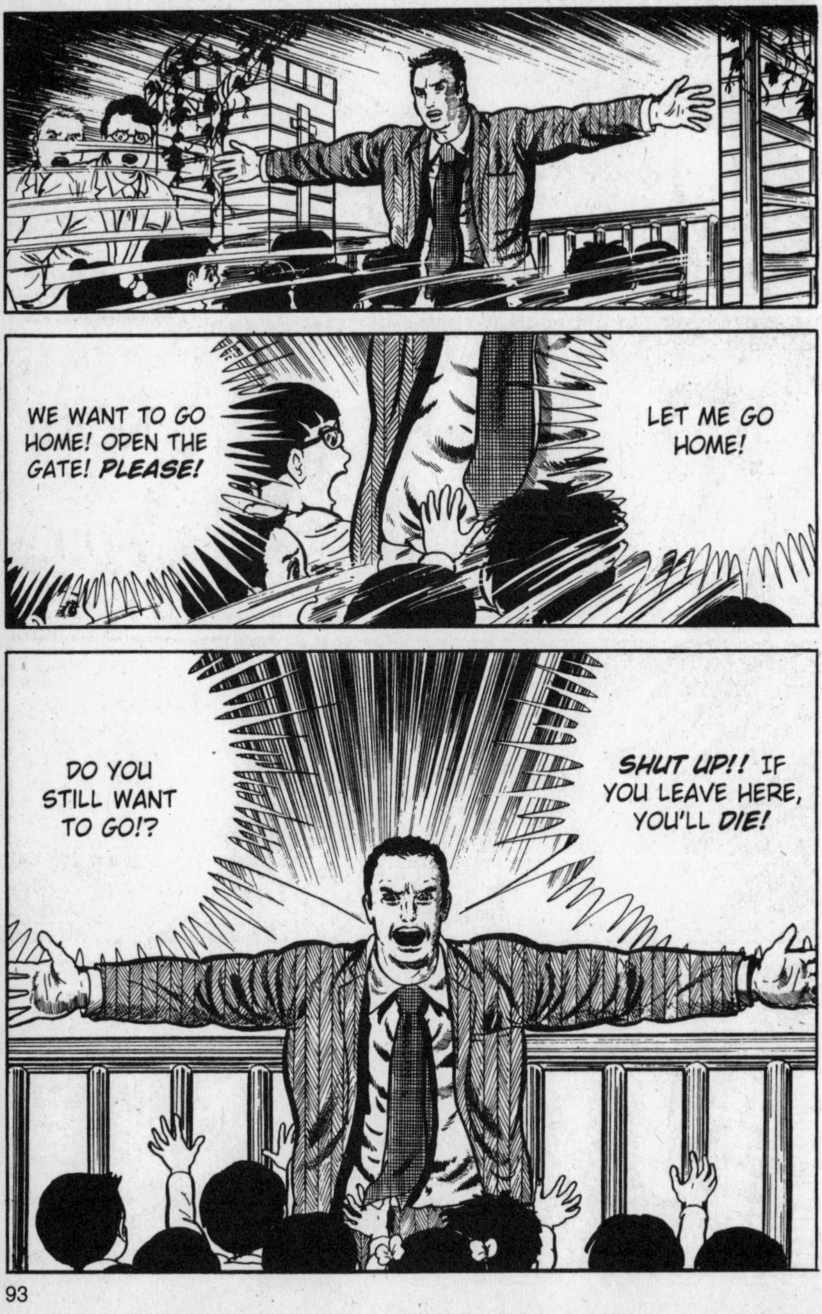
LET ME GO HOME!
WE WANT TO GO HOME! OPEN THE GATE! PLEASE!
SHUT UP!! IF YOU LEAVE HERE, YOU'LL DIE!
DO YOU STILL WANT TO GO!?

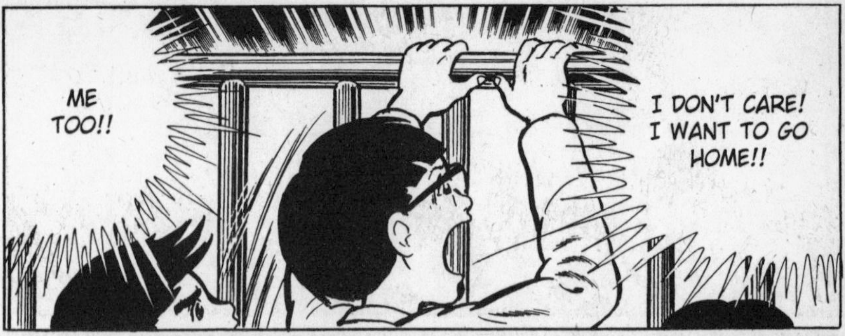
I DON'T CARE! I WANT TO GO HOME!!
ME TOO!!

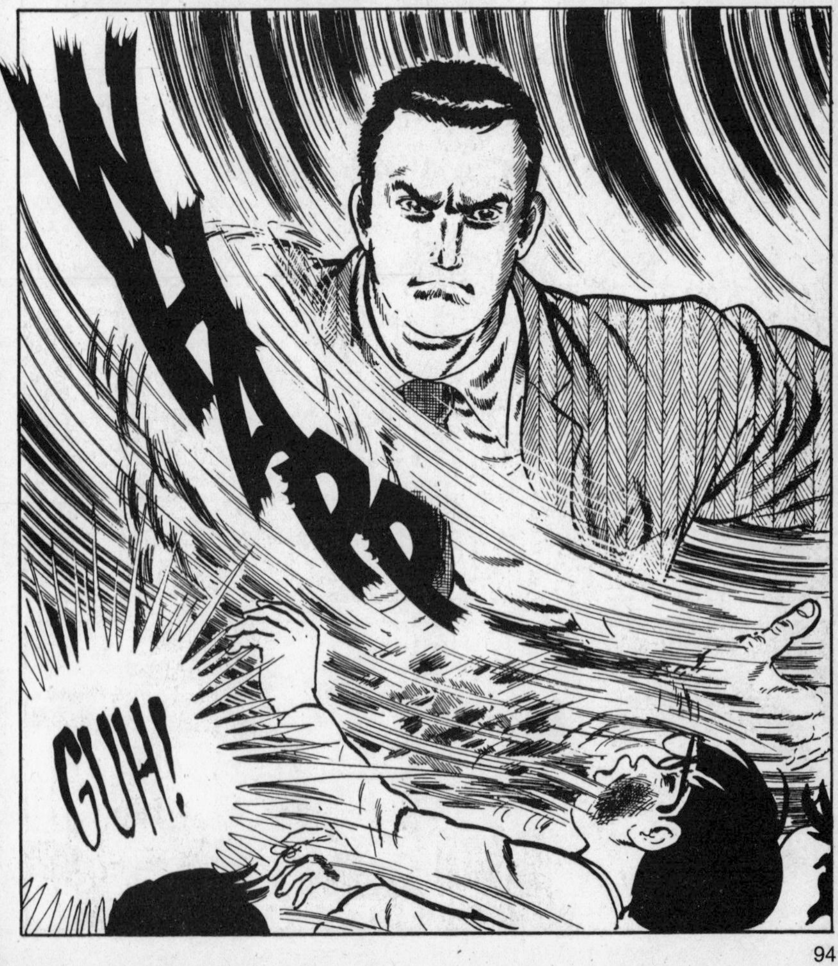
WHAPP
GUH!

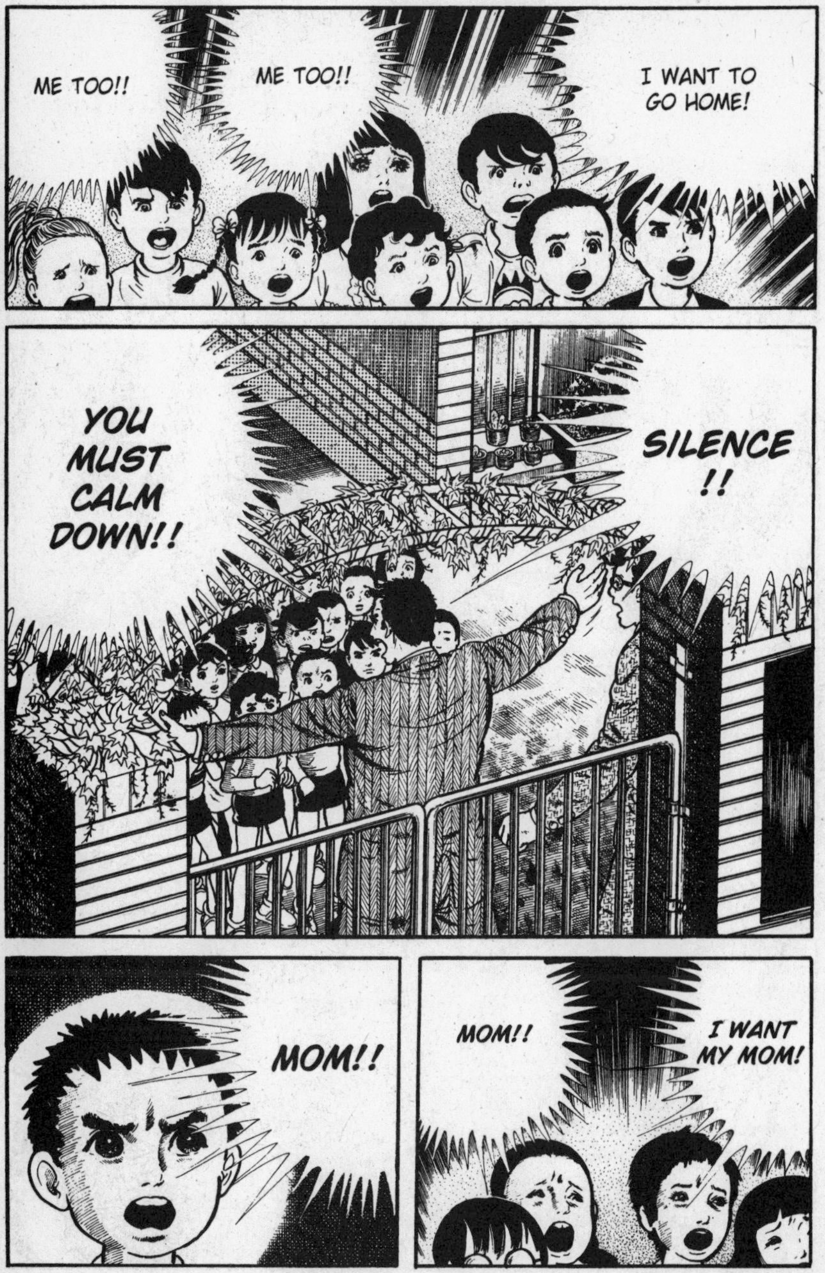
I WANT TO GO HOME!
ME TOO!!
ME TOO!!
SILENCE !!
YOU MUST CALM DOWN!!
I WANT MY MOM!
MOM!!
MOM!!

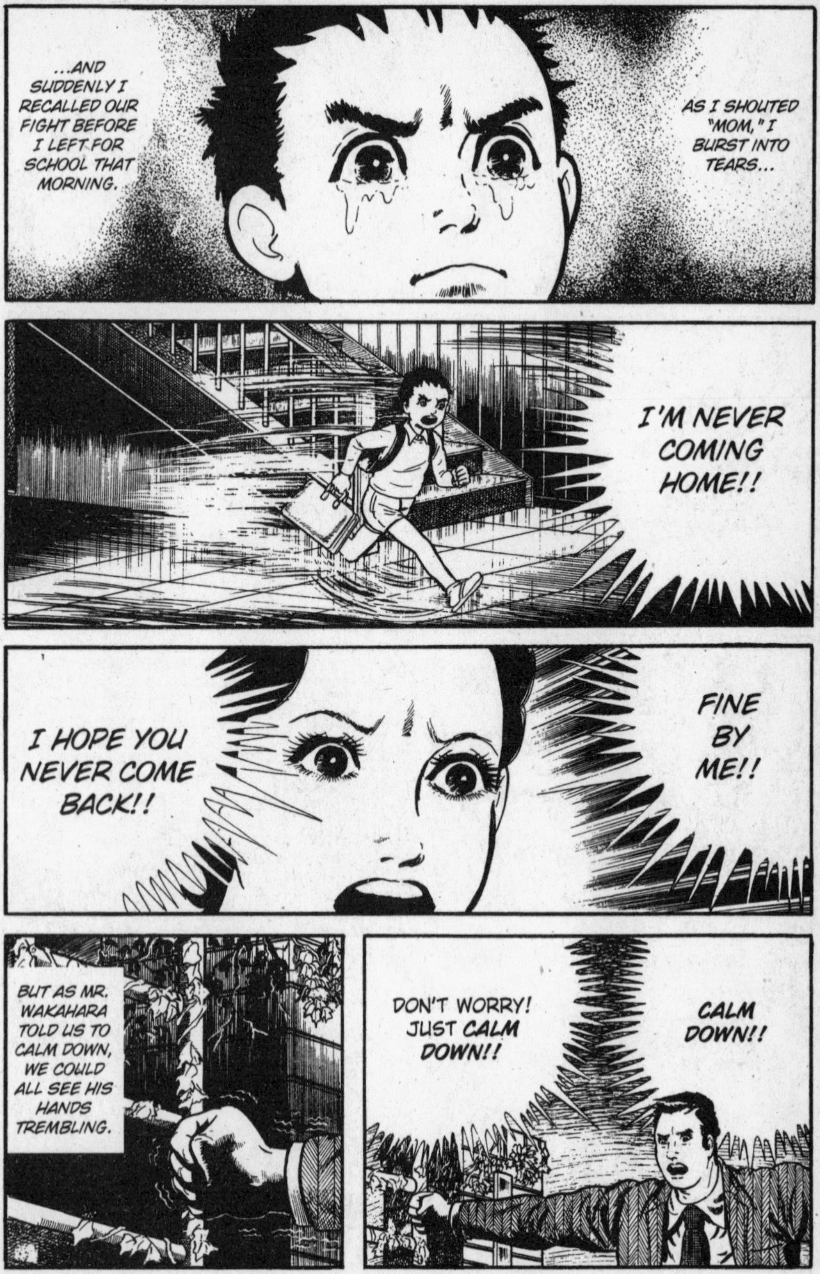
AS I SHOUTED "MOM," I BURST INTO TEARS...
...AND SUDDENLY I RECALLED OUR FIGHT BEFORE I LEFT FOR SCHOOL THAT MORNING.
I'M NEVER COMING HOME!!
FINE BY ME!!
I HOPE YOU NEVER COME BACK!!
CALM DOWN!!
DON'T WORRY! JUST CALM DOWN!!
BUT AS MR. WAKAHARA TOLD US TO CALM DOWN, WE COULD ALL SEE HIS HANDS TREMBLING.

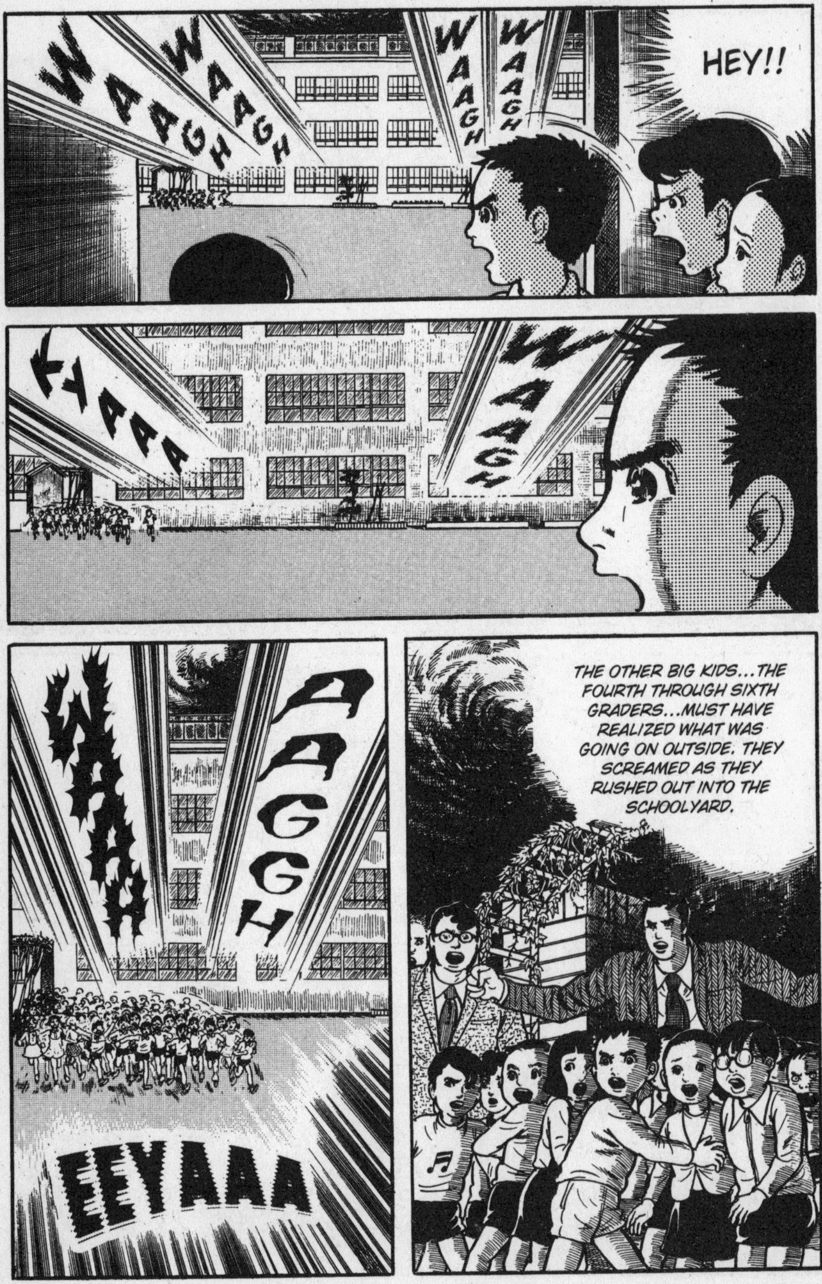
HEY!!
WAAAGH
WAAGH
WAAAGH
THE OTHER BIG KIDS...THE FOURTH THROUGH SIXTH GRADERS...MUST HAVE REALIZED WHAT WAS GOING ON OUTSIDE. THEY SCREAMED AS THEY RUSHED OUT INTO THE SCHOOLYARD.
AAGGH
EEYAAA

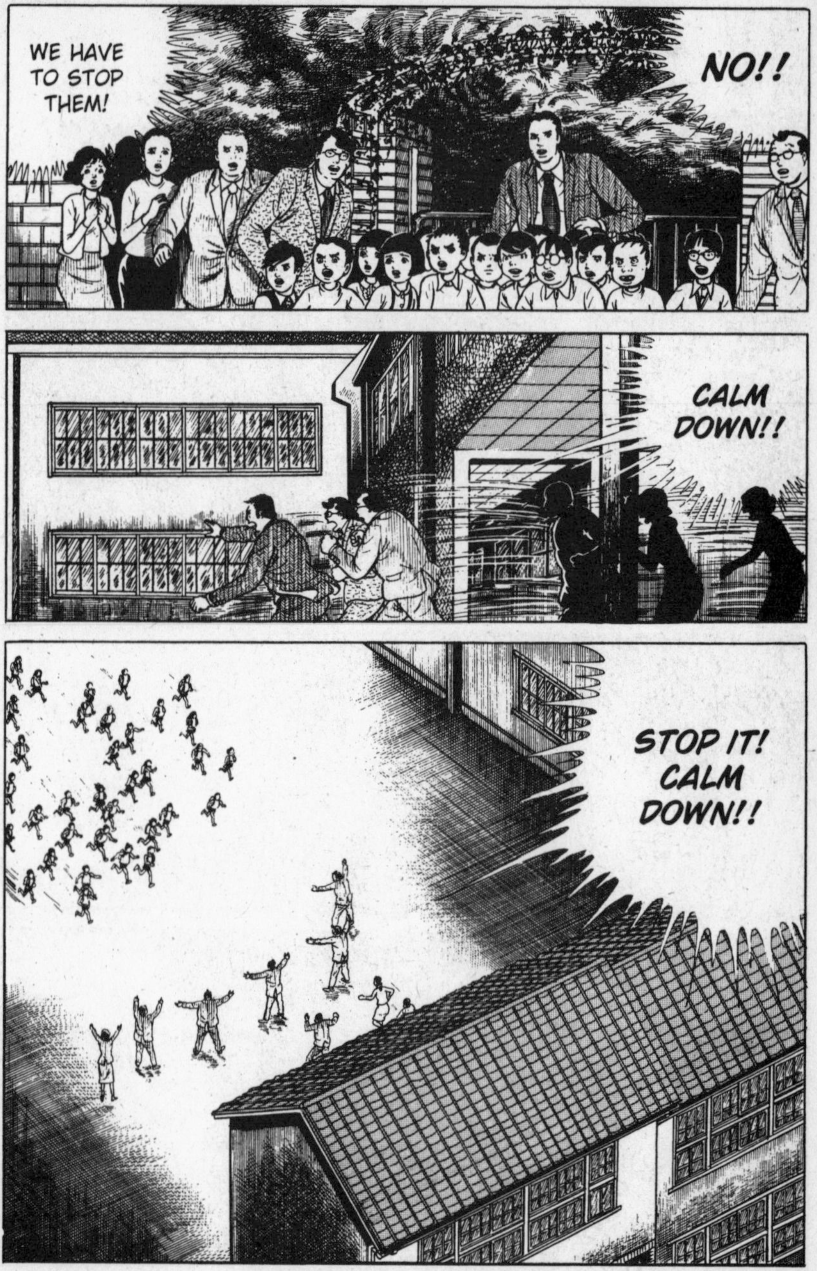

NO!!
WE HAVE TO STOP THEM!
CALM DOWN!!
STOP IT! CALM DOWN!!

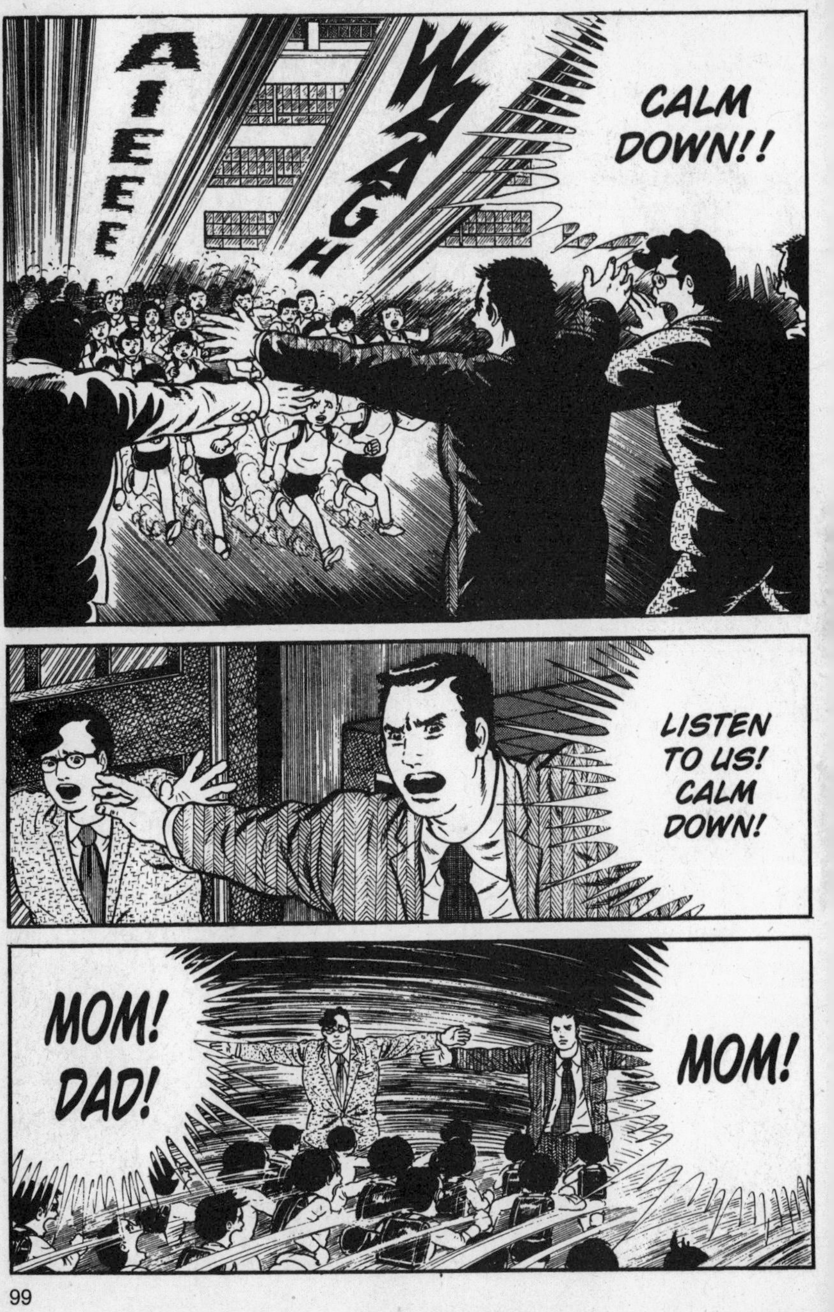
CALM DOWN!!
WAAGH
AIEEEE
LISTEN TO US! CALM DOWN!
MOM!
MOM! DAD!

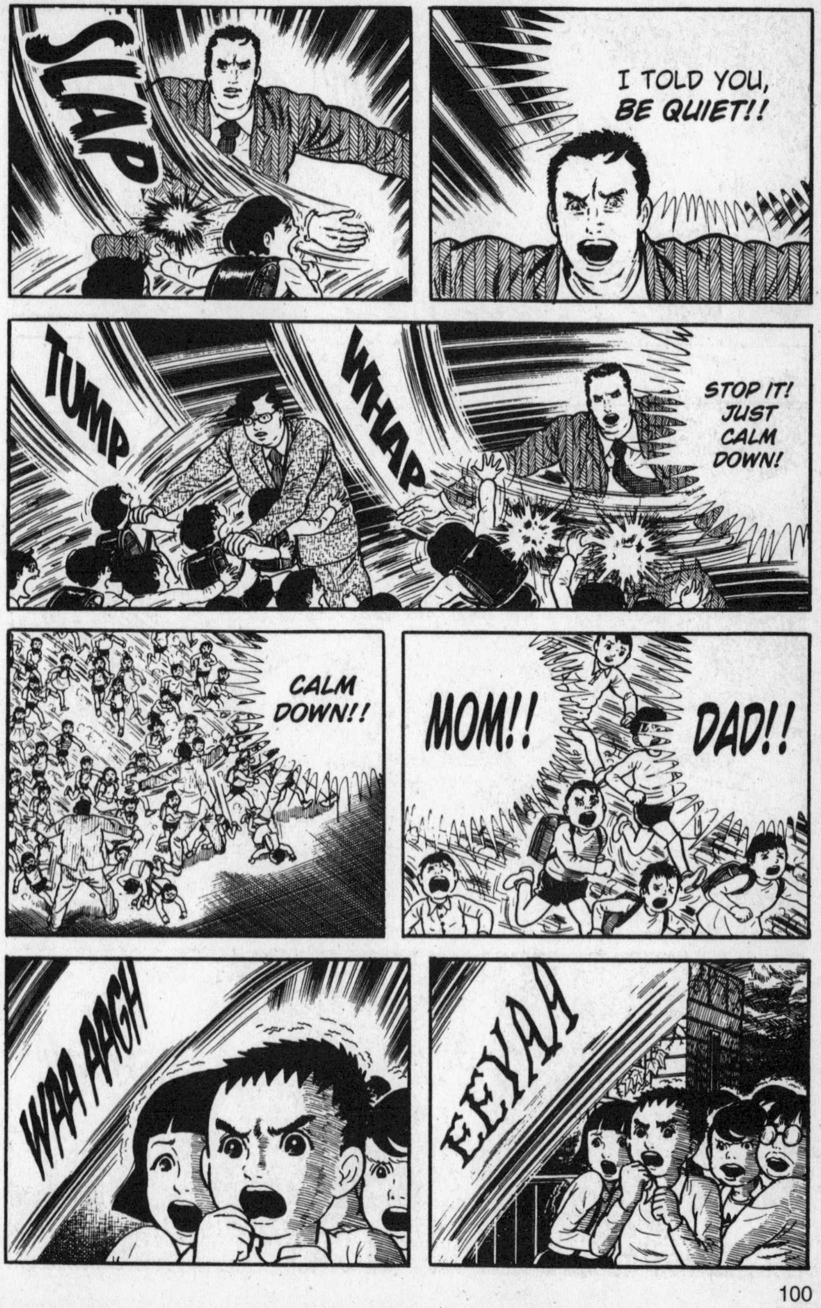
I TOLD YOU, BE QUIET!!
SLAP
STOP IT! JUST CALM DOWN!
WHAP
TUMP
DAD!!
MOM!!
CALM DOWN!!
EEYAA
WAA AAGH

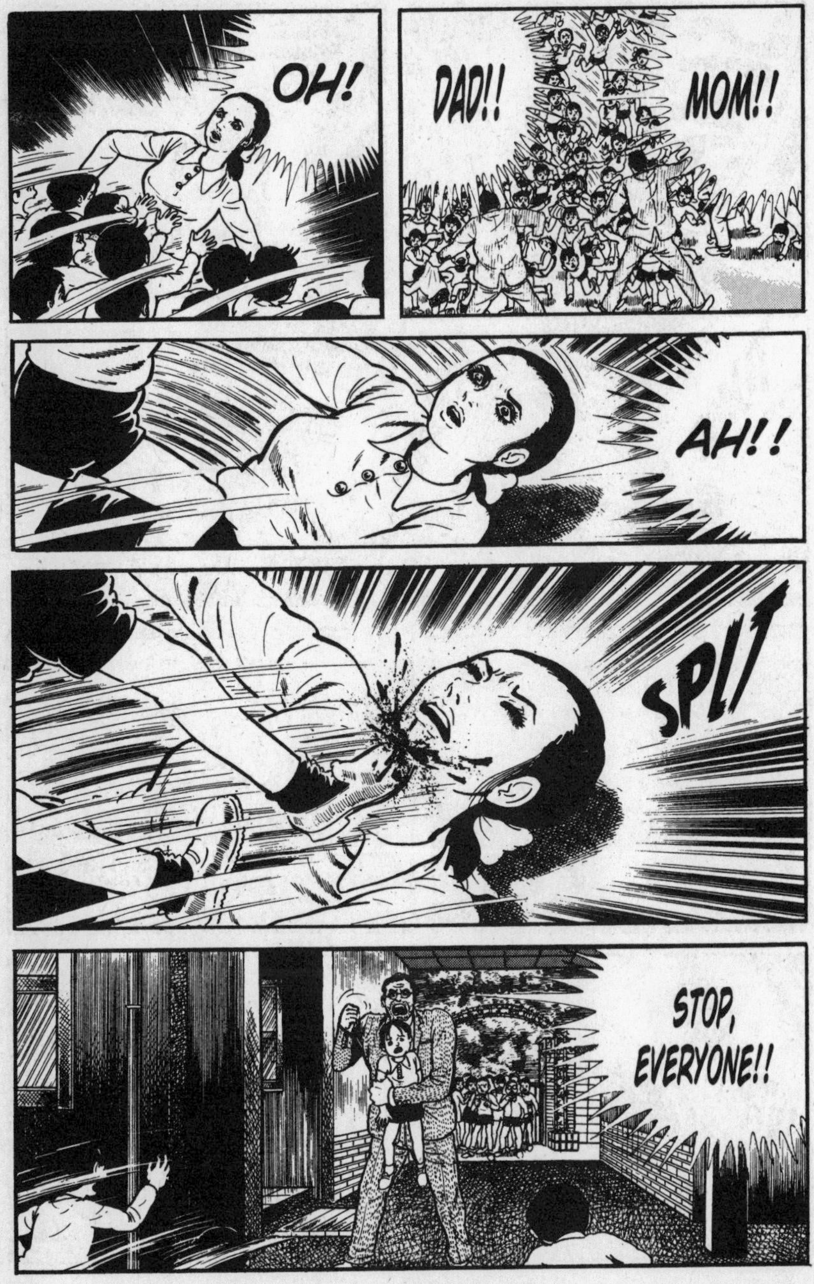
MOM!!
DAD!!
OH!
AH!!
SPLIT
STOP, EVERYONE!!

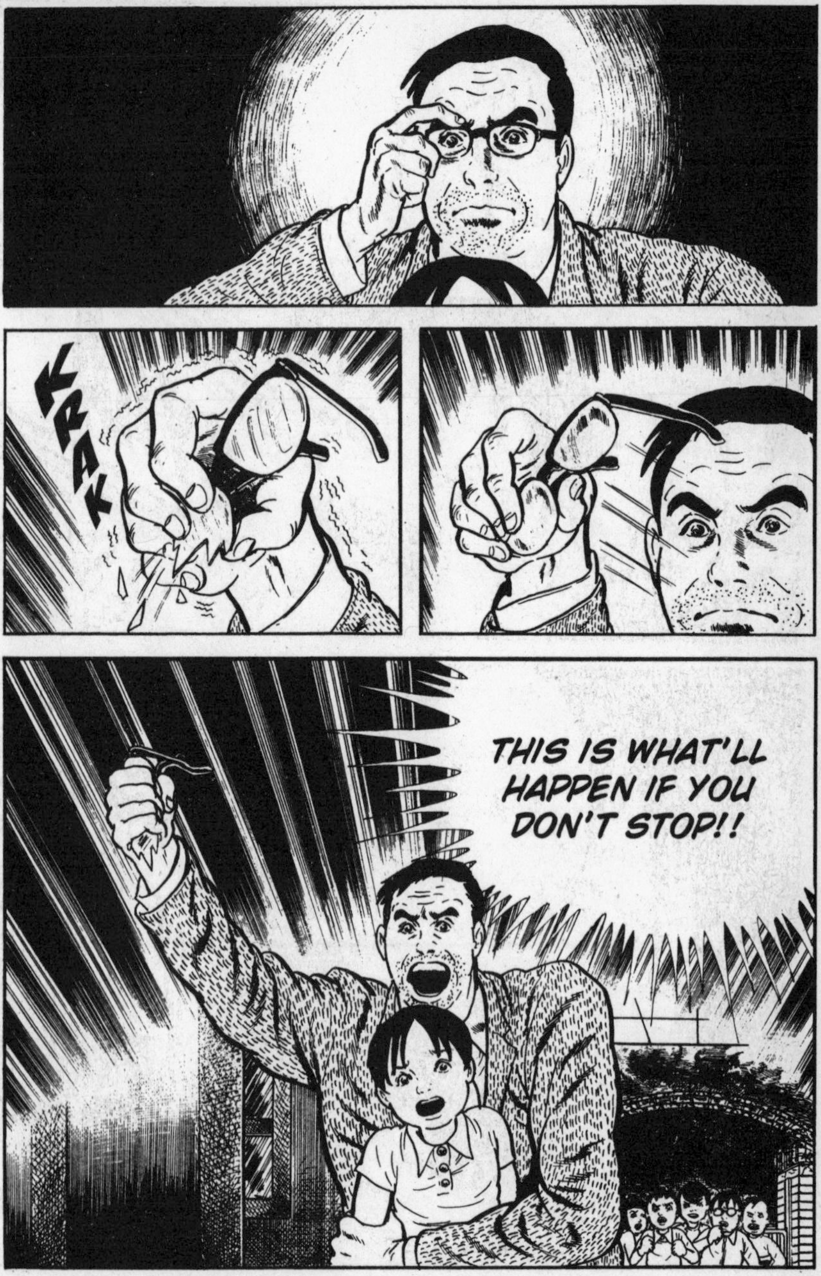
KRAK
THIS IS WHAT'LL HAPPEN IF YOU DON'T STOP!!

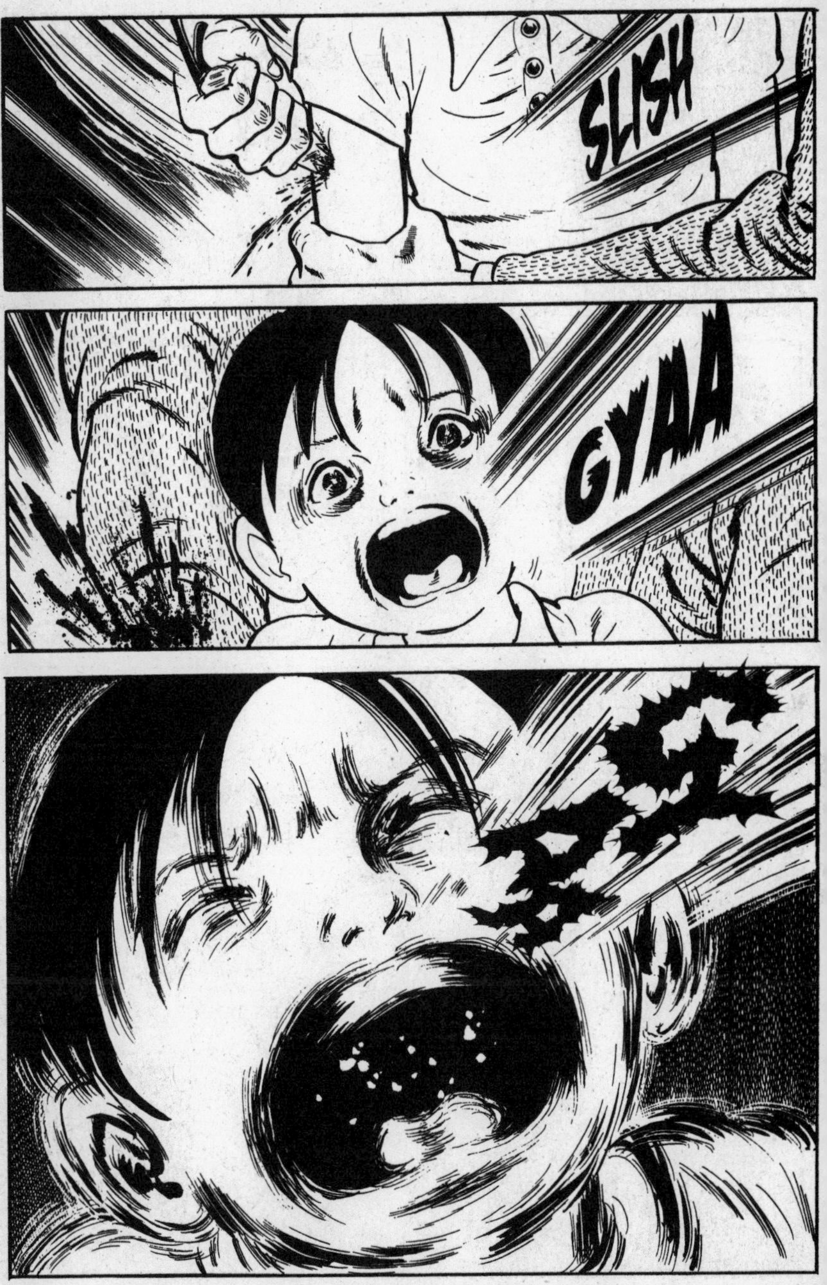
SLISH
GYAA

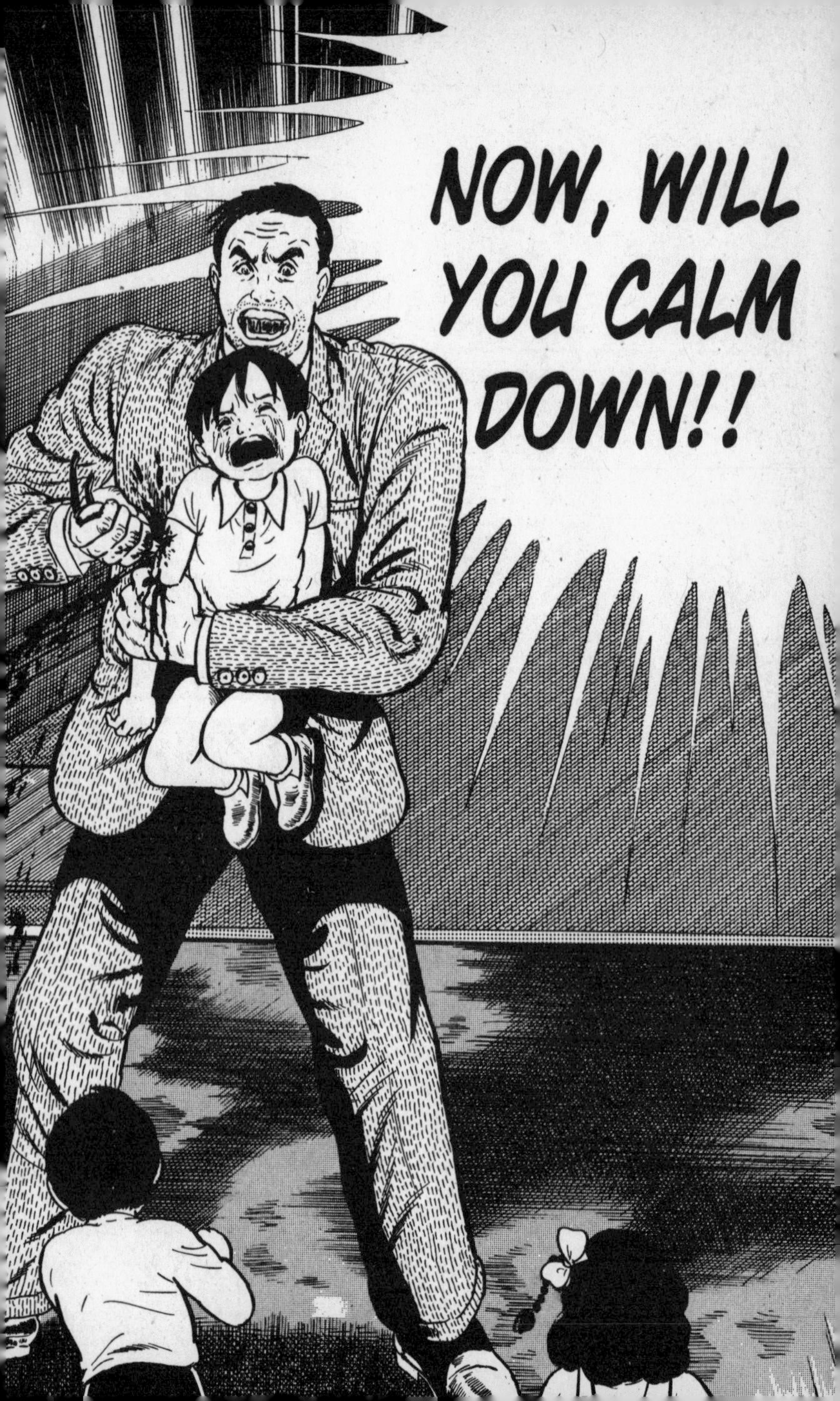
NOW, WILL YOU CALM DOWN!!

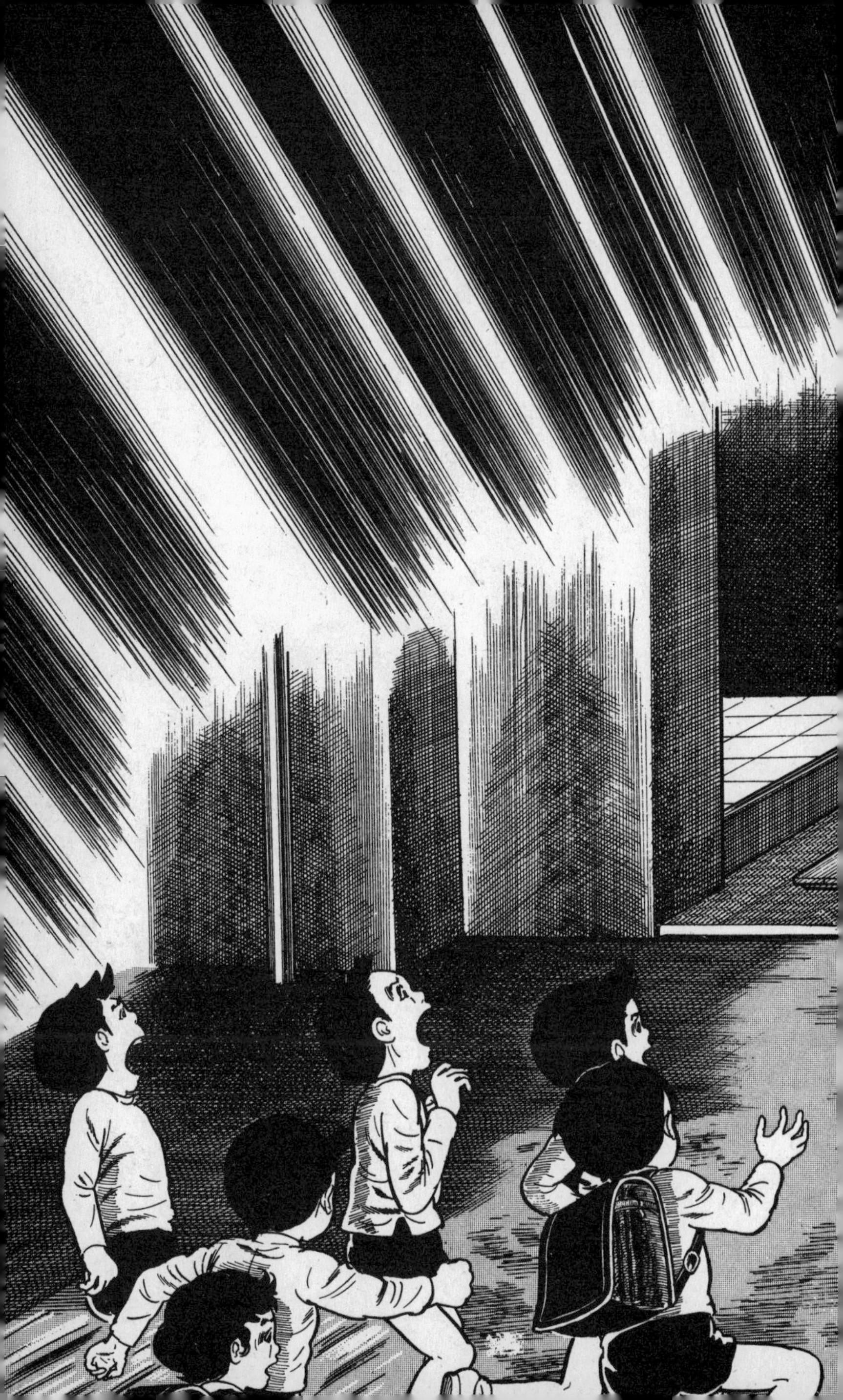

NOW WILL YOU PLEASE CALM DOWN?

EEYAAA

EEYAA!

GET BACK! GET BACK TO YOUR SEATS!

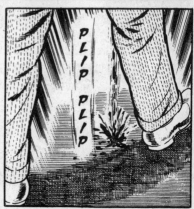

PLIP PLIP

106

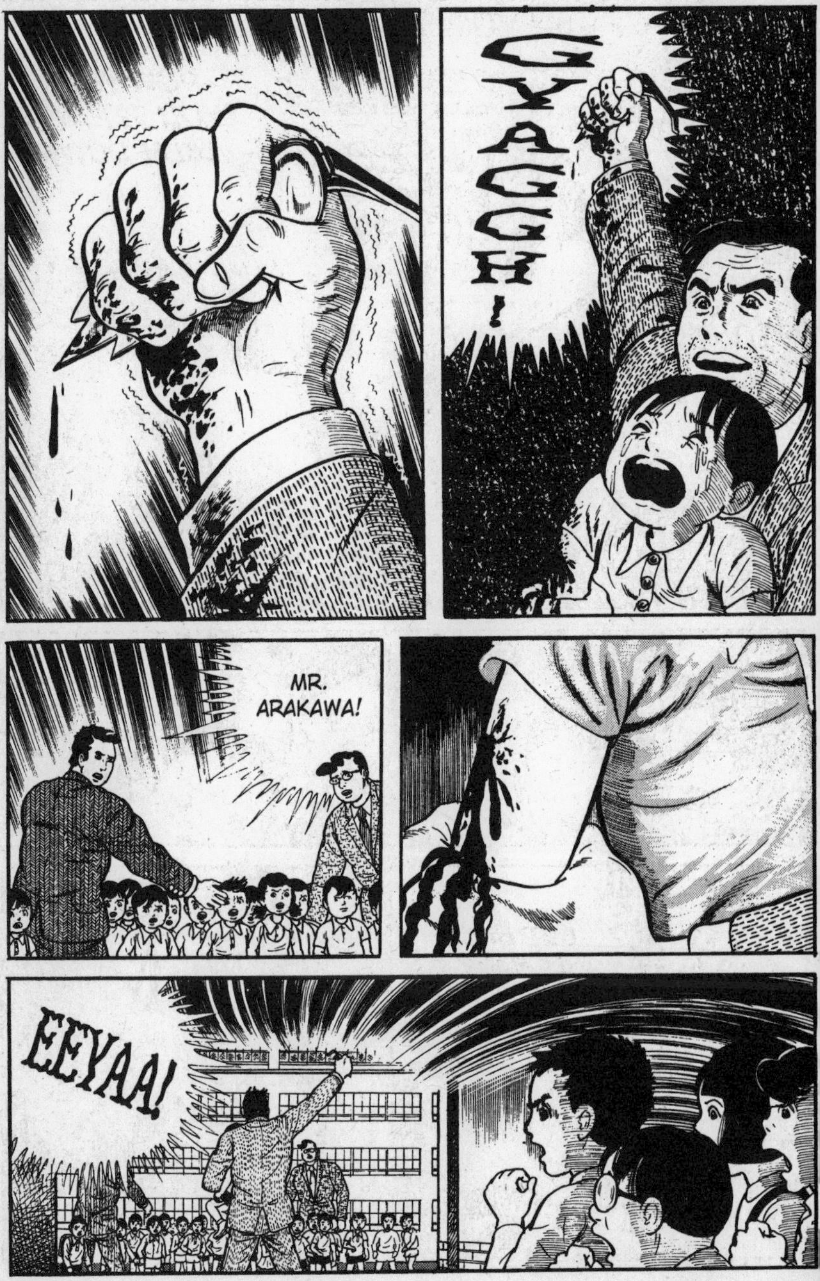
GYAGGH!
MR. ARAKAWA!
EEYAA!

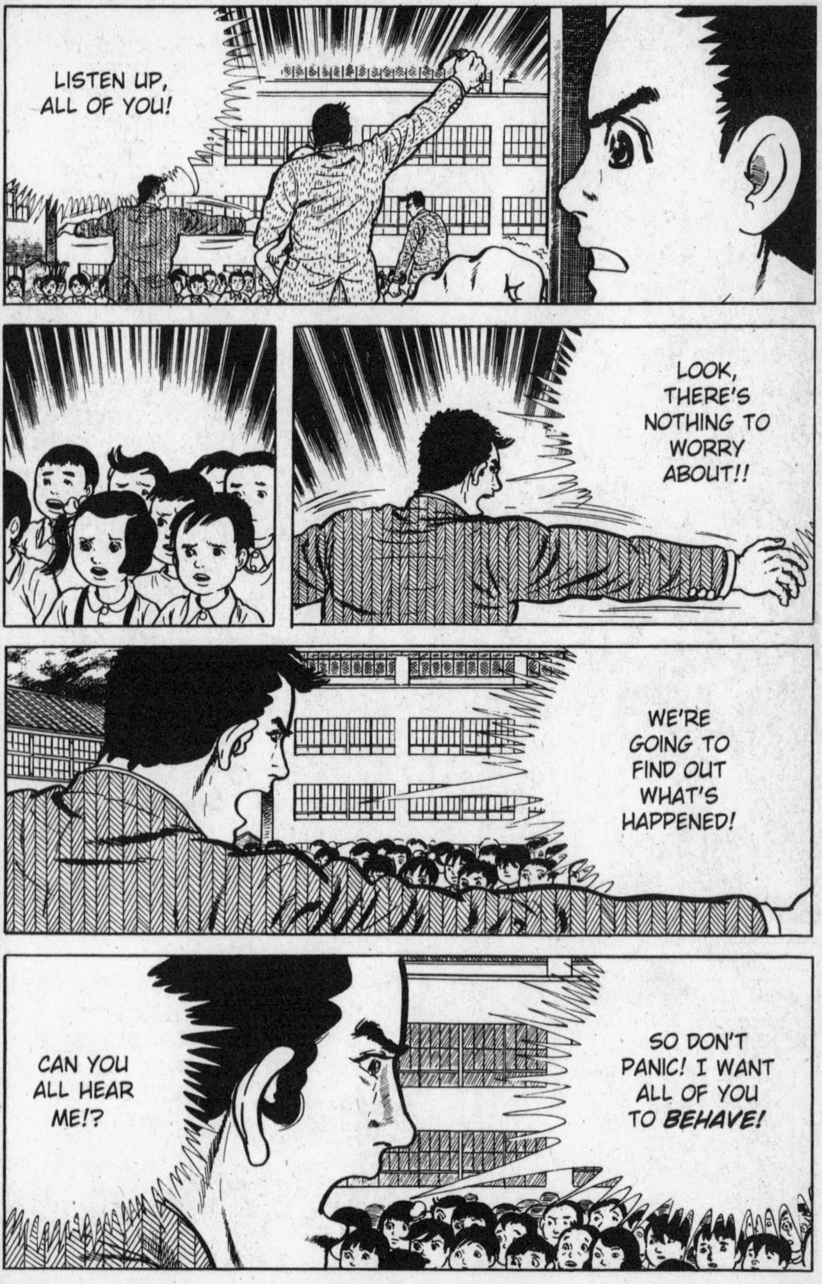
LISTEN UP, ALL OF YOU!
LOOK, THERE'S NOTHING TO WORRY ABOUT!!
WE'RE GOING TO FIND OUT WHAT'S HAPPENED!
SO DON'T PANIC! I WANT ALL OF YOU TO *BEHAVE!*
CAN YOU ALL HEAR ME!?

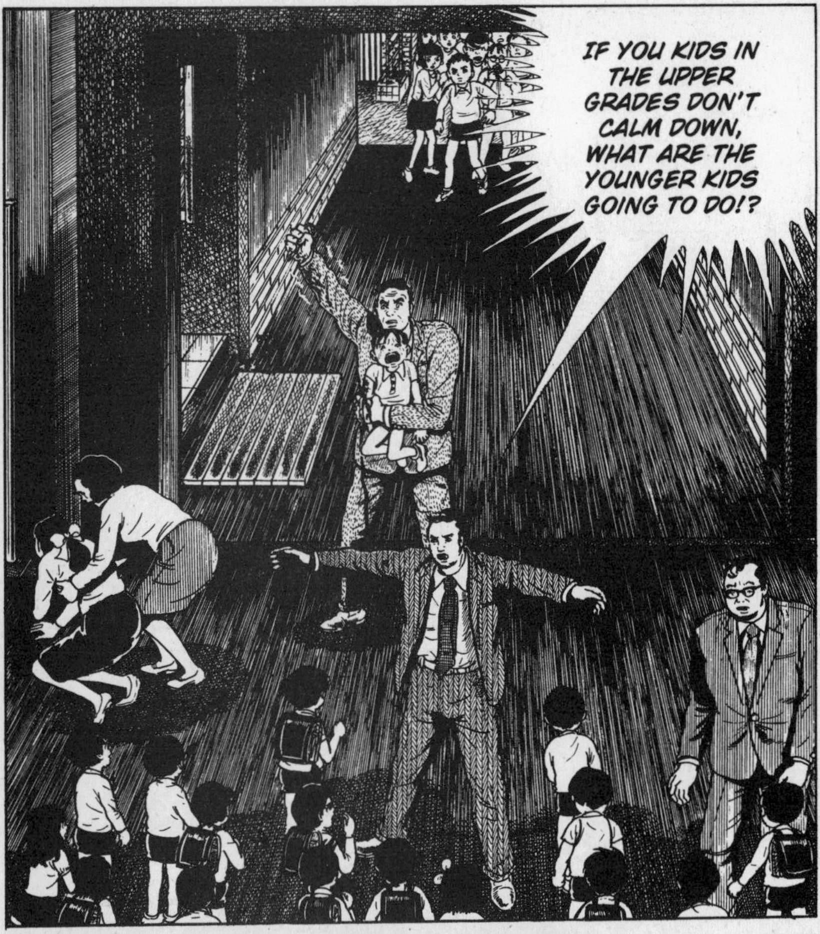
IF YOU KIDS IN THE UPPER GRADES DON'T CALM DOWN, WHAT ARE THE YOUNGER KIDS GOING TO DO!?
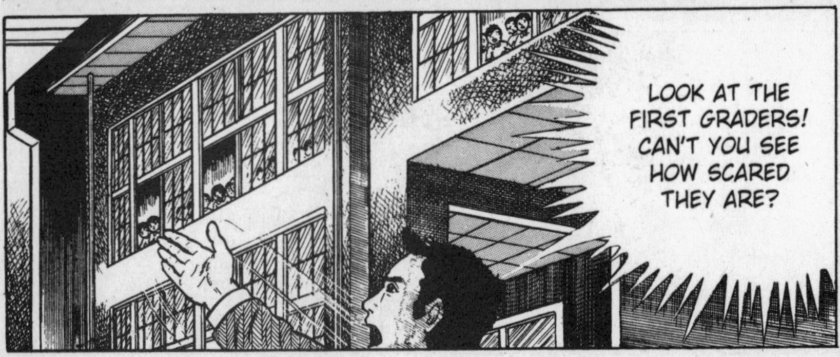
LOOK AT THE FIRST GRADERS! CAN'T YOU SEE HOW SCARED THEY ARE?

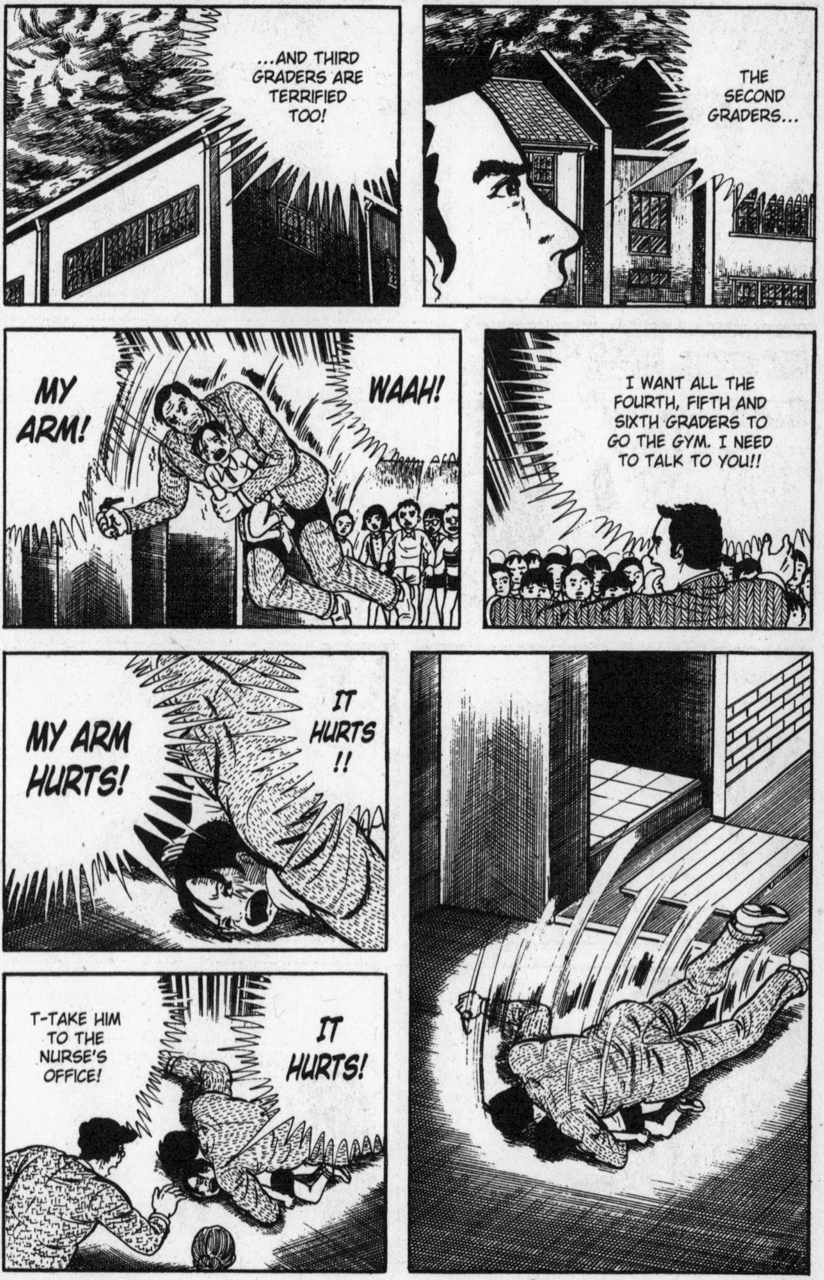
THE SECOND GRADERS...
...AND THIRD GRADERS ARE TERRIFIED TOO!
I WANT ALL THE FOURTH, FIFTH AND SIXTH GRADERS TO GO THE GYM. I NEED TO TALK TO YOU!!
WAAH!
MY ARM!
IT HURTS !!
MY ARM HURTS!
IT HURTS!
T-TAKE HIM TO THE NURSE'S OFFICE!

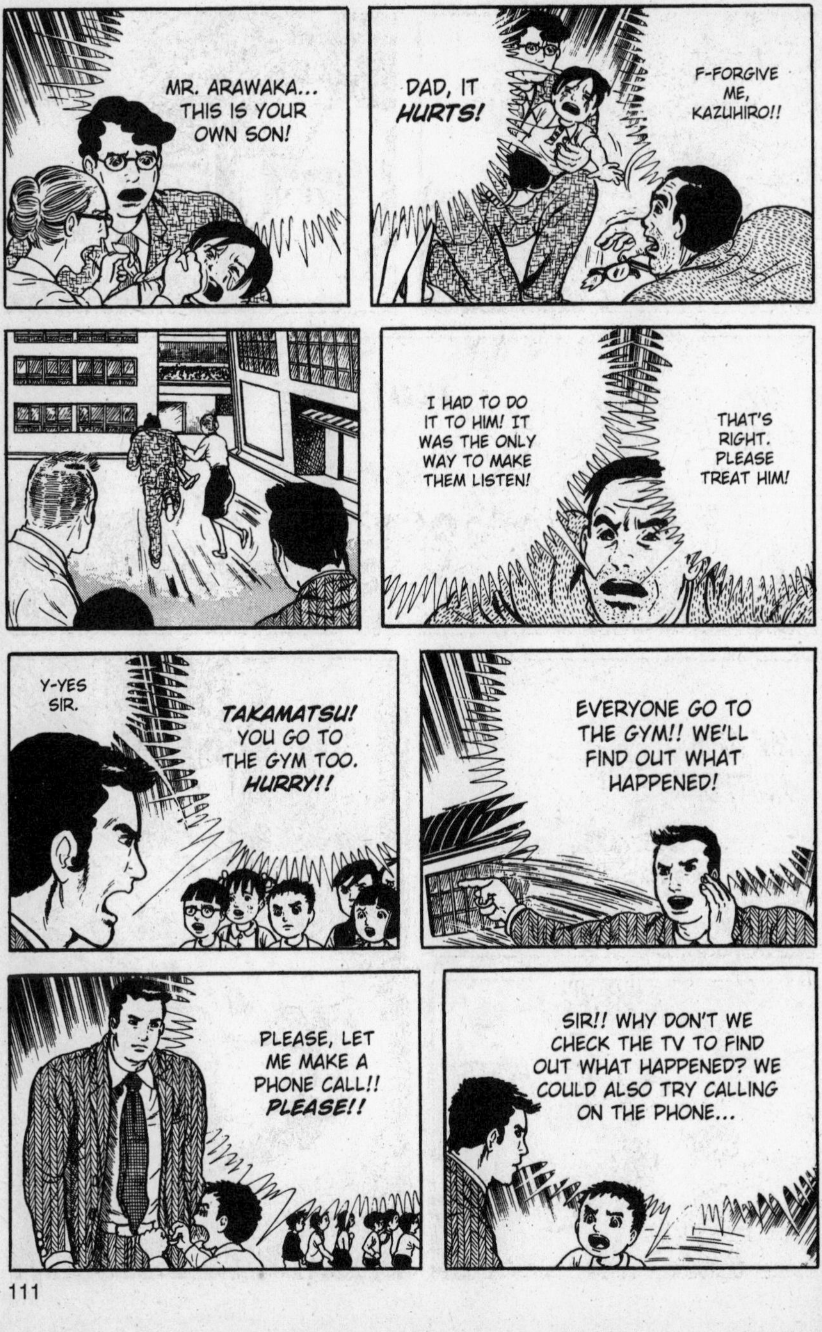
F-FORGIVE ME, KAZUHIRO!!
DAD, IT *HURTS!*
MR. ARAWAKA... THIS IS YOUR OWN SON!
THAT'S RIGHT. PLEASE TREAT HIM!
I HAD TO DO IT TO HIM! IT WAS THE ONLY WAY TO MAKE THEM LISTEN!
EVERYONE GO TO THE GYM!! WE'LL FIND OUT WHAT HAPPENED!
TAKAMATSU! YOU GO TO THE GYM TOO. *HURRY!!*
Y-YES SIR.
SIR!! WHY DON'T WE CHECK THE TV TO FIND OUT WHAT HAPPENED? WE COULD ALSO TRY CALLING ON THE PHONE...
PLEASE, LET ME MAKE A PHONE CALL!! *PLEASE!!*

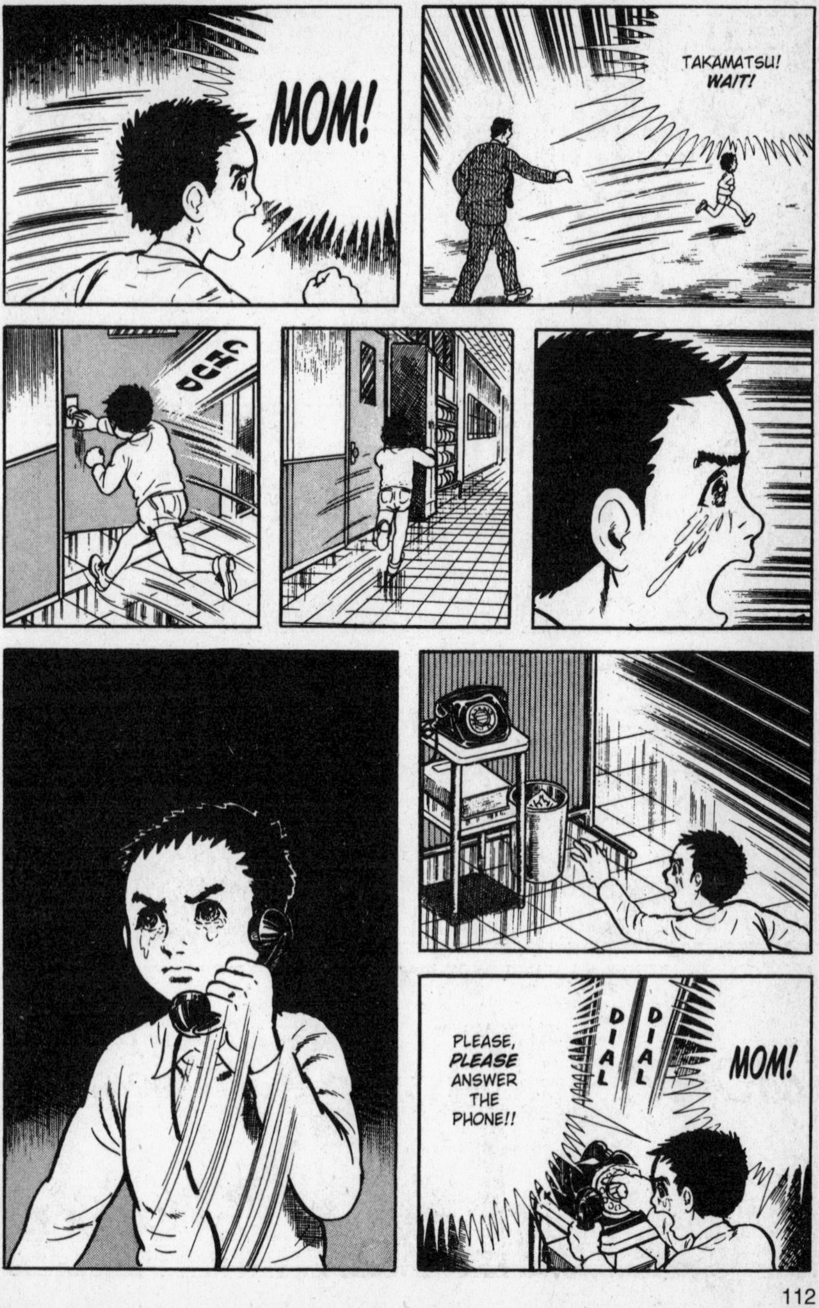
TAKAMATSU! WAIT!
MOM!
MOM!
DIAL DIAL
PLEASE, PLEASE ANSWER THE PHONE!!

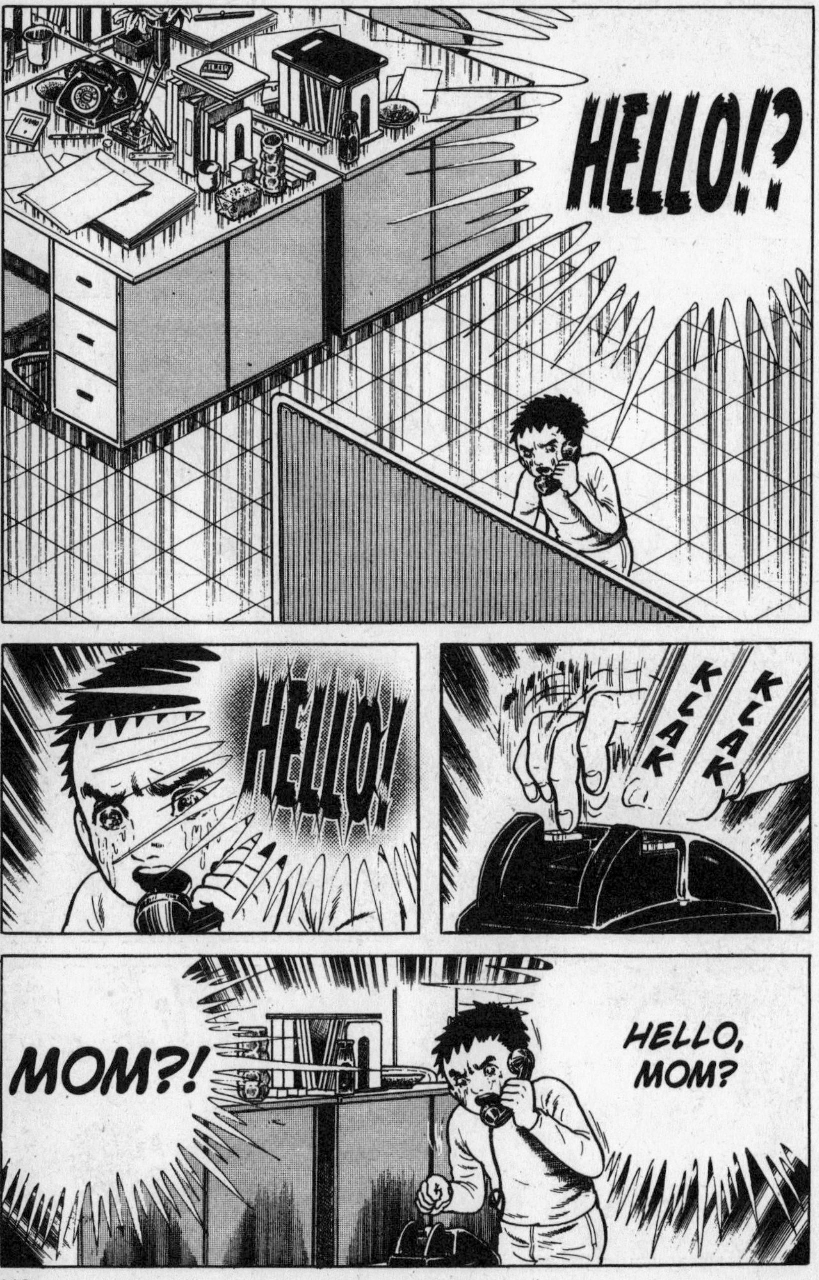
HELLO!?
KLAK
KLAK
HELLO!
HELLO, MOM?
MOM?!

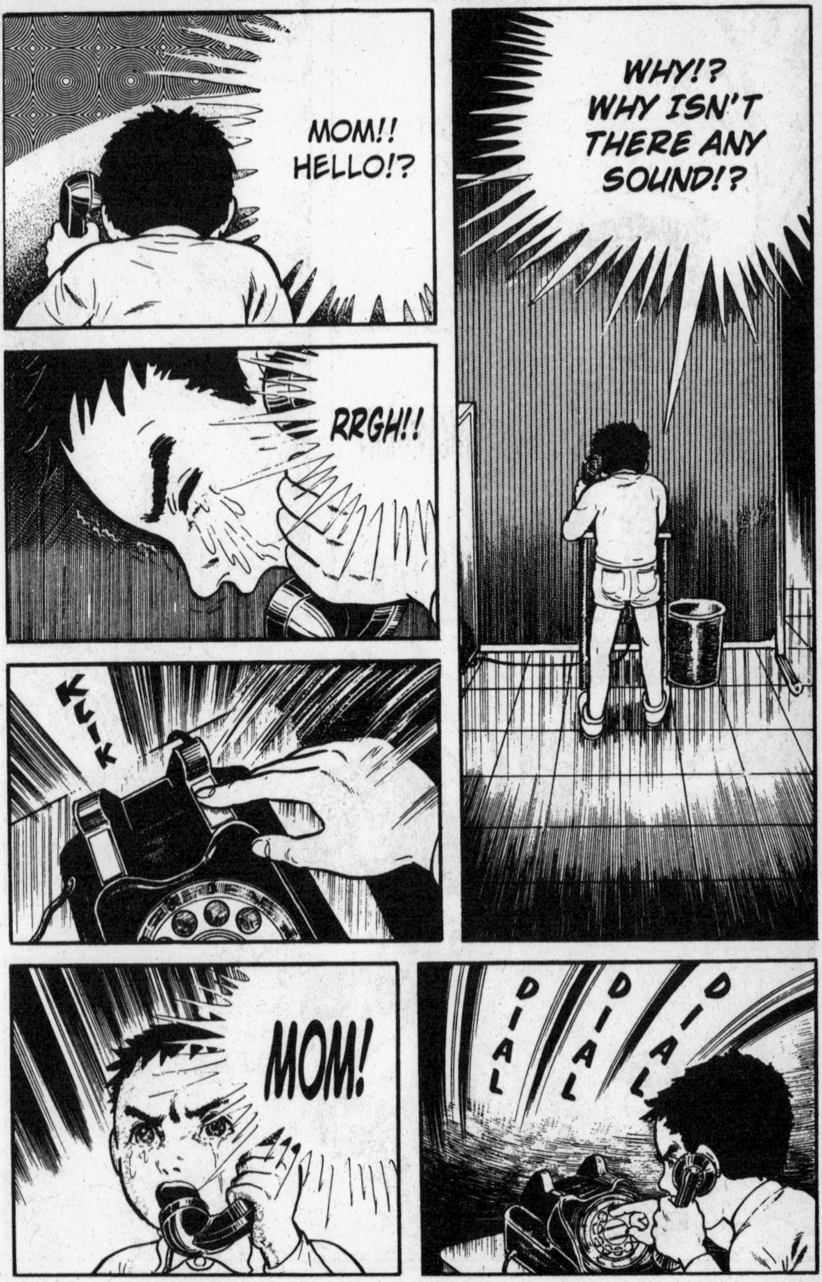
WHY!? WHY ISN'T THERE ANY SOUND!?
MOM!! HELLO!?
RRGH!!
KLIK
DIAL
DIAL
DIAL
MOM!

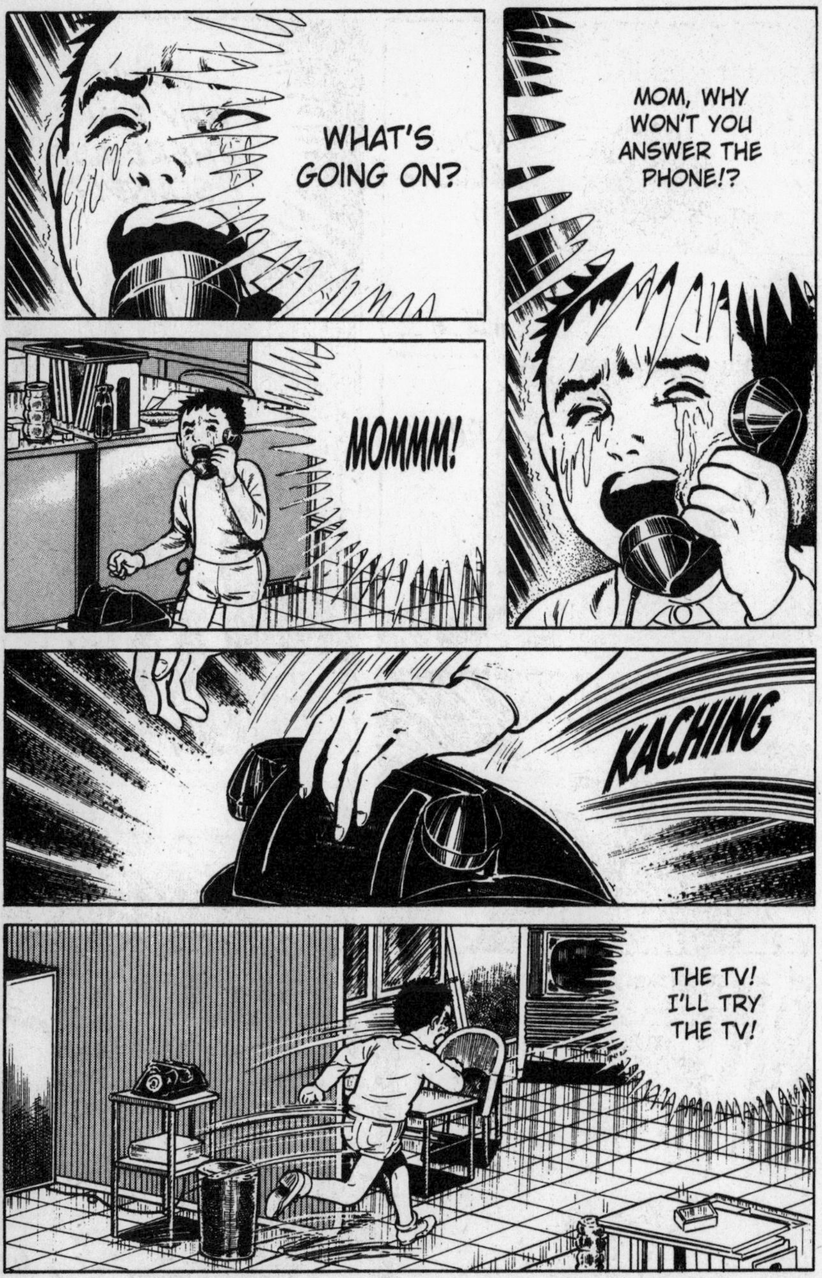
MOM, WHY WON'T YOU ANSWER THE PHONE!?
WHAT'S GOING ON?
MOMMM!
KACHING
THE TV! I'LL TRY THE TV!

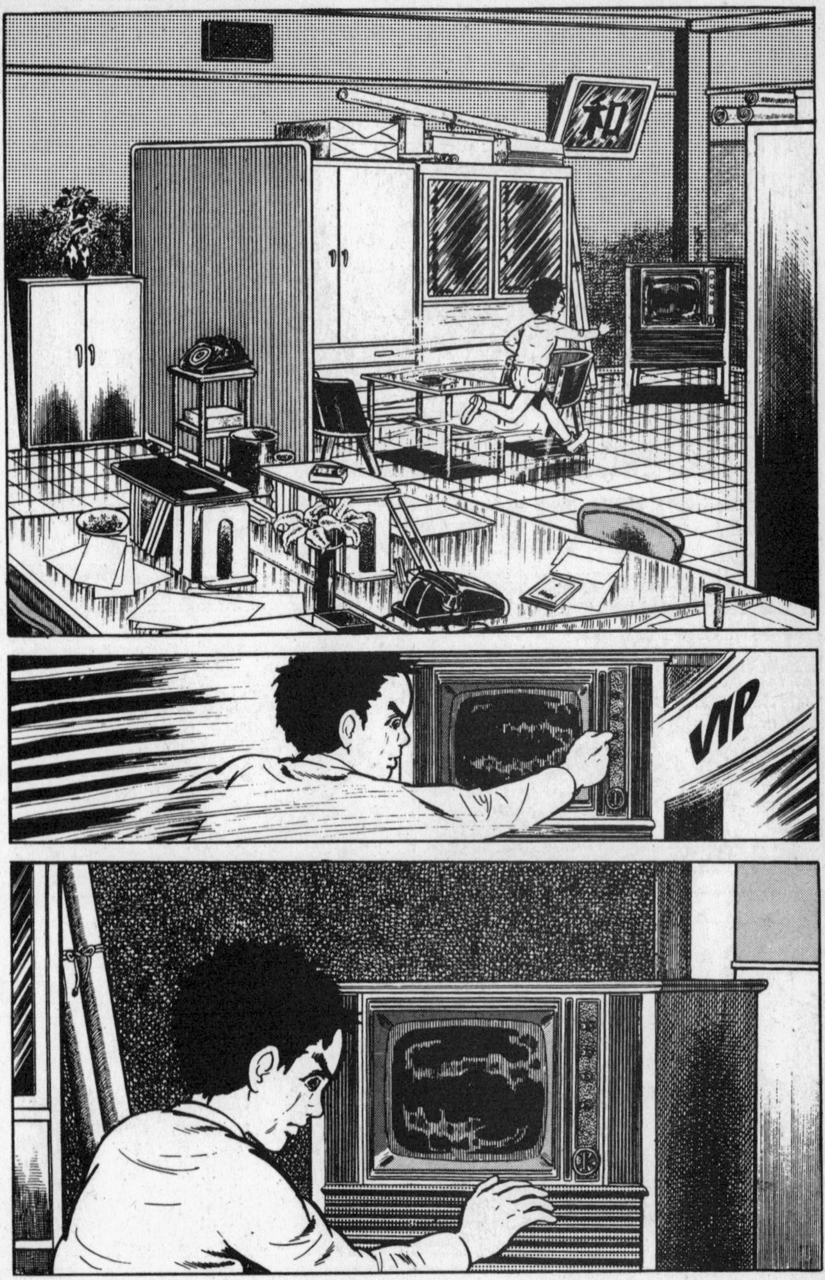
和
VIP

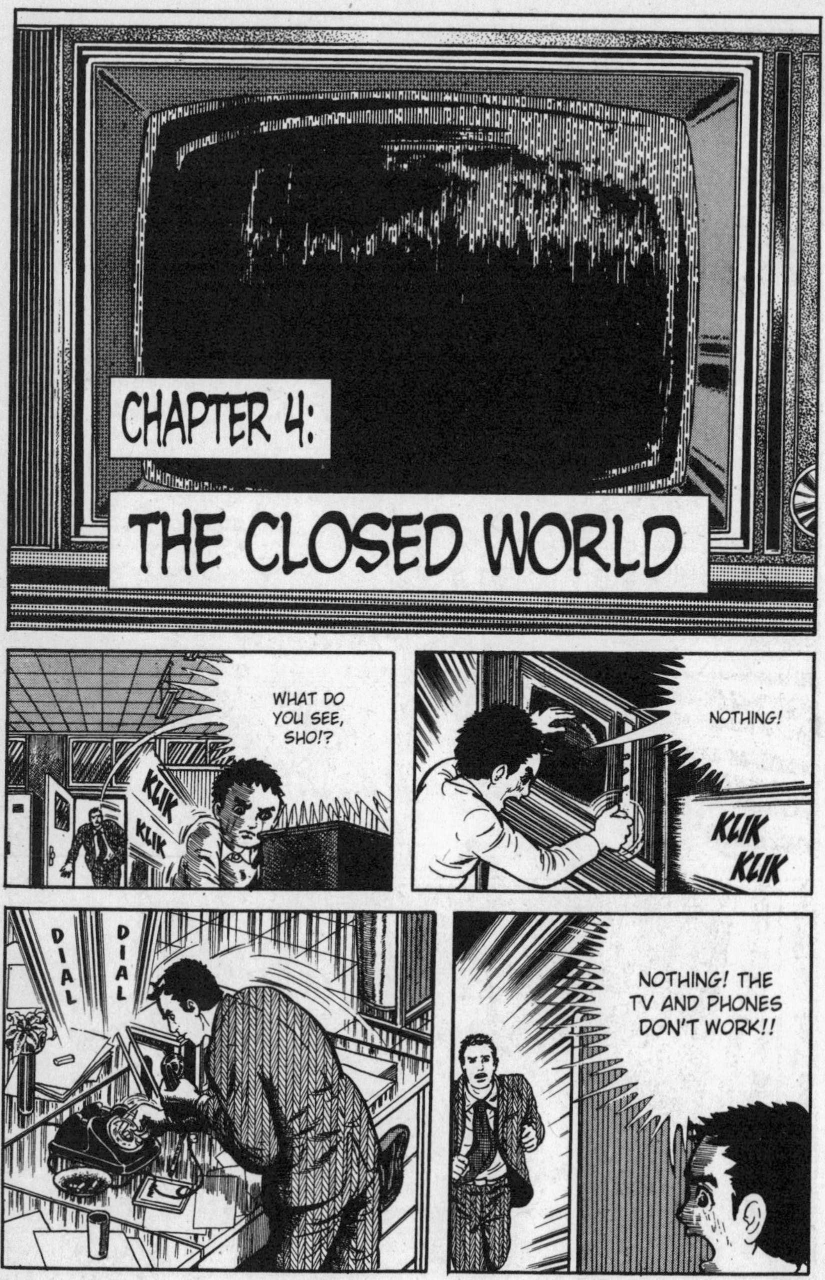
CHAPTER 4:
THE CLOSED WORLD
WHAT DO YOU SEE, SHO!?
KLIK
KLIK
NOTHING!
KLIK
KLIK
DIAL
DIAL
NOTHING! THE TV AND PHONES DON'T WORK!!

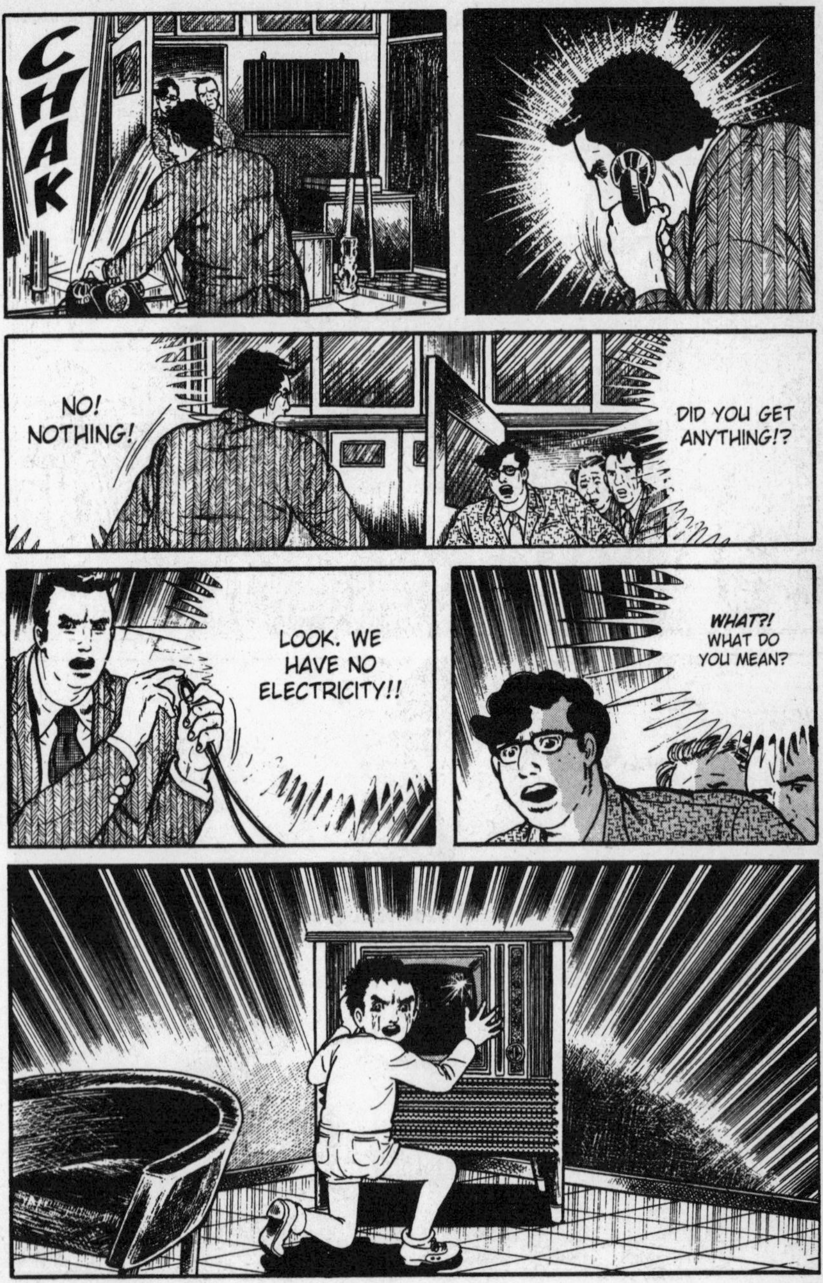
CHAK
DID YOU GET ANYTHING!?
NO! NOTHING!
WHAT?! WHAT DO YOU MEAN?
LOOK. WE HAVE NO ELECTRICITY!!

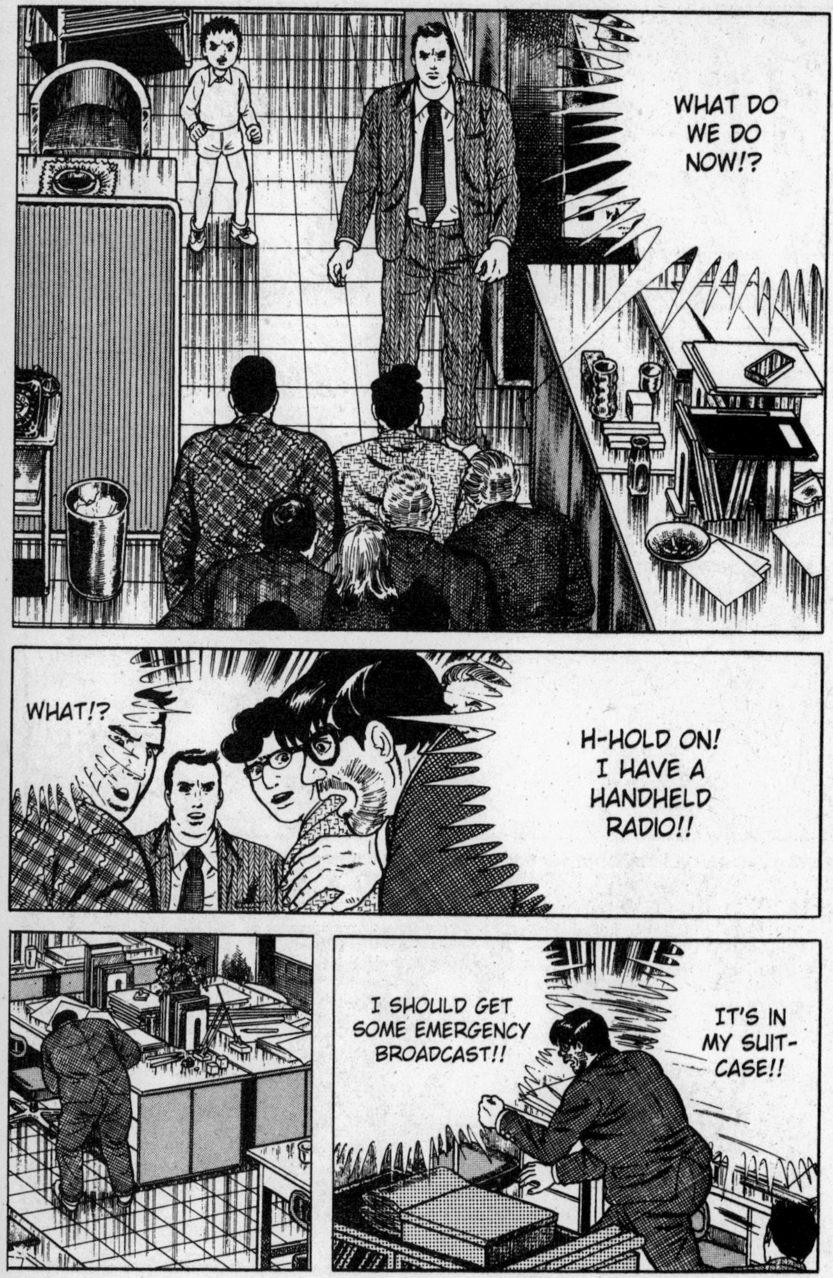
WHAT DO WE DO NOW!?
H-HOLD ON! I HAVE A HANDHELD RADIO!!
WHAT!?
IT'S IN MY SUIT-CASE!!
I SHOULD GET SOME EMERGENCY BROADCAST!!

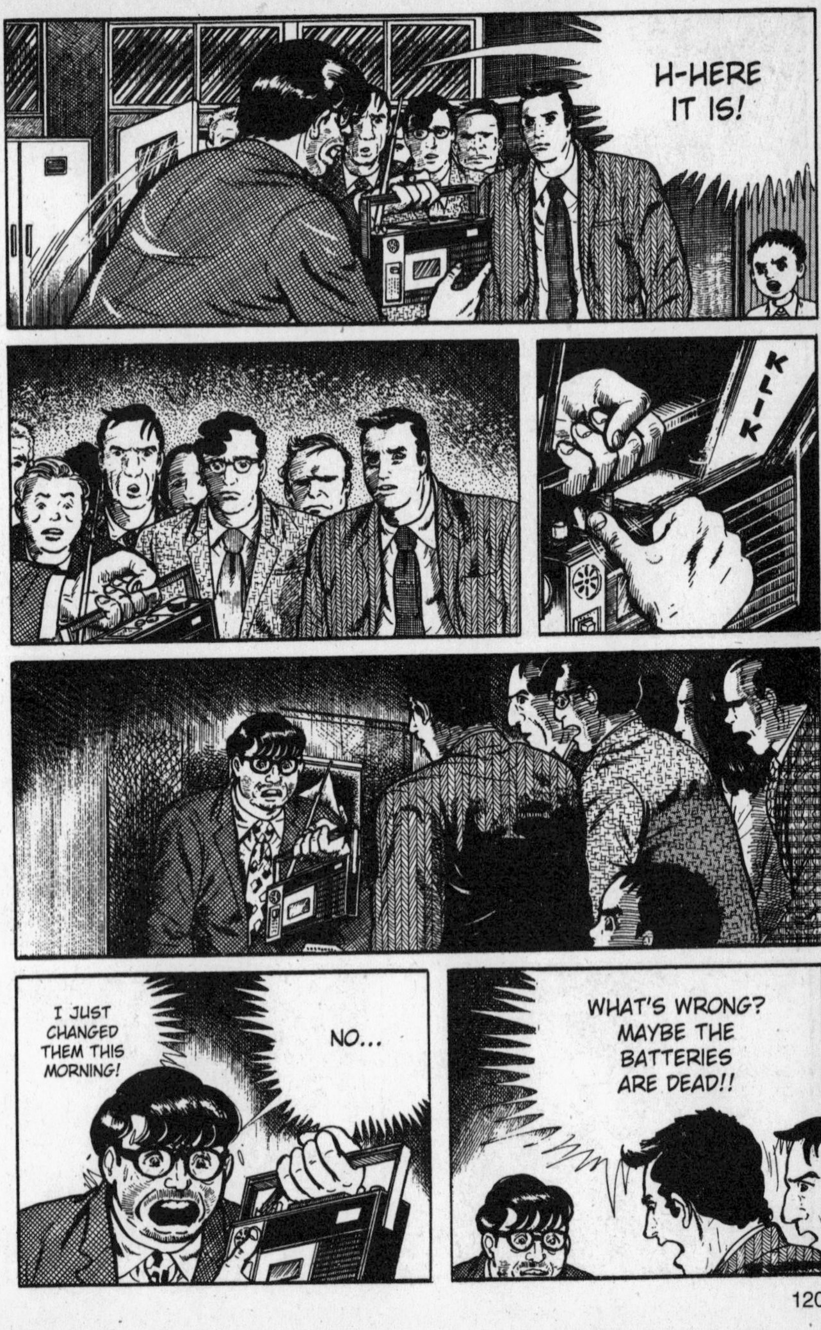
H-HERE IT IS!
KLIK
WHAT'S WRONG? MAYBE THE BATTERIES ARE DEAD!!
NO...
I JUST CHANGED THEM THIS MORNING!

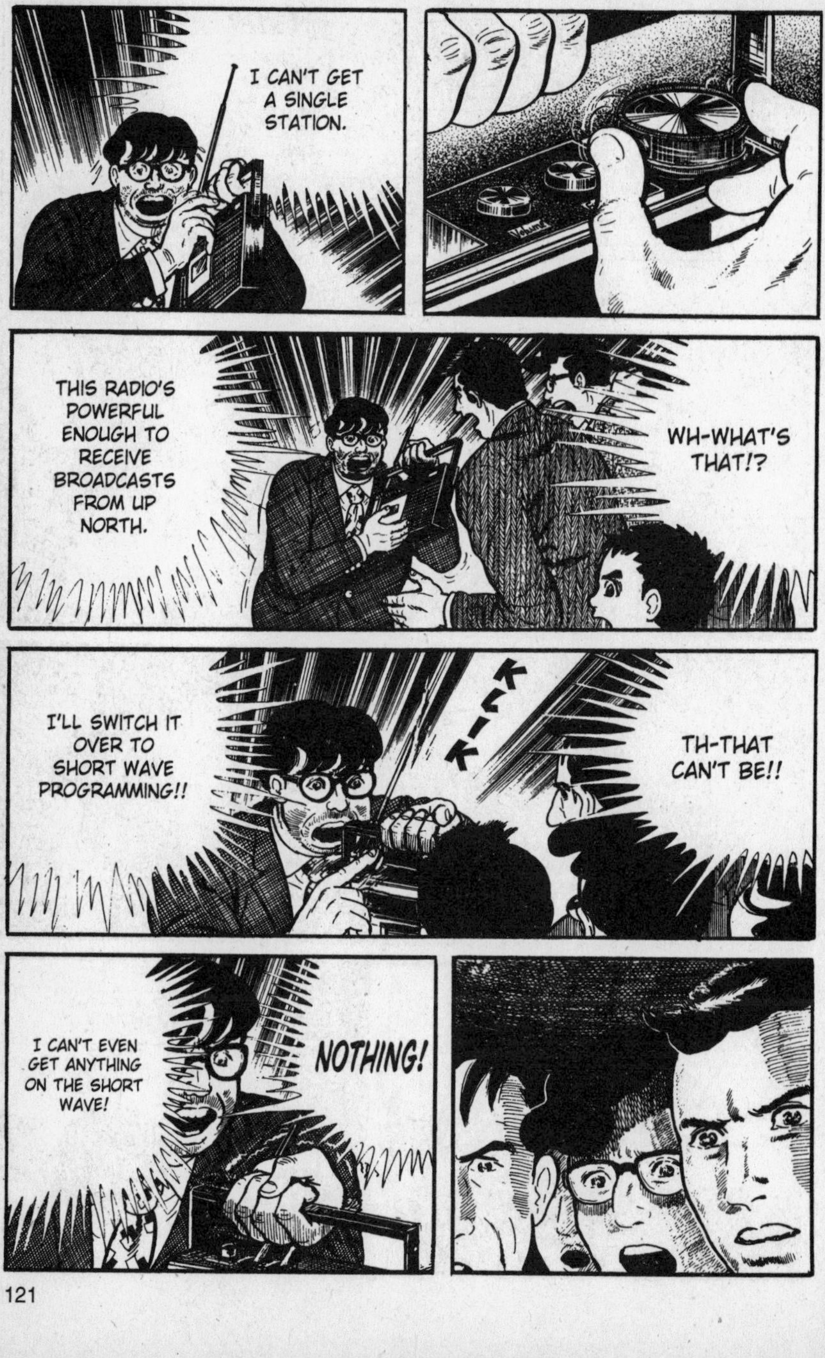
I CAN'T GET A SINGLE STATION.
WH-WHAT'S THAT!?
THIS RADIO'S POWERFUL ENOUGH TO RECEIVE BROADCASTS FROM UP NORTH.
KLIK
TH-THAT CAN'T BE!!
I'LL SWITCH IT OVER TO SHORT WAVE PROGRAMMING!!
NOTHING!
I CAN'T EVEN GET ANYTHING ON THE SHORT WAVE!

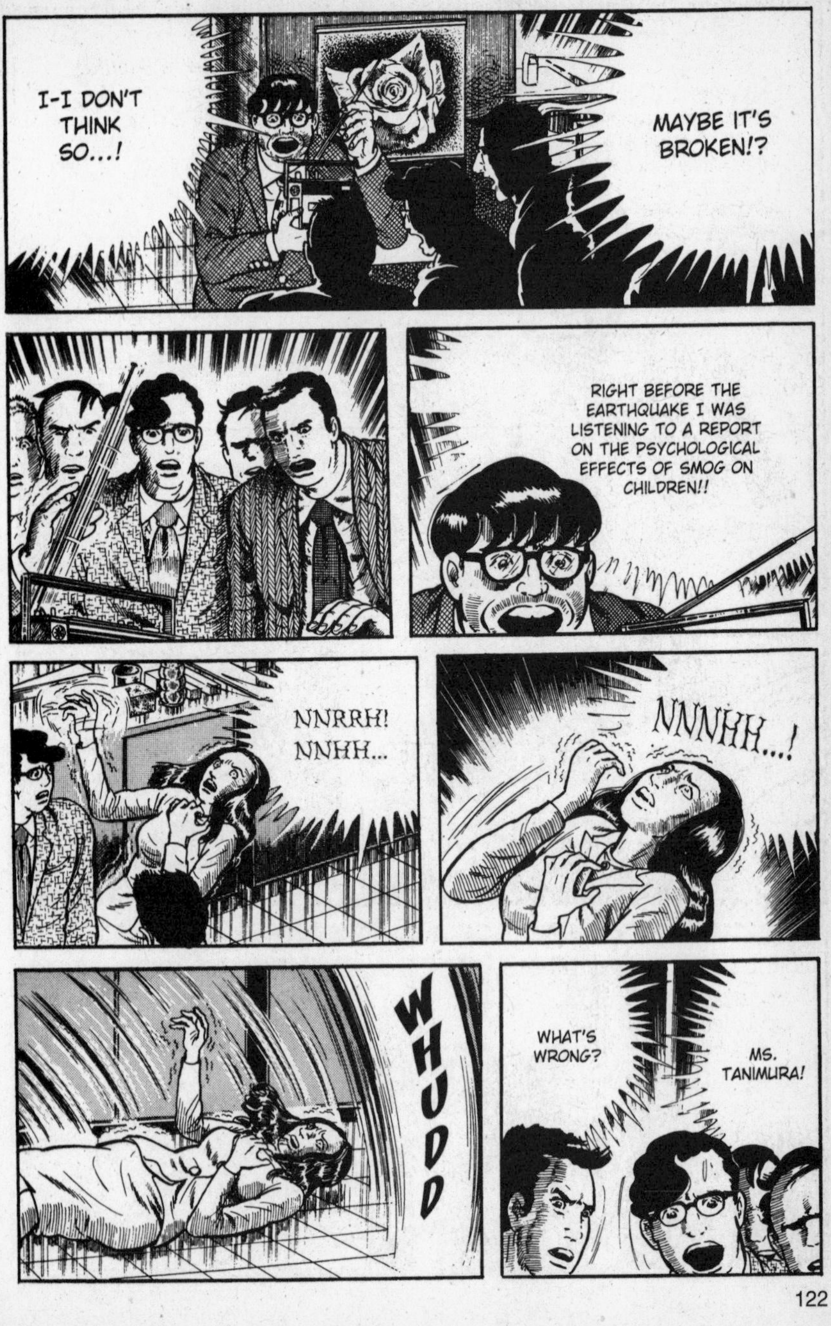
MAYBE IT'S BROKEN!?
I-I DON'T THINK SO...!
RIGHT BEFORE THE EARTHQUAKE I WAS LISTENING TO A REPORT ON THE PSYCHOLOGICAL EFFECTS OF SMOG ON CHILDREN!!
NNNHH...!
NNRRH! NNHH...
MS. TANIMURA!
WHAT'S WRONG?
WHUDD

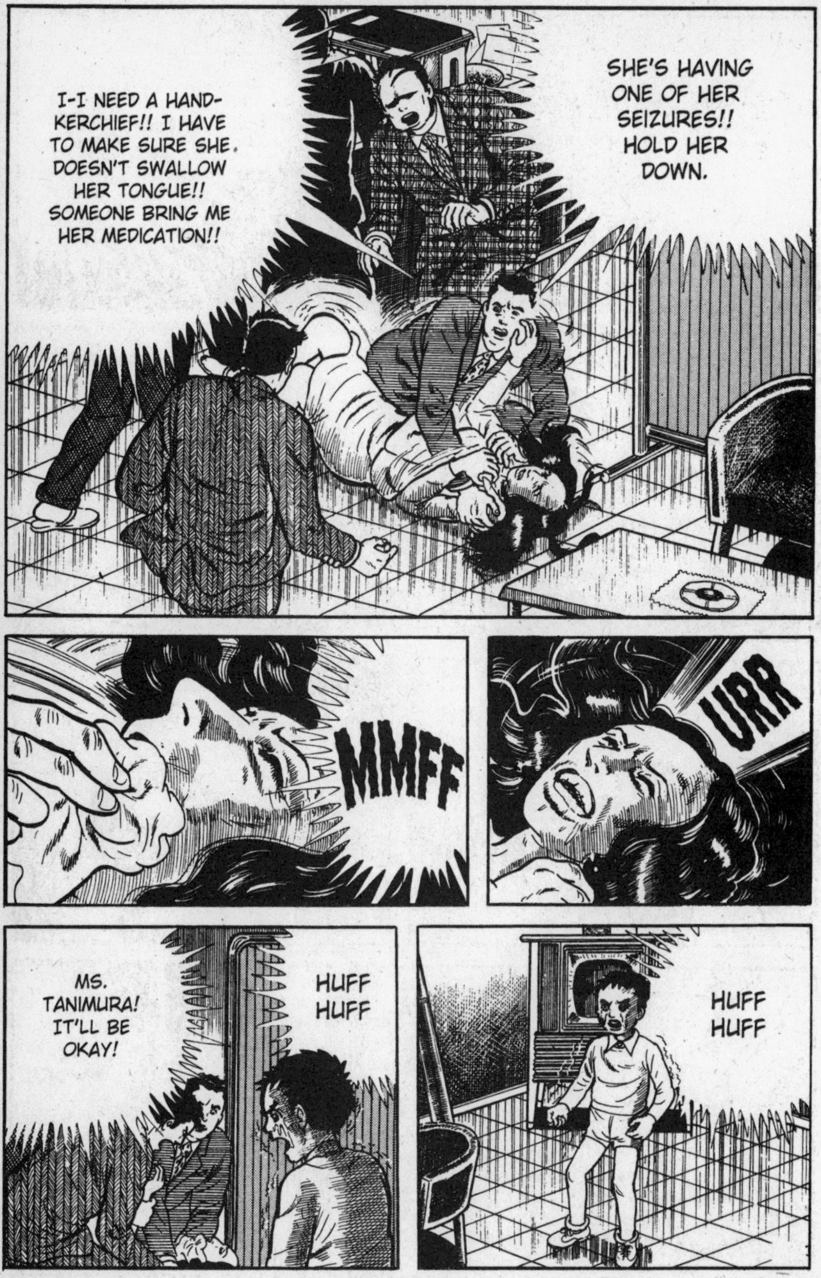
SHE'S HAVING ONE OF HER SEIZURES!! HOLD HER DOWN.
I-I NEED A HAND-KERCHIEF!! I HAVE TO MAKE SURE SHE DOESN'T SWALLOW HER TONGUE!! SOMEONE BRING ME HER MEDICATION!!
URR
MMFF
HUFF HUFF
HUFF HUFF
MS. TANIMURA! IT'LL BE OKAY!

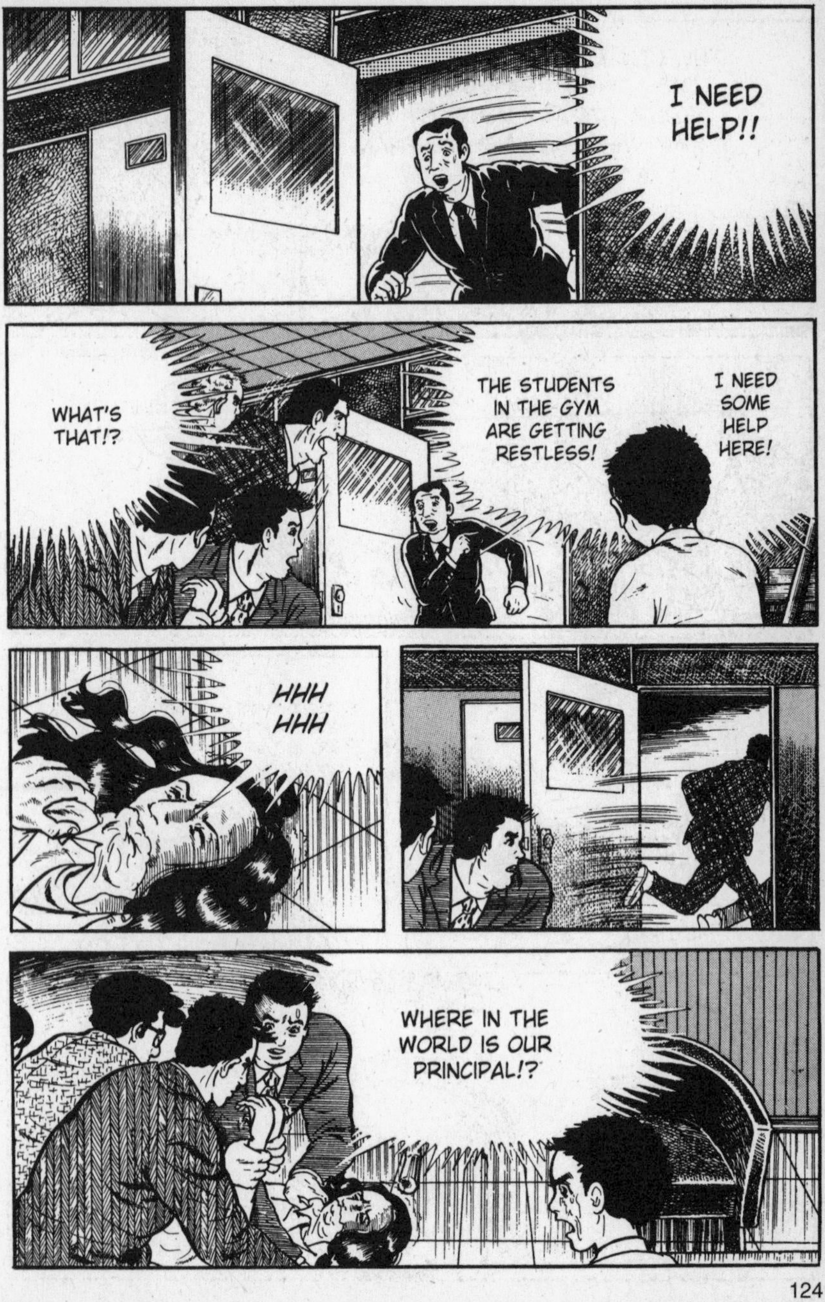
I NEED HELP!!
I NEED SOME HELP HERE!
THE STUDENTS IN THE GYM ARE GETTING RESTLESS!
WHAT'S THAT!?
HHH HHH
WHERE IN THE WORLD IS OUR PRINCIPAL!?

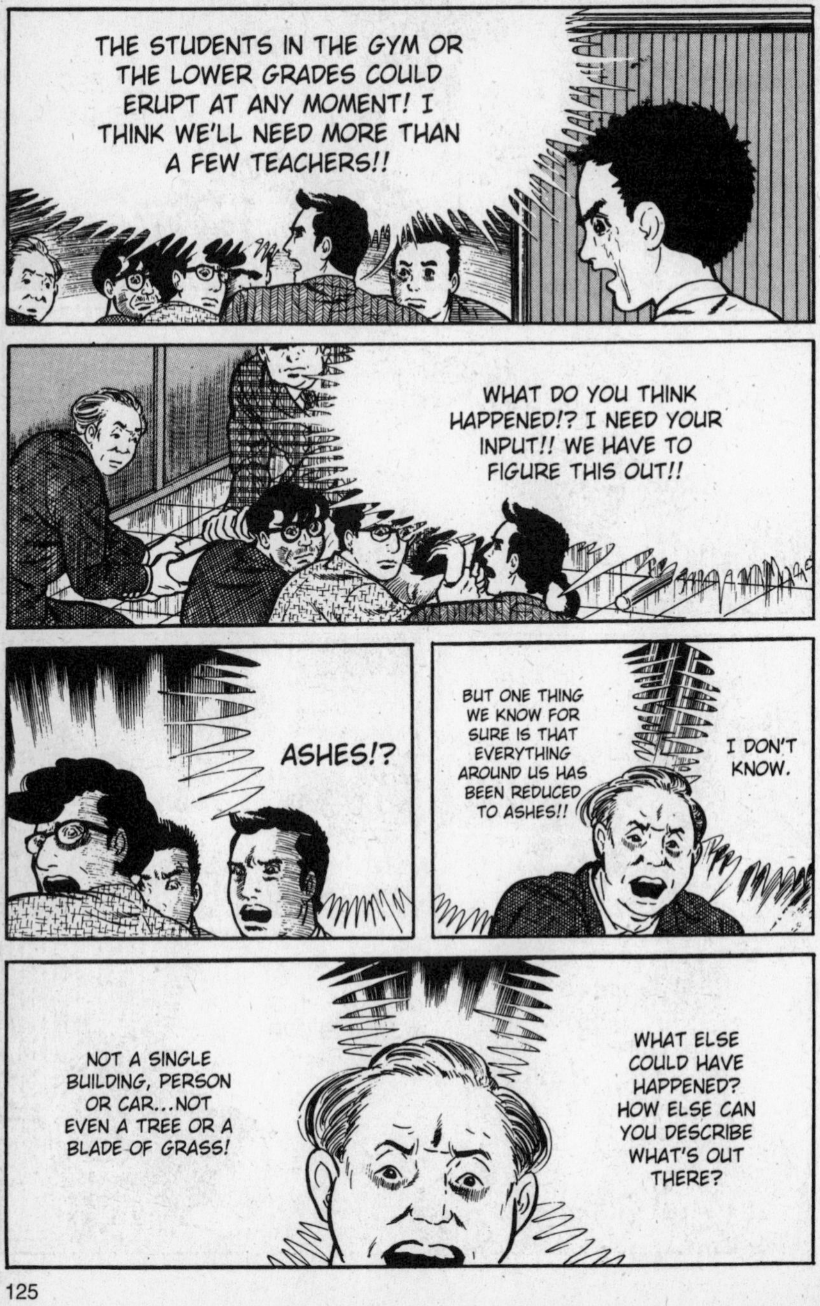
THE STUDENTS IN THE GYM OR THE LOWER GRADES COULD ERUPT AT ANY MOMENT! I THINK WE'LL NEED MORE THAN A FEW TEACHERS!!
WHAT DO YOU THINK HAPPENED!? I NEED YOUR INPUT!! WE HAVE TO FIGURE THIS OUT!!
I DON'T KNOW.
BUT ONE THING WE KNOW FOR SURE IS THAT EVERYTHING AROUND US HAS BEEN REDUCED TO ASHES!!
ASHES!?
WHAT ELSE COULD HAVE HAPPENED? HOW ELSE CAN YOU DESCRIBE WHAT'S OUT THERE?
NOT A SINGLE BUILDING, PERSON OR CAR...NOT EVEN A TREE OR A BLADE OF GRASS!

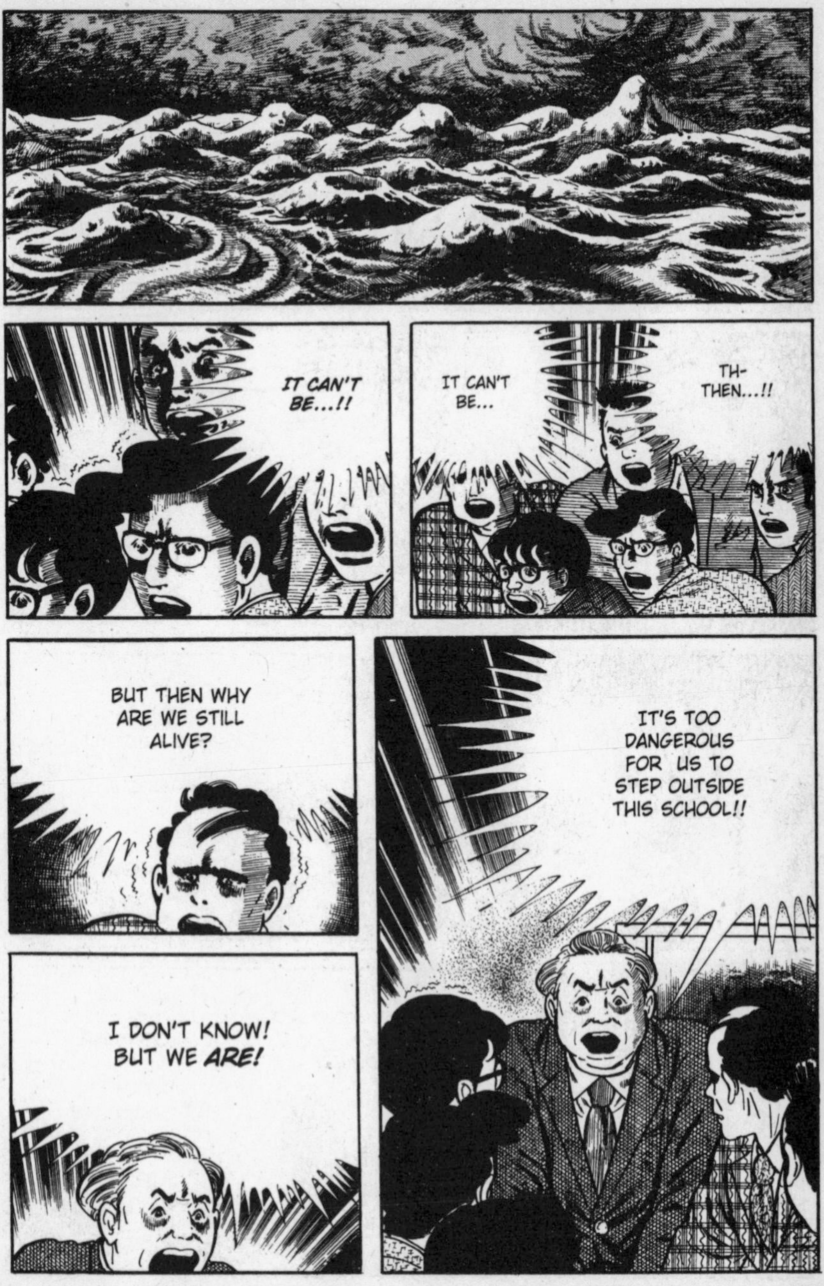
TH- THEN...!!
IT CAN'T BE...
IT CAN'T BE...!!
IT'S TOO DANGEROUS FOR US TO STEP OUTSIDE THIS SCHOOL!!
BUT THEN WHY ARE WE STILL ALIVE?
I DON'T KNOW! BUT WE ARE!

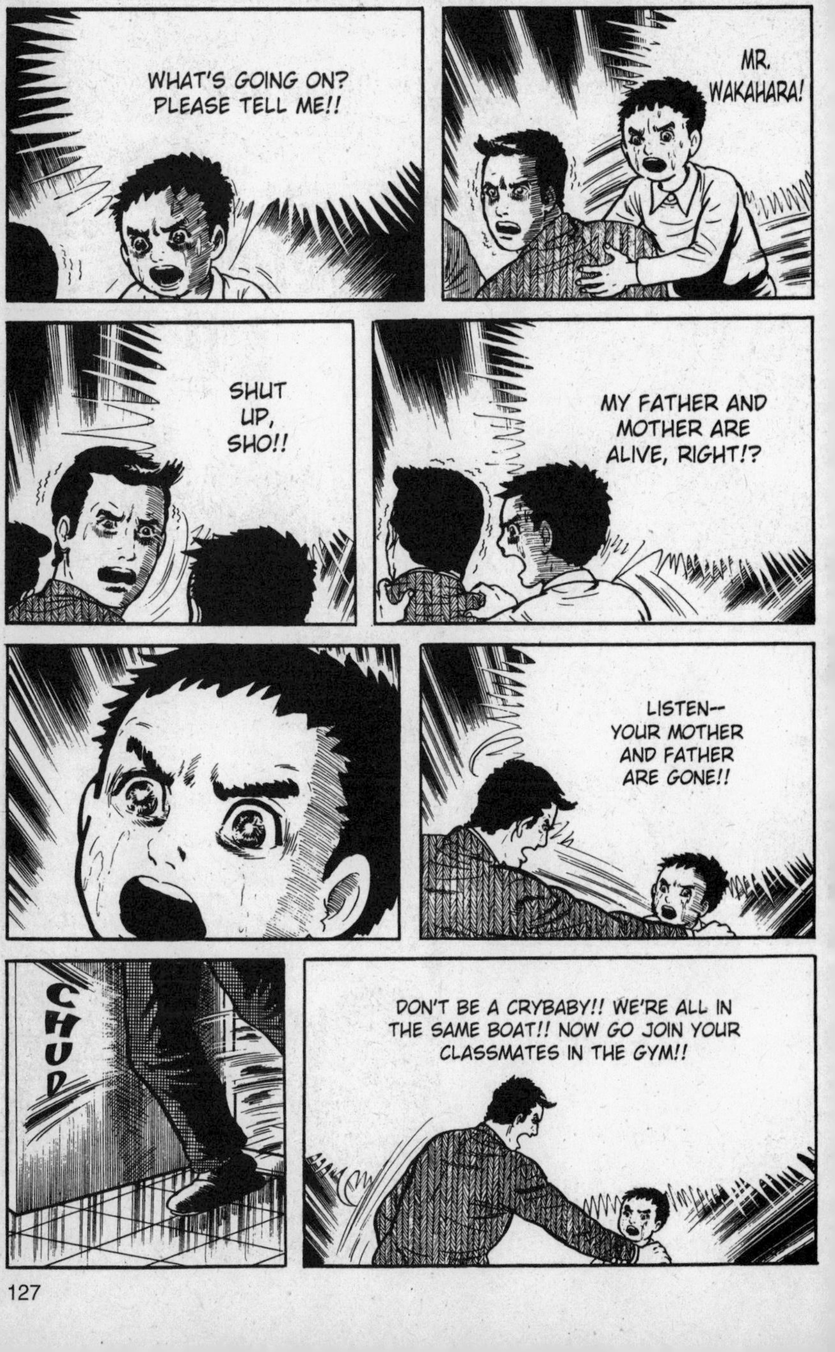
MR. WAKAHARA!
WHAT'S GOING ON? PLEASE TELL ME!!
MY FATHER AND MOTHER ARE ALIVE, RIGHT!?
SHUT UP, SHO!!
LISTEN-- YOUR MOTHER AND FATHER ARE GONE!!
DON'T BE A CRYBABY!! WE'RE ALL IN THE SAME BOAT!! NOW GO JOIN YOUR CLASSMATES IN THE GYM!!
CHUD

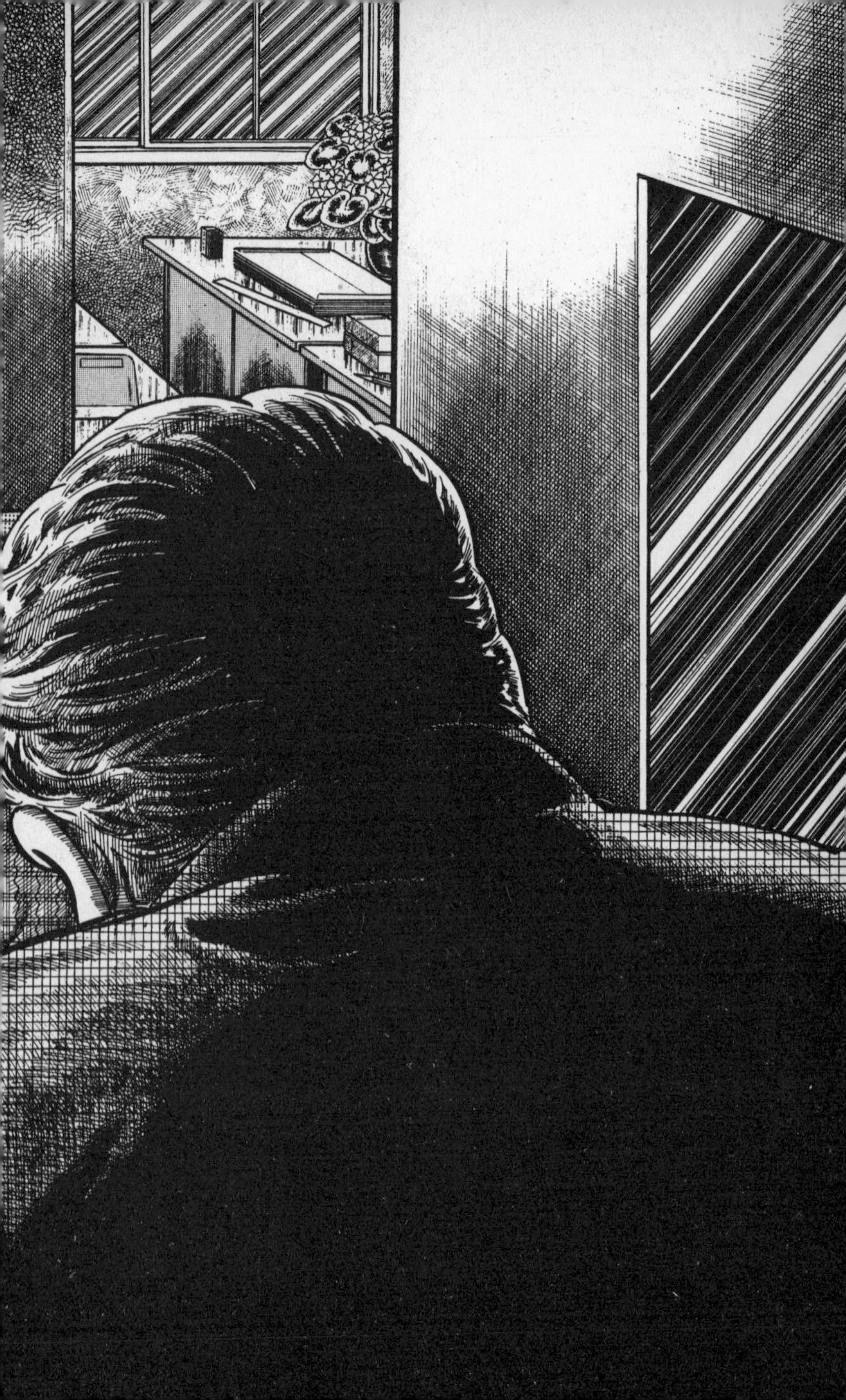

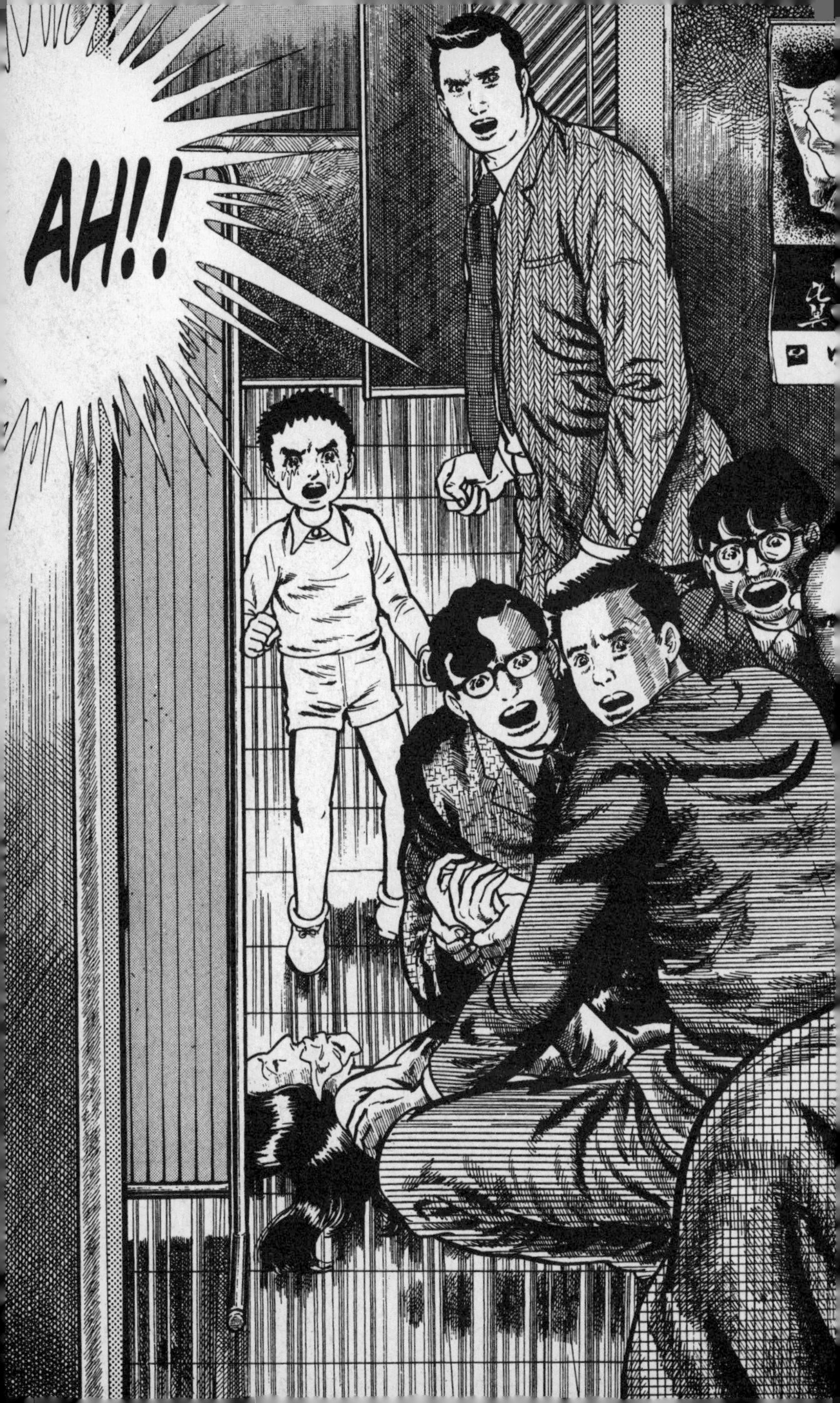
AH!!

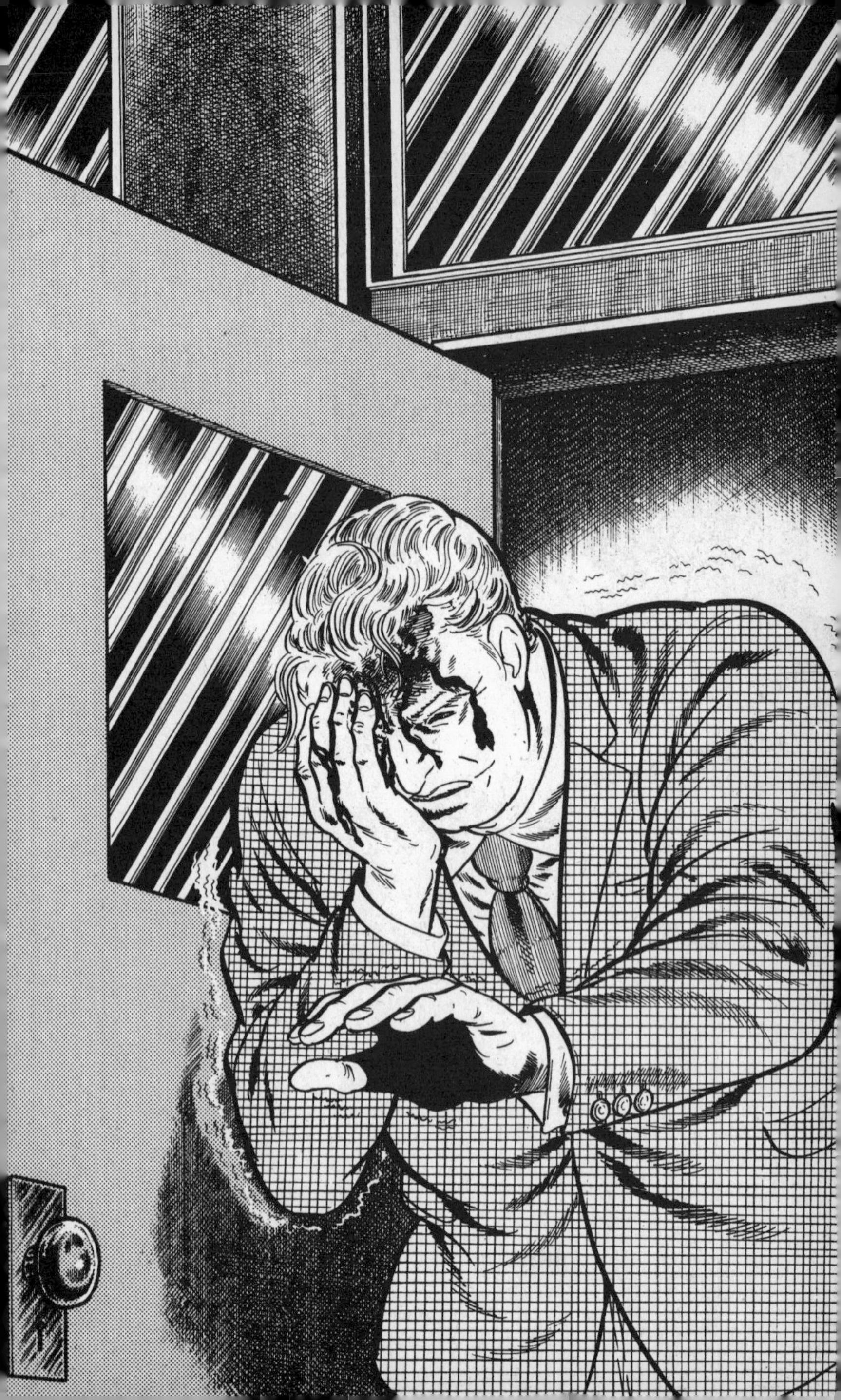

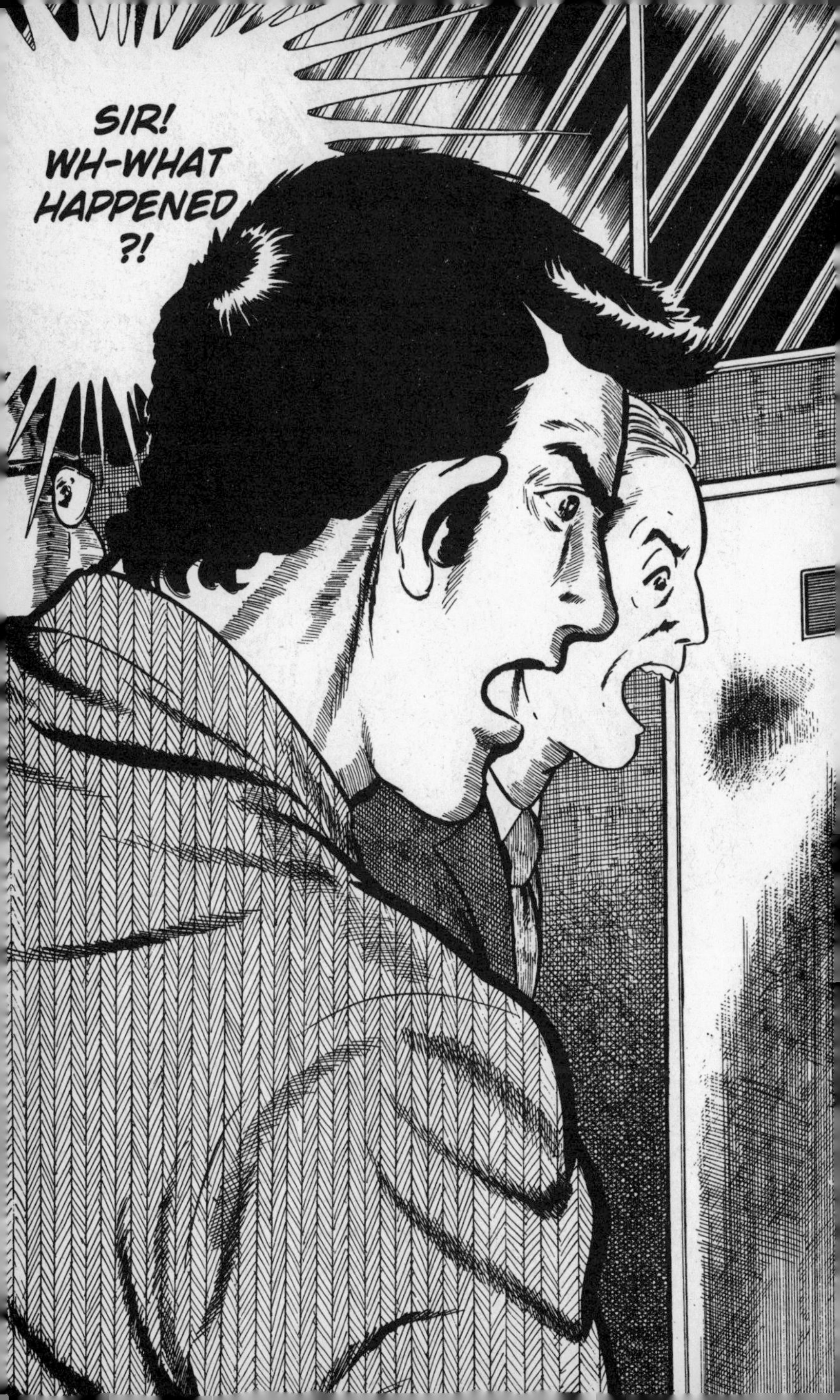
SIR! WH-WHAT HAPPENED ?!

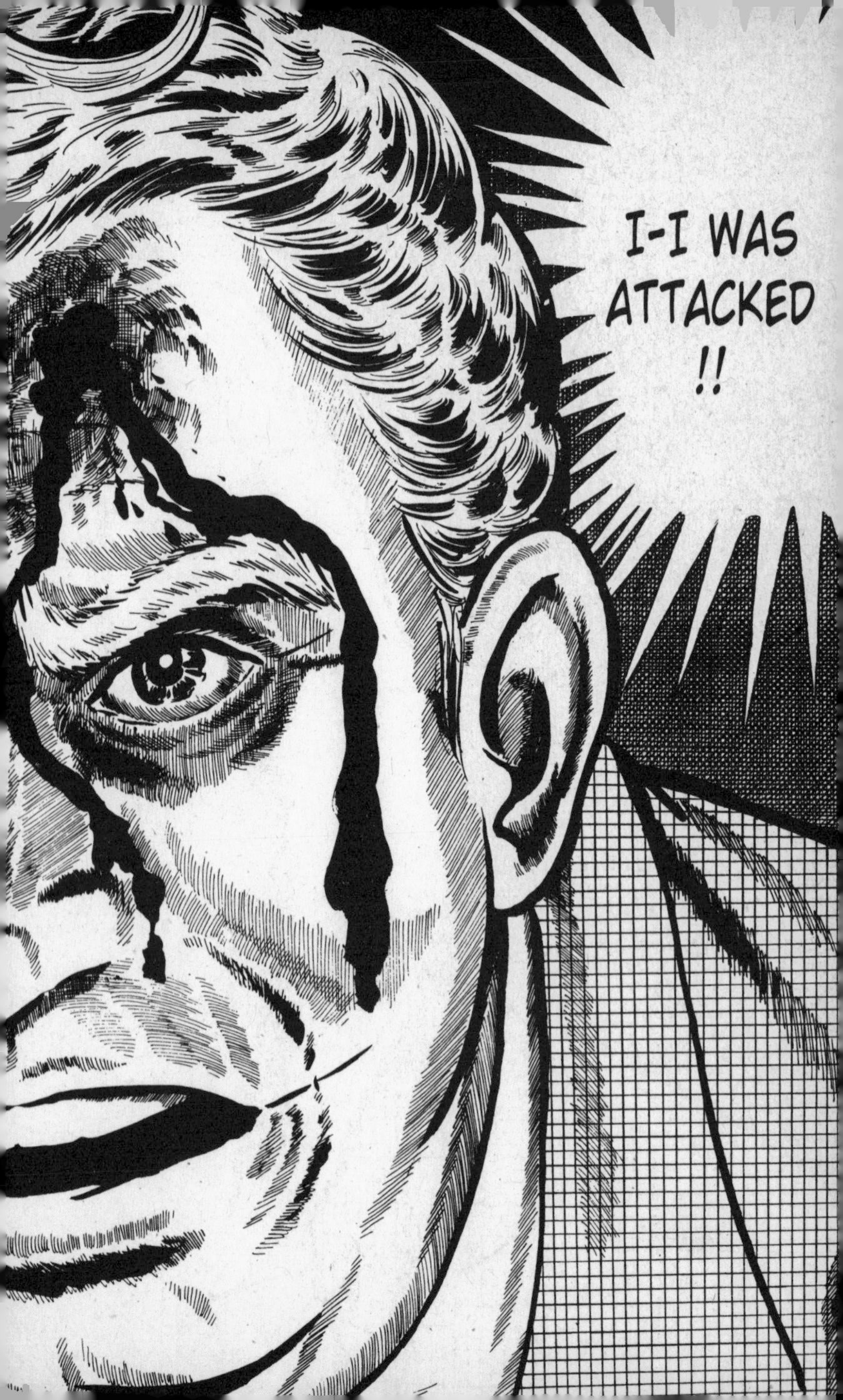
I-I WAS ATTACKED !!

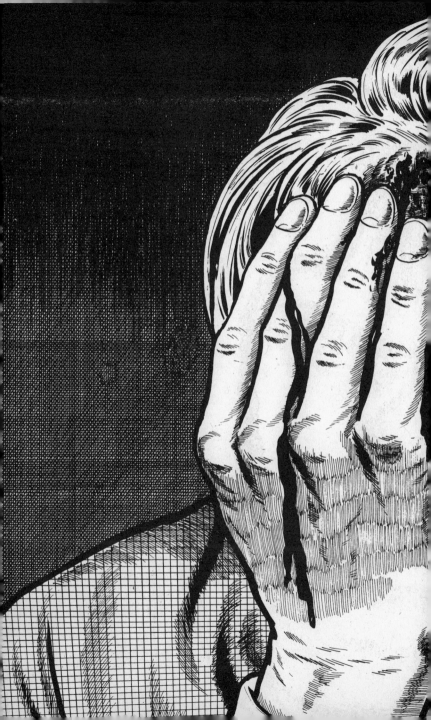

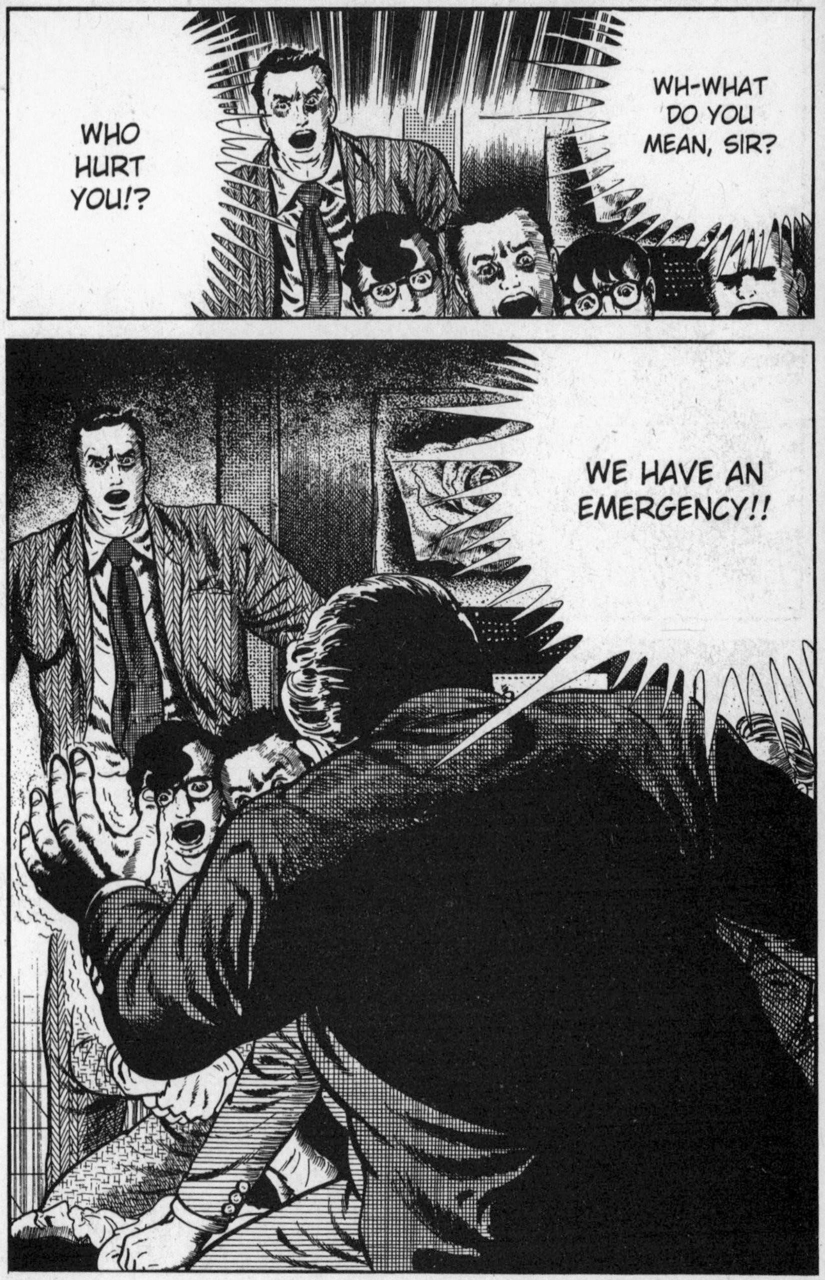
WH-WHAT DO YOU MEAN, SIR?
WHO HURT YOU!?
WE HAVE AN EMERGENCY!!

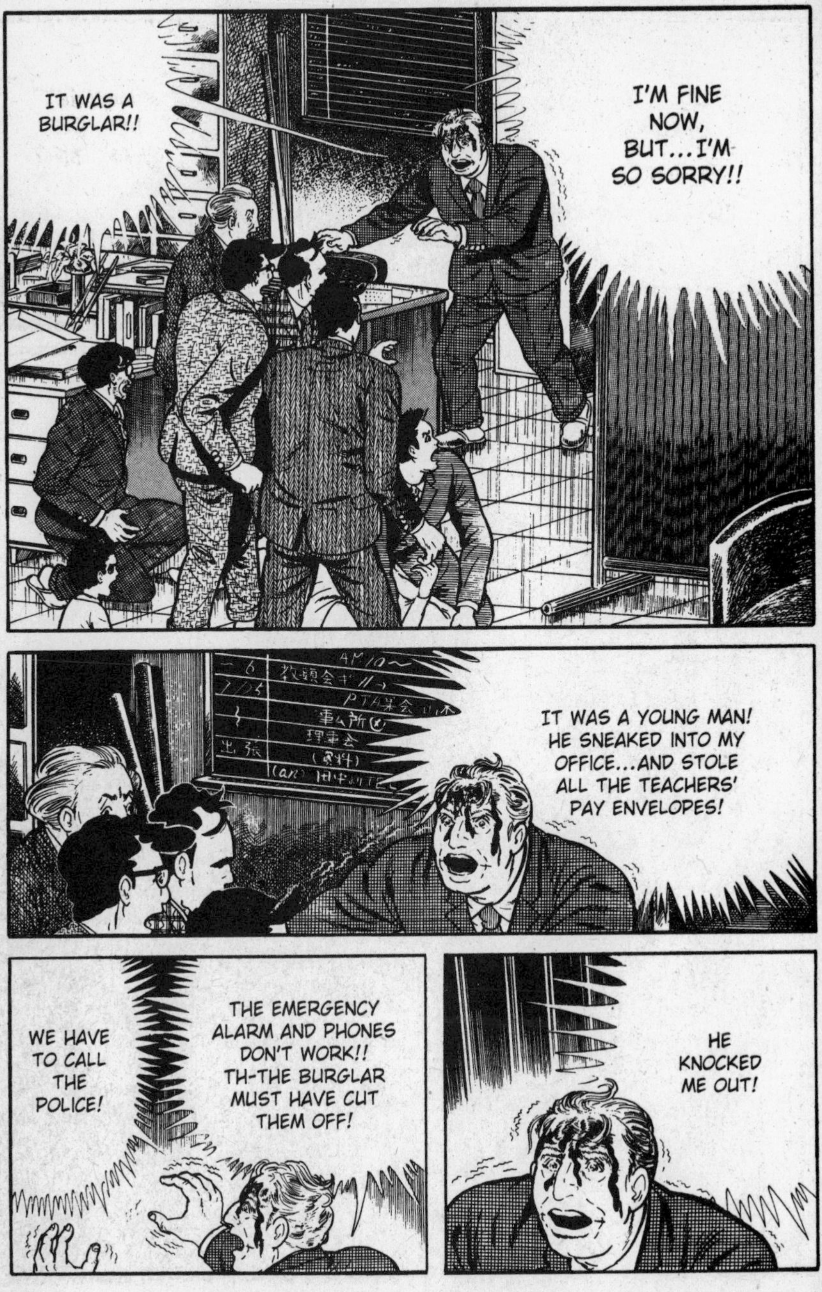
I'M FINE NOW, BUT...I'M SO SORRY!!
IT WAS A BURGLAR!!
IT WAS A YOUNG MAN! HE SNEAKED INTO MY OFFICE...AND STOLE ALL THE TEACHERS' PAY ENVELOPES!
HE KNOCKED ME OUT!
THE EMERGENCY ALARM AND PHONES DON'T WORK!! TH-THE BURGLAR MUST HAVE CUT THEM OFF!
WE HAVE TO CALL THE POLICE!

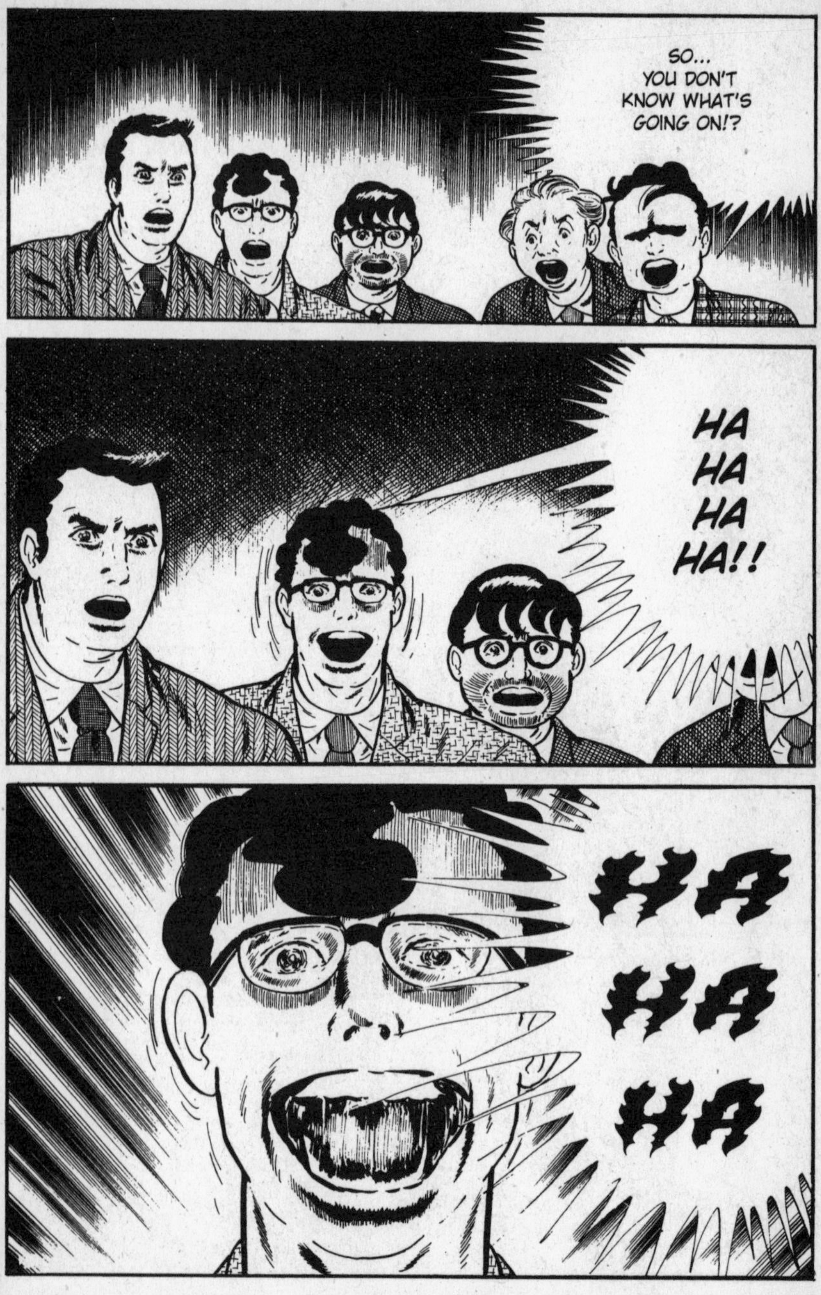
SO... YOU DON'T KNOW WHAT'S GOING ON!?
HA HA HA HA!!
HA HA HA

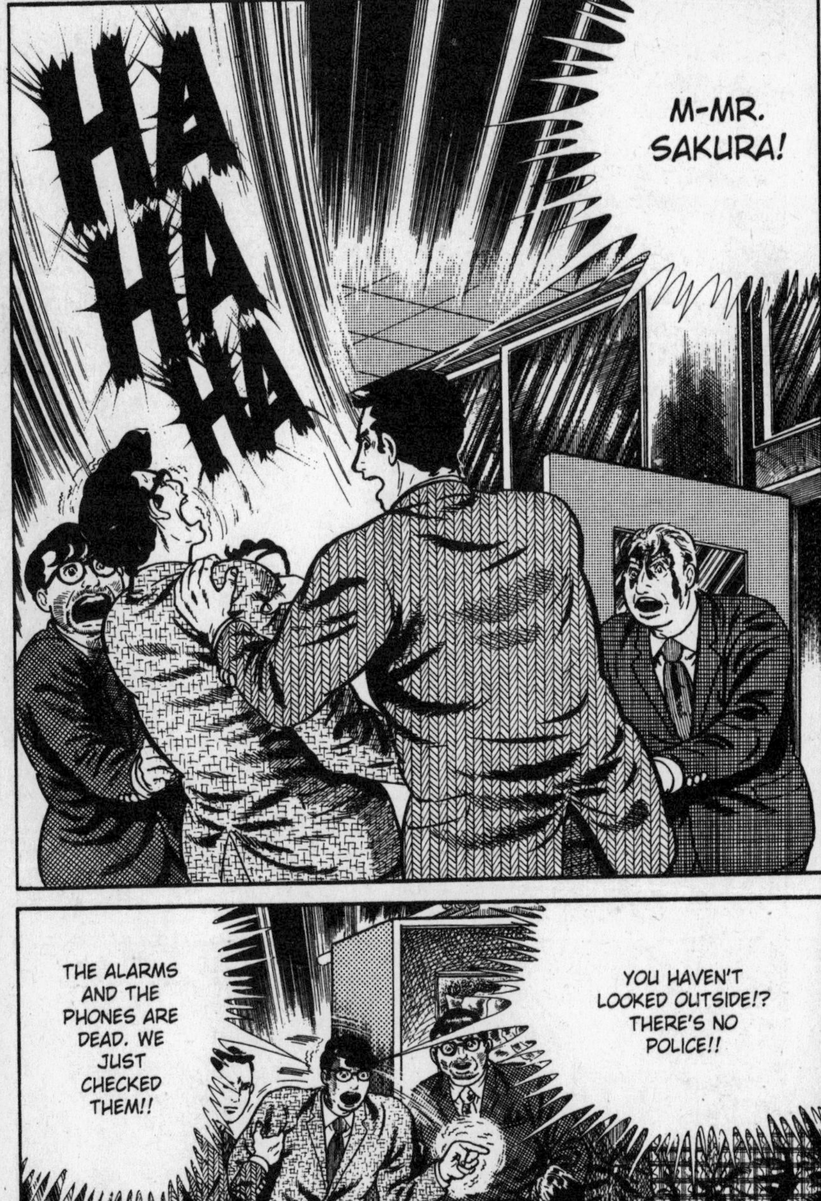
M-MR. SAKURA!
HA HA HA
YOU HAVEN'T LOOKED OUTSIDE!? THERE'S NO POLICE!!
THE ALARMS AND THE PHONES ARE DEAD. WE JUST CHECKED THEM!!

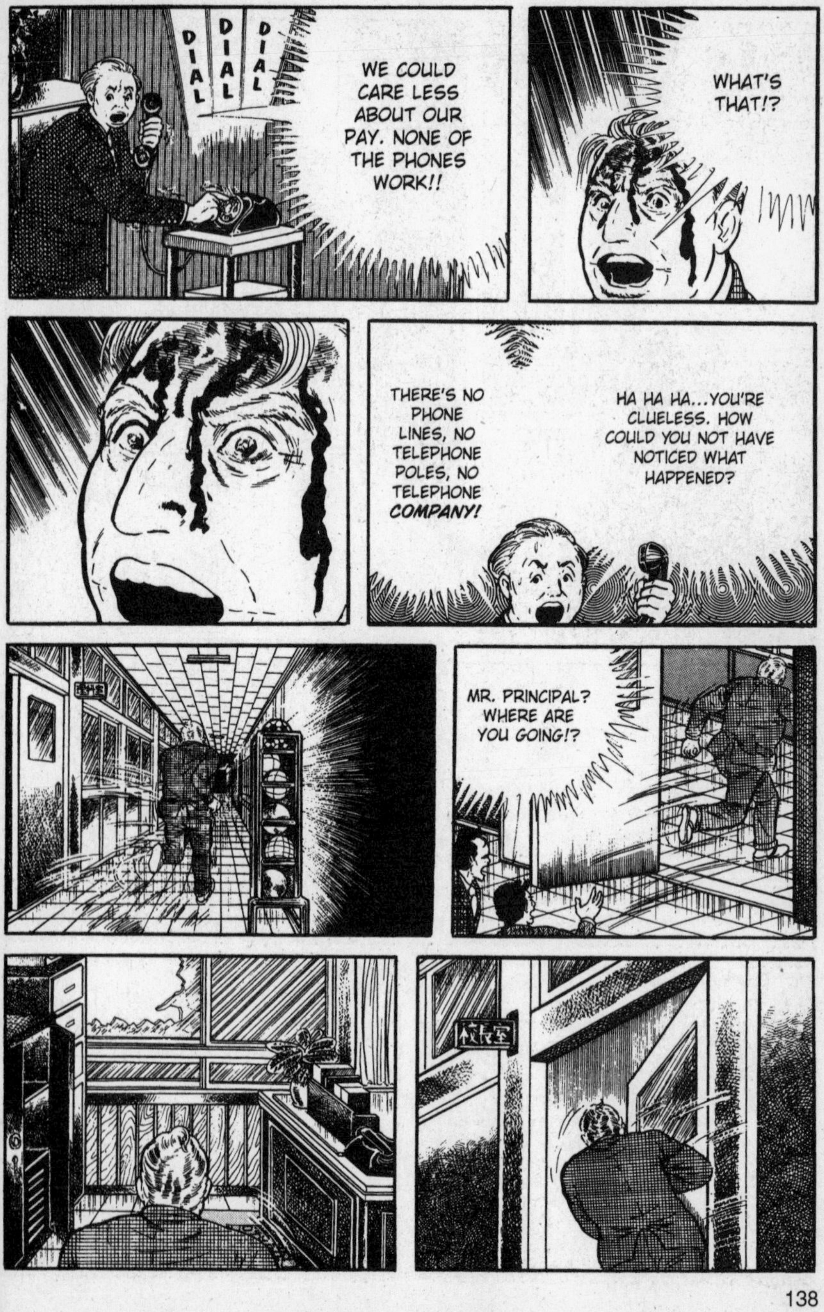
WHAT'S THAT!?
DIAL DIAL DIAL
WE COULD CARE LESS ABOUT OUR PAY. NONE OF THE PHONES WORK!!
HA HA HA...YOU'RE CLUELESS. HOW COULD YOU NOT HAVE NOTICED WHAT HAPPENED?
THERE'S NO PHONE LINES, NO TELEPHONE POLES, NO TELEPHONE *COMPANY!*
MR. PRINCIPAL? WHERE ARE YOU GOING!?

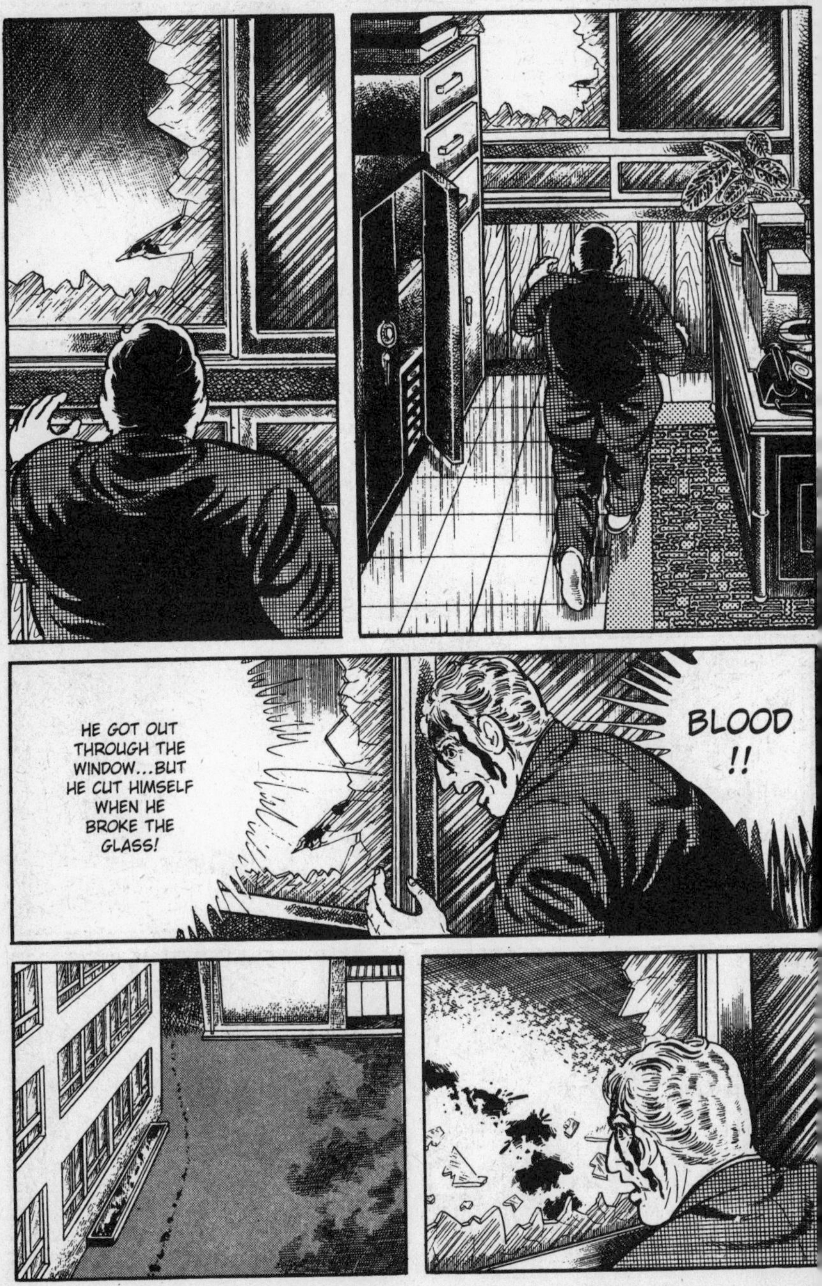
BLOOD !!
HE GOT OUT THROUGH THE WINDOW...BUT HE CUT HIMSELF WHEN HE BROKE THE GLASS!

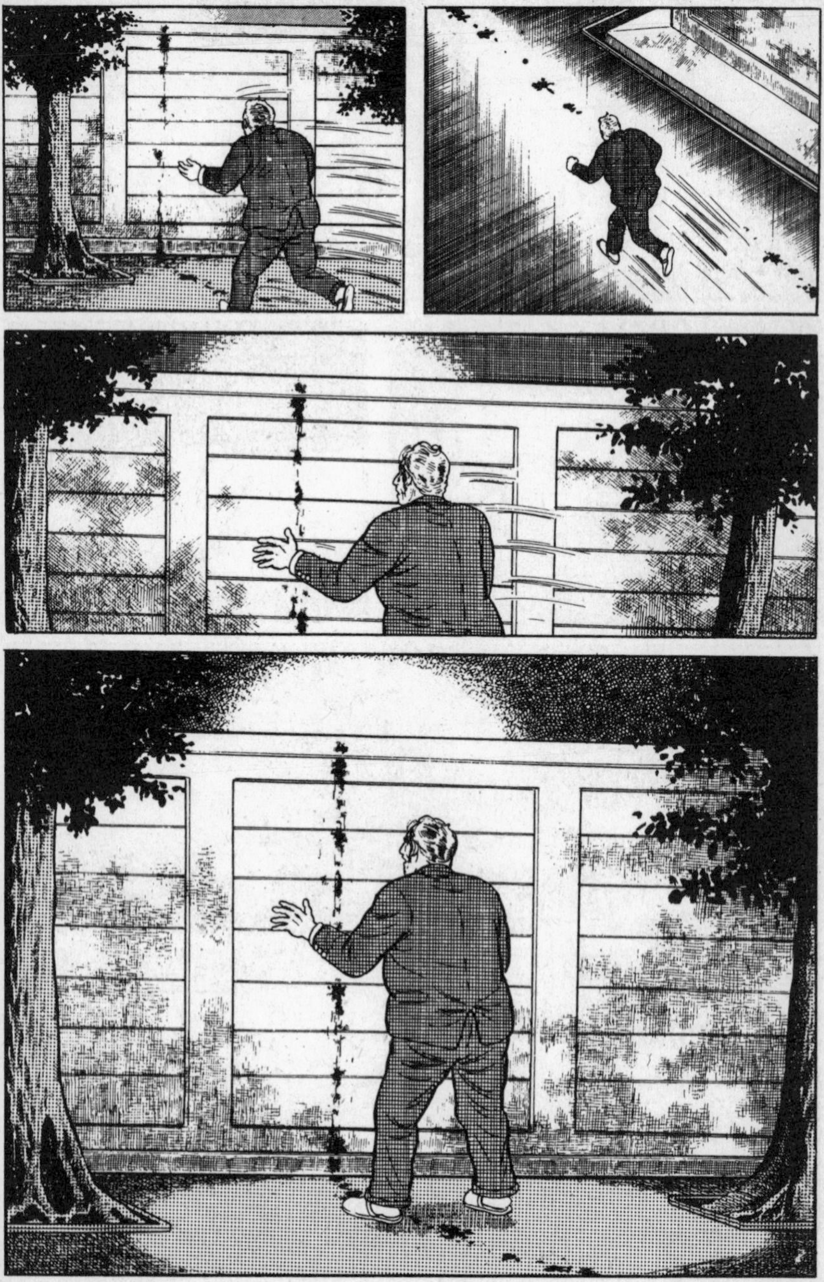

HE CLIMBED OVER THE FENCE!!

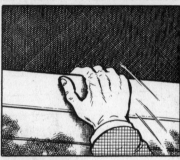

AH--

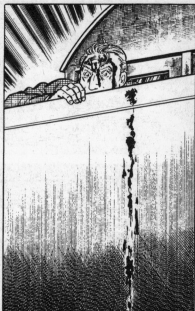

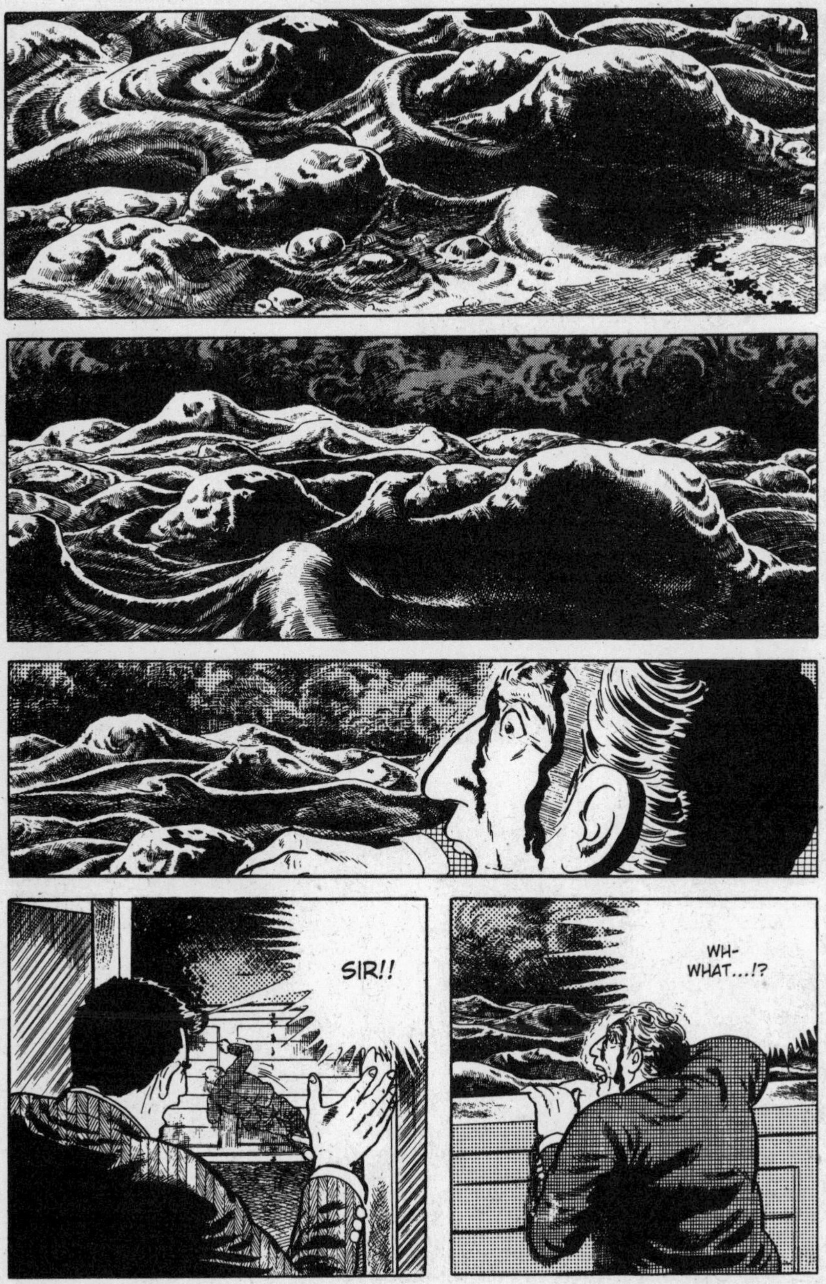
WH-
WHAT...!?
SIR!!

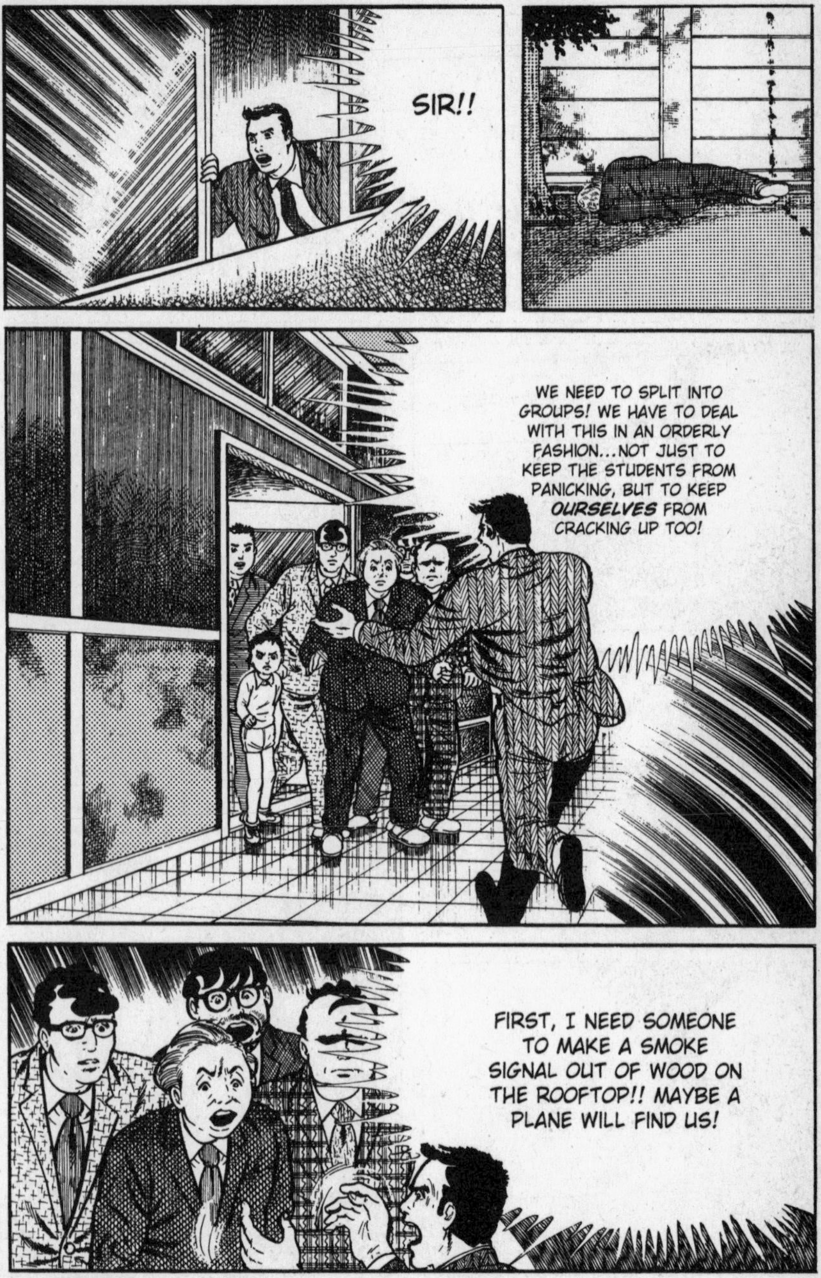
SIR!!
WE NEED TO SPLIT INTO GROUPS! WE HAVE TO DEAL WITH THIS IN AN ORDERLY FASHION...NOT JUST TO KEEP THE STUDENTS FROM PANICKING, BUT TO KEEP *OURSELVES* FROM CRACKING UP TOO!
FIRST, I NEED SOMEONE TO MAKE A SMOKE SIGNAL OUT OF WOOD ON THE ROOFTOP!! MAYBE A PLANE WILL FIND US!

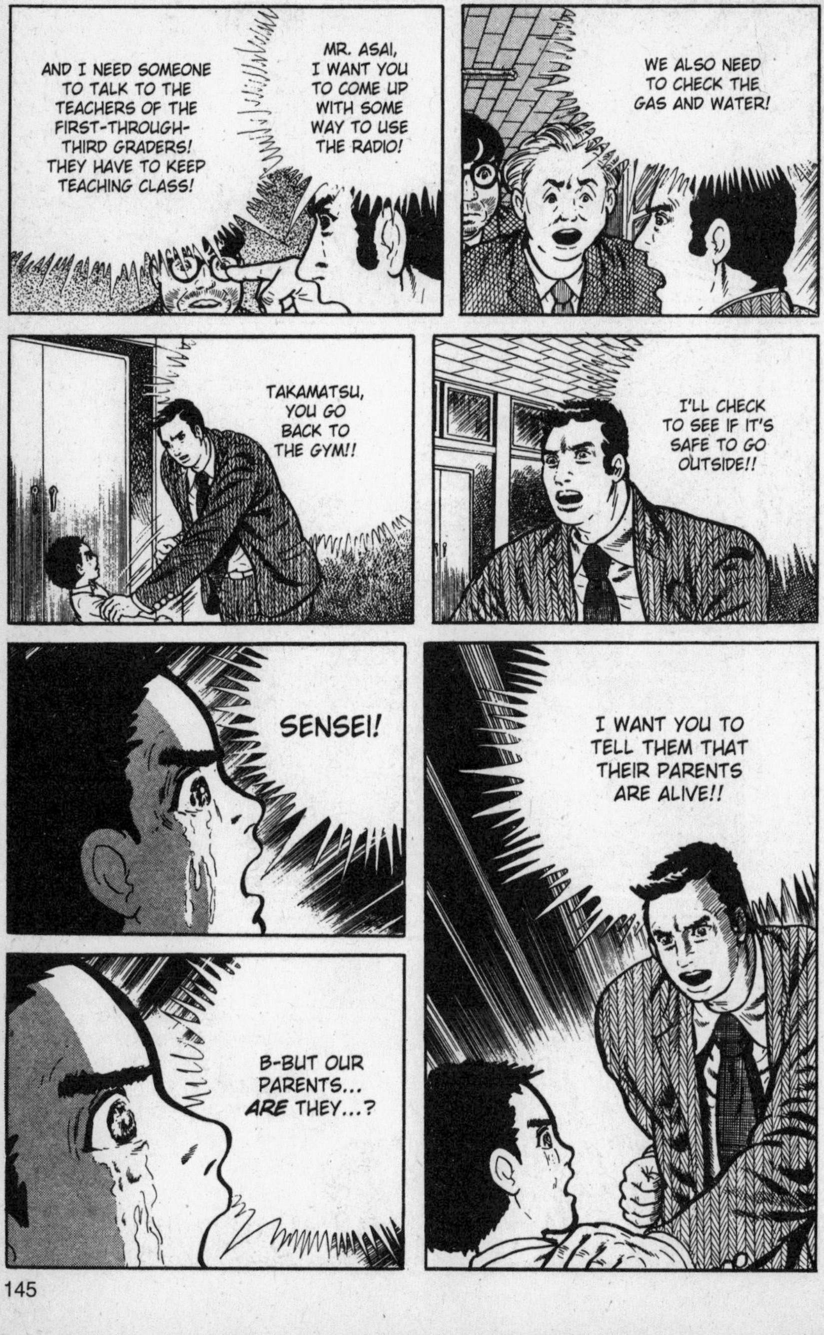

WE ALSO NEED TO CHECK THE GAS AND WATER!
MR. ASAI, I WANT YOU TO COME UP WITH SOME WAY TO USE THE RADIO!
AND I NEED SOMEONE TO TALK TO THE TEACHERS OF THE FIRST-THROUGH-THIRD GRADERS! THEY HAVE TO KEEP TEACHING CLASS!
I'LL CHECK TO SEE IF IT'S SAFE TO GO OUTSIDE!!
TAKAMATSU, YOU GO BACK TO THE GYM!!
I WANT YOU TO TELL THEM THAT THEIR PARENTS ARE ALIVE!!
SENSEI!
B-BUT OUR PARENTS... *ARE* THEY...?

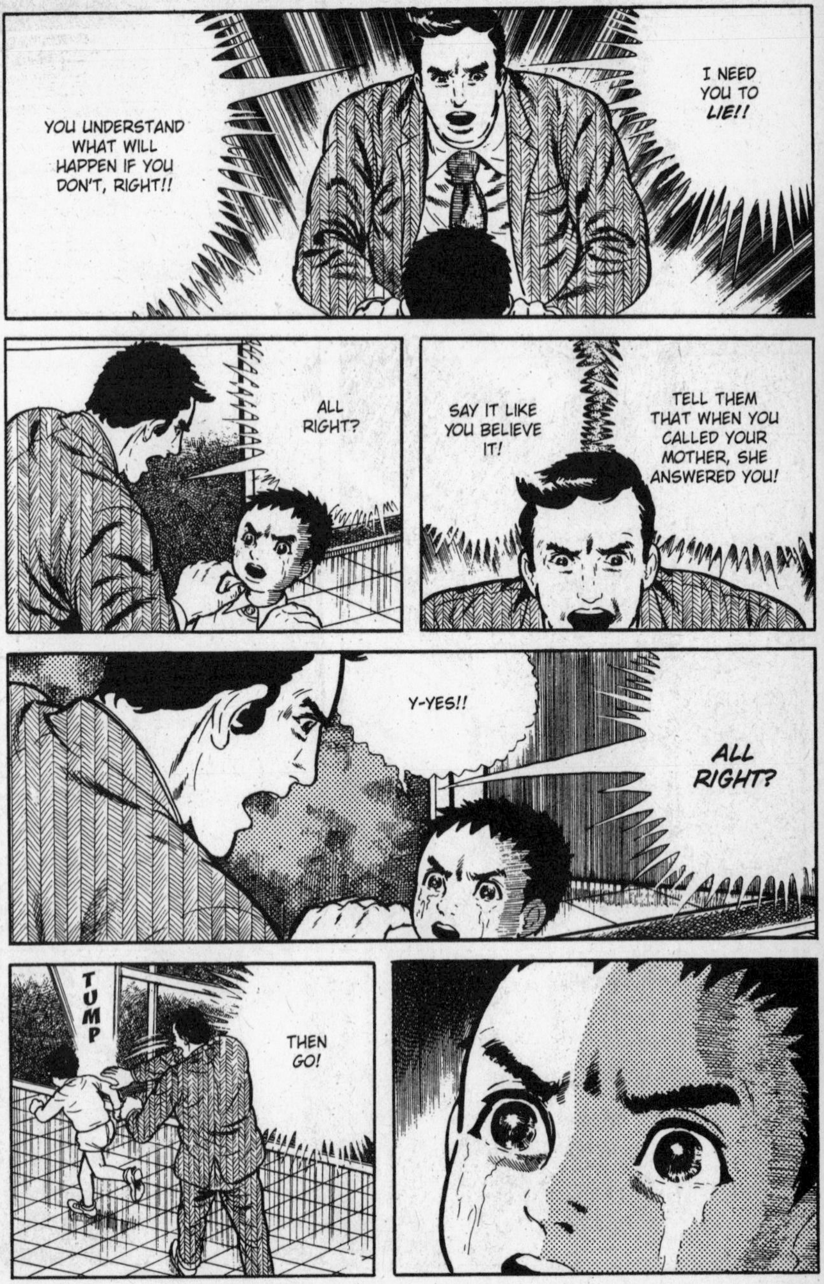
I NEED YOU TO *LIE!!*
YOU UNDERSTAND WHAT WILL HAPPEN IF YOU DON'T, RIGHT!!
TELL THEM THAT WHEN YOU CALLED YOUR MOTHER, SHE ANSWERED YOU!
SAY IT LIKE YOU BELIEVE IT!
ALL RIGHT?
ALL RIGHT?
Y-YES!!
THEN GO!
TUMP

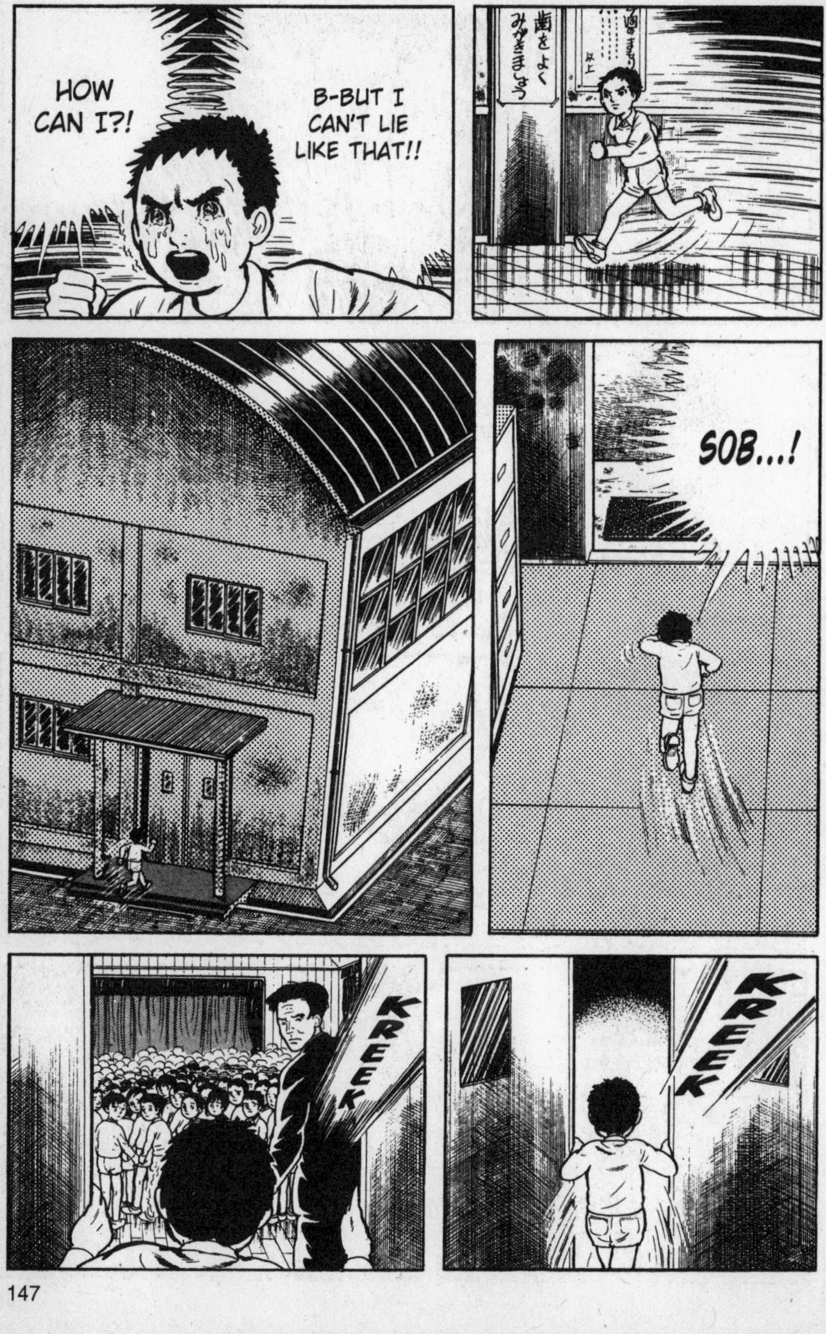
歯をよく みがきましょう
B-BUT I CAN'T LIE LIKE THAT!!
HOW CAN I?!
SOB...!
KREEK
KREEK

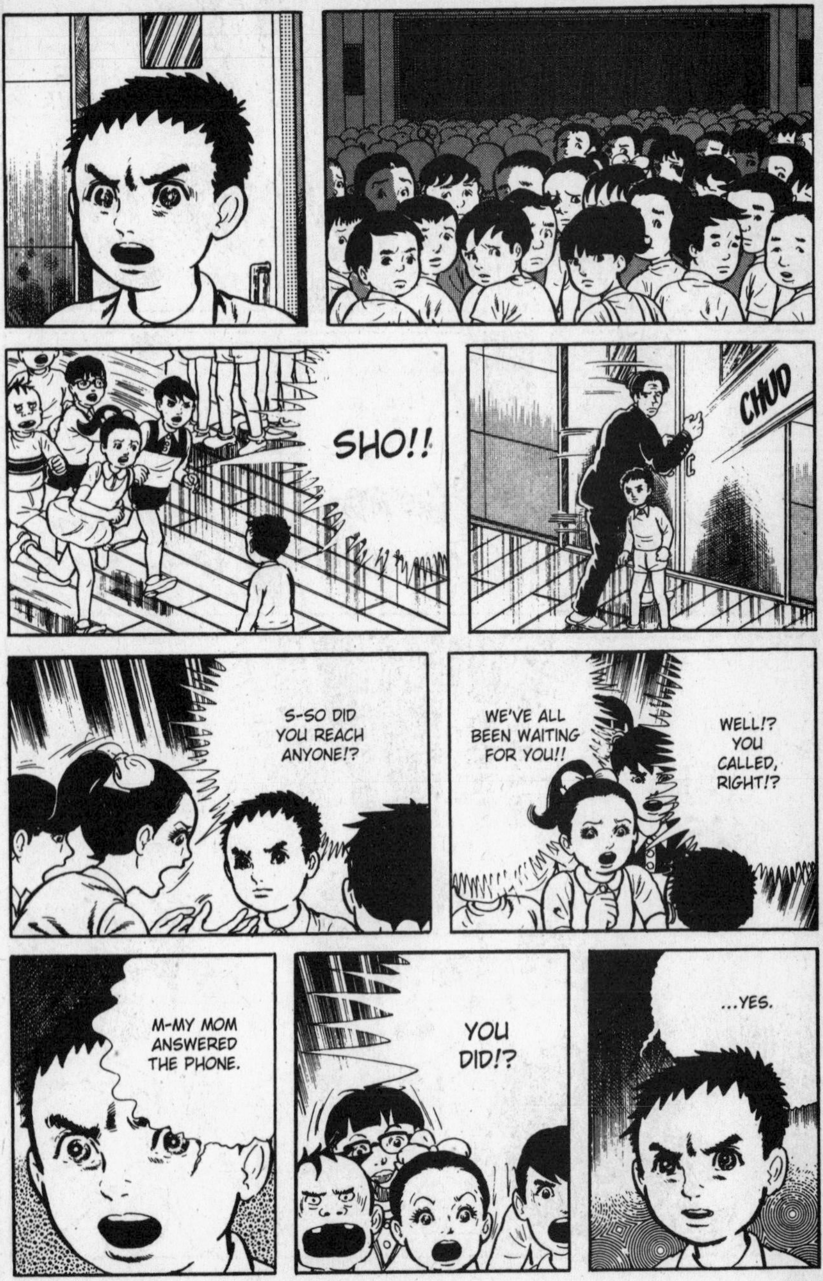
CHUD
SHO!!
WELL!? YOU CALLED, RIGHT!?
WE'VE ALL BEEN WAITING FOR YOU!!
S-SO DID YOU REACH ANYONE!?
...YES.
YOU DID!?
M-MY MOM ANSWERED THE PHONE.

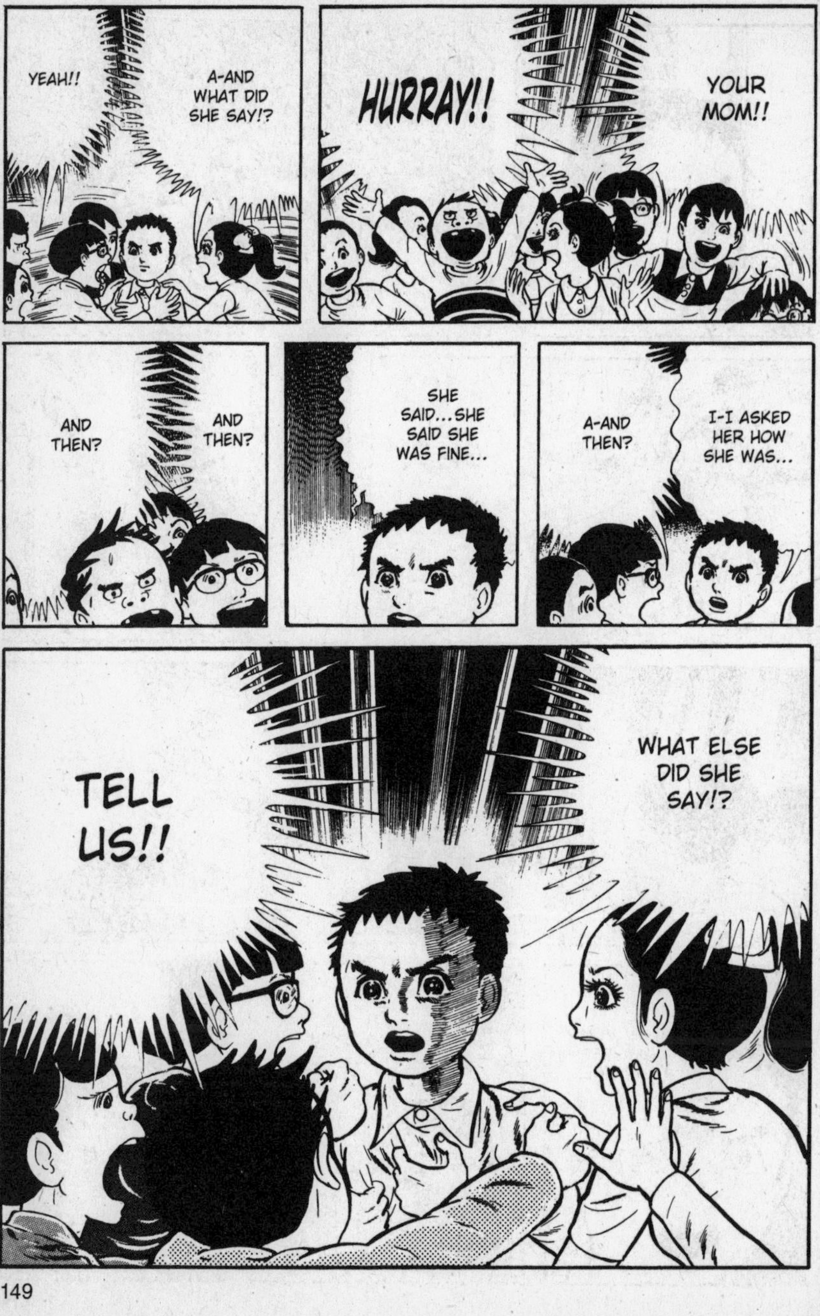
YOUR MOM!!
HURRAY!!
A-AND WHAT DID SHE SAY!?
YEAH!!
I-I ASKED HER HOW SHE WAS...
A-AND THEN?
SHE SAID...SHE SAID SHE WAS FINE...
AND THEN?
AND THEN?
WHAT ELSE DID SHE SAY!?
TELL US!!

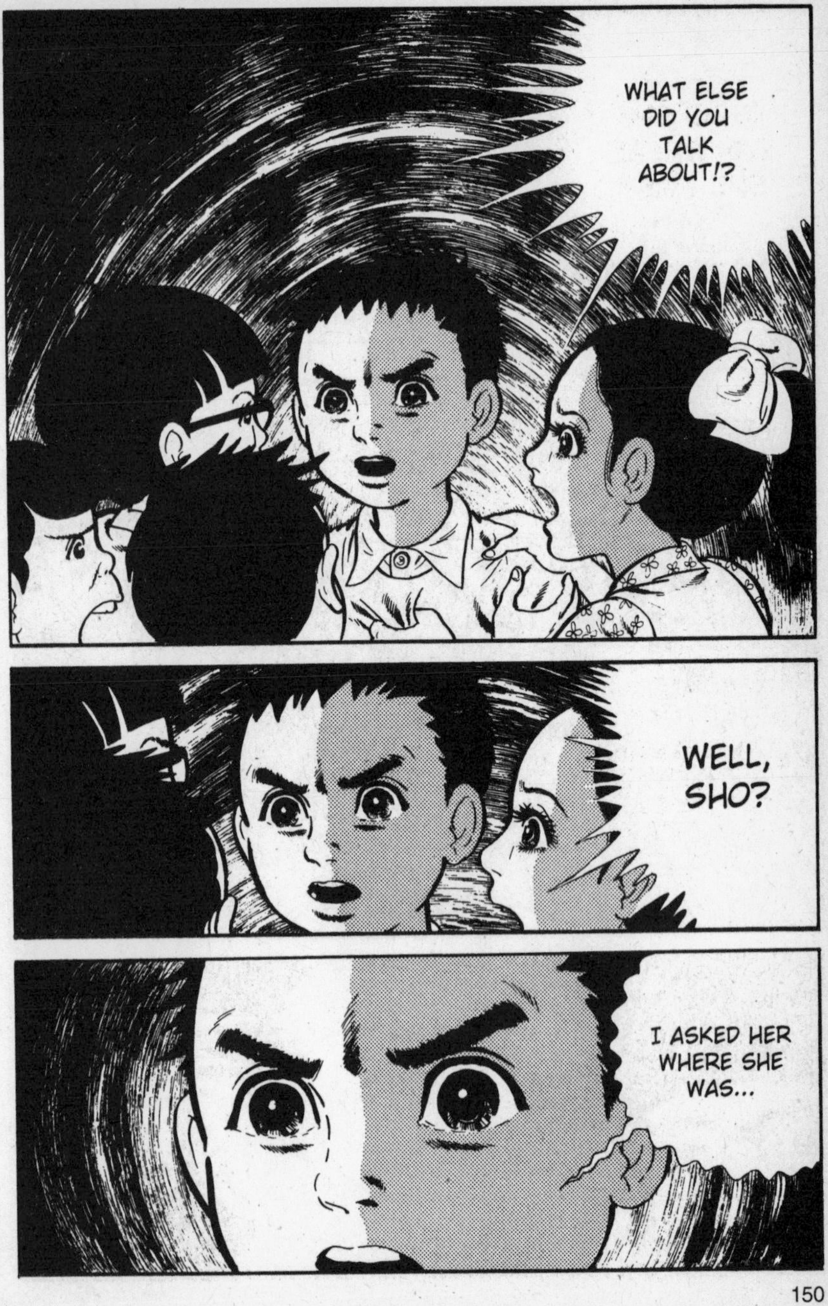
WHAT ELSE DID YOU TALK ABOUT!?
WELL, SHO?
I ASKED HER WHERE SHE WAS...

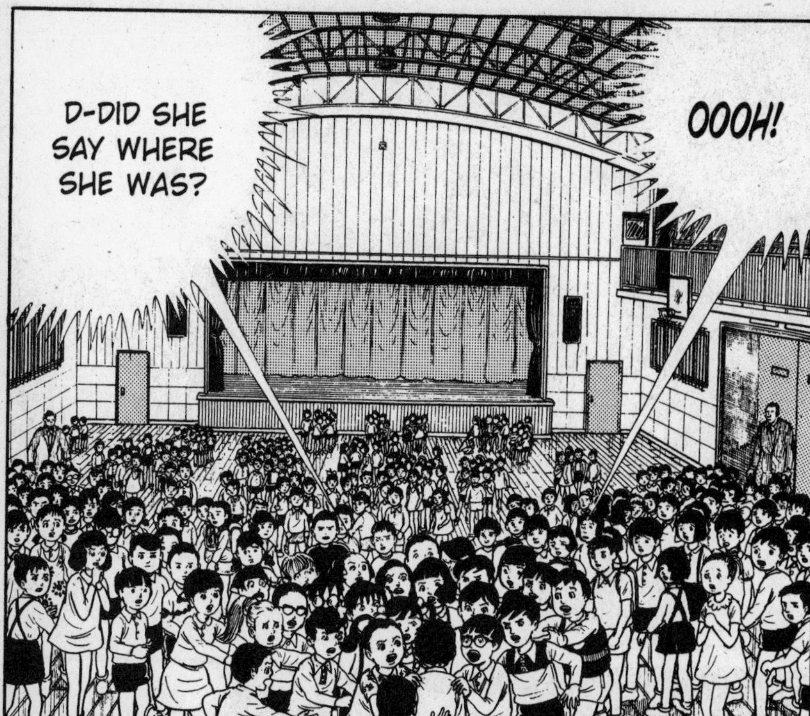
OOOH!
D-DID SHE SAY WHERE SHE WAS?

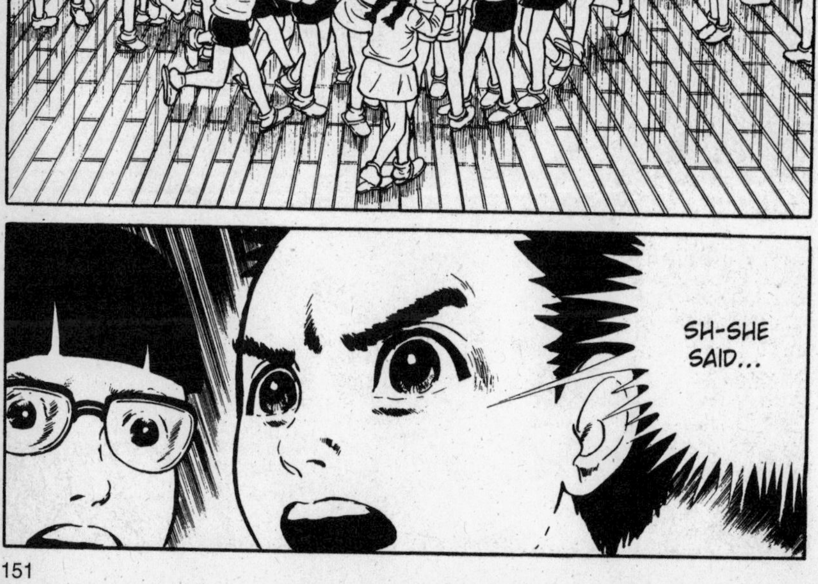
SH-SHE SAID...

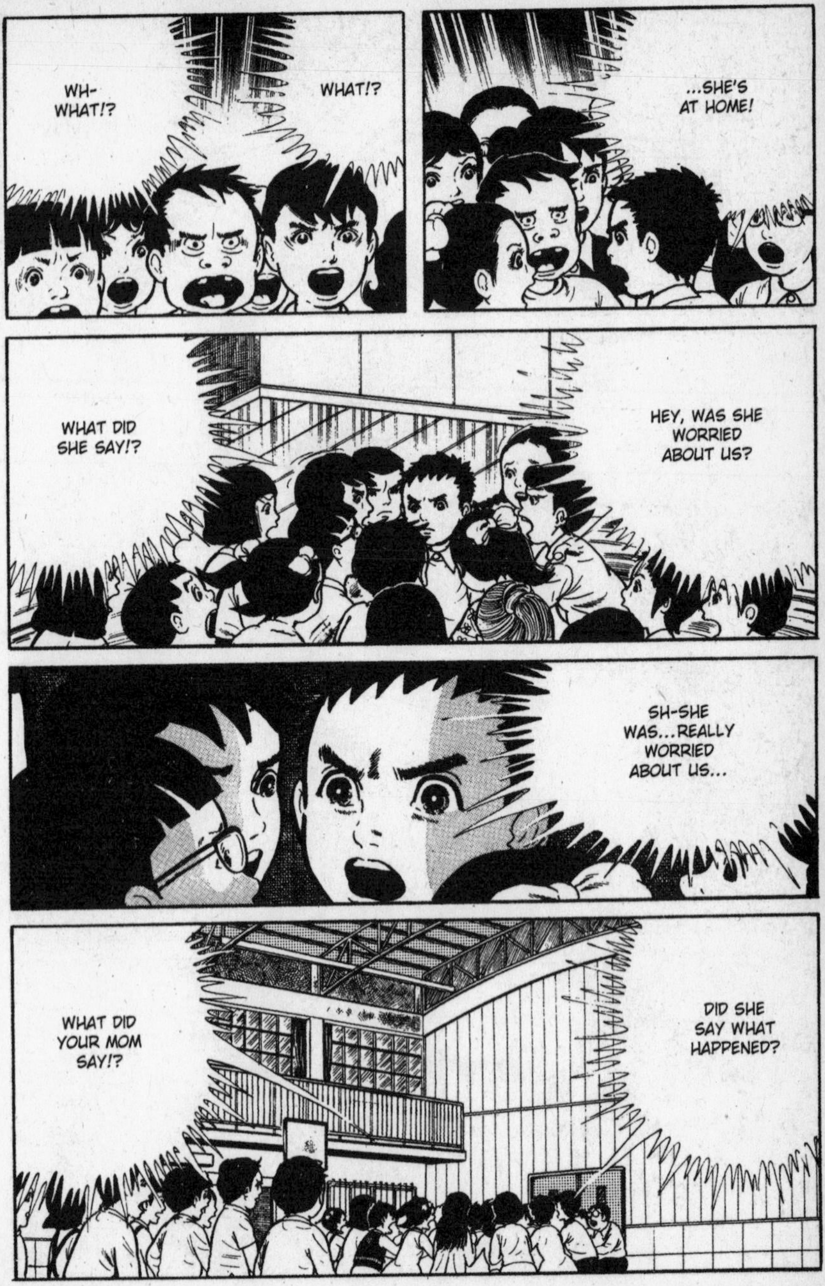
...SHE'S AT HOME!
WHAT!?
WH- WHAT!?
HEY, WAS SHE WORRIED ABOUT US?
WHAT DID SHE SAY!?
SH-SHE WAS...REALLY WORRIED ABOUT US...
DID SHE SAY WHAT HAPPENED?
WHAT DID YOUR MOM SAY!?

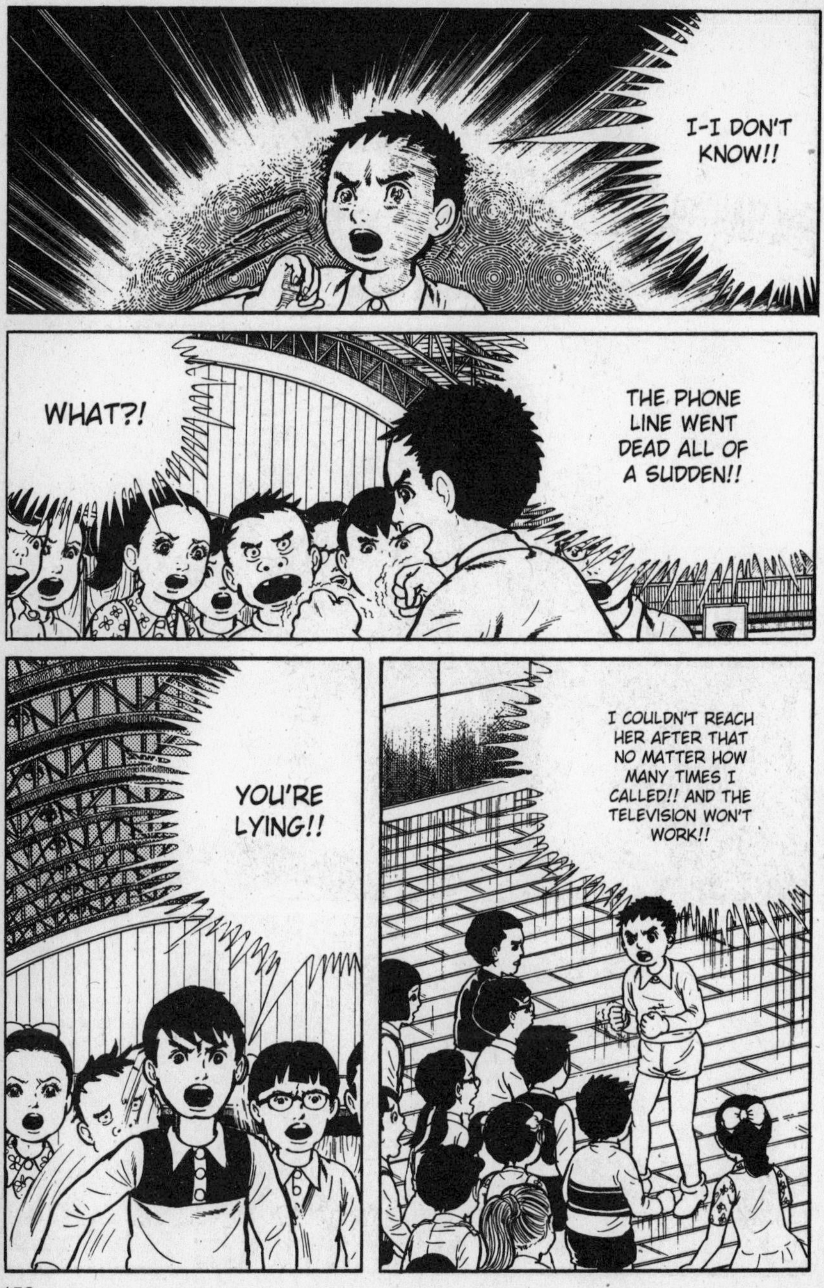
I-I DON'T KNOW!!
THE PHONE LINE WENT DEAD ALL OF A SUDDEN!!
WHAT?!
I COULDN'T REACH HER AFTER THAT NO MATTER HOW MANY TIMES I CALLED!! AND THE TELEVISION WON'T WORK!!
YOU'RE LYING!!

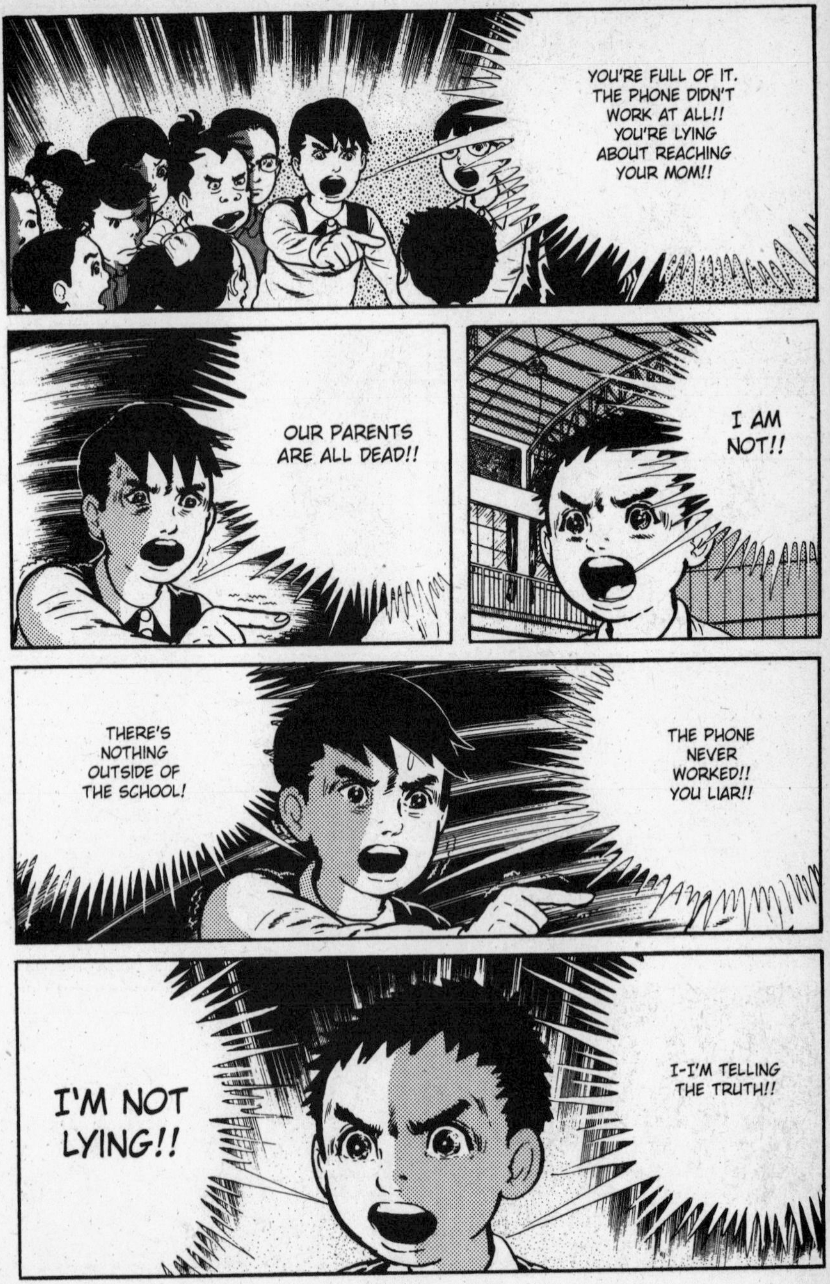
YOU'RE FULL OF IT. THE PHONE DIDN'T WORK AT ALL!! YOU'RE LYING ABOUT REACHING YOUR MOM!!
I AM NOT!!
OUR PARENTS ARE ALL DEAD!!
THE PHONE NEVER WORKED!! YOU LIAR!!
THERE'S NOTHING OUTSIDE OF THE SCHOOL!
I-I'M TELLING THE TRUTH!!
I'M NOT LYING!!

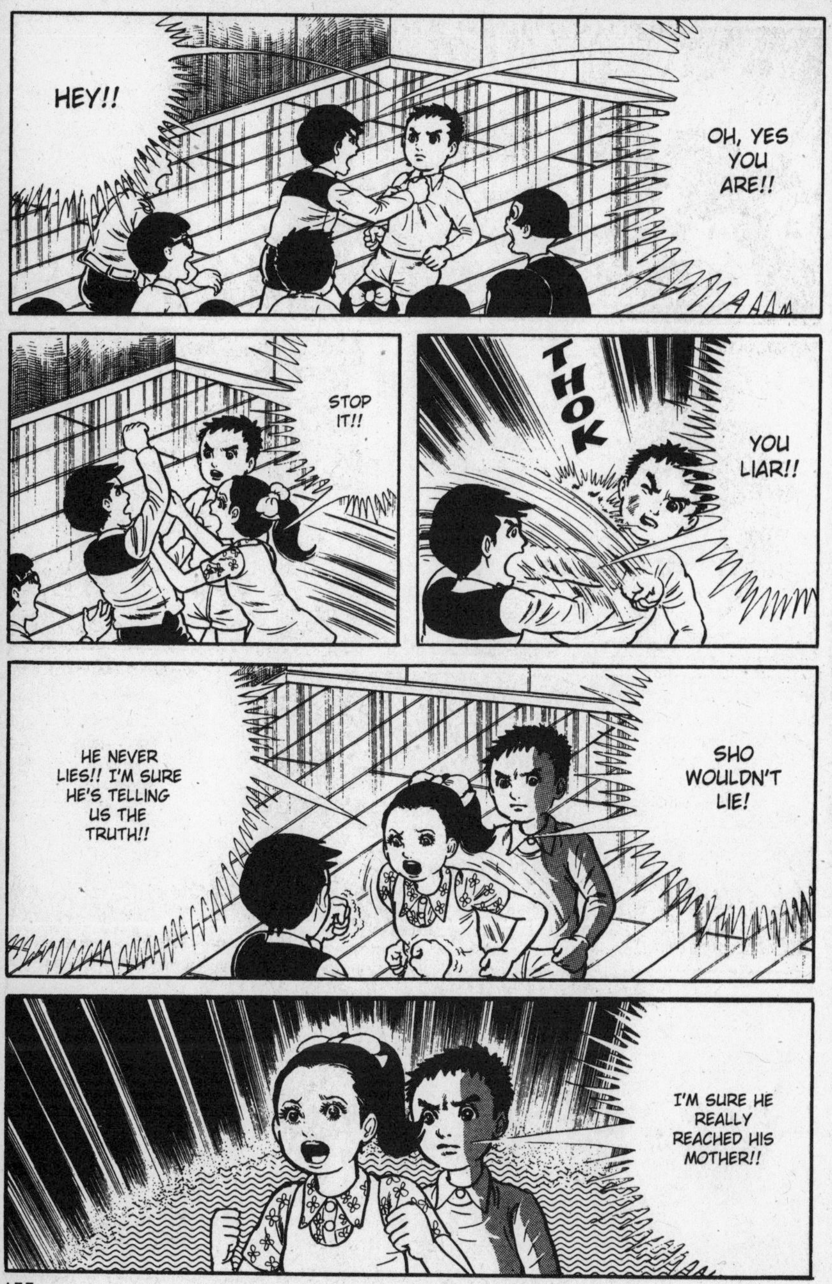
OH, YES YOU ARE!!
HEY!!
THOK
YOU LIAR!!
STOP IT!!
SHO WOULDN'T LIE!
HE NEVER LIES!! I'M SURE HE'S TELLING US THE TRUTH!!
I'M SURE HE REALLY REACHED HIS MOTHER!!

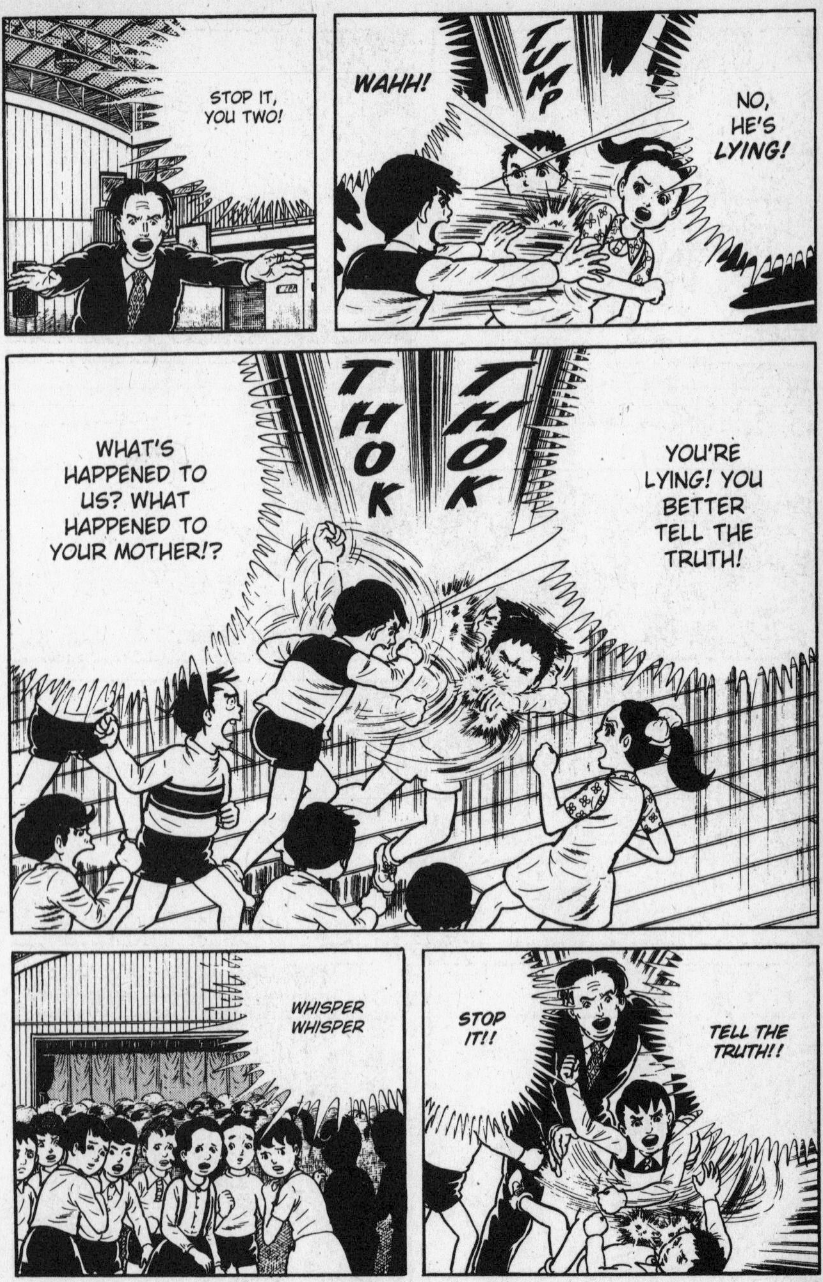
NO, HE'S LYING!
TUMP
WAHH!
STOP IT, YOU TWO!
THOK
THOK
YOU'RE LYING! YOU BETTER TELL THE TRUTH!
WHAT'S HAPPENED TO US? WHAT HAPPENED TO YOUR MOTHER!?
TELL THE TRUTH!!
STOP IT!!
WHISPER WHISPER

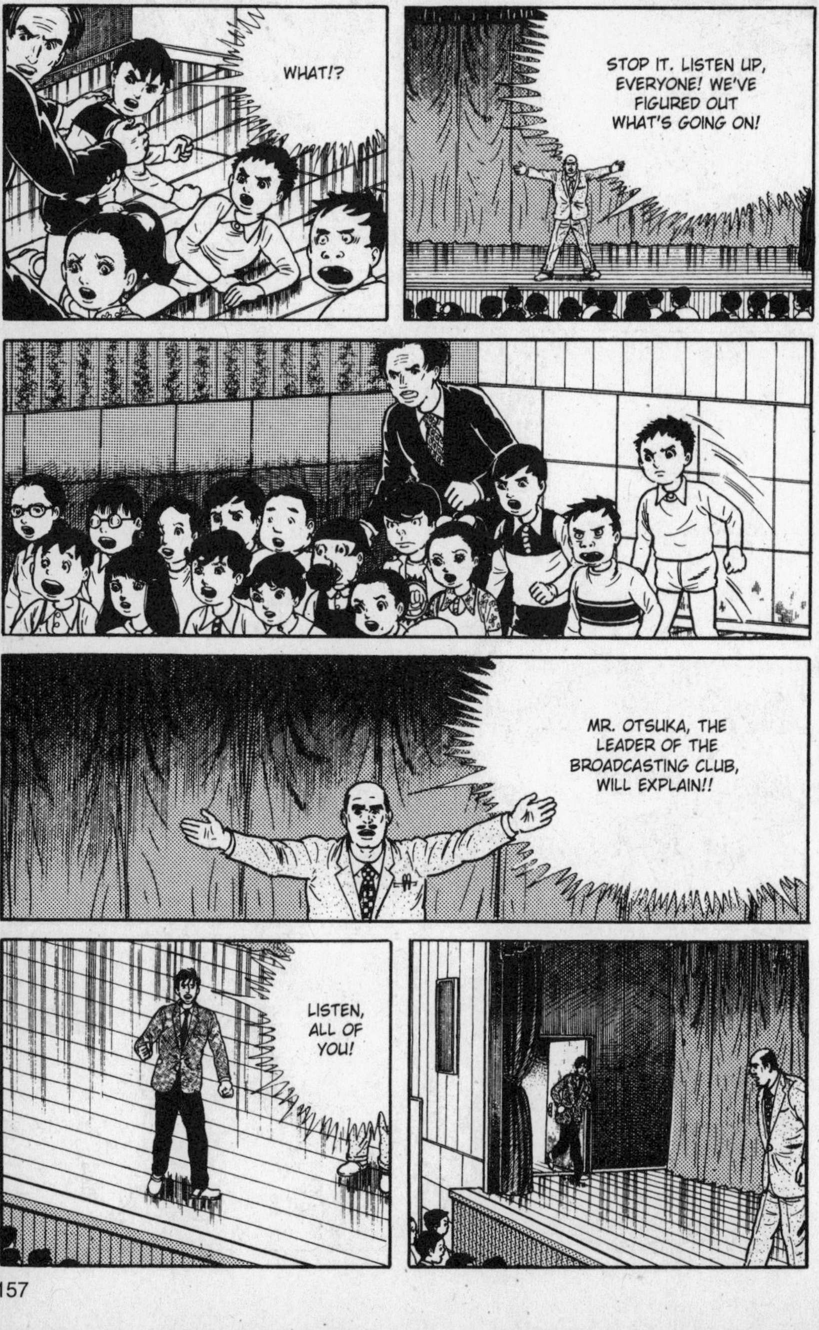
STOP IT. LISTEN UP, EVERYONE! WE'VE FIGURED OUT WHAT'S GOING ON!
WHAT!?
MR. OTSUKA, THE LEADER OF THE BROADCASTING CLUB, WILL EXPLAIN!!
LISTEN, ALL OF YOU!

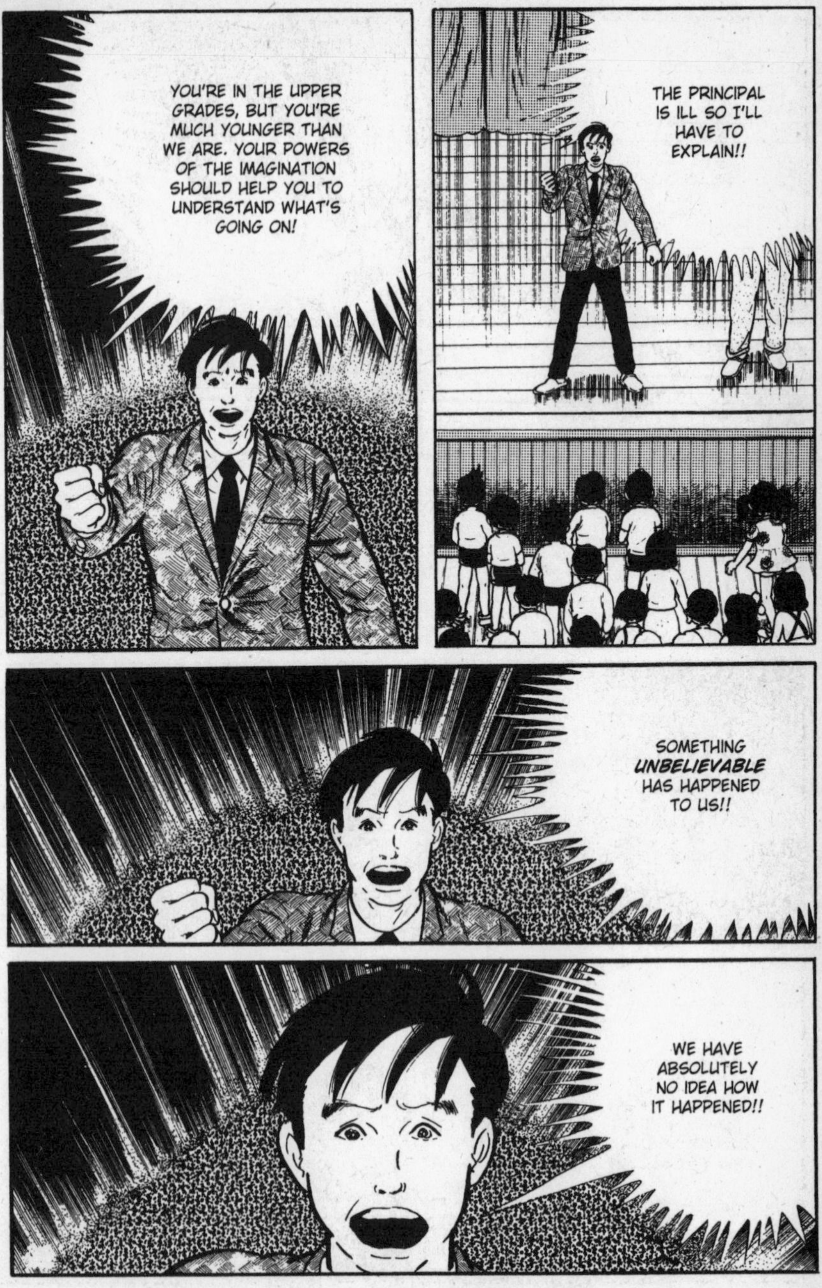
THE PRINCIPAL IS ILL SO I'LL HAVE TO EXPLAIN!!
YOU'RE IN THE UPPER GRADES, BUT YOU'RE MUCH YOUNGER THAN WE ARE. YOUR POWERS OF THE IMAGINATION SHOULD HELP YOU TO UNDERSTAND WHAT'S GOING ON!
SOMETHING *UNBELIEVABLE* HAS HAPPENED TO US!!
WE HAVE ABSOLUTELY NO IDEA HOW IT HAPPENED!!

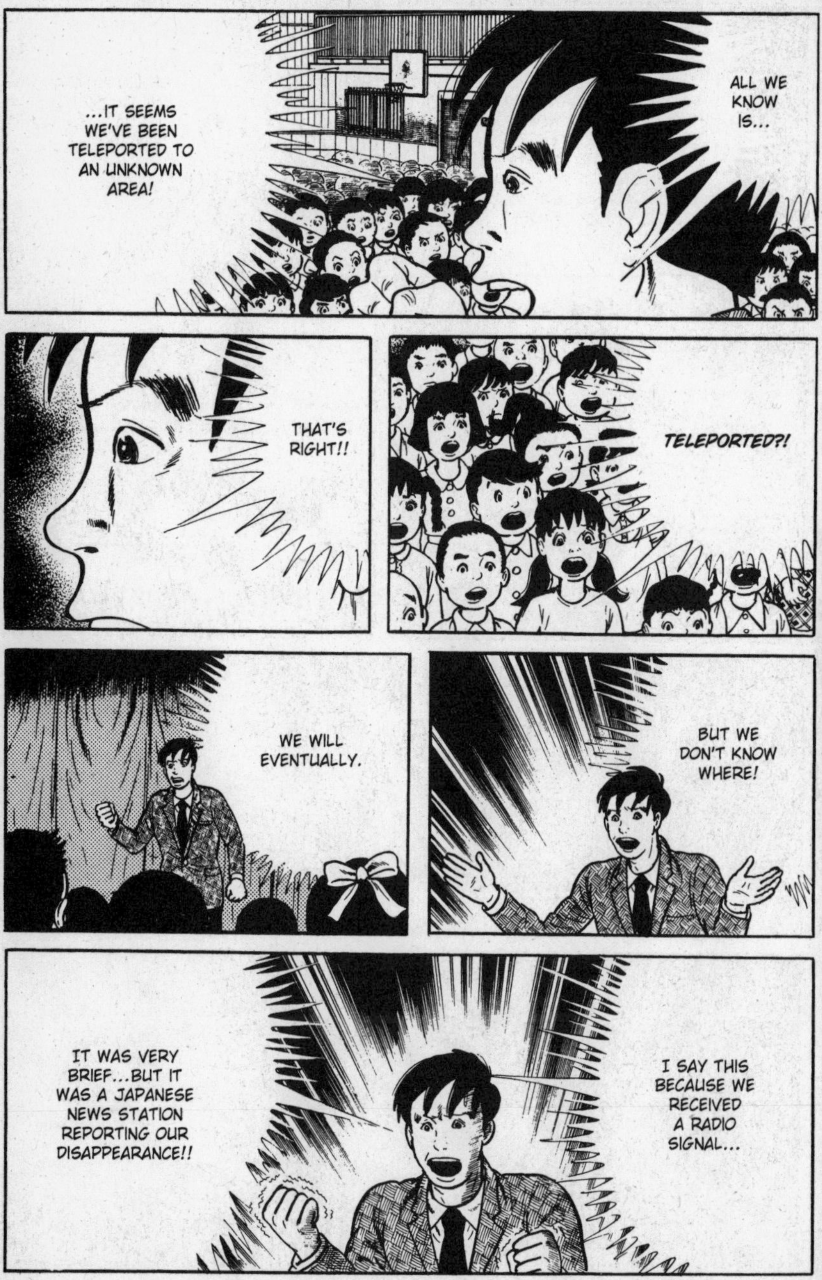
ALL WE KNOW IS...
...IT SEEMS WE'VE BEEN TELEPORTED TO AN UNKNOWN AREA!
TELEPORTED?!
THAT'S RIGHT!!
BUT WE DON'T KNOW WHERE!
WE WILL EVENTUALLY.
I SAY THIS BECAUSE WE RECEIVED A RADIO SIGNAL...
IT WAS VERY BRIEF...BUT IT WAS A JAPANESE NEWS STATION REPORTING OUR DISAPPEARANCE!!

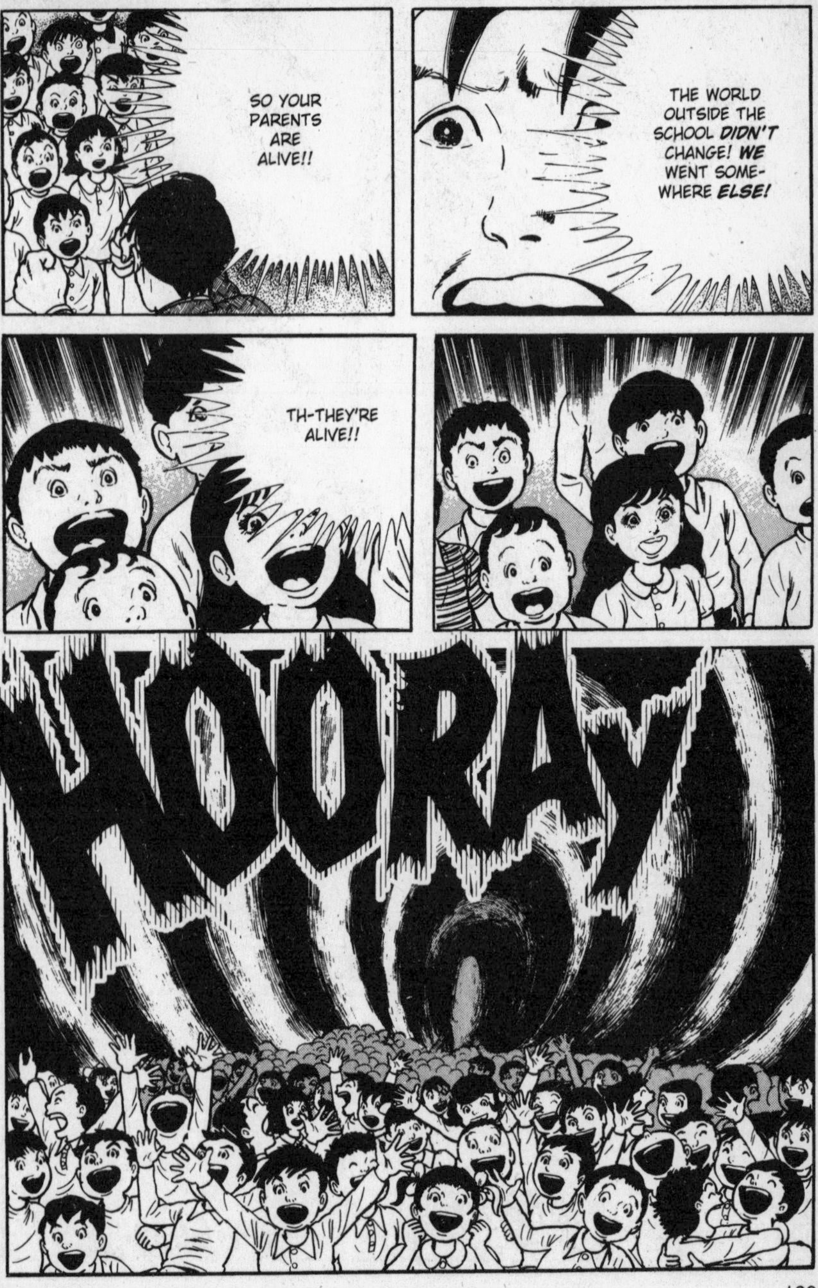
THE WORLD OUTSIDE THE SCHOOL *DIDN'T* CHANGE! *WE* WENT SOMEWHERE *ELSE!*
SO YOUR PARENTS ARE ALIVE!!
TH-THEY'RE ALIVE!!
HOORAY

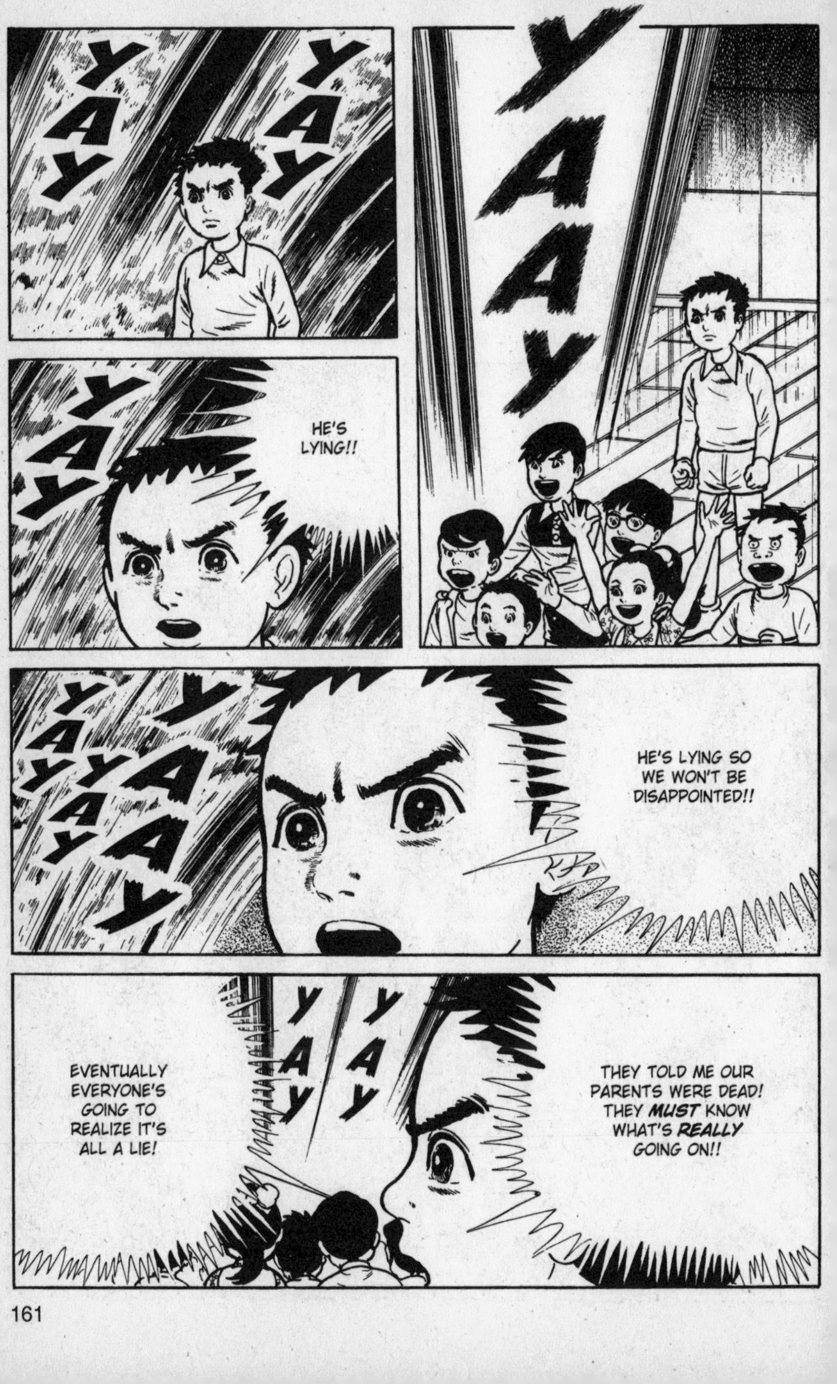
YAAAY
YAY
YAY
YAY
HE'S LYING!!
HE'S LYING SO WE WON'T BE DISAPPOINTED!!
YAAAY
YAY
YAY
THEY TOLD ME OUR PARENTS WERE DEAD! THEY MUST KNOW WHAT'S REALLY GOING ON!!
YAY
YAY
EVENTUALLY EVERYONE'S GOING TO REALIZE IT'S ALL A LIE!

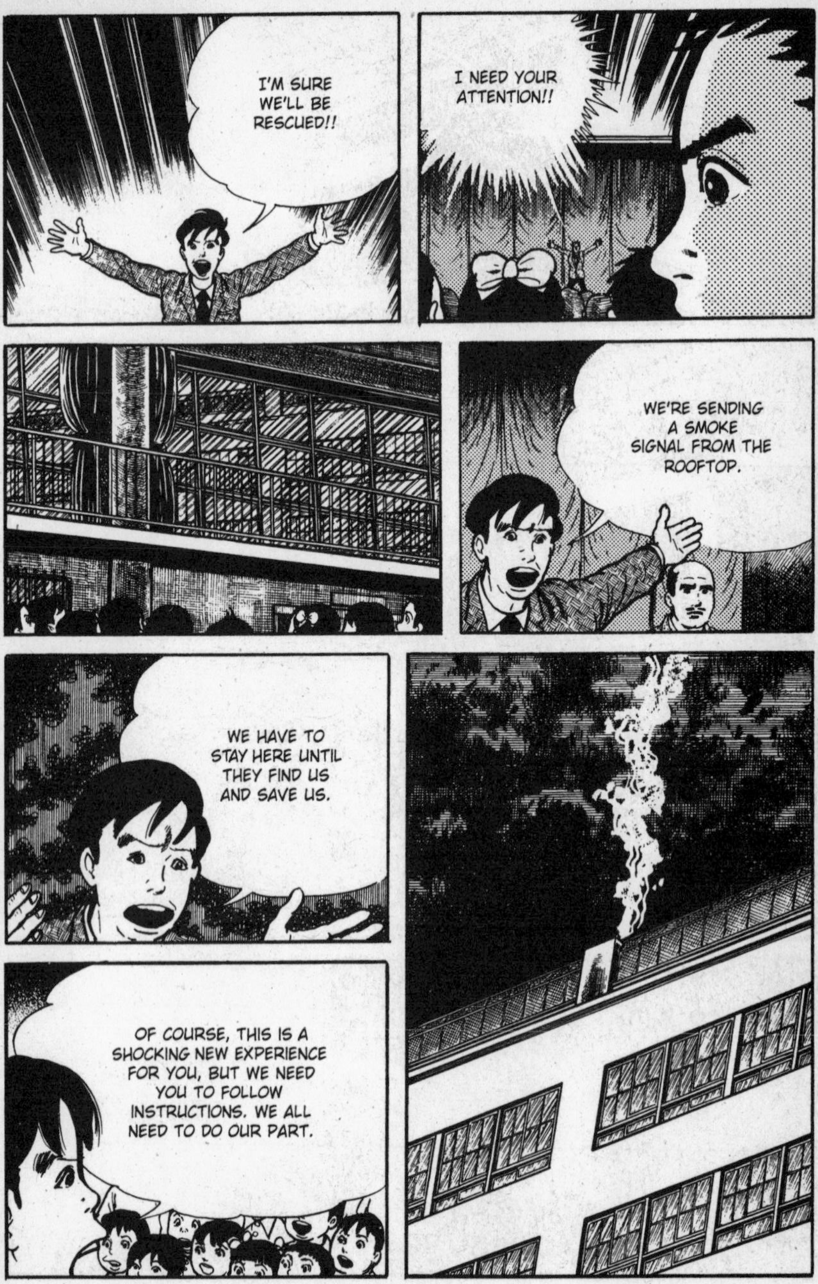
I NEED YOUR ATTENTION!!
I'M SURE WE'LL BE RESCUED!!
WE'RE SENDING A SMOKE SIGNAL FROM THE ROOFTOP.
WE HAVE TO STAY HERE UNTIL THEY FIND US AND SAVE US.
OF COURSE, THIS IS A SHOCKING NEW EXPERIENCE FOR YOU, BUT WE NEED YOU TO FOLLOW INSTRUCTIONS. WE ALL NEED TO DO OUR PART.

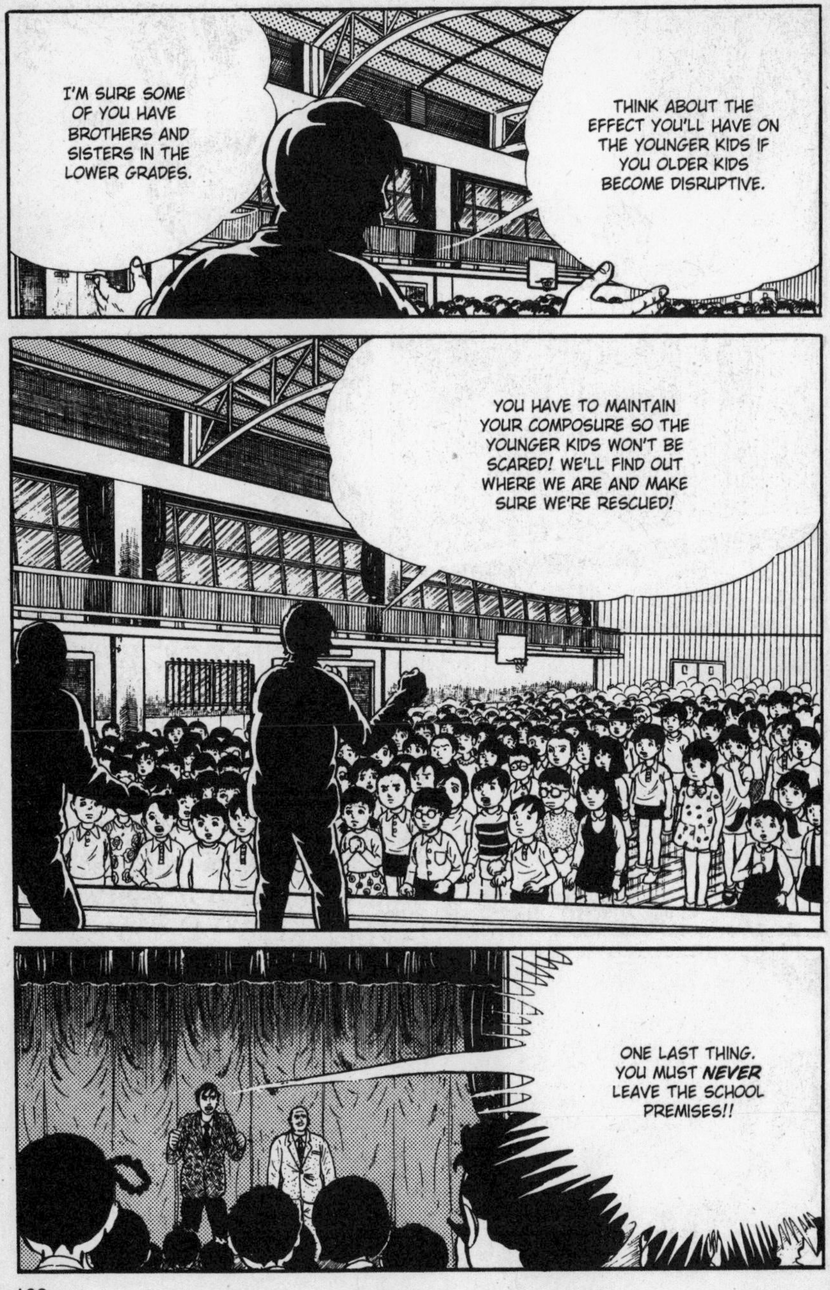
THINK ABOUT THE EFFECT YOU'LL HAVE ON THE YOUNGER KIDS IF YOU OLDER KIDS BECOME DISRUPTIVE.
I'M SURE SOME OF YOU HAVE BROTHERS AND SISTERS IN THE LOWER GRADES.
YOU HAVE TO MAINTAIN YOUR COMPOSURE SO THE YOUNGER KIDS WON'T BE SCARED! WE'LL FIND OUT WHERE WE ARE AND MAKE SURE WE'RE RESCUED!
ONE LAST THING. YOU MUST ***NEVER*** LEAVE THE SCHOOL PREMISES!!

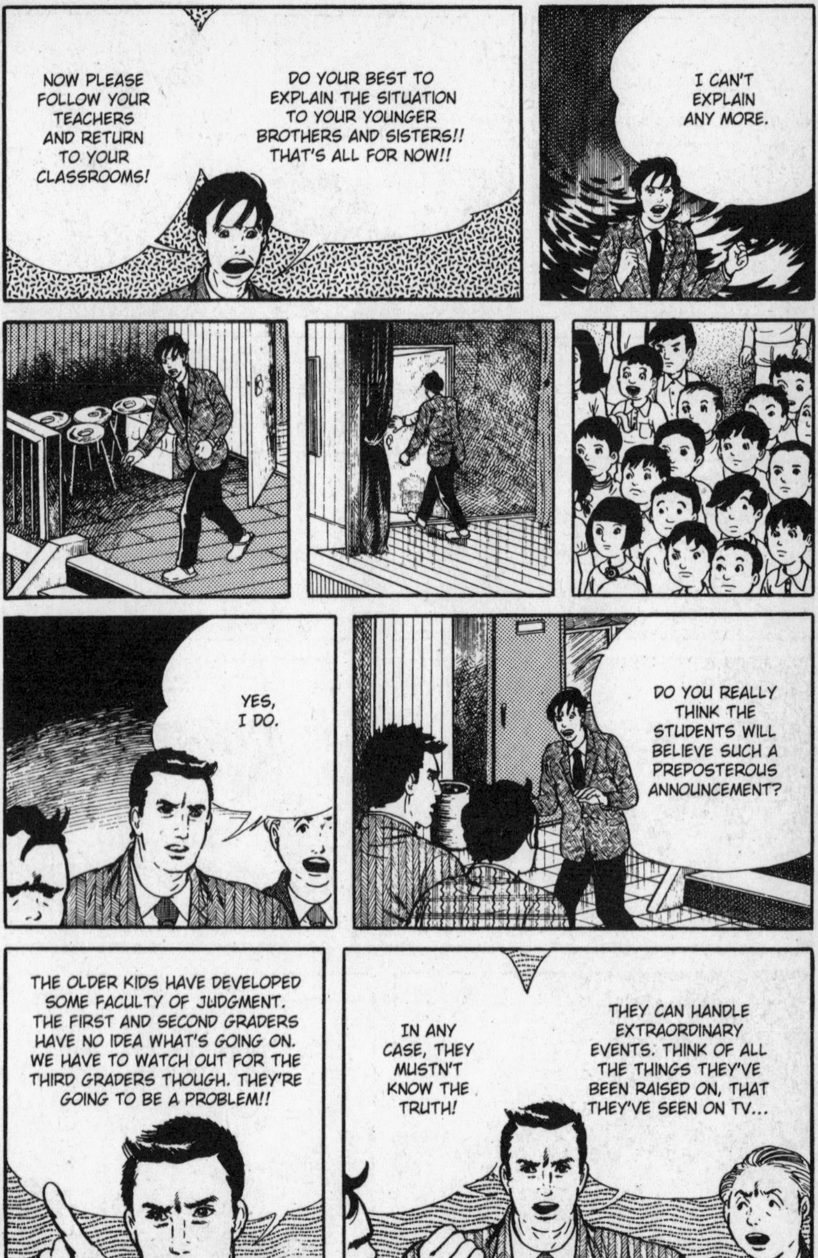
I CAN'T EXPLAIN ANY MORE.
DO YOUR BEST TO EXPLAIN THE SITUATION TO YOUR YOUNGER BROTHERS AND SISTERS!! THAT'S ALL FOR NOW!!
NOW PLEASE FOLLOW YOUR TEACHERS AND RETURN TO YOUR CLASSROOMS!
DO YOU REALLY THINK THE STUDENTS WILL BELIEVE SUCH A PREPOSTEROUS ANNOUNCEMENT?
YES, I DO.
THEY CAN HANDLE EXTRAORDINARY EVENTS. THINK OF ALL THE THINGS THEY'VE BEEN RAISED ON, THAT THEY'VE SEEN ON TV...
IN ANY CASE, THEY MUSTN'T KNOW THE TRUTH!
THE OLDER KIDS HAVE DEVELOPED SOME FACULTY OF JUDGMENT. THE FIRST AND SECOND GRADERS HAVE NO IDEA WHAT'S GOING ON. WE HAVE TO WATCH OUT FOR THE THIRD GRADERS THOUGH. THEY'RE GOING TO BE A PROBLEM!!

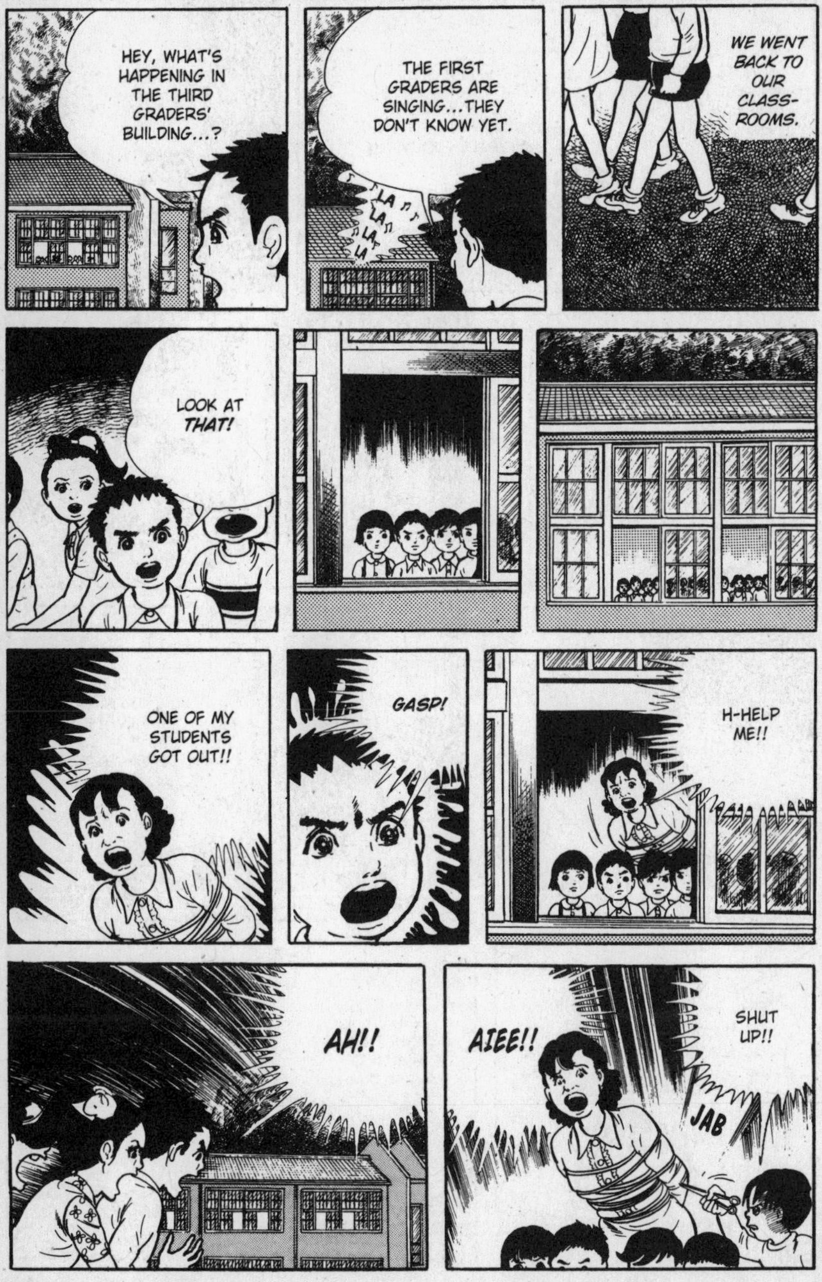
WE WENT BACK TO OUR CLASS-ROOMS.
THE FIRST GRADERS ARE SINGING...THEY DON'T KNOW YET.
LA LA LA LA
HEY, WHAT'S HAPPENING IN THE THIRD GRADERS' BUILDING...?
LOOK AT *THAT!*
H-HELP ME!!
GASP!
ONE OF MY STUDENTS GOT OUT!!
SHUT UP!!
AIEE!!
JAB
AH!!

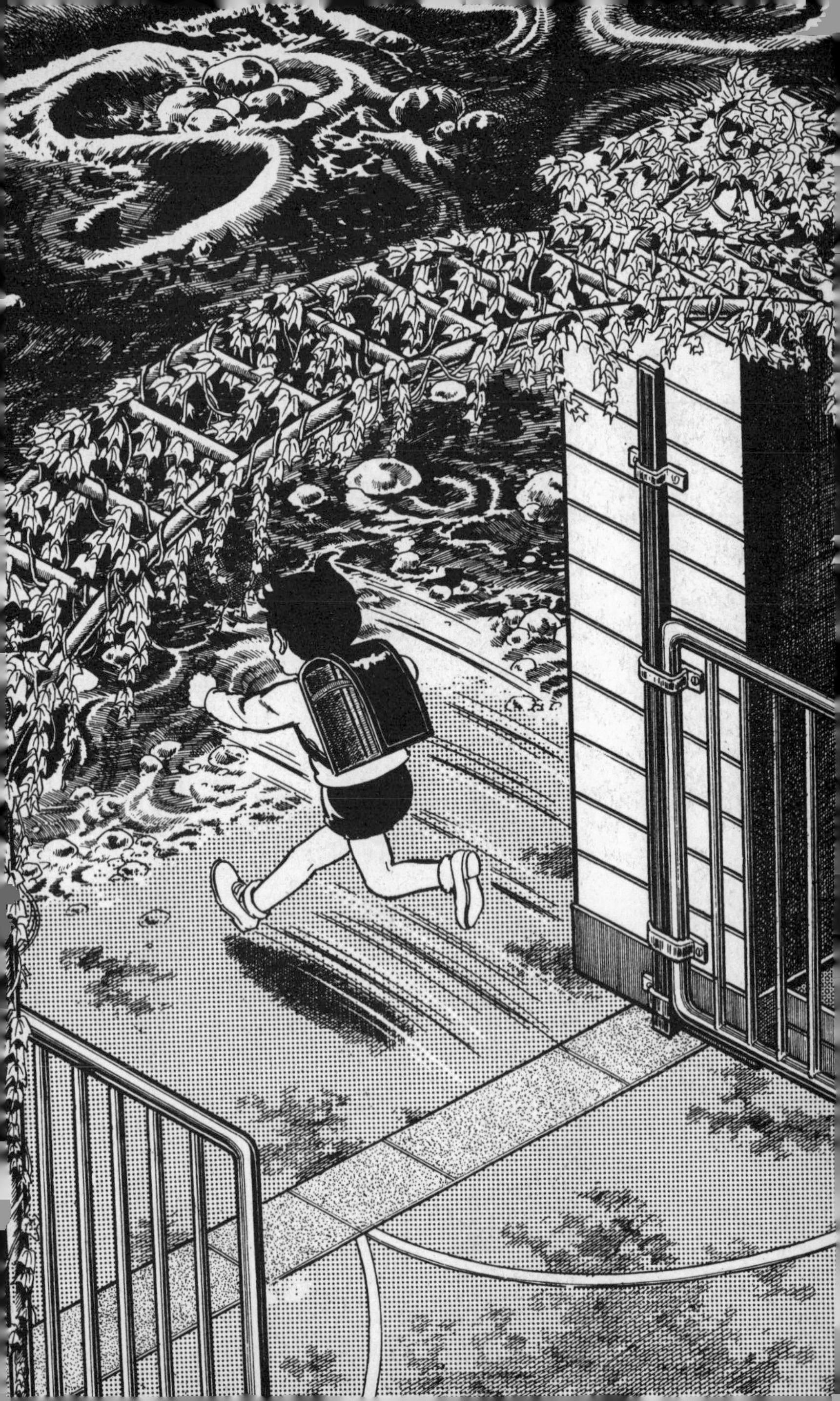

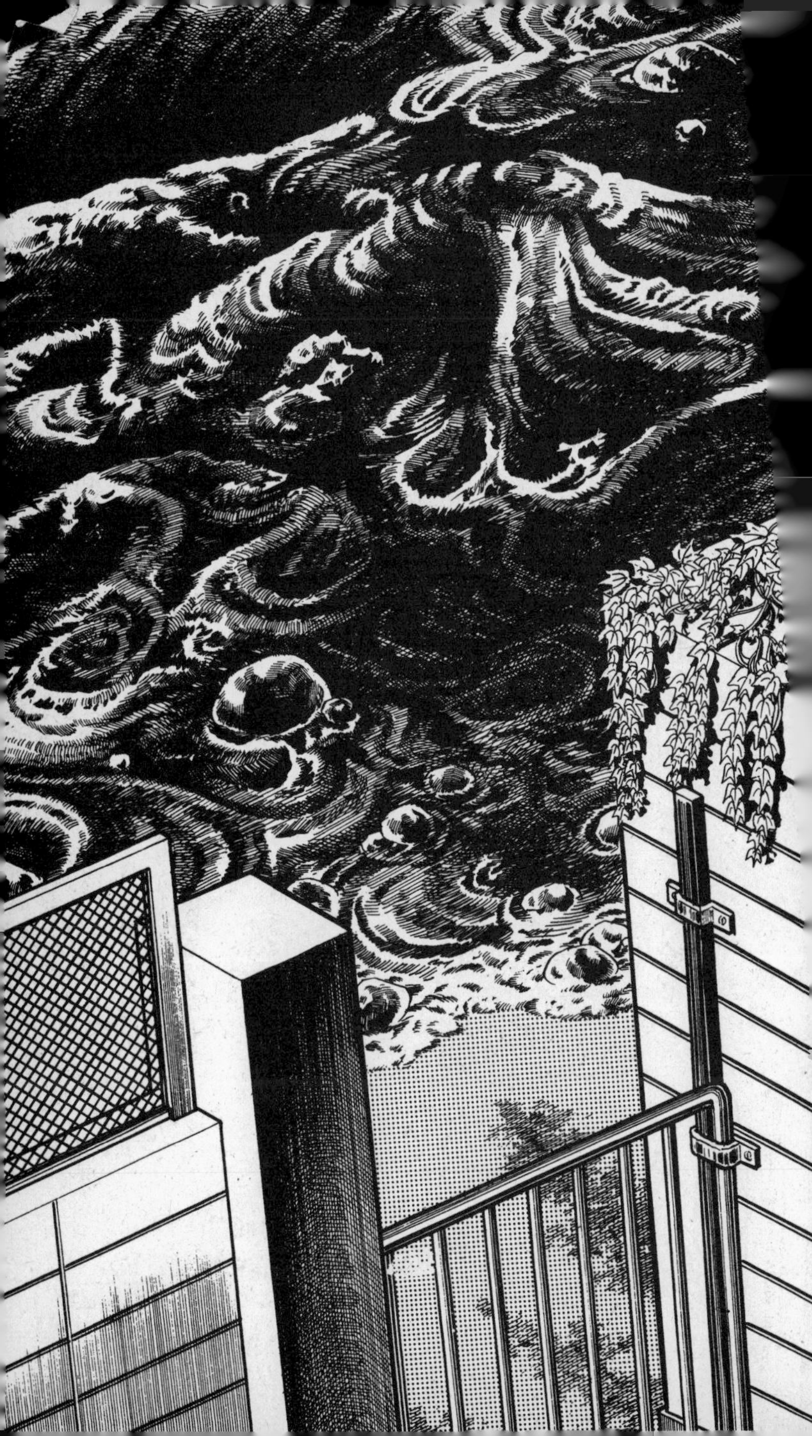

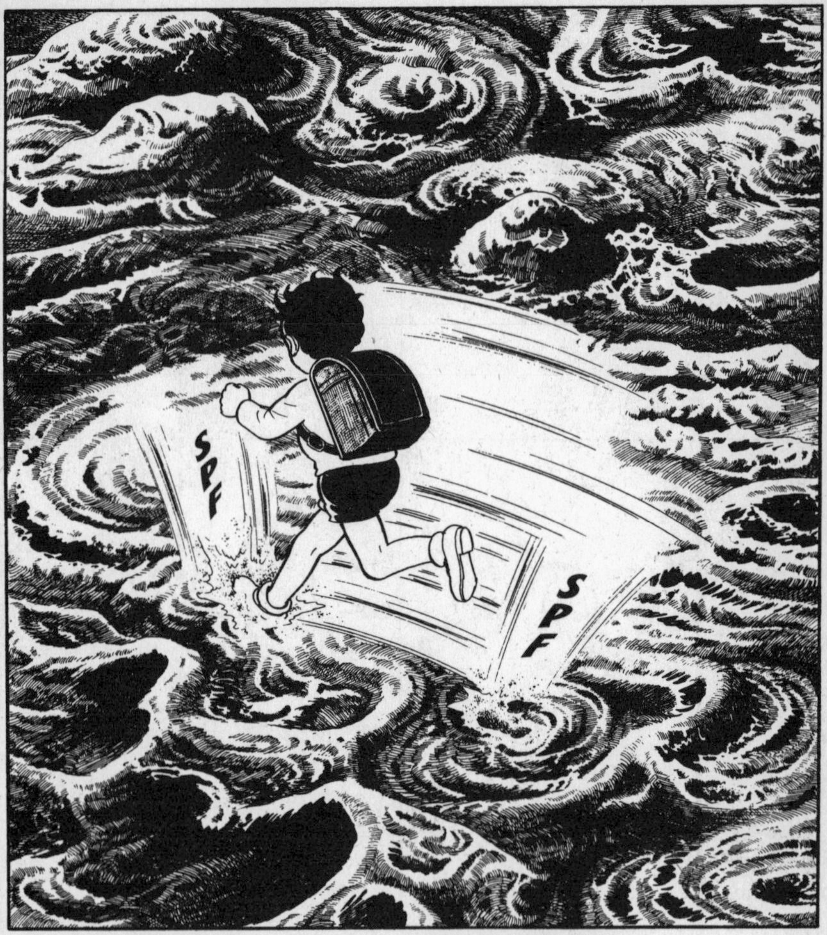
SPF
SPF
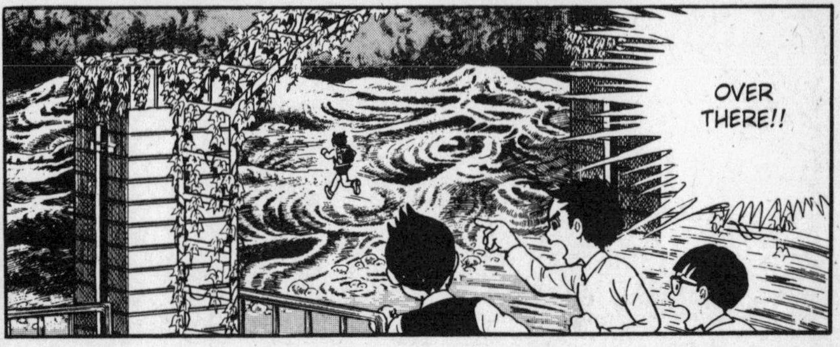
OVER THERE!!

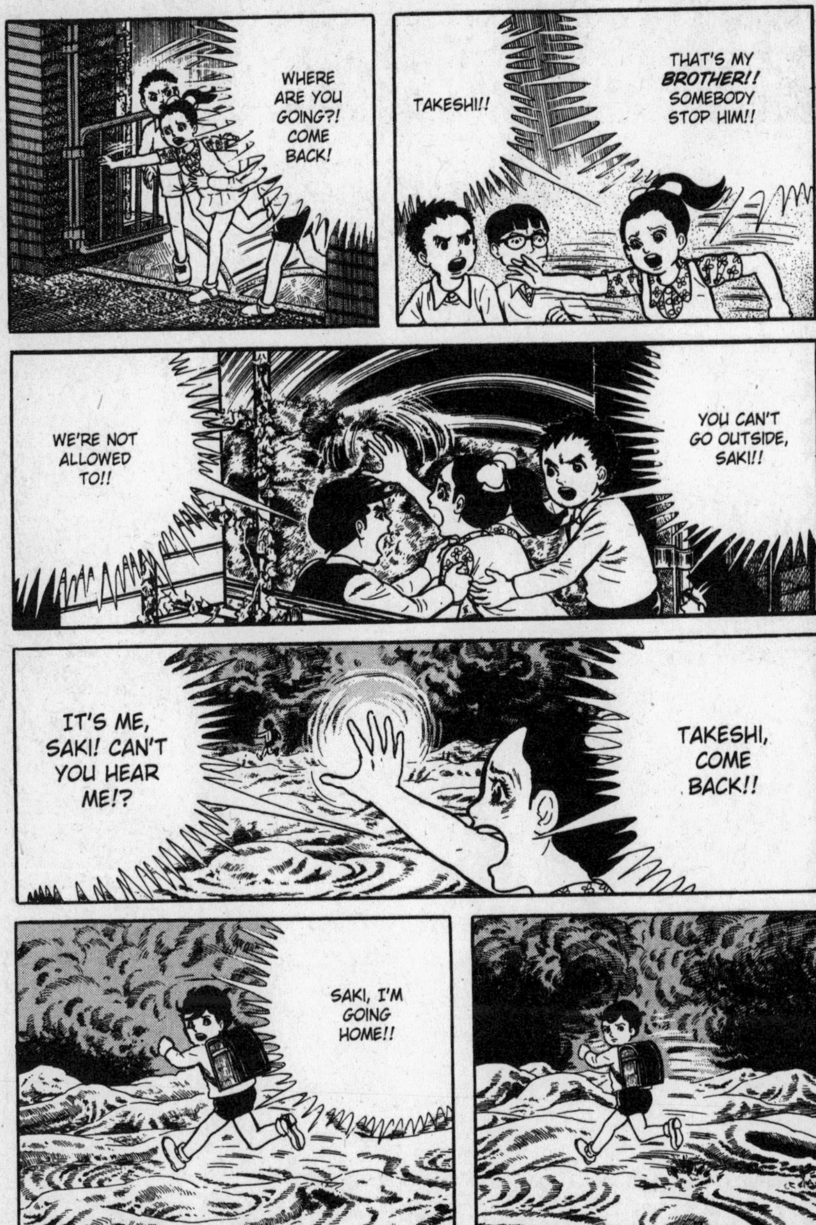
THAT'S MY BROTHER!! SOMEBODY STOP HIM!!
TAKESHI!!
WHERE ARE YOU GOING?! COME BACK!
YOU CAN'T GO OUTSIDE, SAKI!!
WE'RE NOT ALLOWED TO!!
TAKESHI, COME BACK!!
IT'S ME, SAKI! CAN'T YOU HEAR ME!?
SAKI, I'M GOING HOME!!

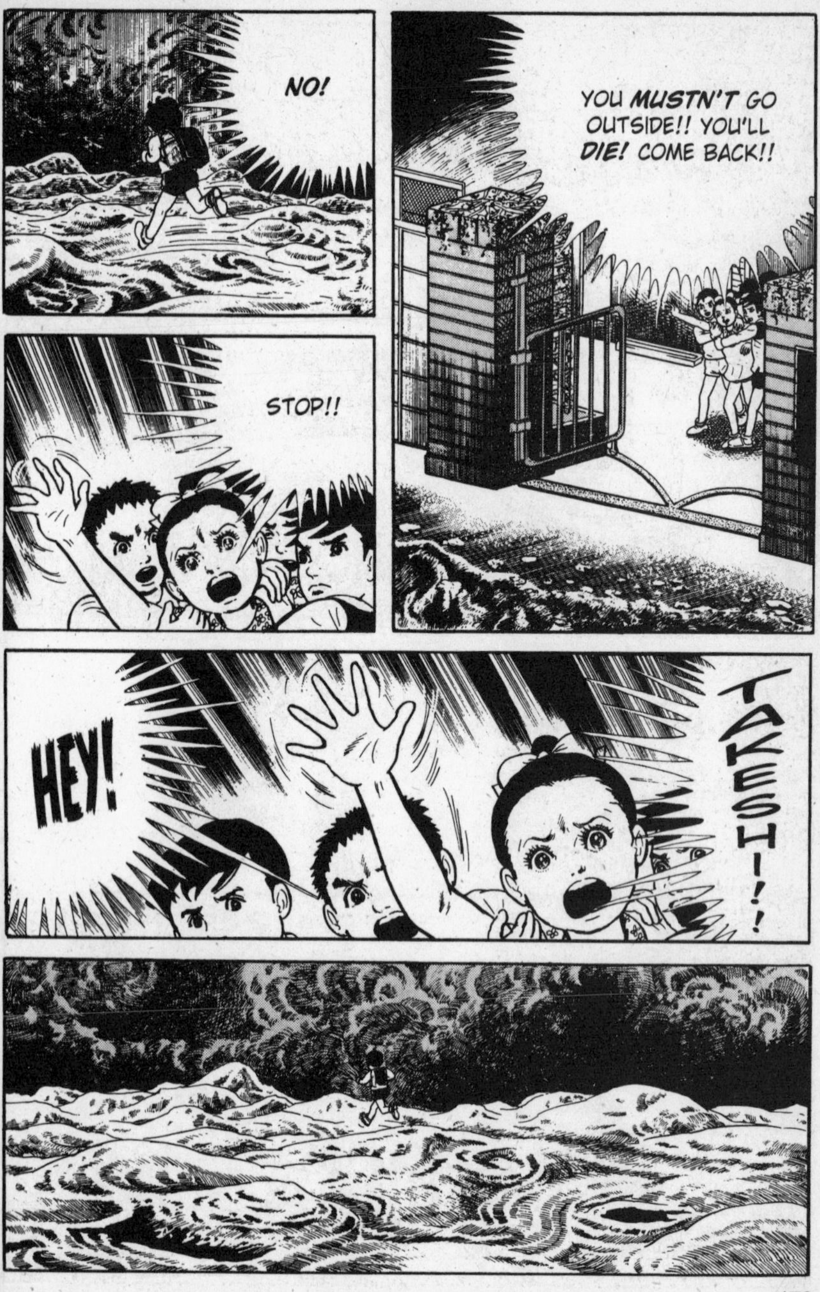

YOU MUSTN'T GO OUTSIDE!! YOU'LL DIE! COME BACK!!
NO!
STOP!!
TAKESHI!!
HEY!

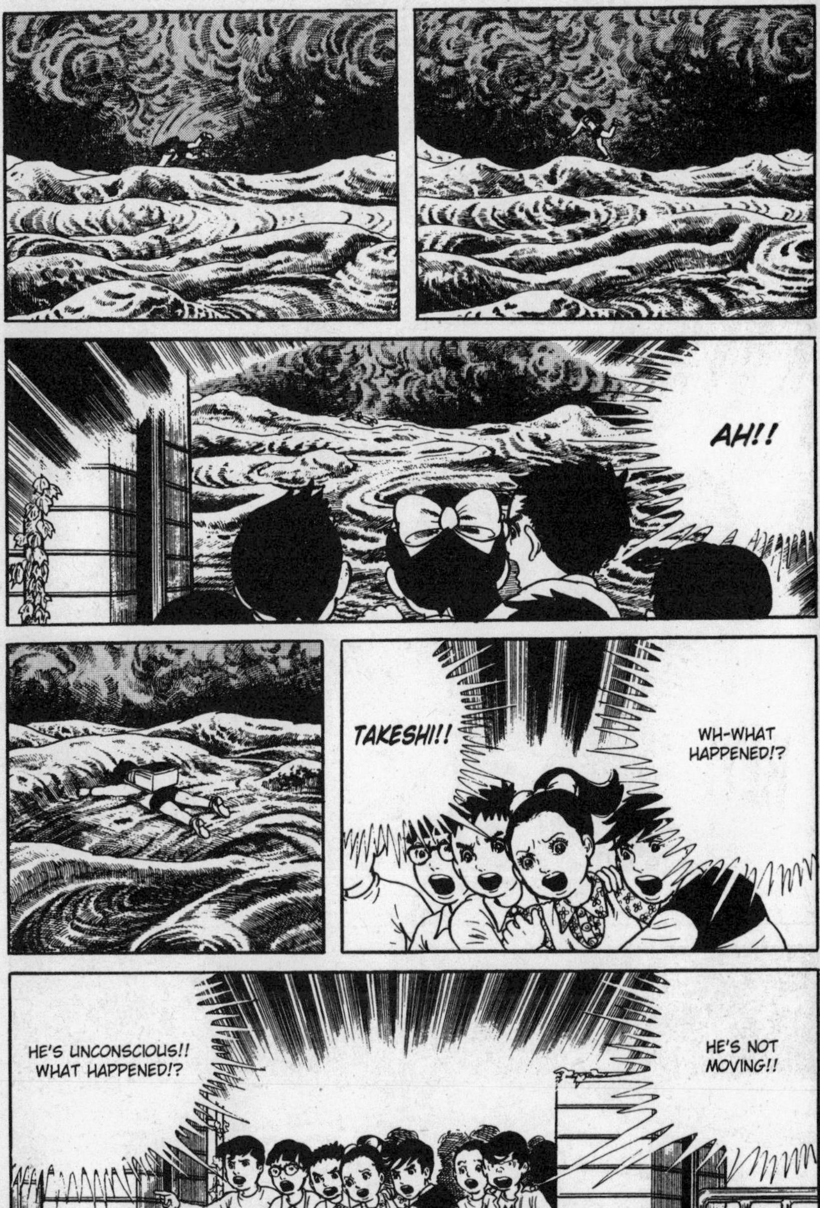
AH!!
WH-WHAT HAPPENED!?
TAKESHI!!
HE'S NOT MOVING!!
HE'S UNCONSCIOUS!! WHAT HAPPENED!?

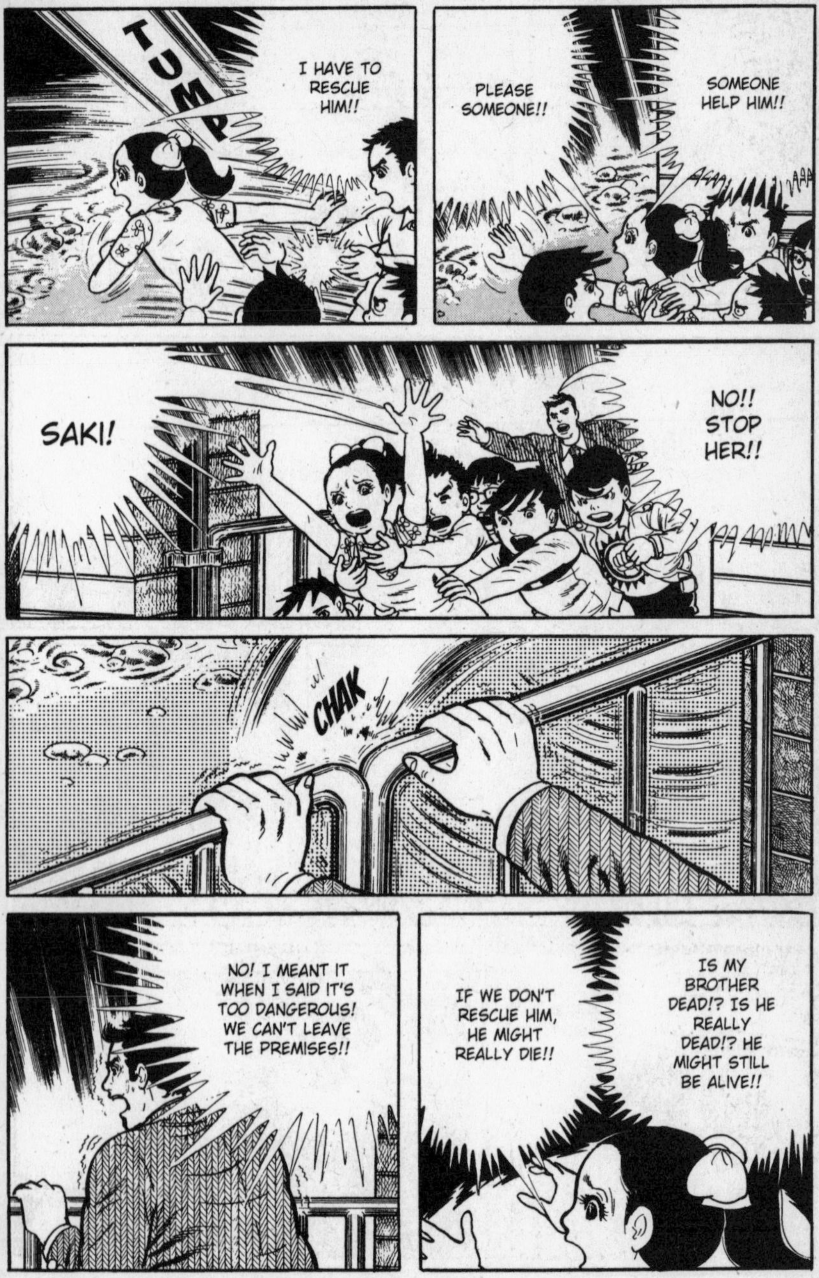
SOMEONE HELP HIM!!
PLEASE SOMEONE!!
TUMP
I HAVE TO RESCUE HIM!!
NO!! STOP HER!!
SAKI!
CHAK
IS MY BROTHER DEAD!? IS HE REALLY DEAD!? HE MIGHT STILL BE ALIVE!!
IF WE DON'T RESCUE HIM, HE MIGHT REALLY DIE!!
NO! I MEANT IT WHEN I SAID IT'S TOO DANGEROUS! WE CAN'T LEAVE THE PREMISES!!

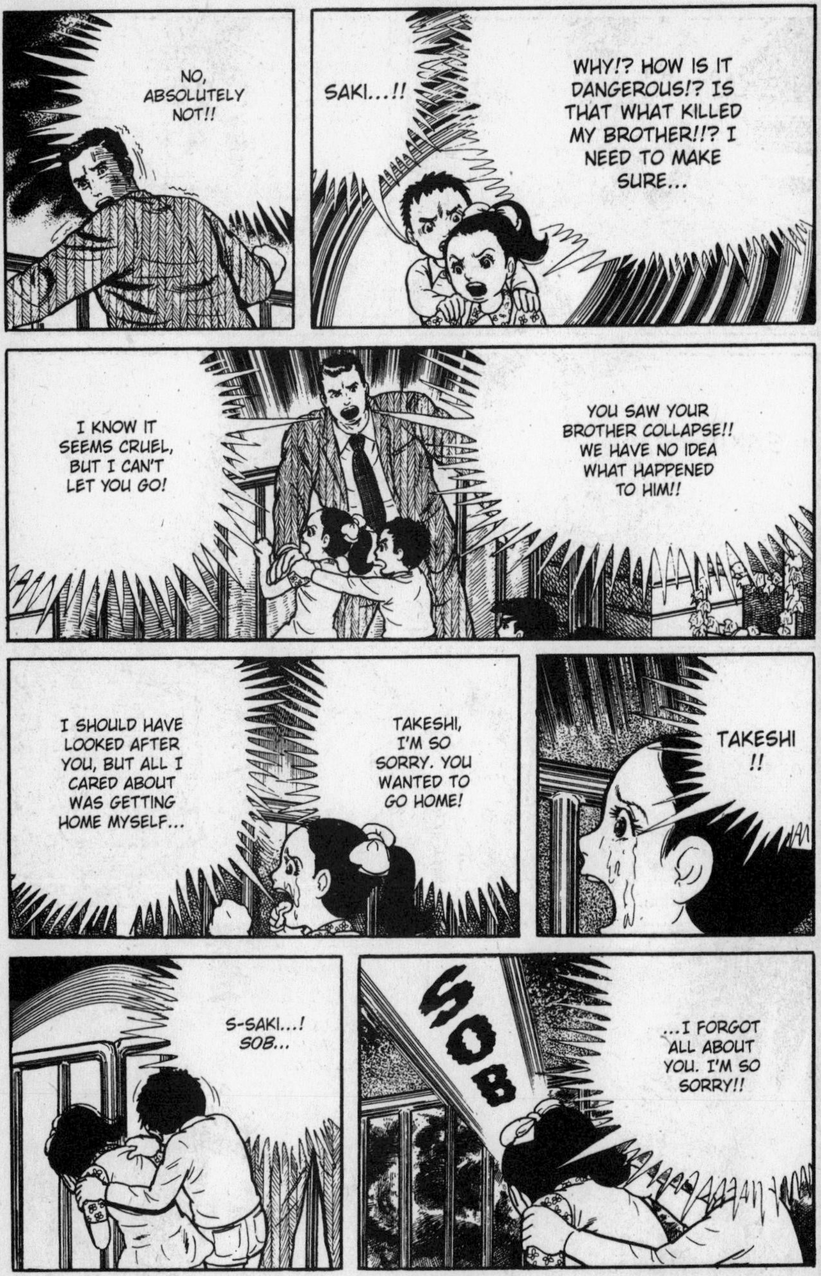
WHY!? HOW IS IT DANGEROUS!? IS THAT WHAT KILLED MY BROTHER!!? I NEED TO MAKE SURE...
SAKI...!!
NO, ABSOLUTELY NOT!!
YOU SAW YOUR BROTHER COLLAPSE!! WE HAVE NO IDEA WHAT HAPPENED TO HIM!!
I KNOW IT SEEMS CRUEL, BUT I CAN'T LET YOU GO!
TAKESHI !!
TAKESHI, I'M SO SORRY. YOU WANTED TO GO HOME!
I SHOULD HAVE LOOKED AFTER YOU, BUT ALL I CARED ABOUT WAS GETTING HOME MYSELF...
...I FORGOT ALL ABOUT YOU. I'M SO SORRY!!
SOB
S-SAKI...! SOB...

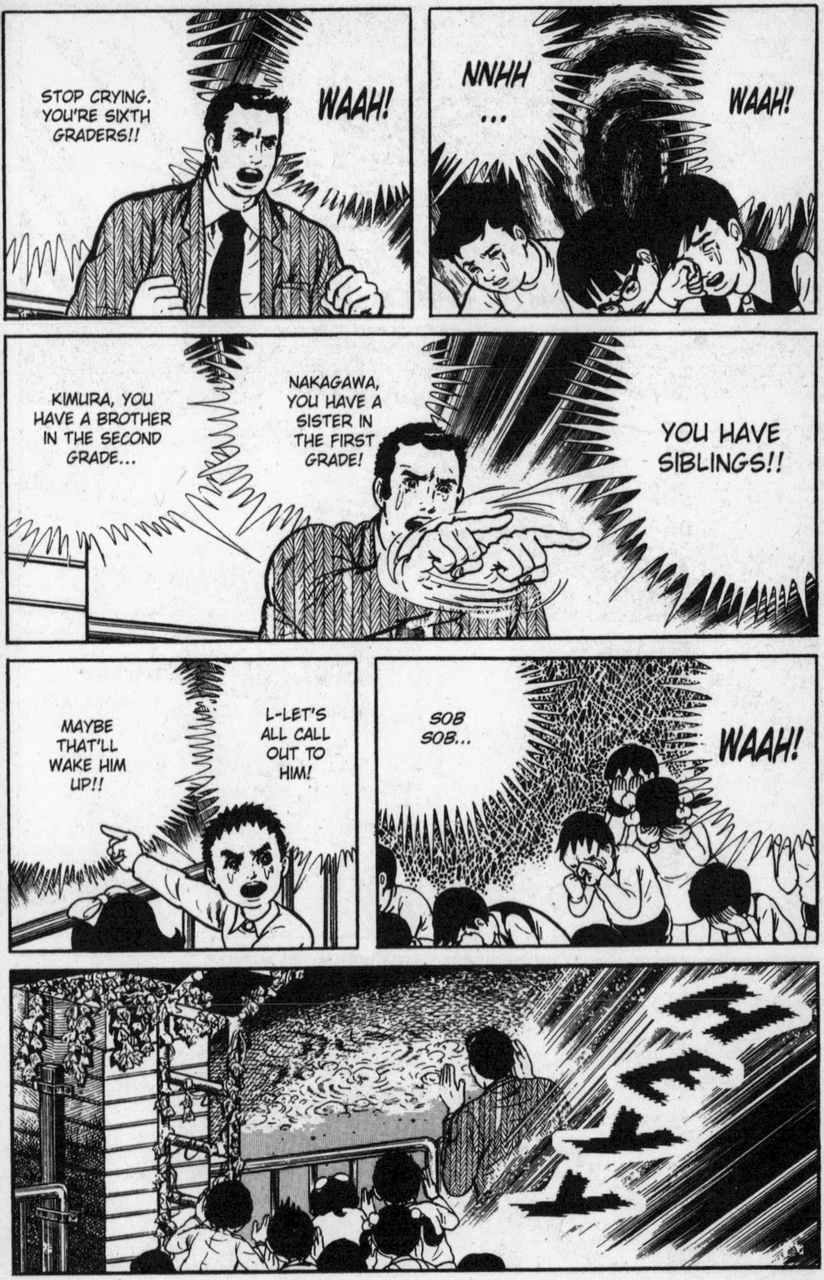
WAAH!
NNHH ...
WAAH!
STOP CRYING. YOU'RE SIXTH GRADERS!!
YOU HAVE SIBLINGS!!
NAKAGAWA, YOU HAVE A SISTER IN THE FIRST GRADE!
KIMURA, YOU HAVE A BROTHER IN THE SECOND GRADE...
WAAH!
SOB SOB...
L-LET'S ALL CALL OUT TO HIM!
MAYBE THAT'LL WAKE HIM UP!!

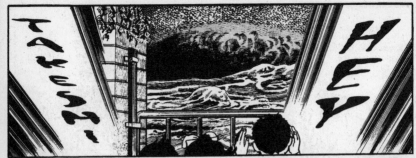

HEY
TAKESHI!
NO MATTER HOW LOUD WE YELLED, SAKI'S BROTHER DIDN'T MOVE.
WAAAH!
AS WE WERE SHOUTING, I SUDDENLY RECALLED MY MOTHER'S FACE.
BUT WHERE WAS SHE? DID YOU REALLY DIE, MOTHER? IT COULDN'T BE TRUE!

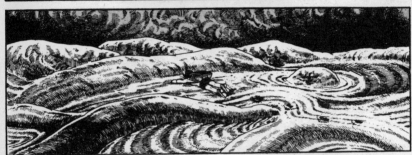

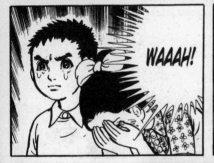

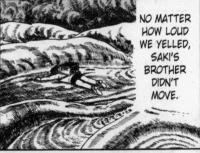

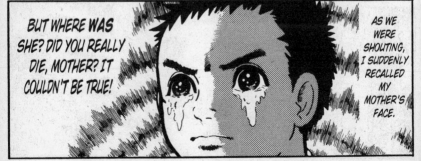

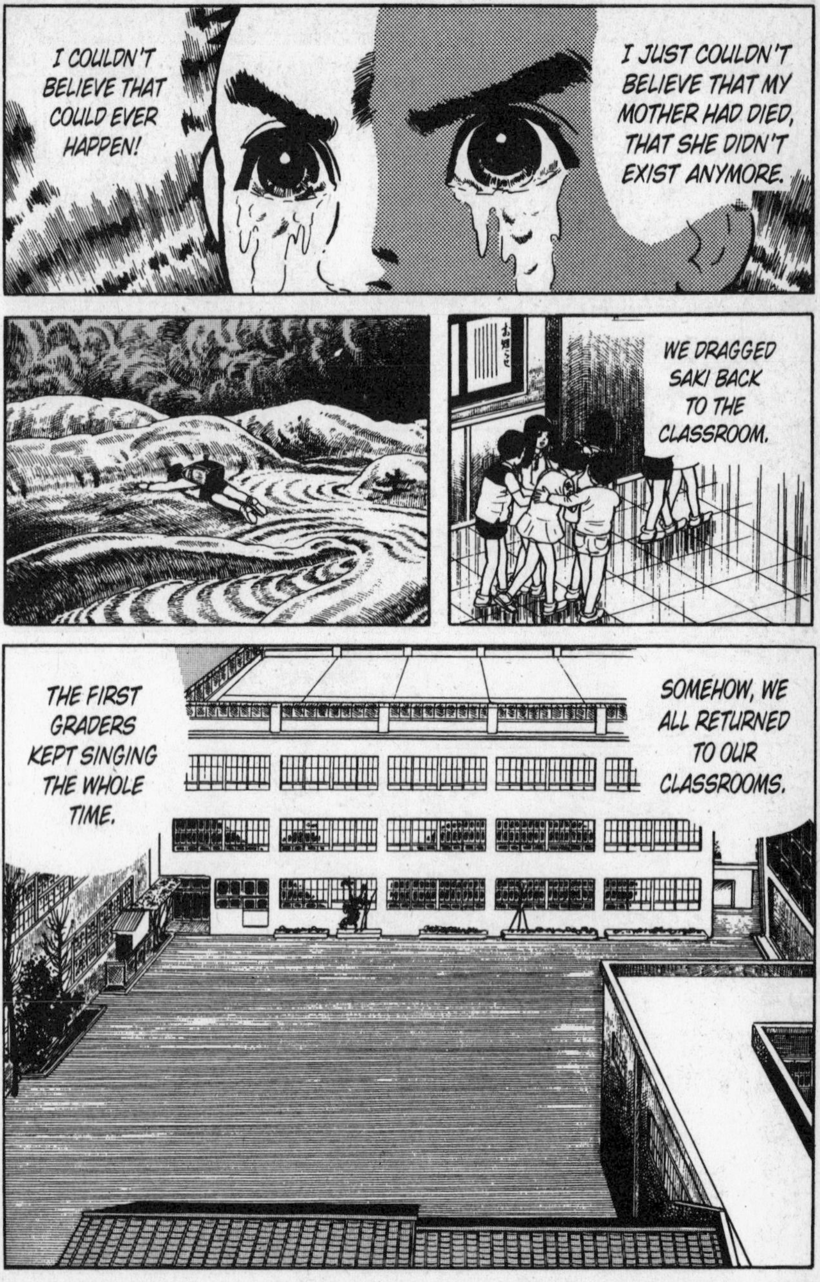
I JUST COULDN'T BELIEVE THAT MY MOTHER HAD DIED, THAT SHE DIDN'T EXIST ANYMORE.
I COULDN'T BELIEVE THAT COULD EVER HAPPEN!
WE DRAGGED SAKI BACK TO THE CLASSROOM.
SOMEHOW, WE ALL RETURNED TO OUR CLASSROOMS.
THE FIRST GRADERS KEPT SINGING THE WHOLE TIME.

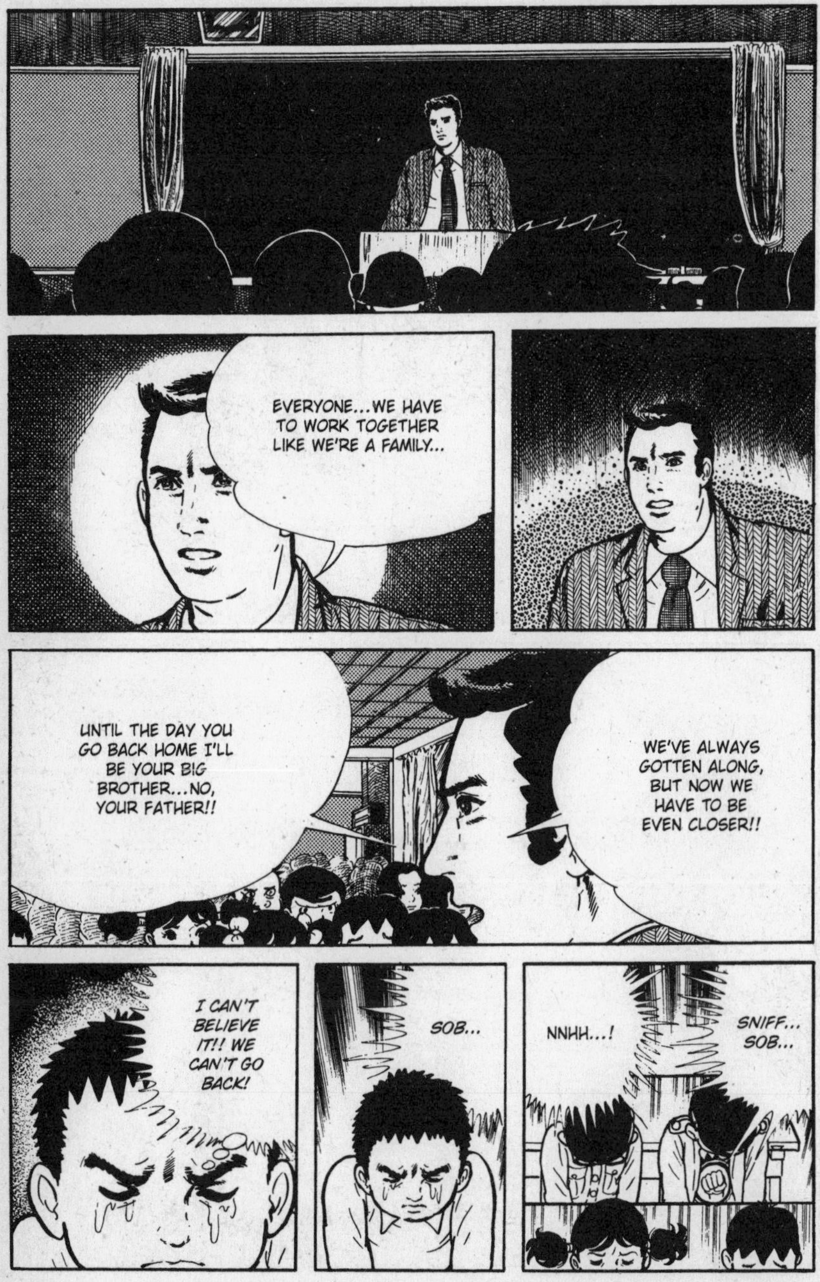
EVERYONE...WE HAVE TO WORK TOGETHER LIKE WE'RE A FAMILY...
WE'VE ALWAYS GOTTEN ALONG, BUT NOW WE HAVE TO BE EVEN CLOSER!!
UNTIL THE DAY YOU GO BACK HOME I'LL BE YOUR BIG BROTHER...NO, YOUR FATHER!!
SNIFF... SOB...
NNHH...!
SOB...
I CAN'T BELIEVE IT!! WE CAN'T GO BACK!

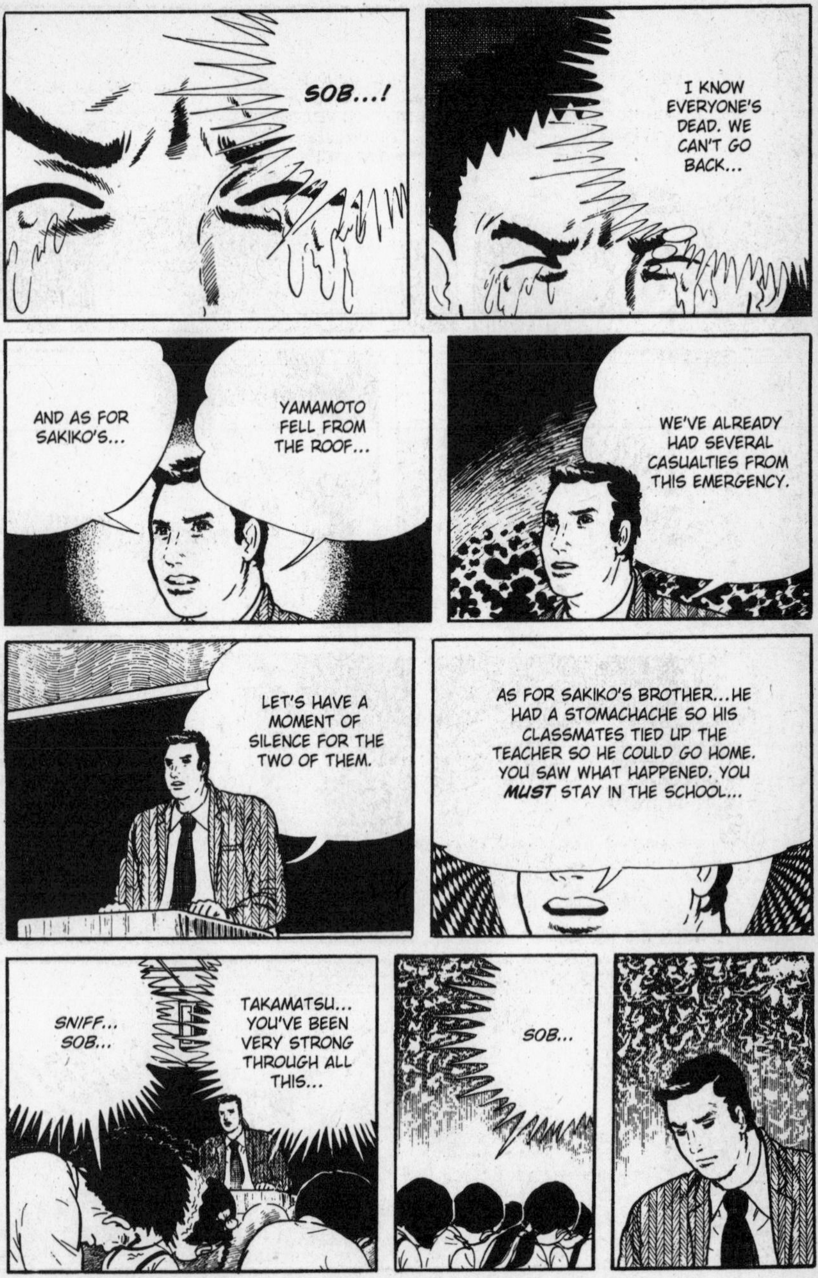
I KNOW EVERYONE'S DEAD. WE CAN'T GO BACK...
SOB...!
WE'VE ALREADY HAD SEVERAL CASUALTIES FROM THIS EMERGENCY.
YAMAMOTO FELL FROM THE ROOF...
AND AS FOR SAKIKO'S...
AS FOR SAKIKO'S BROTHER...HE HAD A STOMACHACHE SO HIS CLASSMATES TIED UP THE TEACHER SO HE COULD GO HOME. YOU SAW WHAT HAPPENED. YOU ***MUST*** STAY IN THE SCHOOL...
LET'S HAVE A MOMENT OF SILENCE FOR THE TWO OF THEM.
SOB...
TAKAMATSU... YOU'VE BEEN VERY STRONG THROUGH ALL THIS...
SNIFF... SOB...

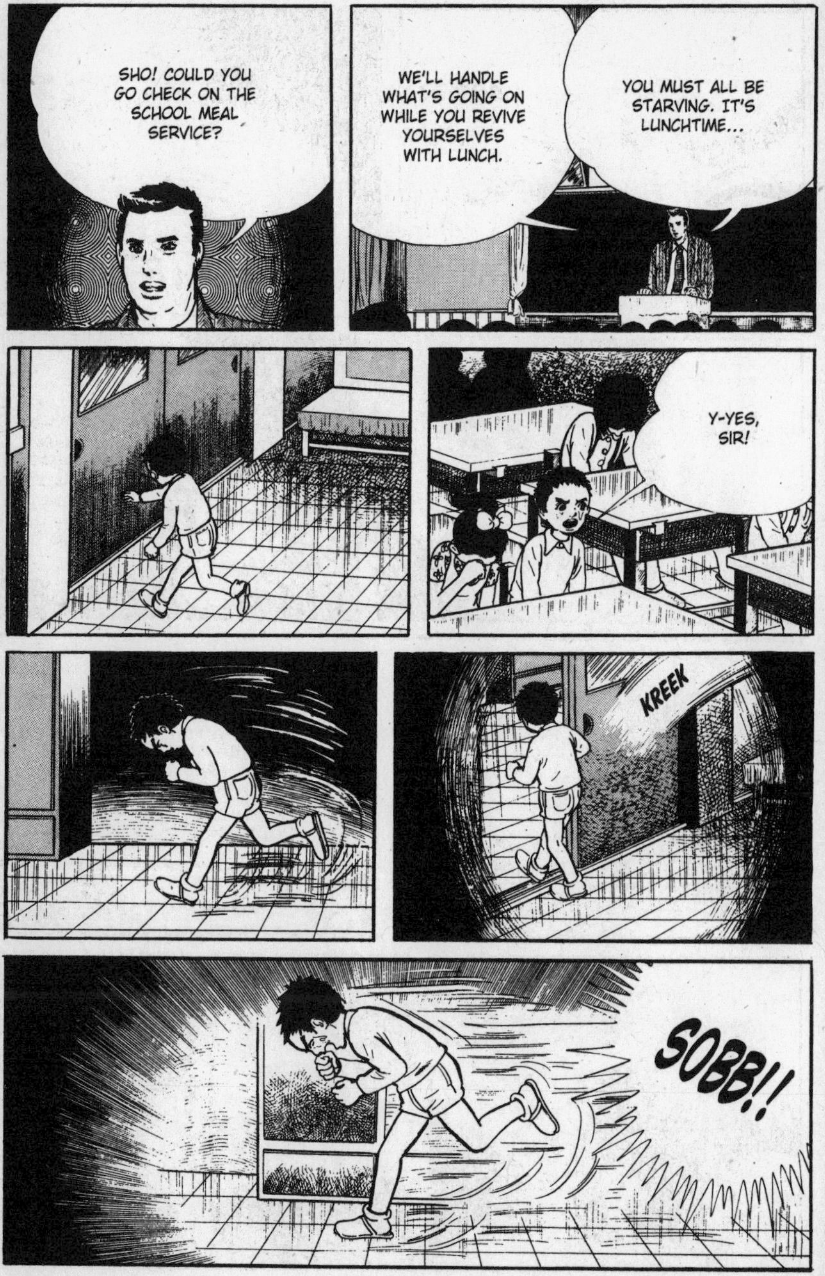
YOU MUST ALL BE STARVING. IT'S LUNCHTIME...
WE'LL HANDLE WHAT'S GOING ON WHILE YOU REVIVE YOURSELVES WITH LUNCH.
SHO! COULD YOU GO CHECK ON THE SCHOOL MEAL SERVICE?
Y-YES, SIR!
KREEK
SOBB!!

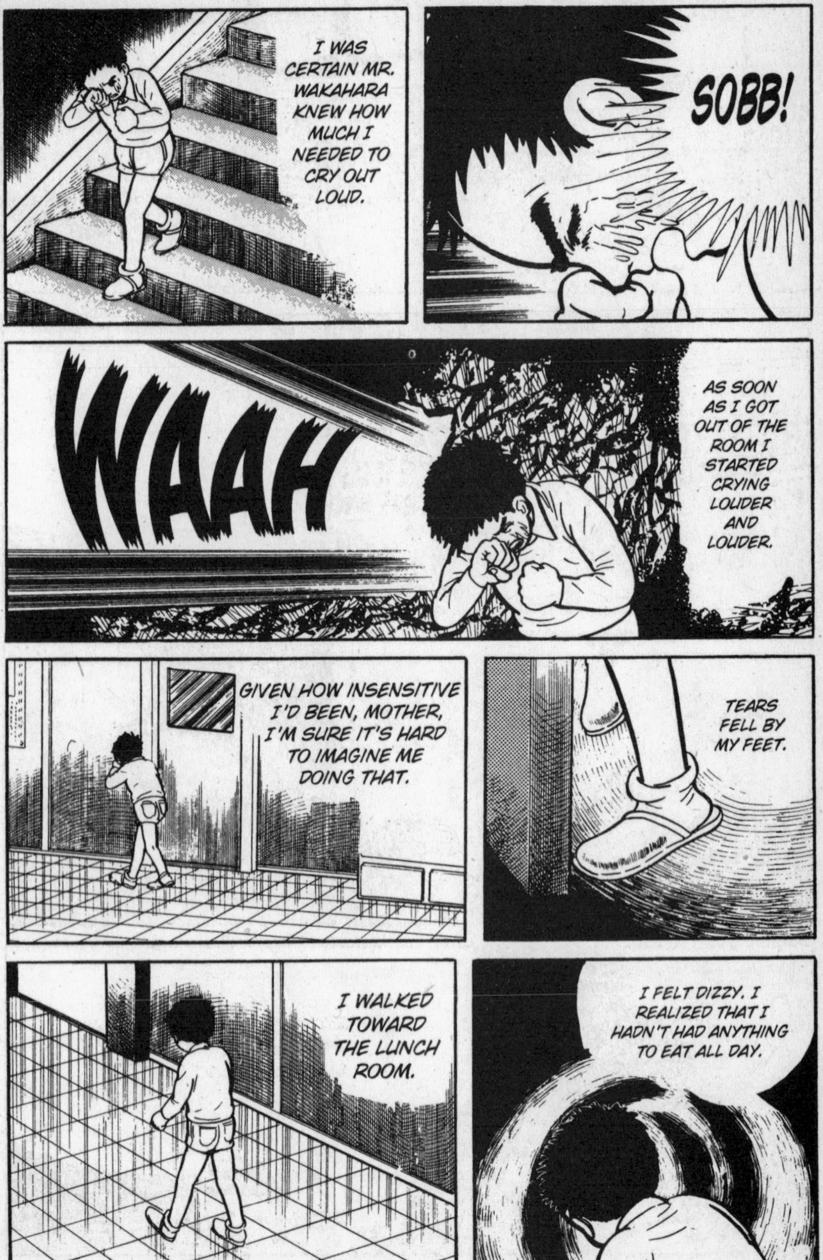
SOBB!
I WAS CERTAIN MR. WAKAHARA KNEW HOW MUCH I NEEDED TO CRY OUT LOUD.
AS SOON AS I GOT OUT OF THE ROOM I STARTED CRYING LOUDER AND LOUDER.
WAAH
TEARS FELL BY MY FEET.
GIVEN HOW INSENSITIVE I'D BEEN, MOTHER, I'M SURE IT'S HARD TO IMAGINE ME DOING THAT.
I FELT DIZZY. I REALIZED THAT I HADN'T HAD ANYTHING TO EAT ALL DAY.
I WALKED TOWARD THE LUNCH ROOM.

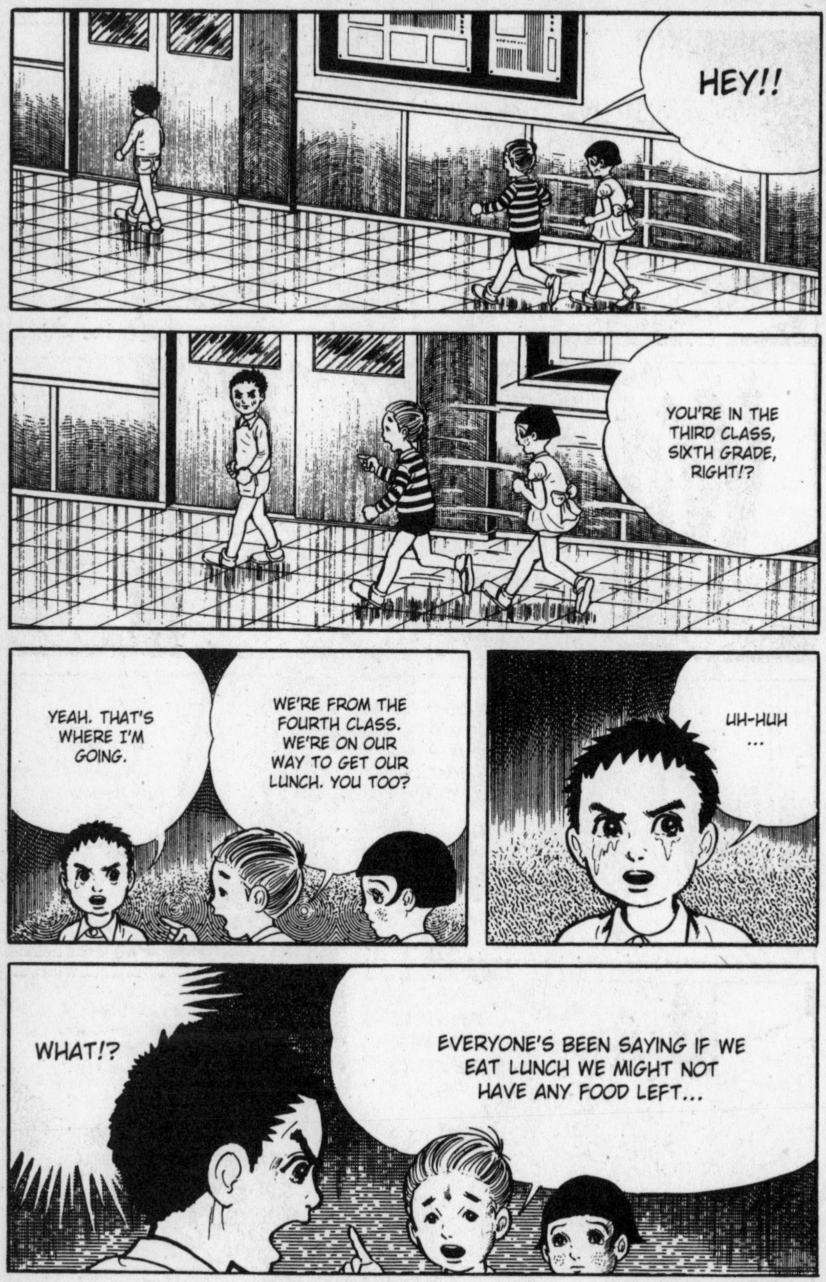
HEY!!
YOU'RE IN THE THIRD CLASS, SIXTH GRADE, RIGHT!?
UH-HUH ...
WE'RE FROM THE FOURTH CLASS. WE'RE ON OUR WAY TO GET OUR LUNCH. YOU TOO?
YEAH. THAT'S WHERE I'M GOING.
EVERYONE'S BEEN SAYING IF WE EAT LUNCH WE MIGHT NOT HAVE ANY FOOD LEFT...
WHAT!?

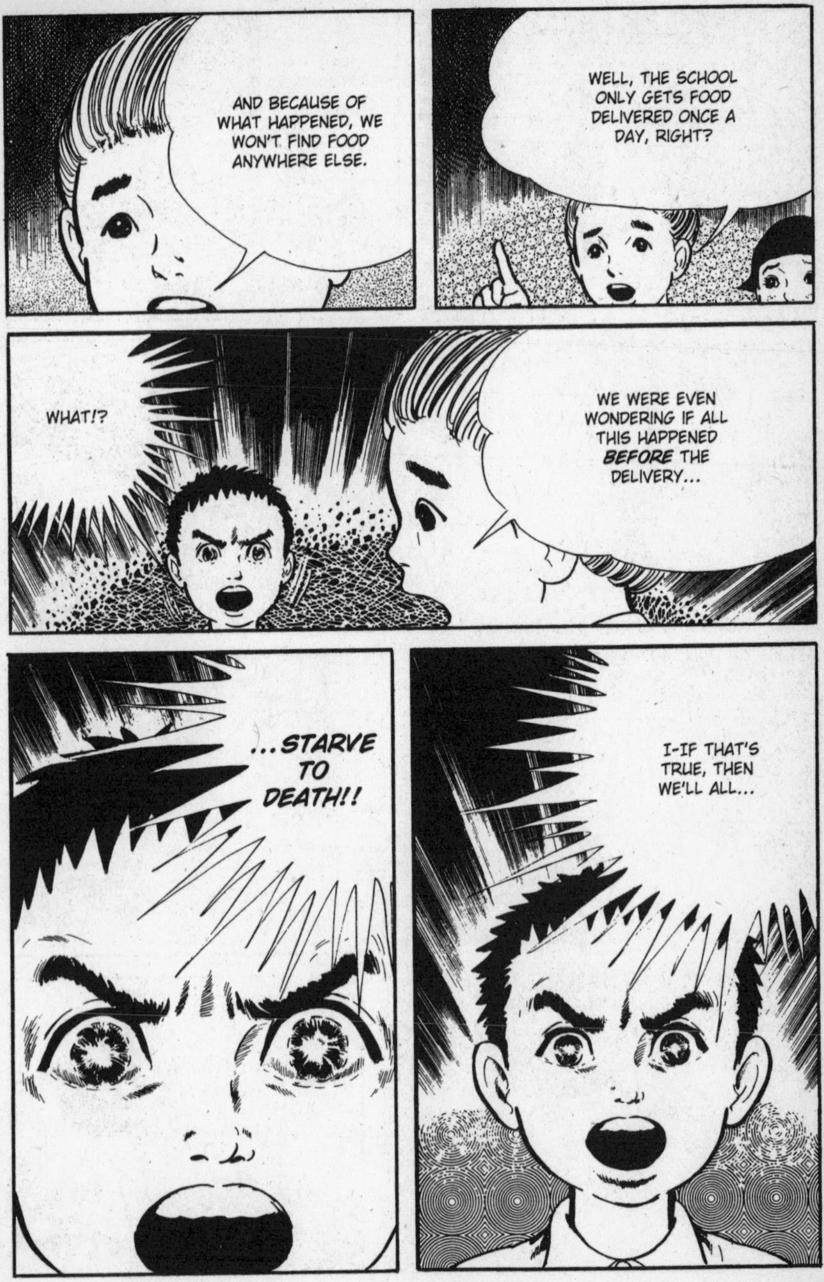

WELL, THE SCHOOL ONLY GETS FOOD DELIVERED ONCE A DAY, RIGHT?
AND BECAUSE OF WHAT HAPPENED, WE WON'T FIND FOOD ANYWHERE ELSE.
WE WERE EVEN WONDERING IF ALL THIS HAPPENED *BEFORE* THE DELIVERY...
WHAT!?
I-IF THAT'S TRUE, THEN WE'LL ALL...
...STARVE TO DEATH!!

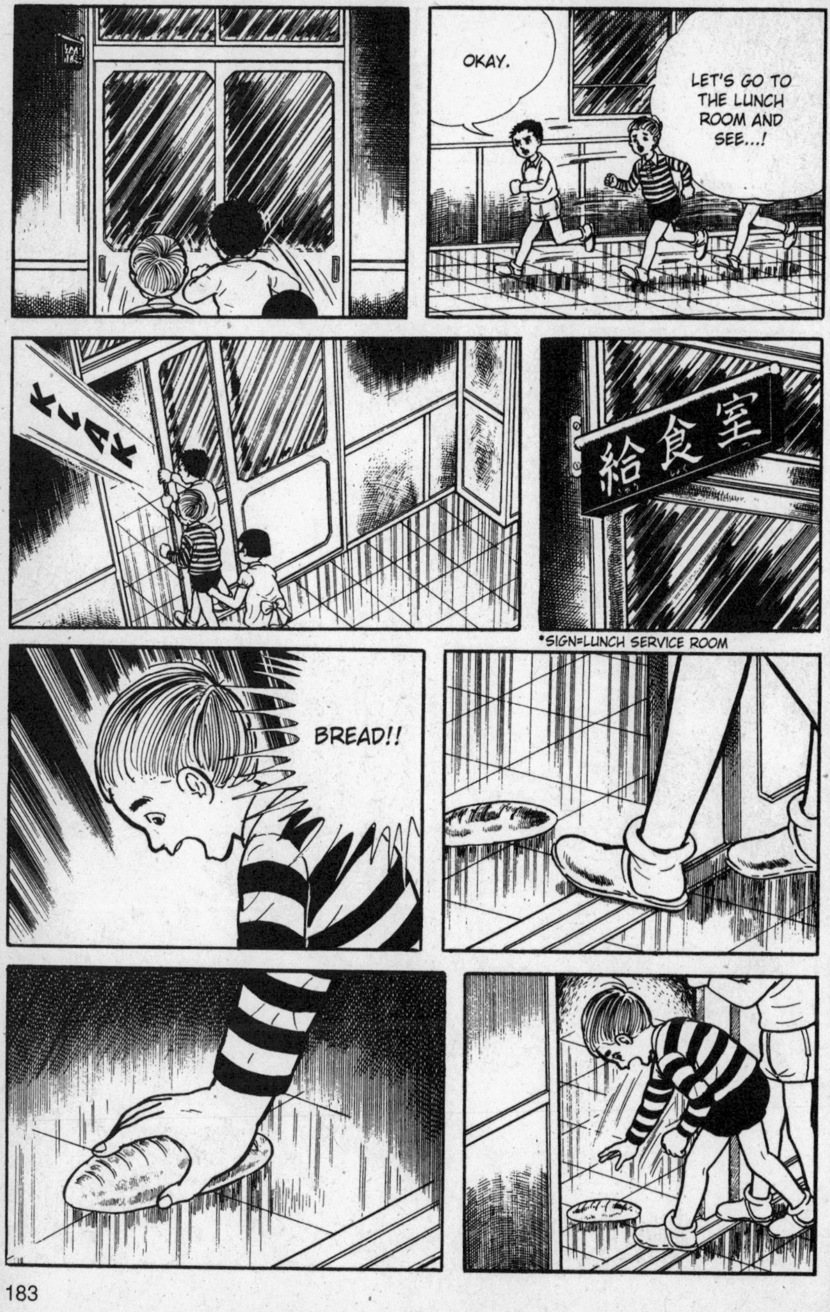
LET'S GO TO THE LUNCH ROOM AND SEE...!
OKAY.
給食室
*SIGN=LUNCH SERVICE ROOM
KLAK
BREAD!!

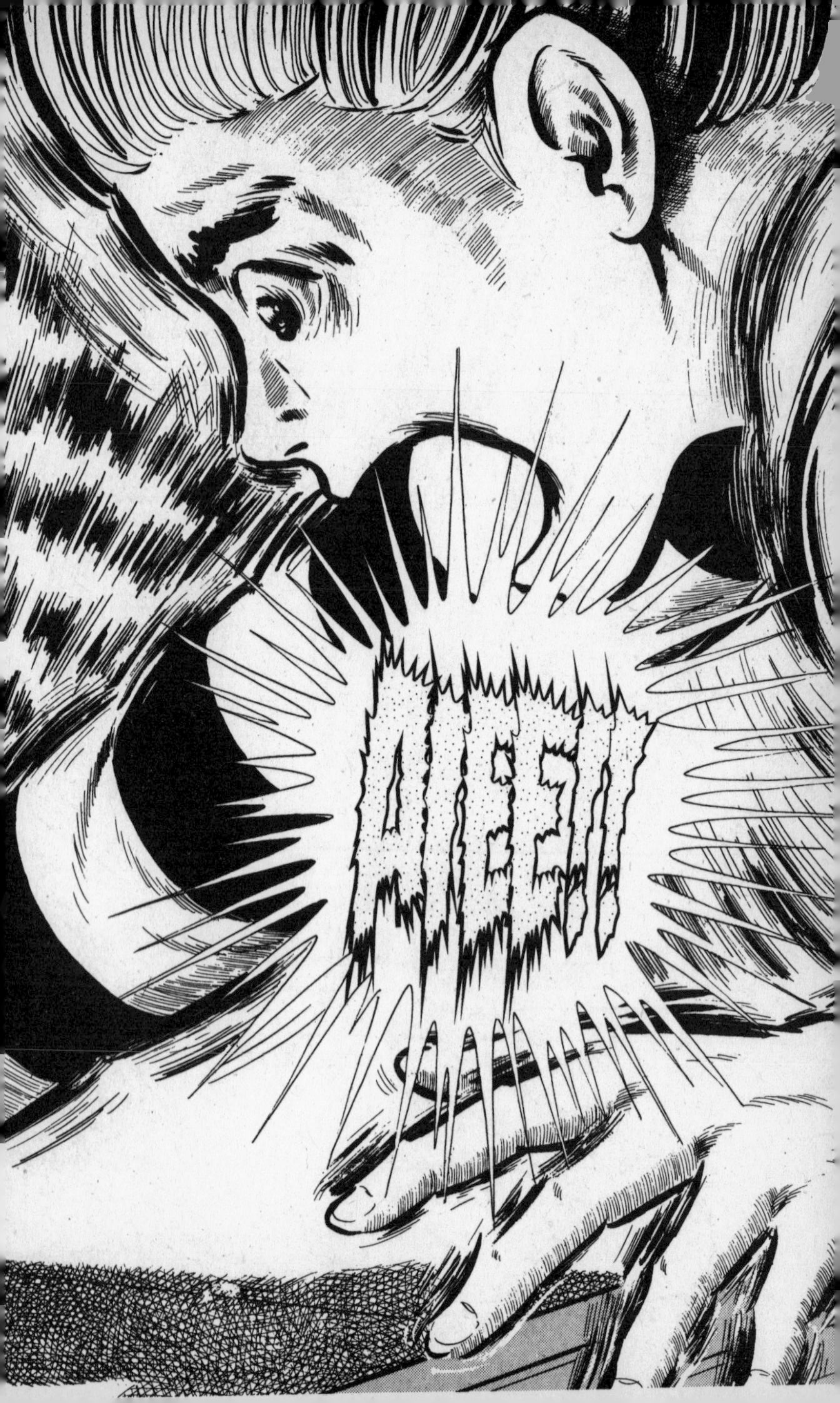

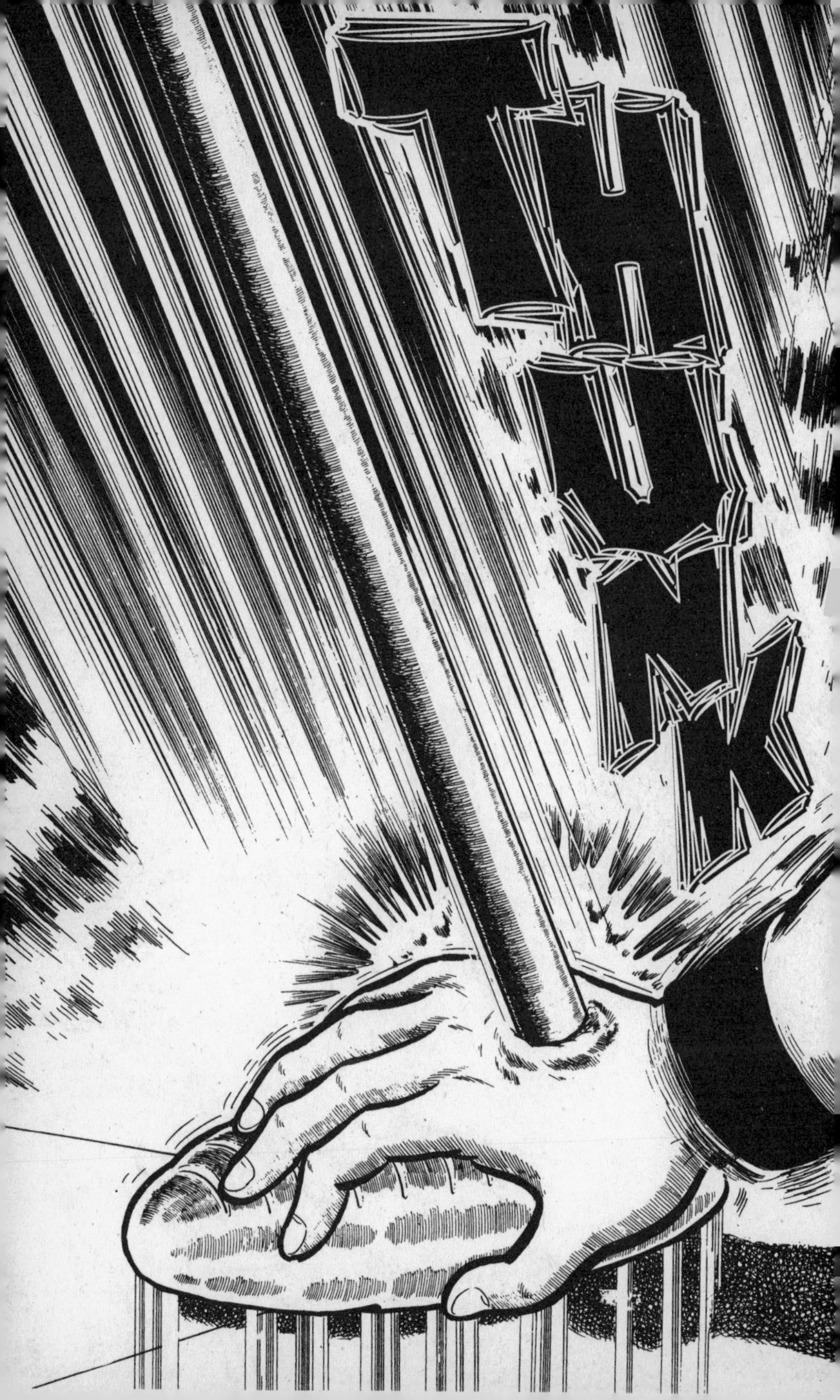
THWACK

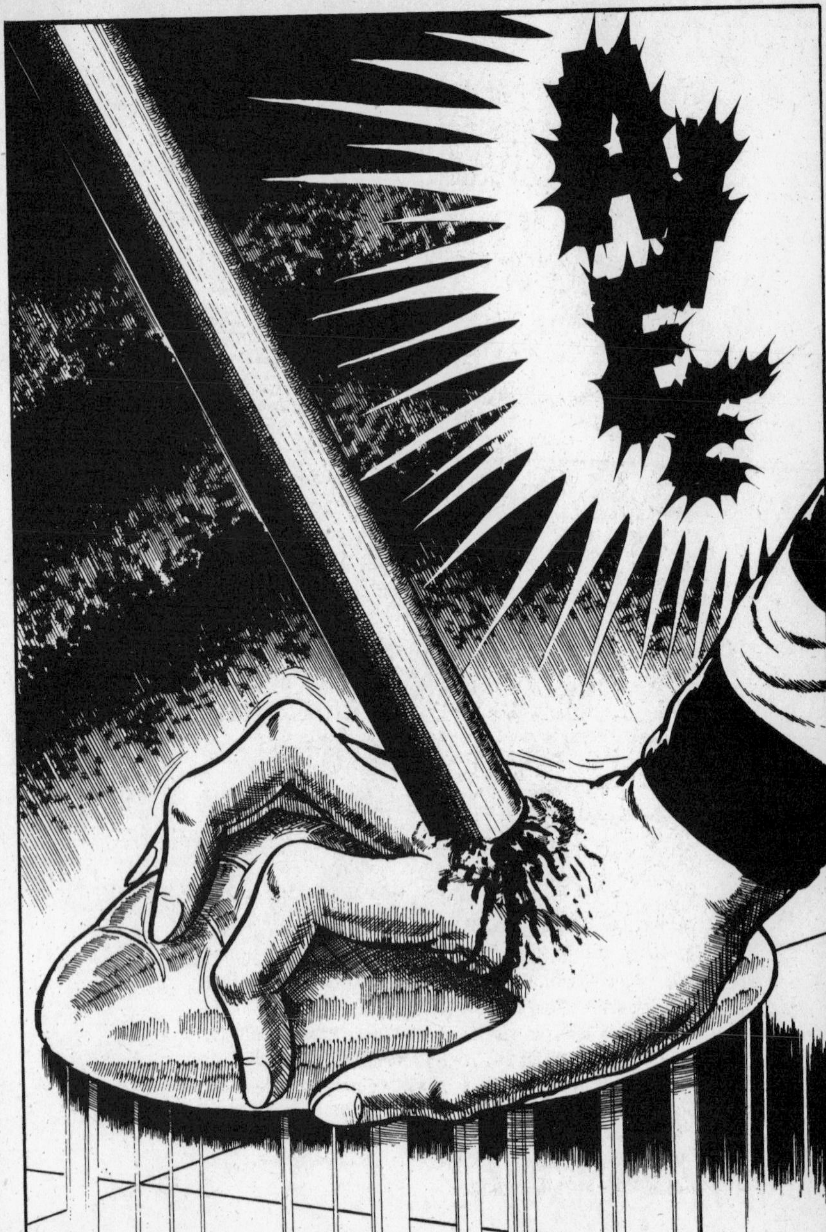

TO BE CONTINUED...

IN THE NEXT VOLUME...

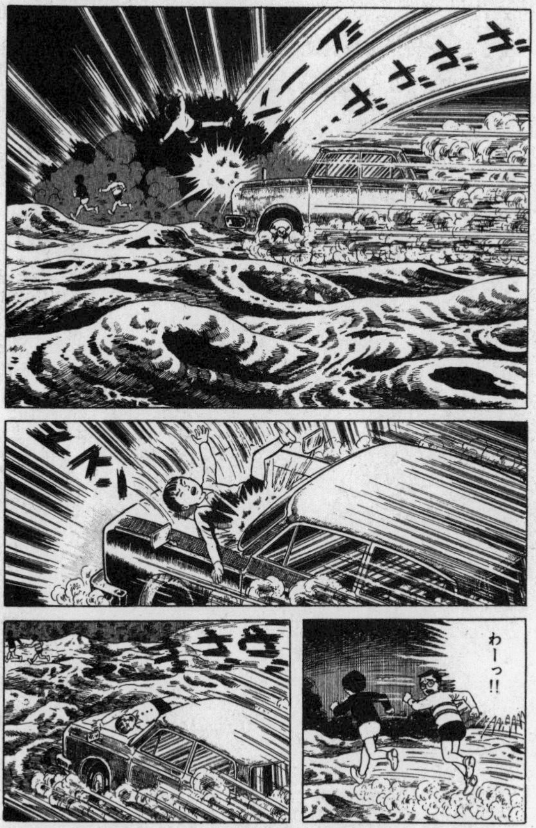
わーっ!!

Madness takes hold as the teachers and students realize they are trapped in a lifeless world! Sekiya, the cafeteria worker, takes control of the school's food supplies, enforcing his authority with a gun. As the adults start to fight among one another, sixth-grader Sho makes the startling discovery of where they are and what has happened to them. Soon, Sho and his classmates must venture into the wasteland beyond the school gates...and make the choice between a slow death from hunger or a quick death at a killer's hands...

AVAILABLE OCTOBER 2006!

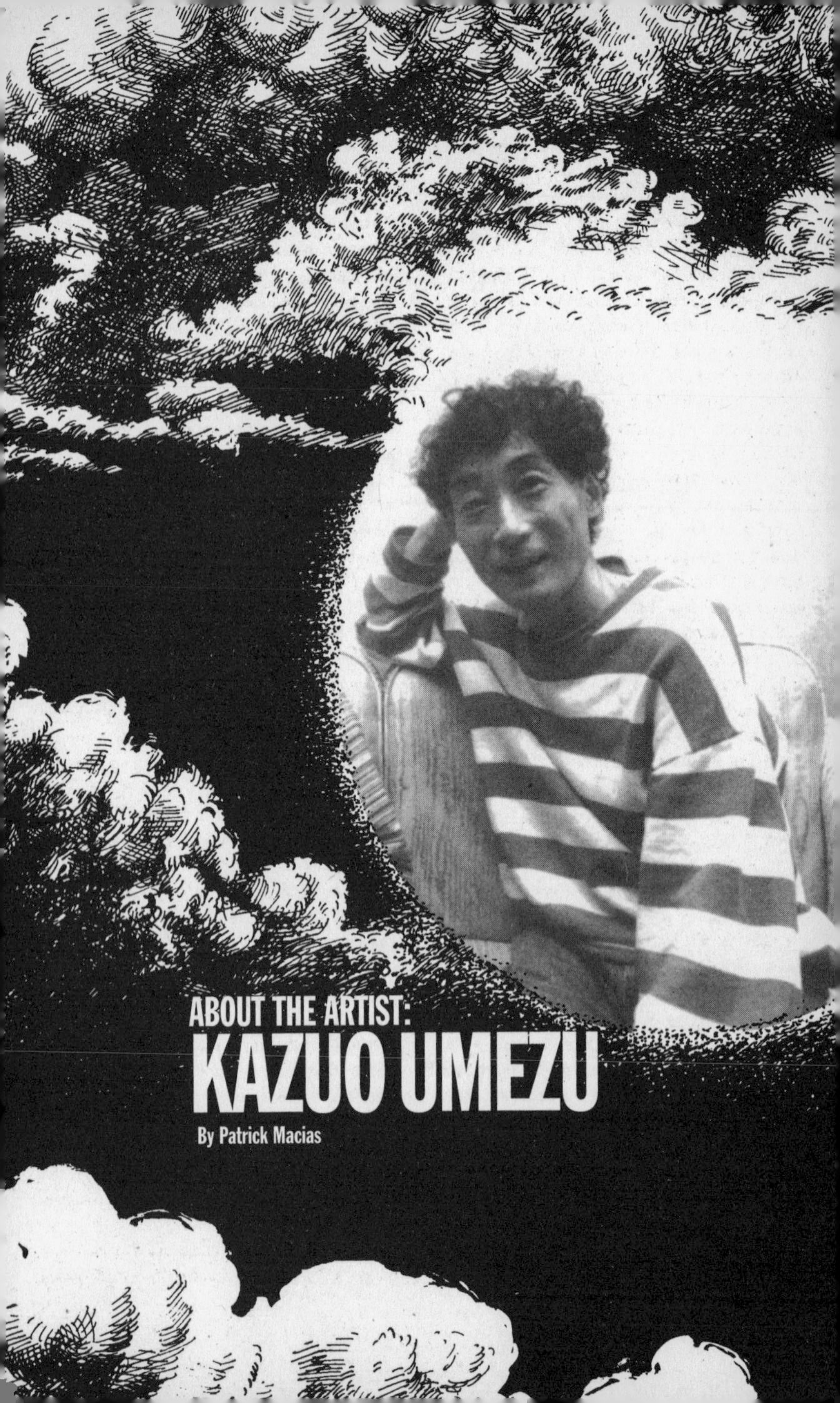

ABOUT THE ARTIST:
KAZUO UMEZU

By Patrick Macias

"**Y**ou'll never believe who just passed by," my neighbor's excited voice on the phone was saying. "Kazuo Umezu! I didn't see him, but my wife did. Now I'm going around the neighborhood to see if I can track him down!"

I live in Tokyo (at least part of the year, anyway), on the west side, near Kichijoji station. This laid-back part of town is known for its animation studios. The Studio Ghibli museum is here also. And, to cap it all off, it's where Kazuo Umezu, the author of *The Drifting Classroom,* makes his home.

One reason my friend was reacting as if a mythological creature (a leprechaun, maybe) had just been sighted in the vicinity is that, according to the locals, to see Umezu in his natural habitat means you've been blessed with good luck. (But of course, it's more complicated than that. Exactly *what* kind of luck depends on the color of striped sweater he's wearing that day. Umezu only wears striped sweaters, with his red and white ones being the best known.)

It's a strange and wonderful thing to imagine, but apparently, it happens quite a bit: the inhabitants of Kichijoji dashing through the streets to get a peek at the famed manga-ka. Because, as Umezu himself once said in interview, "If you are chasing someone, it is a joke. But if you are the one being chased, this is horror."

In Japan, "Kazuo Umezu" is as much of a brand name of horror as "Edgar Allan Poe" or "Stephen King." Audiences have eagerly consumed his distinctive works in the genre for generations, through his original manga or numerous television and movie adaptations. His moniker even graces the famed Kazuo Umezu Haunted Mansion, a seasonal attraction in Tokyo top-rated by connoisseurs of that type of thing.

There's also Umezu the "gag manga" artist. The single most popular creation associated with "Kazz" (as he's often referred to) is the snot-nosed and scatologically obsessed wild child Makoto-chan. First introduced in 1971, the grotesque and rudely funny *Makoto-chan* series became a national sensation, spawning an animated film as well as a lucrative merchandising boom in the guise of Makoto-chan key chains, pencil sharpeners, and miniature toilets.

It's been a lifetime of alternating between fits of laughter and bouts of terror, much like the imagination and moods of a child.

Kazuo Umezu was born September 3, 1936 in Wakayama, a rural prefecture located on the coast of southwest Japan. Nurtured on *Grimm's Fairy Tales*, encouraged by his parents, and inspired—like so many others of his generation—by Osamu Tezuka's groundbreaking postwar comics, the young Umezu produced amateur manga at a prodigious rate. At age 18, two of his comics, both of which he'd authored while still in junior high school, were acquired and published by a regional rental comics library. Umezu spent the first phase of his professional career in the mid-fifties creating works exclusively for the rental market.

As the pay library market began to shrink, artists flocked to Tokyo to find employment with the major publishers, who were themselves hungry for new talent to fill the pages of their burgeoning weekly and monthly manga magazines. Umezu created new works for both shojo (girls) and shonen (boys) anthologies. His early- to mid-sixties titles (which are said to have intimidated Tezuka himself) were amazingly diverse and ran the gamut from starry-eyed romance to adventure, from science fiction to giant monster stories—including a very strange *Ultraman* adaptation.

As the decade neared conclusion, Umezu finally shook the strong Tezuka influence that had dominated his youth and began to work in an increasingly original and uncanny vein. His horror works culminated in his 1969-1970 serial *Orochi,* a mix of heavy gothic atmosphere and tight pulp storytelling in the best *Alfred Hitchcock Presents* tradition.

Following *Orochi,* Umezu became a full-blown multimedia star with his *Makoto-chan* manga. He even made forays into rock and roll as the front man of the Makoto-chan band (whose hit single was "Diarrhea Pants Rock").

Somewhere in the midst of all this activity, Umezu began serializing *The Drifting Classroom* in 1972 in the pages of *Shonen Sunday* magazine. So began the next, most ambitious phase of Umezu's body of work.

With their emphasis on biology, evolution, and Big Ideas, *The Drifting Classroom, My Name Is Shingo*

KAZUO UMEZU'S SELECTED BIBLIOGRAPHY

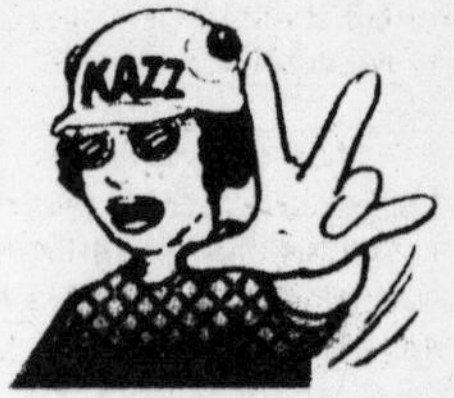
KAZZ

1

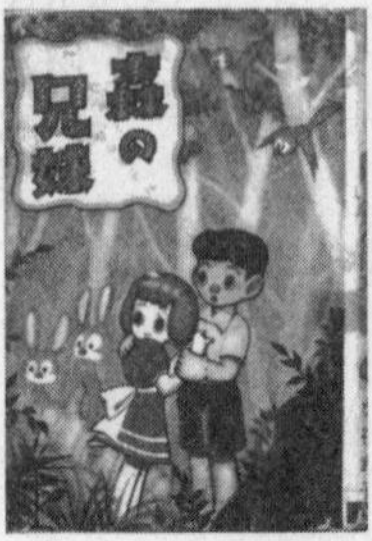

2

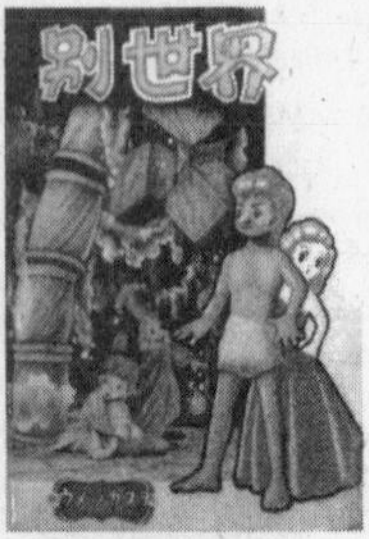
別世界

3

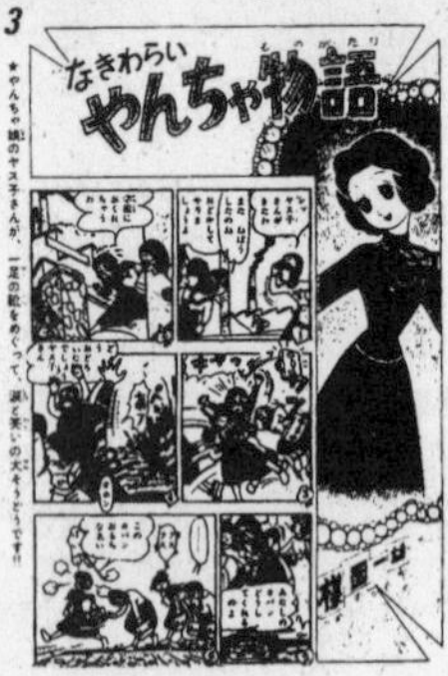
なきわらい
やんちゃ物語

4

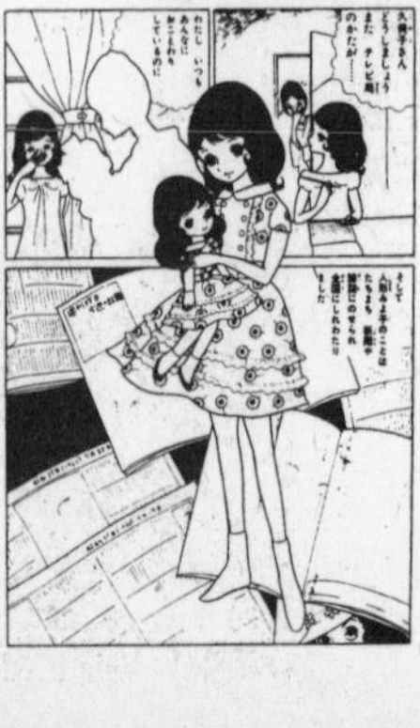

(1982-86), and *Fourteen* (1990-95) (see Selected Bibliography, below) were unprecedented epics in the field of manga, and were certainly Umezu's most impressive artistic statements. And of the bunch, *The Drifting Classroom* is the best known and most widely read.

In the career-overview book *Kazuo Umezu* (Kawada Shobo Shinsha, 2004), critic Yuuichiro Kurihara speculates on *Drifting Classroom's* popularity: "It appears to be a human drama about children who begin from a state of no hope, and eventually come back to hopefulness."

But what about the world they inherit?

Kurihara again: "You have to consider that Umezu's later work depicts the end of humanity. In that respect, *Drifting Classroom* is really the doorway to the extinction of the human race."

In later works, such as the apocalyptic *Fourteen*, a spiraling cosmic madness quickly eclipses concerns like survival and feeling good about the future. By contrast, *Drifting Classroom* still seems like an oasis, a fountain of hope surrounded by ruins. After all, despite the death, despair, and treachery, the children in the story also become fully realized human beings—adults on their own terms, really—by overcoming the adults around them.

Umezu himself is now well into his sixties, but he remains the portrait of the eternal child. And in the same books where we are asked to consider *The Drifting Classroom* as an entryway to the abyss, there is a picture of Kazz himself swinging like a loon from the branches of the cherry blossom trees.

Looks like fun to me.

Patrick Macias is the author of *TokyoScope: The Japanese Cult Film Companion* (Cadence Books) and the co-author of *Cruising the Anime City: An Otaku Guide to Neo-Tokyo* (Stone Bridge Press).

1 Brother and Sister's Forest (*Mori no kyôdai,* 1955) Umezu's first published work—a "Hansel and Gretel" story he drew in junior high school.

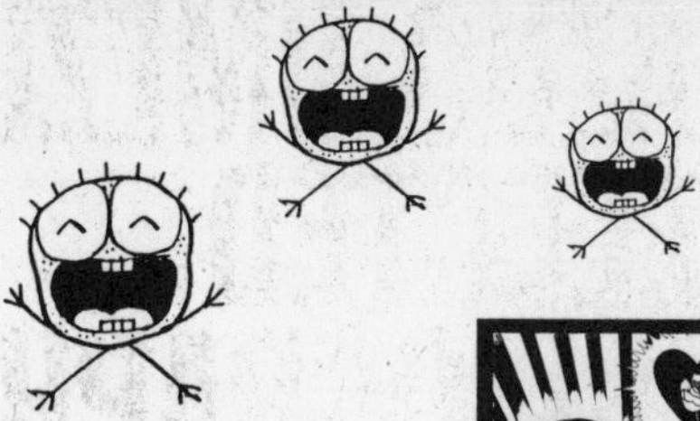

2 Another World (*Bessekai,* 1955) Neolithic kids in prehistoric times stumble into a strange world of cannibalism and giant mosquito people. Umezu's second published work.

3 Comical Naughty Story (*Nakiwarai yancha monogatari,* 1955) Loud and obnoxious Osaka-style gag comedy strip about a mischievous girl named Yasuko.

4 Doll Girl (*Ningyo shojo,* 1959) Umezu first began drawing classically big-eyed shojo manga with this tear-jerking story about a poor girl adopted by a nice family. The catch is, to earn her keep, she must babysit a doll. Realistic postwar setting.

5

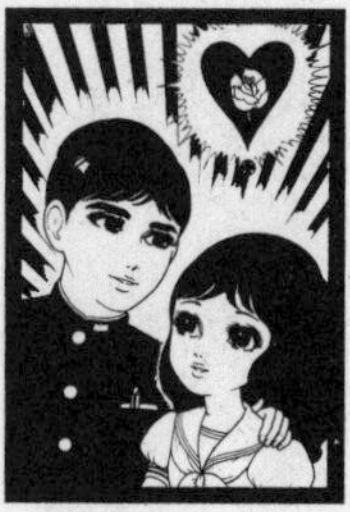

5 Medicine of Romance (*Romance no kusuri,* 1961) Starry-eyed female protagonist struggles to make the man of her dreams take "Love Potion #9." The first in the *Romance* series.

6

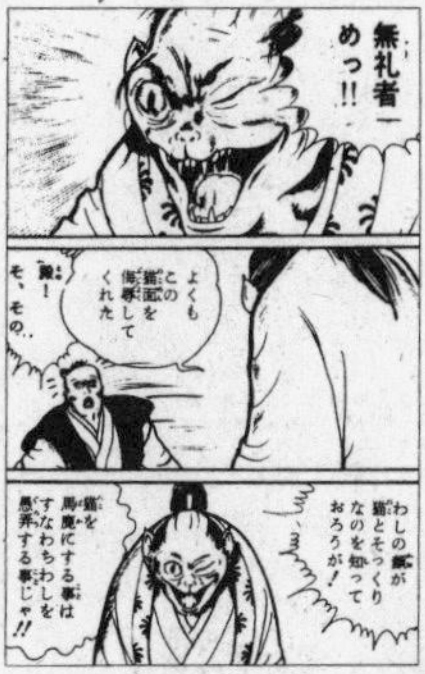
無礼者一めっ!!
よくもこの猫面を侮辱してくれた
殿! そ、その…
わしの顔が猫とそっくりなのを知っておろうが!
猫を馬鹿にする事はすなわちわしを愚弄する事じゃ!!

6 Cat Face (*Neko men,* 1963) Deformed peeping tom falls in love with a beautiful woman and starts torturing her suitors. Supernatural revenge story set in ancient Japan drawn in a raw, brutal style.

7

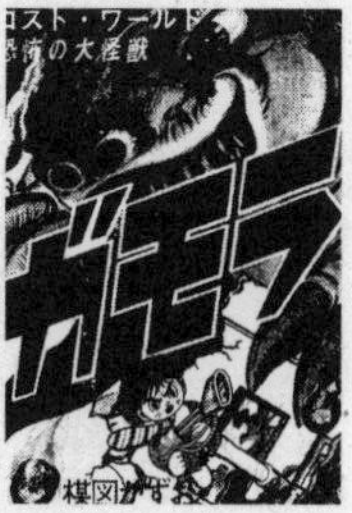
ロスト・ワールド
ガモラ

7 Lost World—Gamora (1964-1965) Giant monster action in the Godzilla tradition. Multi-generational plot begins in ancient Japan, then jumps to the present day for massive city stomping.

8

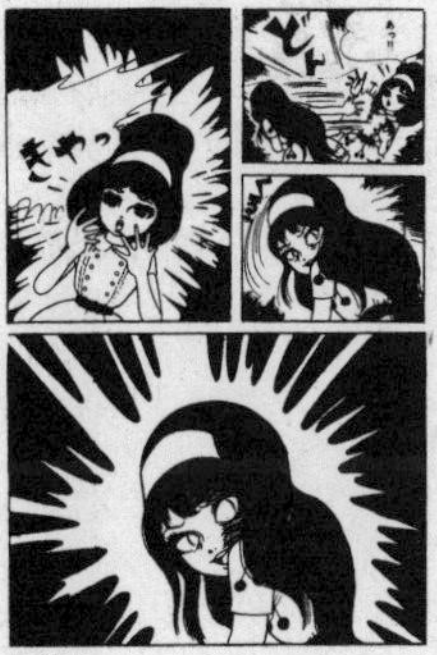
きゃっ

8 Girl with Cat's Eyes (*Nekome no shojo,* 1965) Poe's "Black Cat" given the Umezu twist. The Master of the House hates cats—unfortunately his daughter looks like one. He poisons her, and she makes wooden cat statues to enact revenge.

9

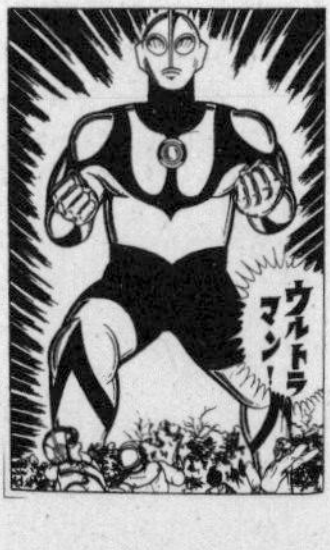
ウルトラマン!

9 Ultraman (1966-1967) Adaptation of the classic superhero TV show. Deviates from televised version in bizarre and wonderful ways as Umezu had only seen the pilot episode.

10 ***Laughing Mask*** (*Warai kamen,* 1967) As a result of a government conspiracy, a biologist is forced to wear a ghoulish mask. Two boy detectives cross his path and learn the truth about the giant ants he's studying. Sci-fi-adventure-mystery mix points toward later works such as *The Drifting Classroom.*

11 ***Face of Scales*** (*Uroko no kao,* 1968) Seemingly another snake-girl story, but this time the transformation of the heroine into a giant serpent is astonishingly grotesque.

12 ***Shadow*** (*Kage,* 1968) Beautiful girl obsessed with her mirror begins to battle her own demonic reflection. Umezu's art and background details take giant leaps.

13 ***The Snake Girl and the Silver-Haired Witch*** (*Hebi musume to hakuhatsu ma*, 1968) A home invasion by the title characters scares the hell out of a little girl. Also a 1968 movie from Daiei, in which Umezu has a cameo as a cab driver.

14 ***Cat's Eye Kid*** (*Nekome kozo*, 1967-1968, 1976) A ghost-story anthology built around the wanderings of a strange little kid with cat's eyes through Japan.

15 ***Orochi*** (1969-1970) A mysterious girl named Orochi (an old Japanese word for "serpent") drifts across a gloomy landscape in a loosely connected series of short suspense stories. In 2002, VIZ released a single volume in the series as *Orochi: Blood.*

16 ***Dali's Man*** (*Dali no otoko,* 1969) Disturbing fun with artists and models. Visuals inspired by Salvador Dali.

17 ***Iara*** (1970) A man searching for the meaning of the word "Iara" travels through time and space in a strange short story anthology. The adult-strength version of *Orochi*.

18 ***Again*** (1970-1972) Old man takes medicine that turns him into a high school kid. Hangs out with his grandson. This shonen gag breakthrough led to *Makoto-chan.*

19 ***Makoto-chan*** (1971) See intro.

20 ***The Drifting Classroom*** (*Hyouryû kyôshitsu,* 1972-1974) See intro.

21 ***Album of the Dark*** (*Yami no album,* 1974-1975) Twenty-four black-humor short stories of free-flowing surrealism. Relentless graphic experimentation—also spawned a concept LP by Umezu.

19

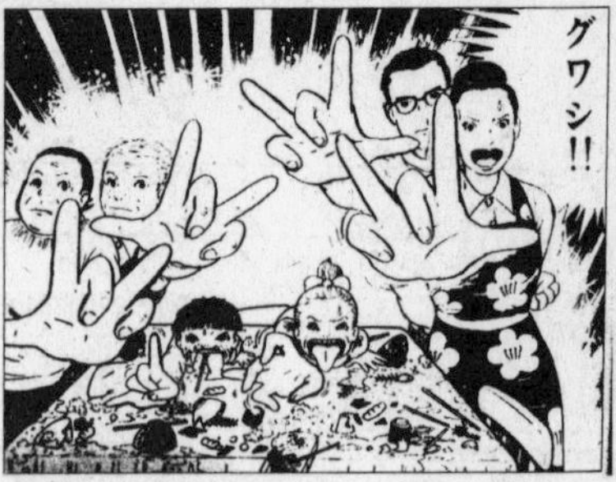
グワシ!!

20

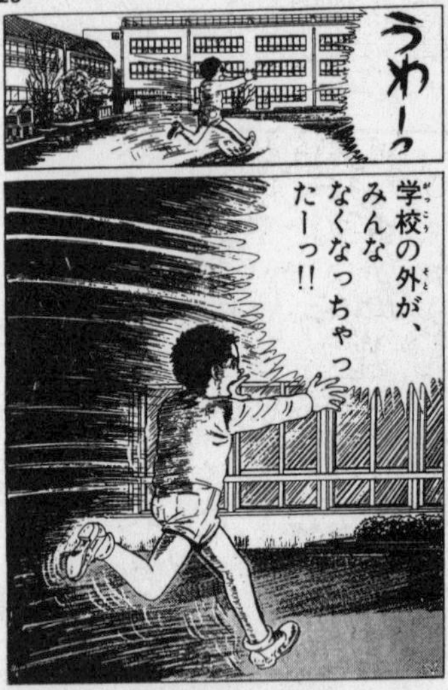
うわーっ
学校の外が、みんななくなっちゃったーっ!!

21

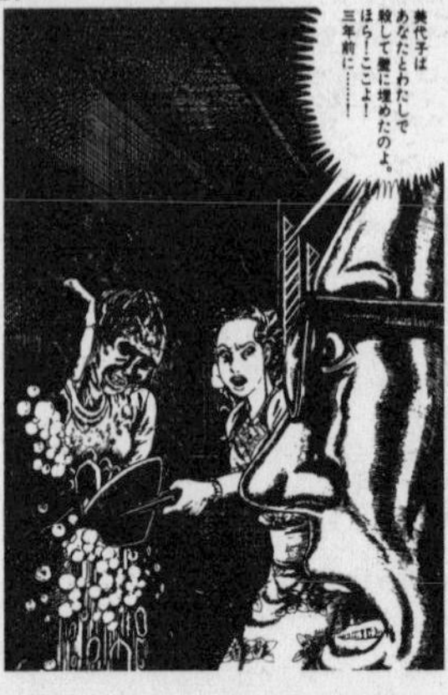
美代子はあなたとわたしで殺して庭に埋めたのよ。ほら!ここよ!三年前に……!

10

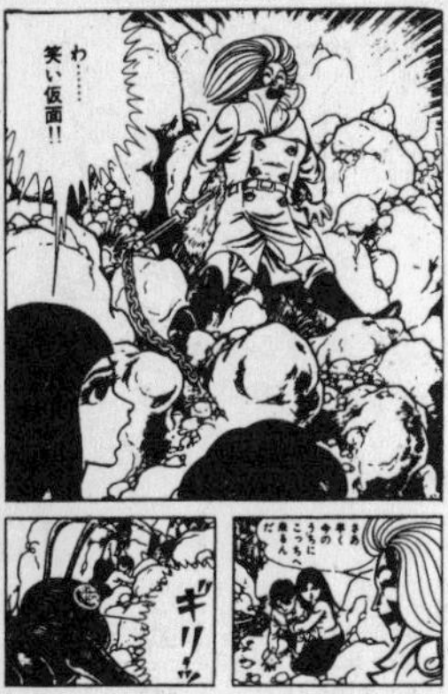
わ……
笑い仮面!!
まあ早く今のうちにこっちへ来るんだ
ギリッ

11

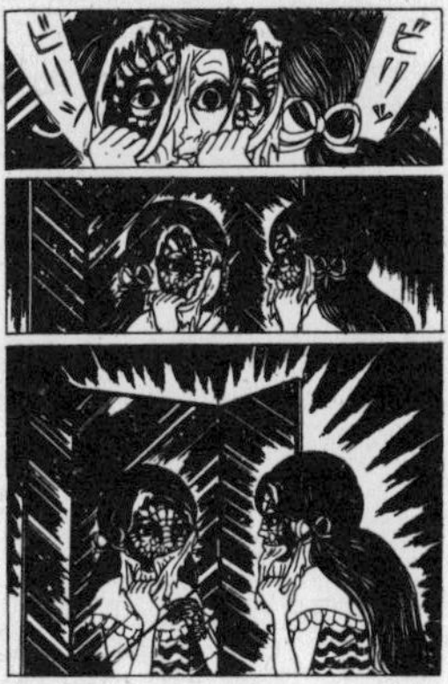
ビリッ
ビリッ

12

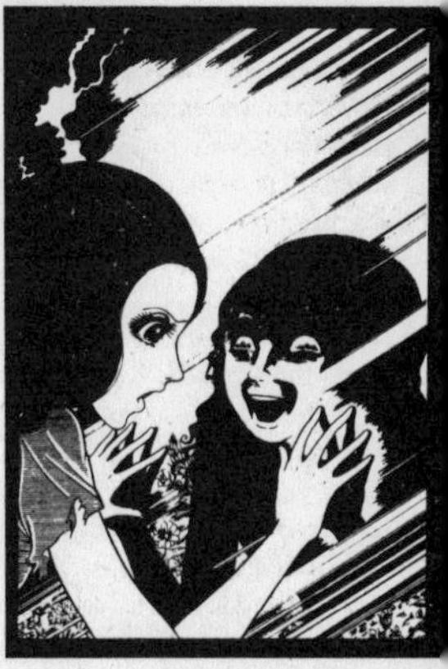

13

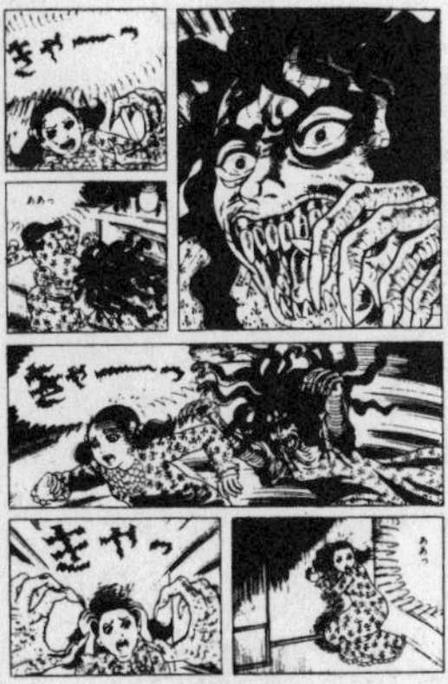
きゃーっ
ああっ
きゃーっ
ああっ
きゃっ

14

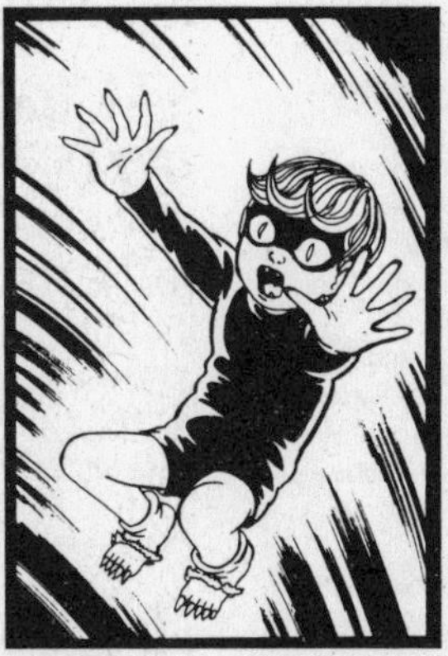

15

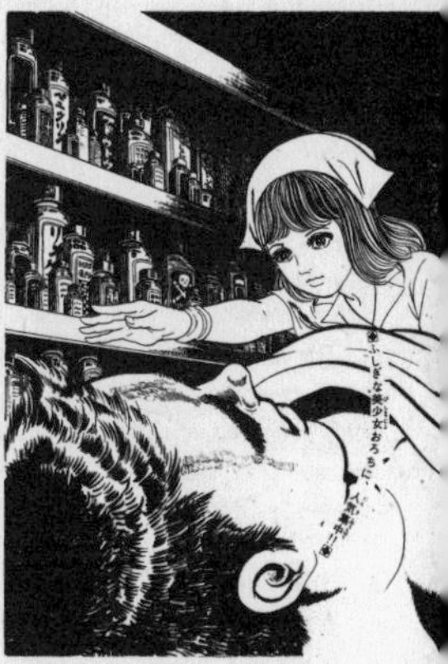
ふしぎな美少女おろちに、

16

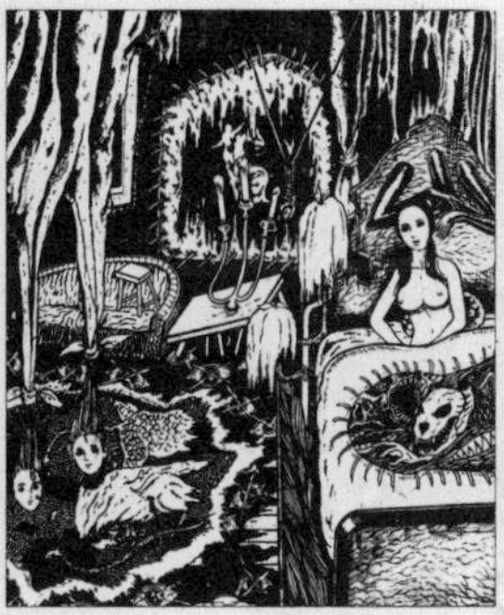

17

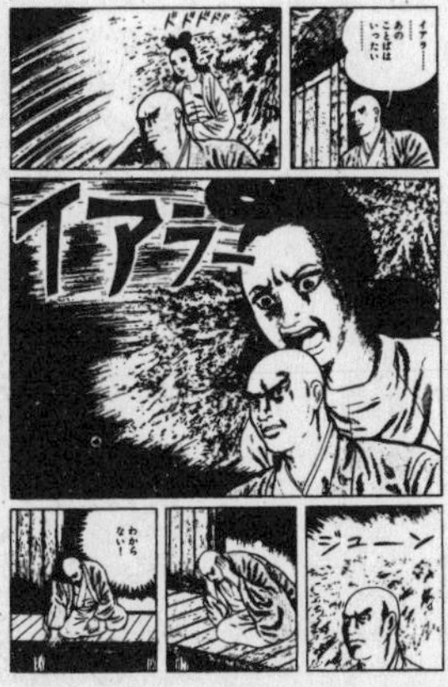
イアラ……
あのことばはいったい……
ドドドド
イアラー
ジューン
わからない!

18

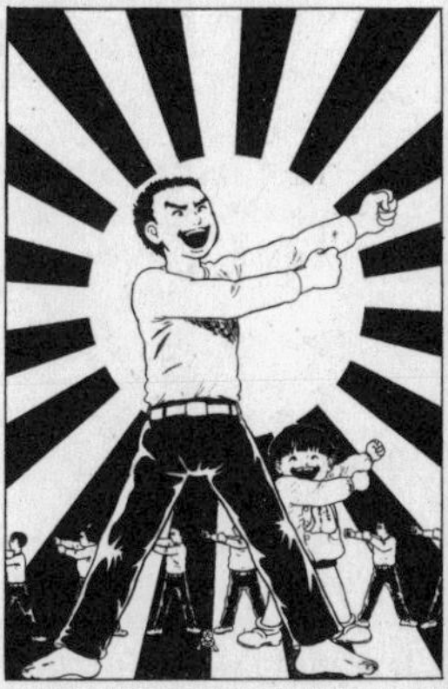

23

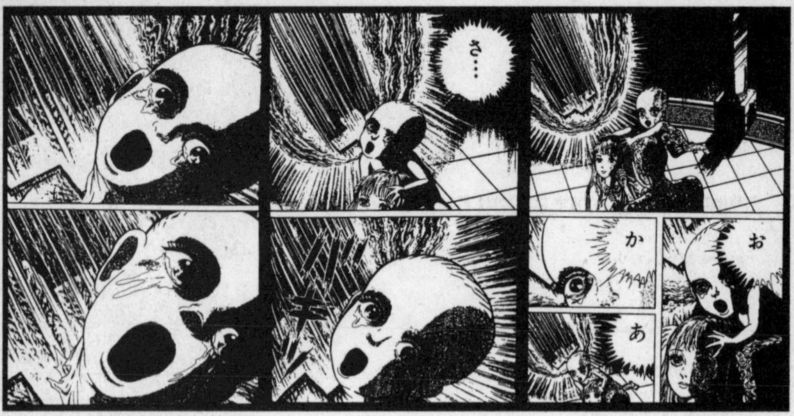
さ…
お
か
あ

22

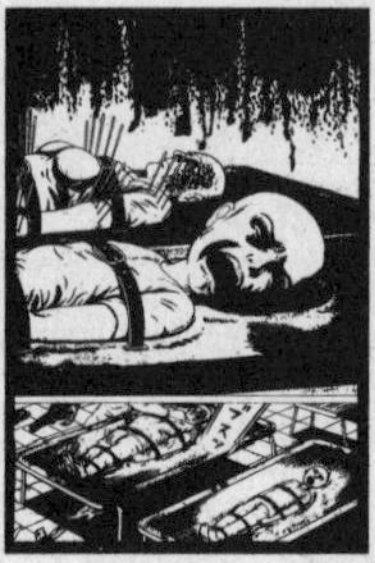

24

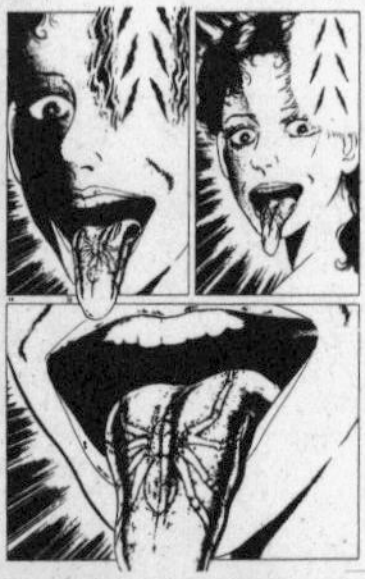

25

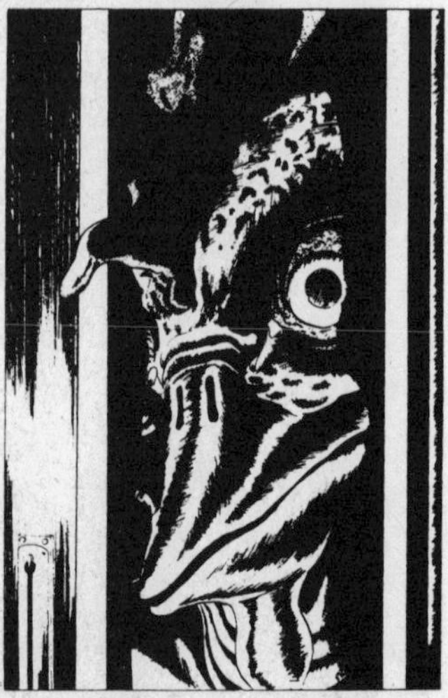

22 Baptism (*Senrei,* 1974-1976) An aging actress plots to switch brains with her beautiful young daughter so she can relive her youth. Things don't quite work out, though. Film adaptation available on video in US as *Baptism of Blood.*

23 My Name Is Shingo (*Watashi wa Shingo*, 1982-1986) Star-crossed lovers, a boy and girl, inadvertently program a factory robot arm into sentience. After the boy and girl are separated, the robot arm wanders the earth. This popular love-story sci-fi classic is an epic account of the human experience.

24 The Left Hand of God, the Right Hand of the Devil (*Kami no hidarite, akuma no migite*, 1986-1989) Umezu's most relentless "pure horror" work: a masterpiece of the abnormal, of dream and reality colliding head on. A young boy experiences visions and nightmares as his sister suddenly begins vomiting forth stranger and stranger objects. It all goes back to a gruesome serial killing spree that occurred before they were born and still haunts the local community.

25 Fourteen (1990-1995) One day in the bleak near-future, a scientist discovers that a lump of chicken meat is becoming sentient. The lump eventually grows into Chicken George, a half-chicken, half-man creature who seeks revenge on humanity for their mistreatment of animals. Things get complicated when he falls in love with a human girl.

Thanks to Izumi Evers, Tomo Machiyama, and Yuji Oniki. •

THE DRIFTING CLASSROOM
Vol. 1

STORY AND ART BY KAZUO UMEZU

Translation/Yuji Oniki
Touch-up Art & Lettering/Kelle Han
Design/Izumi Evers
Editor/Jason Thompson

Managing Editor/Annette Roman
Director of Production/Noboru Watanabe
VP of Publishing/Alvin Lu
Sr. Director of Acquisitions/Rika Inouye
VP of Sales & Marketing/Liza Coppola
Publisher/Hyoe Narita

Printed in the U.S.A.

Published by VIZ Media, LLC
P.O. Box 77010
San Francisco, CA 94107

10 9 8 7 6 5 4 3 2 1
First printing, August 2006

www.viz.com
store.viz.com

PARENTAL ADVISORY
THE DRIFTING CLASSROOM is rated M for Mature and is recommended for mature readers. Contains strong language and graphic violence.

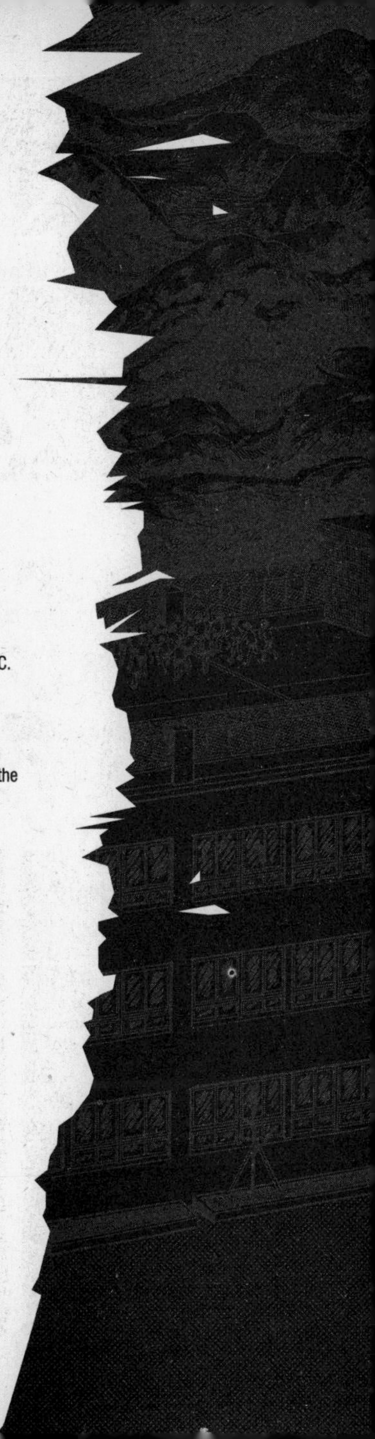

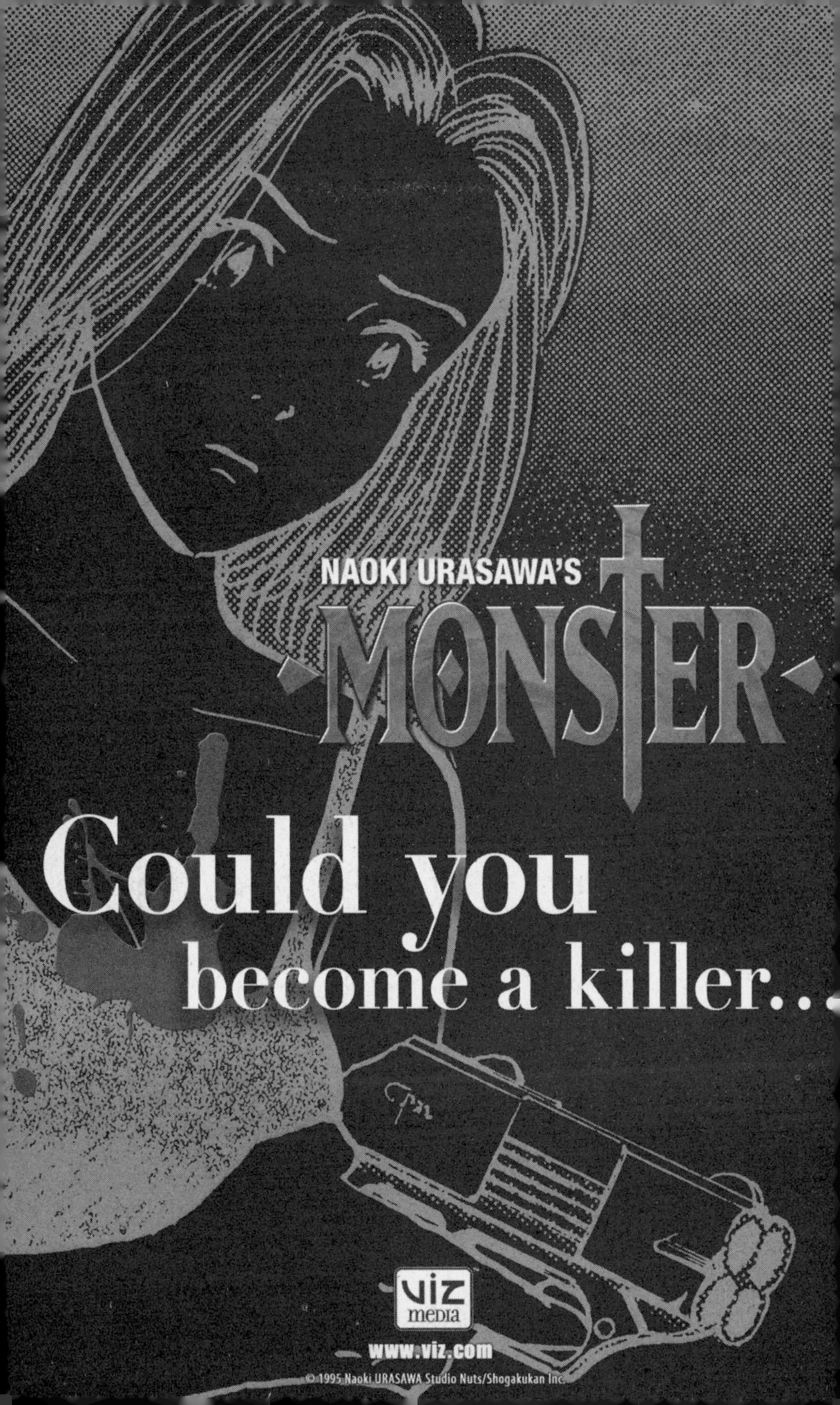
NAOKI URASAWA'S
MONSTER
Could you
become a killer...
VIZ MEDIA
www.viz.com
© 1995 Naoki URASAWA Studio Nuts/Shogakukan Inc.